SANDRA GUSTAFSON'S

GREAT EATS
PARIS

NINTH EDITION

CHRONICLE BOOKS

SAN FRANCISCO

Printed in the United States of America.

NINTH EDITION
ISBN: 0-8118-2920-0
ISSN: 1074-5068

Cover design: Benjamin Shaykin
Book design: Words & Deeds
Typesetting: Jack Lanning
Series editor: Jeff Campbell
Author photograph: Marv Summers

Distributed in Canada by Raincoast Books
9050 Shaughnessy Street
Vancouver, British Columbia V6P 6E5

10 9 8 7 6 5 4 3 2 1

Chronicle Books LLC
85 Second Street
San Francisco, CA 94105

www.chroniclebooks.com
www.greateatsandsleeps.com

For Sara, with love

Contents

To the Reader

Paris is a feast, but the banquet has become painfully expensive.

—*Anthony Dias Blue*

Eating is a serious venture, if not a patriotic duty, in France.

—*Patricia Roberts*

Paris is famous for its fashion, acclaimed for its art, and notorious for its nightlife, but to visit Paris and bypass the endless opportunities for sampling its wonderful cuisine is absolutely unthinkable. Thus, along with visits to the Louvre, the Eiffel Tower, and the Champs-Élysées, dining is almost always an integral part of any successful trip to Paris. The French know how to eat; if there is something a French person would rather do, no one has yet discovered it. For the French, good food is not a casual pastime reserved only for dining out, but a way of life, a celebration of the bounty of foods available throughout the year. As a result, French cooking is an art form; chefs with great talent and skill are awarded the Legion of Honor and given the same media attention we reserve for rock stars. One of the most well known statements by former French president Charles de Gaulle refers not to politics or war but to cheese. The ritual of Sunday lunch has almost been canonized, and even *Le Monde,* the country's largest and most serious newspaper, runs front-page stories about *cornichons,* types of bread, and the wines and cheeses that go best with them. In Paris you will find this love of eating well reflected in more than twenty thousand cafés, bistros, brasseries, and restaurants, which cater to every taste and budget, from haute cuisine to hole-in-the-wall.

Because the French demand a higher quality of food and preparation, they are usually willing to pay for it. It is easy, if you have unlimited funds, to dine at one of the Parisian cathedrals of cuisine and have an exquisite meal for over $200 per person. For most visitors to Paris, this would be a one-time-only indulgence, if it could be afforded at all. However, too often visitors determined to partake in Paris' ultimate culinary pleasures rush only to those restaurants with at least one Michelin star and, in so doing, overlook many up-and-coming restaurants that serve remarkable food at a fraction of the price. The ongoing demands for *bon rapport et qualité prix* (good value for money), along with the fluctuating French economy, have not been able to sustain the bloated tabs of the culinary all-stars, forcing many to either lower their prices and add affordable *prix fixe* (or set-price) menus or go out of business altogether. At the same time, it has encouraged diners to experiment with less-expensive bistros and family-run restaurants. Hands-on newcomers, who learned their cooking craft from the masters, are redefining the Parisian dining palate by branching out on their own in low-end, off-the-beaten-track establishments. Most seat diners in bare, humdrum surroundings, but the high-quality food and fair prices more than compensate for the lack of elegance. Talented regional chefs have put sizzle into the Paris dining scene with their artfully inspired dishes, giving foreign diners a chance to acquaint themselves with France's many regional cuisines . . . and all for the price of a main course in the restaurants these chefs once cooked in. Many of these places have at least a three- to five-day waiting list for a table, while the three-star shrines only dream of having such lists.

As we all know, selecting a place to eat can be frustrating and time-consuming because it is also quite possible, especially in Paris, to pay too much and eat badly. Whether you're visiting for a day or for several weeks, you don't want to waste time and money on a mediocre meal when you could be eating magnificently and paying less just around the corner. Here is where *Great Eats Paris* comes to the rescue—it takes the uncertainty out of dining and puts you on the inside track to some of the best dining deals in Paris. *Great Eats Paris* will improve the quality of your Parisian dining experiences and save you money by leading you away from the tourist-packed, high-priced restaurants and toward the well-located, picturesque ones serving reasonably priced meals of good value to mostly French patrons. With *Great Eats Paris* in hand, you will discover a world of good taste and affordable food in a wide array of genuinely Parisian establishments: crowded, noisy cafés with a haze of pungent smoke and a coterie of colorful regulars; family-run bistros with red-and-white-checked tablecloths and sawdust on the floor; sophisticated wine bars; cozy tearooms; big brasseries serving steaming platters of *choucroute;* and candlelit restaurants that inspire couples to leave more in love than when they arrived. Some of these are classics everyone has heard about. Others, until now, have been virtually unknown to foreigners. A few are Big Splurges that have been selected for special occasions, for when you want to sample an abundance of the very best.

My research trip for this edition took me to parts of Paris I otherwise would not have visited and led me to many new and exciting dining discoveries. In an effort to help you save money and, as much as possible, keep you from making mistakes, I revisited every listing in the eighth edition, and I tried countless others that for one reason or another did not make the final cut. I dined anonymously and paid my own way, which enabled me to objectively evaluate the good and the bad and to report the findings to you freely, fairly, and honestly. In the process, I walked more than seven hundred miles in all types of weather, was asked directions almost every day, wore out my umbrella and two pairs of shoes, and of course, ate out every day. I was seated in English-speaking Siberia near the kitchen, under the fan, and behind a post; suffered through nearly inedible meals; was overcharged by condescending waiters who thought I didn't know beans when the bag was open; sat on chairs that must have been used during the Inquisition; and received a cool shoulder from apéritif to *digestif* just so you can avoid suffering the same things. Many old favorites remain. Unfortunately, some entries from past editions have been dropped. Places that were once wonderful are now sadly lacking; chefs and owners changed, quality dropped severely, and/or prices rose to a mind-numbing level. Cozy corner cafés fell victim to fast-food joints, and the age of concrete and modernization removed others. The result of my months of research is the ninth edition of *Great Eats Paris,* with more than two hundred cafés, bistros, brasseries, restaurants, tearooms, and wine bars offering good food quality and top value.

In the back of the book is a page for your comments and notes. Naturally, I hope you are as enthusiastic about the restaurants you choose from *Great Eats Paris* as I was in selecting them. I also hope this book will inspire you to strike out on your own and make your own dining discoveries. If you find a place you think I should know about, or want to report a change in a restaurant I've listed, please take a few moments to write me a note telling me about your experience. I answer every letter, and I cannot emphasize enough how important your letters and comments are.

Longtime readers of the *Cheap Eats* series will notice one obvious change from the last edition: the title. I have done this to more accurately reflect the nature of these guides: they are my personal discoveries and hand-picked selections of what I consider the best-value places to dine well in Paris in a range of price categories. But while the title has changed, the purpose of the series remains the same—to save you money without sacrificing quality, and to share with you Paris's greatest eats.

Whether for business, sightseeing, or as a stop on the way to another destination, Paris has been beckoning travelers for hundreds of years, and most visitors have treasured memories of their stay in the City of Light. One of the best souvenirs you can have of your trip to Paris is the memory of a good meal. I hope that by using *Great Eats Paris* you will have some very special memories of Paris to take home with you. If I have helped you do that, I consider my job well done. *Bon voyage,* and of course, *bon appétit!*

Tips for Great Eats in Paris

Animals feed themselves, men eat; but only wise men know the art of eating.

—*Anthelme Brillat-Savarin,*
La Physiologie du Gout, *1825*

1. Eat and drink a block or two away from the main boulevards and tourist attractions. The difference in price for even a coffee can be considerable.

2. In smaller restaurants and cafés, arrive early for the best selection of seats and food. Remember that the last order is usually taken no less than fifteen minutes before closing.

3. If you want to eat outside the normal Parisian lunch or dinner times, go to a brasserie. These places serve continually throughout the day, often until midnight.

4. Eat where you see a crowd of French people. If a restaurant is either empty or full of tourists, or it posts a menu outside in five languages, you can assume the locals know something you do not and move on.

5. French law states that all restaurants must post a menu outside. *Always* read it before going in to make sure the menu has something you want at a price you can afford.

6. Stay within and respect the limits of the kitchen. Don't expect gourmet fare from a corner café, and don't go to a fine restaurant and order only a salad.

7. The set-price menu, called a *prix fixe* or *formule,* will always be the best value. The next best bet is the *plat du jour* ordered à la carte. This is always fresh and usually garnished with potatoes and a vegetable.

8. It's an open secret. In most places, especially more expensive restaurants, the money-saving tactic is to go for lunch and order the prix fixe menu. This usually costs a fraction of what it would for dinner and sometimes includes wine and coffee. But be aware that there are no substitutions on these menus . . . what you see listed on the menu is what you get.

9. Look for restaurants that offer *only* one price for everything, from a kir to start and a coffee to finish to three courses and wine in between. These are popping up all over Paris and represent some of the best dining values.

10. Order the house wine (*vin de la mason* or *vin ordinaire*). Ask for *une carafe de l'eau ordinaire* (tap water), which is free, rather than paying for a bottle of mineral water.

11. Have your morning *café au lait* and croissant standing at the bar at the corner café. It will cost twice as much if it is served at a table, and even more at your hotel.

12. Always double-check the math on your bill. Mistakes are frequent and are usually not in your favor. By law, restaurants must include the service charge (which is the tip) in the price. No additional tip is necessary unless either the food or the service has been very special. If you are drinking at the bar, it is customary to leave small change.

13. Restaurants change their hours and their annual vacations to adjust to the changing patterns of tourism and economics, so call ahead to make sure the place you have selected will be open, especially if you're making a special trip. All of the information given in *Great Eats Paris* was accurate at press time, but closings change frequently around holidays and during July and August.

14. It is always better to arrive at a restaurant with reservations than to not have them and be turned away, with no backup choice close by. If you are a solo diner, always make the reservation for two (see also "Reservations," page 15).

15. For a really cheap meal, the street *marchés* (or markets; see also "Food Shopping," page 34) are the perfect place to pick up fixings for a *déjeuner sur l'herbe* (lunch under a tree in the park). A piece of ripe Brie cheese, a fresh baguette, a juicy apple or pear, and a bottle of young Beaujolais wine . . . ah, that's Paris.

16. You will never get lost if you buy a copy of the *Plan de Paris par Arrondissement.* The free maps you get are worth what they cost: nothing. This invaluable and timeless map is available at all news kiosks and bookstores in Paris and at many travel bookstores in the United States.

17. If you have particularly enjoyed a place recommended by *Great Eats Paris,* be sure to tell the owner or manager where you found out about them. They are always very appreciative.

How to Use Great Eats Paris

Each listing in the book includes the following information: the name of the establishment, the address, the telephone number, the most convenient métro stop, the days and hours it is open and closed, whether reservations are necessary, which credit cards are accepted, the average price for a three-course à la carte meal, the price for a prix fixe meal, and whether or not English is spoken and to what degree. If there is a nonsmoking section, the listing notes it. Most include a map key number in parentheses to the right of the restaurant name; an entry without a number means it is located beyond the parameters of the map. A dollar sign ($) to the right of the name means it is a Big Splurge.

At the end of the book there is a glossary of French dining phrases and menu terms; an index of all restaurants, plus indexes by category, such as Big Splurges, tearooms, vegetarian restaurants, and so on; and finally a Readers' Comments page.

Big Splurges

These restaurants are for those with more flexible budgets or for special occasion dining to celebrate a birthday, anniversary, or just being in Paris. In almost every case, however, these restaurants offer a prix fixe menu that is within the range of most budget-minded diners; they become Big Splurges when you order à la carte. In the text, Big Splurges are marked with a dollar sign ($). Please refer to the index for a complete listing of all the Big Splurge restaurants in Paris.

The Euro

The euro became the official currency of the eleven-nation European Union, of which France is a part, on January 1, 2000, but euro notes and coins will not be made available until January 2002, when they will be used alongside the national currencies until July 2002. At that point, the euro will become the sole legal tender for the European Union. Until then, travelers can continue to use national currencies (such as francs for France and pesetas for Spain). You will also start to notice prices being displayed in both the national currency and the euro. If you need help transforming francs into euros and back again, you can buy small "euro calculators" in Paris that do this for you instantly; they cost anywhere from 20F to 80F (3.05–12.20€).

All prices in *Great Eats Paris* are quoted in francs and euros. At press time, 1 euro = 6.56 French francs, and 1 euro = 1.02 U.S. dollars. But please be aware that these rates fluctuate constantly and will change.

Holidays

Very few Paris eating establishments are open every day of the year. Most close at least one day a week, and sometimes for either lunch or dinner on Saturday and all day Sunday. Many close for public holidays (listed below), as well as for one week at Christmas and Easter. Some smaller family-run operations close for the school holidays in the fall and winter. The French consider their annual holiday time to be a God-given right. In fact, every working person in France is guaranteed a five-week vacation, no matter how long they have been employed in their present job. Despite government pleadings and tourist demands, many still have an annual closing (*fermeture annuelle*) for all or parts of July and August, when 75 percent of all Parisians leave the city. Closures also vary with the mood of the owner and to adjust to the changing patterns of tourism and inflation. More places are opting for a one- or two-week closure and allowing their employees to rotate their vacation times. It is impossible to guarantee that one year's policy will carry over to the next. To avoid arriving at a restaurant only to find it closed, always call ahead to check, especially on a holiday and in July and August.

The restaurant listings note all vacation dates. If a restaurant has no annual closing, this is indicated by the abbreviation NAC, for "no annual closing."

January 1	New Year's Day	*Jour de l'An*
	Easter Sunday and Monday	*Pâques et Lundi de Pâques*
	Ascension Day	*Ascension* (forty days after Easter)
May 1	Labor Day	*Fête du Travail*
May 8	VE Day	Armistice 1945
July 14	Bastille Day	*Quatorze Juillet*/*Fête Nationale*
August 15	Assumption Day	*Assomption*
November 1	All Saints' Day	*Toussaint*
November 11	Armistice Day	Armistice 1918
December 25	Christmas Day	*Noël*

Maps

Most of the Paris arrondissements covered in *Great Eats Paris* have an accompanying map and restaurant key, and in the text, these map key numbers appear in parentheses to the right of the restaurant's name. If a restaurant does not have a number, it is located beyond the boundaries of the map.

Please note that the maps in *Great Eats Paris* are designed to help the reader locate the restaurant listings; they are not meant to replace fully detailed street maps. If you plan on being in Paris for more than a day or two, I strongly suggest you buy *Plan de Paris par Arrondissement*. It is available at all news kiosks and bookstores and contains a detailed map of every arrondissement, with a complete street index, métro and bus routes, tourist sites, and much more. It is pocket-size and every Parisian has one. It is a purchase that will never go out of style or change much.

Nonsmoking Restaurants

The reason the French drink so much is to help them forget what they are doing to themselves by smoking.
—*Art Buchwald,* Vive la Cigarette

Cigarette stubs make up three of the twenty tons of trash collected daily in the Paris métro. There has been a lukewarm attempt to cut down on smoking in public places, but there is no French surgeon general extolling the virtues of a smoke-free environment. The antismoking law stipulates that all places serving food designate separate smoking and nonsmoking sections. Most ignore this completely. Others relegate nonsmokers to a table surrounded by those puffing throughout the entire meal. When the nonsmoker asks about his or her nonsmoking table, he or she will be told in no uncertain terms, "Yours *is* a nonsmoking table." During the busiest times in cafés and bistros, it is nearly impossible to escape from the Gauloise-induced haze. In *Great Eats Paris,* listings where smoking is prohibited or where there is a specific nonsmoking section (though it is sometimes small) have been boldly noted and are listed in the index. Otherwise . . . *bonne chance.*

Paying the Bill

After the mysteries of the French menu, no subject is more confusing to foreigners than French restaurant bills. Your bill will not automatically be brought to your table at the end of the meal; you usually must ask for it (*l'addition, s'il vous plaît*). If you are eating with a group and plan on paying individually, don't expect your waiter to provide separate checks. Appoint a designated mathematician to keep track of everyone's order. Otherwise, you will develop indigestion trying to make sense of the lumped-together charges on *l'addition.*

Credit Cards

The acceptance of plastic money is second nature in Paris, and it is almost always possible to pay for most meals with a credit card. Policies often change, however, so when reserving, it is wise to double-check which cards the restaurant accepts. The most popular cards are Visa, known as Carte Bleu, and MasterCard, known as Eurocard. American Express and Diners Club are much less popular because they charge fees to merchants and are slow to pay.

The following abbreviations are used for the major credit cards:

American Express	AE
Diners Club	DC
MasterCard	MC
Visa	V

Prices

In most cases, the size of the bottom line on your restaurant bill will depend on your choice of wine. All prices quoted in *Great Eats Paris* are for one person and show whether or not drinks are included using the following abbreviations:

Boissons compris	(drinks included)	BC
Boissons non-compris	(drinks *not* included)	BNC

In determining price quotations, the cheapest menu items have been avoided, including such French favorites as *rognons* (kidneys) and *andouillettes* (tripe sausage), which do not appeal to most Americans. The à la carte prices that are quoted represent the median cost of an à la carte meal with a starter (*entrée*), main course (*plat*), and dessert. The prix fixe prices state how many courses you can expect and whether drinks are included or extra. Even though every attempt has been made to ensure the accuracy of the information given, there is a certain margin of error in pricing due to fluctuating exchange rates, inflation, escalating food costs, and the whims of restaurant owners.

Service Charge

In Paris, always remember that *the service charge is the tip*. By law, all restaurants in France must include a 12 to 15 percent service charge in the price of all food and beverages served. This will be stated on the menu by the words *service compris* or *prix nets*. No additional service charge may be added to your bill. Always check your bill very carefully because mistakes are too frequent.

Important! Beware of the service charge/credit card scam. This is a deliberate gouging of the customer that should not be tolerated. If you are paying by credit card, the total should be at the bottom. If the restaurant has left the space on your credit card slip for the "tip/gratuity" blank, they are hoping you will fill in an amount, thus paying the tip twice, since the service charge has already been included. To avoid this, draw a line from the top total to the bottom total and draw an additional line through the space marked "tip/gratuity."

Tipping

Americans seem to have a hard time with this concept, so it bears repeating: *The service charge is the tip*. You do not have to leave one *sou* more than the price of your meal . . . because the tip has already been included. In France you are obliged to tip the butcher, the delivery boy, and the theater usher, but not the waiter, even in the finest restaurants like Jamin and La Tour d'Argent. However, if the waiter has performed some extraordinary service, or if you were particularly pleased, then an additional tip may be in order. Depending on the size and type of place, anything from a few francs to 5 or 10 percent of the bill would be appreciated. In cafés, it is usually expected to leave the small change.

Reservations

To avoid disappointment, it is always better to arrive with reservations. While reservations are not necessary or accepted in a café, they are essential in most restaurants and in popular bistros and brasseries. If you arrive without a reservation, you might be told that the restaurant is *complet* (full) even when there are empty tables. The reason is that those empty tables have been reserved and are being held. If you are a solo diner, always make the reservation for two people. When you arrive, tell the maître d' that your party will arrive shortly. Soon the waiter will inquire about the empty chair. Look soulfully at your watch and say, "Oh, he/she must not be coming. I will order now." Believe me, it works every time. You will not be relegated to a table behind a post (as many single diners are), and the waitstaff will become very solicitous of your predicament and the service will improve immediately.

When you have a reservation, don't be late. French restaurants honor their reservation times and do not relegate patrons to the bar to wait for the present occupants to gulp down the last drop of espresso before relinquishing the table. Many places have only one or two seatings for both lunch and dinner, so if you change your plans after booking, you should always call to cancel so that your table can be rebooked.

All entries in *Great Eats Paris* state the reservation policy, so you will know exactly what to do and expect. If you do not feel comfortable making the reservation yourself, the hotel desk personnel can do it for you, possibly getting a better table than if you had tried yourself.

Transportation

In *Great Eats Paris,* the nearest Paris métro stop is given for each restaurant, and in central Paris the métro is so comprehensive there are often two or three stops that are equally convenient. The Paris métro is safe, efficient, and fast, and it is the best way to get around. While buses are not hard to figure out and are more interesting, since you can see the neighborhoods you are passing through, they often get stuck in traffic, and you could walk to your destination in the time the bus will take. The same can sometimes be said of taxis, though now and then I recommend using them late at night in some of the outer arrondissements.

General Information about French Dining

Where to Eat

"Is this a café, a bistro, a brasserie, or a restaurant?" This is the first question many foreigners ask, with the second one usually being, "What's the difference?" In the pecking order of eateries, a bistro is a cut above a café and a notch below a restaurant, and brasseries can fall anywhere among them all. The following explanations should help to clear away some of the confusion while giving you the flavor of these various establishments.

Cafés

The last time I saw Paris
Her heart was warm and gay.
I heard the laughter of her heart in
Ev'ry street café.
—Oscar Hammerstein II

The French don't go to priests, doctors, or psychiatrists to talk over their problems; they sit in a café over a cup of coffee or a glass of wine and talk to each other.
—Eric Sevareid, "Town Meeting of the World," CBS Television, March 1966

For the visitor to Paris, the café is a living stage and the perfect place to feel the heartbeat of the city. The café experience lets anyone become a Parisian in the space of an hour or so, since by coming here, you are immediately cast into one of the best scenes in the city. For the French, it would be easier to change their religion than their favorite café. Depending on the area, it can be a café pouring a wake-up Calvados to workers at 4 A.M., the lunch spot for local merchants, a lively afternoon rendezvous for students and gossiping civil servants, or a meeting place to have "a few with the boys" on the way home from work. People who are lonely find company, foreigners find a place to write postcards, countesses rub elbows with cab drivers, and everyone finds *égalité*.

In a café, you can eat, drink, and sleep it off afterward, flirt, meet your lover, play pinball, hide from your boss, talk, listen, dream, read, write, order takeout sandwiches, make telephone calls, use the toilet, pet the lazy dog sprawled across the entrance, and sit at a table for as long as you like, engaging in prime people-watching. If the café is also a tabac, you can buy cigarettes, pipes, postcards, stamps, razor blades, cheap watches, lottery tickets, and telecartes, the wallet-size cards that take the place of coins in most public telephone booths in Paris. If the café has a PMU sign, you can place a bet on your favorite horse or political candidate. Talk about convenience! No wonder there are fifty thousand cafés in France and ten thousand in Paris, which means you can find a café on almost every corner in the city.

Cafés don't try to be trendy. The management will never consult a decorator, and they don't listen to talk about *nouvelle cuisine,* lowering cholesterol, or controlling fat grams. You can expect cafés to be smoky. Even though the government is trying to curtail cigarette smoking, puffing away remains a solid fact of café life in Paris. At peak hours, the hectic, noisy, smoky ambience is part of the café's charm. The lunch hour is always lively, with service by acrobatic waiters who commit orders to memory, run with plates full of food, and never mix an order or spill a drop. The hearty *bonne maman* food is offered at prices that even struggling students can afford.

Parisians are masters of the art of the café. Almost any time of year, the most popular tables are those on the sidewalk. Even when the temperatures are in the single digits, you will find bundled Parisians huddled outside under heat lamps. Cafés offer a window on contemporary life in Paris and allow you to linger for hours over a single drink and perfect the Parisian art of doing nothing while watching the world pass by. Of course, if you stand at the bar, whatever you order will cost less, but by paying the premium and occupying a table, you acquire privileges bordering on squatter's rights. If the table has a cloth or paper placemat, that means that the table is only for patrons who want to eat. If it is bare, you are welcome to sit, have a drink, and stay as long as you like. No one will rush you or ask you to pay until you are ready to leave, unless the waiters are changing shifts and need to settle their daily take or if the café is about to close. Don't complain when the bill comes; you are not paying $3.50 for a tiny, strong cup of coffee, you are paying for the privilege of sitting in a pleasant environment for as long as your heart desires.

As a nod to the digitial revolution, cyber cafés have been included in this edition of the guide, but it should be noted that in most respects they usually don't qualify as true French cafés. Along with a host of Internet-ready terminals, most provide only candy bars, soda, and bad coffee, but a few actually serve sandwiches and light meals. However, they merit the name in one important way: they are places to hang out and meet like-minded travelers, both in person and online. If you will be depending on them, I suggest you call ahead to make sure the one you are headed to is still open, as their individual fortunes change about as rapidly as those of high-tech stocks.

Bistros

After the fall of Napoléon, the Russian soldiers who occupied Paris would bang on the zinc bars and shout *bistrot!*—which means "hurry" in Russian. Many say that bistros served the world's first fast food. In the past, when bistros were all simple *maman et papa* places, fast food was the order of the day. Today, bistros still make up the heart and soul of Parisian dining. Some are small, unpretentious, and family run, with handwritten menus and a waitstaff and decor that have not changed in thirty years, which is just the way their equally dedicated and unchanging customers like it. Others are elegant, with starched linens, formally clad waiters, and prices to match. Culinary habits in Paris are changing, thanks to the new generation of chefs who, having trained with the culinary maestros, now offer a similar, more affordable cuisine in bistros located in lower-rent, out-of-the-way neighborhoods. In any bistro, the atmosphere is friendly, and the room is packed with loyalists who know every dish on the menu. When you are hungry enough to dig in to a steaming platter of rib-sticking fare, head for a bistro. Farm-kitchen renditions of *pot-au-feu, boeuf bourguignon,* Lyonnaise sausages, thick *cassoulets,* duck *confit,* salt cod, and the quintessential bistro dessert, *tarte Tatin,* are the once-lost and now-found dishes that salute the robust, nostalgic bistro cooking firmly rooted in the French past.

Brasseries

The earliest brasseries began in Alsace, along the eastern border between France and Germany. Open from early morning until past midnight, they are big, brightly lit, and perpetually packed with a noisy, high-energy crowd enjoying service in the best long-aproned tradition. As opposed to bistros and restaurants, you can order food at almost any time of the day, delving into platters of *choucroute,* fresh shellfish, steaks, and chicory salad loaded with bacon and topped with a poached egg. Everything is washed down with bottles of Alsatian wine and cold beer. While reservations are appreciated, you can usually get a table without them.

Restaurants

To eat is a necessity; to eat well is an art.
—*Anthelme Brillat-Savarin,*
La Physiologie du Gout, *1825*

With more than twenty thousand places to eat, Paris can accommodate any dining mood or whim. A restaurant serves only full, three-course meals at set times for lunch and/or dinner. It is not the place to go if you want a quick sandwich or a big salad on the go. Restaurants offer a complete menu with impressive wine lists, and diners are expected to order accordingly. They are more formal in service, food preparation, and presentation than cafés, bistros, and brasseries. Because eating is such a serious business in France, especially in Paris, most restaurants have only one seating to allow for leisurely dining. No waiter worth his or her white apron or black tie would ever rush a French person through a meal in order to free the table for other diners. You can count on spending almost two hours for a serious lunch and at least three for a nice dinner. Do as the French do: relax, take your time, enjoy each course and the wine, and above all, be happy you are in Paris.

Tearooms

Tearooms play an important part in the lives of most Parisians. In fact, there are more tearooms in Paris than there are in London! The French *salons de thé* are romantic, hospitable places where you are encouraged to get comfortable and stay awhile. Hidden away in all corners of Paris, they are a welcome stop for those looking for a relaxing lunch, a sightseeing or shopping break, or an afternoon of quiet, unhurried conversation with an old friend over a rich dessert and a pot of brewed tea. In addition, they are havens for single diners, and they are nice places to go for a light lunch, brunch, or late-afternoon snack if you know dinner will be very late. Almost every neighborhood has its *salon de thé,* and each is as different as its owner: some are elegant, some quaint, and others high-tech modern. They often have a friendly cat to pet, periodicals to glance through, and an air of intellectualism.

Wine Bars

Un bon repas favorise la conversation. Un bon vin lui donne de l'espirit.
("A good meal favors conversation. A good wine gives it spirit.")
—*Note found on the back of a napkin*
in a Parisian wine bar

Average life of a drinker of water: 56 years
Average life of a drinker of wine: 77 years
Choose!
—*Sign in a French railroad station*

The popularity of *bars à vin* continues in the City of Light. Most wine bar owners not only have a passion for good wine but an interest in good food. The friendly rendezvous for Parisian pacesetters, wine bars are a smart solution for those looking for a place to relax over a glass or two of nice wine while enjoying a light meal from noon until late in the evening. Ranging from rustic to futuristic, they serve fine wines as well as little-known vintages by the glass or bottle, along with simple meals of salads, *tartines* (slices of baguette or country bread spread with pâté or cheese), cold meats, cheeses, and usually hot main dishes.

The French Menu

Dining in Paris is often anticipated as the most pleasurable aspect of any visit, but for foreigners it can sometimes be a very disappointing and unsettling experience. Let's face it: whether it is neatly printed on an oversized menu in a fine restaurant, whitewashed on a bistro window, written in fading chalk on a blackboard, or handwritten on a sheet pinned to a café curtain, the French menu can be intimidating. This section will take the mystery out of the menu, so that you will feel confident to go anywhere and order with style and ease.

All French eating establishments must, by law, post a menu outside showing the prices of the food they serve. *Great Eats Paris* gives you enough information about each restaurant listed so that you will know generally what to expect before you get there. Still, when you arrive at your destination, read the posted menu *before* going in. This avoids unpleasant surprises and embarrassment in the event that what is offered that day does not appeal to your taste or budget.

Once inside and seated, do not ask for *le menu,* ask for *la carte.* That way you will get the complete listing of all the foods served, from appetizers to desserts, on *both* the prix fixe and à la carte menus. If you say, *le menu, s'il vous plaît* ("the menu, please"), you could get a strange look from the waiter, cause some confusion, and possibly end up with the prix fixe meal, which is also referred to as *le menu.*

When reading a menu, look at the *menu prix fixe* (sometimes called a *formule* or *menu conseille*) as well as the à la carte menu. The prix fixe menu usually consists of a combination of two or three courses—the *entrée* (first course), the *plat* (main course), and cheese and/or dessert—all for one price. The drinks (wine, beer, or mineral water, and sometimes coffee) may or may not be included. The prix fixe is often a terrific bargain, especially in higher-priced restaurants and during lunch, enabling those on a tighter budget to dine in luxury. Very often the same dishes are offered at night at more than double what savvy diners paid in the afternoon. The prix fixe choices may be limited, but the value is always there. If you opt for this menu, you will be expected to take all of the courses offered and not make any substitutions. If you want only one or two, and three are offered, there will generally be no reduction in price, but don't think that a three- or even four-course meal will be too much to eat. A good French meal is balanced, and the portions are not large. Enjoy your meal the way the French do—slowly—and you will not feel overfed.

Most restaurants also offer à la carte choices, and for those with lighter appetites, this often makes good sense because you are not paying for courses you do not want. Another smart, money-saving tactic in a café, bar, or brasserie is to order just a main course, or the *plat du jour*. However, exercise caution when ordering à la carte: if you start to order more than one dish, remember that each course is priced separately—and that the sum of the parts may add up to a very expensive meal compared to the prix fixe menu.

When ordering, keep in mind what is likely to be fresh and in season, and consider, too, the specialties of the chef. No matter what the size or scope of the eating establishment, always consider the *entrée* or *plat du jour* (the daily special starter and main course). They usually change every day, the ingredients are fresh and seasonal, and there is a rapid turnover because the dishes are proven winners with the regulars. They will not be dishes whose ingredients have been languishing in the refrigerator for several days or relegated to the freezer due to lack of interest. The specialties of the house are sometimes starred or underlined in red on the menu. You will also see the word *maison* (house) written by some choices, which means that it is made "in house" and therefore considered a specialty. If you want a green salad and don't see one on the menu, almost every kitchen will have the fixings to put together a *salade verte* or *salade mixe* if you ask. It won't test the skill of the chef, but sometimes a light starter is in order. The day of the week is also important. Fish can be a poor choice on Sunday, when the wholesale food market at Rungis is closed, and on Monday, when most outdoor markets are closed. Also keep in mind where you are. If you are in a corner café, complete with pinball machines and a tabac in the corner, don't expect the chef to perform magic with wild game or to dazzle you with high-rising soufflés.

Meals

Every good meal in Paris is like a *petite vacance*.
—*Ray Lampard*

Proper French meals usually consist of three courses—an *entrée* (starter), a *plat* (main course), and cheese or dessert—but they can also be just the *plat* with either the *entrée* or the dessert. At more formal restaurants, you can expect to be served additional courses up to as many as seven. Bread, an essential part of any French meal, is served free, and it is usually freshly cut just before it is brought to your table; you are entitled to as much as you want. Unless you are given a separate bread plate, place your bread on the table, not on your plate. Butter is usually not served with the bread, but you can always ask for it.

Here is a list of the traditional French courses:

apéritif	before-dinner drink, generally a kir
amuse bouche or *amuse gueule*	a plate of little hors d'oeuvres served with your apéritif
entrée	appetizer or starter
fish course	
plat	main course
salad or cheese	
dessert	
petits fours	plate of cookies served with after-dinner coffee
coffee	always espresso

The best way to experience Parisian life (or, for that matter, the way people live in any place) is to dine the way the locals do, at the same times, and on the native dishes and specialties that constitute their culinary heritage. The French take dining very seriously. In most French restaurants, no matter how big or small, time is not of the essence. A meal is to be savored and enjoyed, not dispatched in a rush to some other destination. This especially applies to dinner, which is often an event lasting the entire evening.

There was a time when one could honestly say, "You can't get a bad meal in Paris." With the influx of golden arches, pizza parlors, ethnic restaurants, and *le fast food,* it is definitely possible to suffer a bad Paris meal. Despite this, there are few cities in the world where you can consistently eat as well as you can in Paris, and if you plan carefully, you can have the gastronomic experience of a lifetime for much less than you would spend in any other major city in the world.

Just as Paris fashions change, so do the demands of restaurant patrons. Not too long ago dining before 8 P.M. was almost unheard of. Now, more and more restaurants are opening at 7 or 7:30 P.M. for dinner and staying open much later on Friday and Saturday nights. Many, too, are now staying open part of August, which a few years ago was absolutely unthinkable. Unfortunately, many of the long-standing restaurant standards regarding the waitstaff dress code have been dramatically relaxed. Levi's, T-shirts, and jogging shoes have replaced black pants, bow ties, and long white aprons, especially in the cheaper places.

As a result of the desire for lighter meals, wine bars and tearooms continue to flourish. Formula restaurants are booming—these places offer either a limited two-course, rapid-service menu or a three-course meal with several selections for each course and wine, but no à la carte. In order to keep the cost of meals down and still cope with rising inflation, more and more restaurants are adopting the use of paper napkins and paper table coverings, the corners of which are then used by the waiter to tally the bill. The Parisian love affair with anything American, especially food, shows no signs of diminishing. Weekend brunch, chocolate chip cookies, cheesecake, brownies, apple crumble, baby back ribs, and pizza delivered to the door win converts daily.

No matter what the recipe or the time of year, a good French chef insists on the freshest ingredients, ignores frozen or, heaven forbid, canned, and does not cut corners or use artificial flavorings or preservatives. French eating establishments, from humble cafés to the great temples of gastronomy, seldom have teenagers working part-time in the kitchen or waiting tables between classes. From the chef on down, the employees are dedicated personnel who consider their jobs permanent, not way stations on the road to somewhere else. This makes a difference in everything from the quality of food on your plate to the service at your table.

Breakfast (*Petite Déjeuner*)

Breakfast is served from 7 to 10 A.M. in most cafés.

Parisians do not have a good grasp of what constitutes a real American breakfast, so do yourself a favor and follow the French example: start the day at the corner café with a *café au lait, grande crème,* or a *chocolat chaud* and a flaky croissant. If you are willing to eat standing at the bar, you will save significantly, and of course, you will save money eating breakfast almost any place but your hotel, where the markup can be 100 percent. If your hotel has a buffet breakfast, *please* do not try to bag enough extra to sustain you through lunch. *Hôteliers* take a very dim view of this practice, and if you attempt it, you will label yourself as a greedy tourist without a *soupçon* of manners. If you do insist on bacon and eggs or other staples of the American breakfast table, be prepared to pay dearly for them. Astute diners save their omelettes or ham and eggs for lunch.

Lunch (*Déjeuner*)

The midday meal is served from noon to 2:30 P.M., with the last order taken about thirty minutes before closing.

If you face a deadline, or do not want a full-blown meal at lunch, grab a sandwich from the nearest *boulangerie* or *pâtisserie;* go to a café, wine bar, or tearoom; or put together *le snack.* Do not try to rush through a meal at a restaurant, and please do not go into a restaurant and order just a salad or an appetizer. It just is not done, and you will not be regarded well by the staff, which can result in embarrassment on your part.

A surprising number of French eat their main meal at noon. Recognizing this, many places offer very good value prix fixe menus at lunch *only.* If you are on a shoestring budget, or are willing to eat a large lunch, there are bargains in all categories of eateries. Many places have their biggest crowds at lunch, so if you do not have a reservation, keep this in mind and try to arrive early to be assured a good seat. Remember, too, that the specials often run out, making yet another reason to arrive earlier rather than later.

Paris has many delightful parks—such as the Luxembourg Gardens, the Tuileries, Champ-de-Mars, Jardin des Plantes, and the Bois de Boulogne—not to mention the romantic banks along the Seine and the many pretty squares throughout the city. The street *marchés* and shopping streets are the perfect places to shop for a satisfying and inexpensive al fresco *piquenique* lunch (see "Food Shopping," page 34). If you have your picnic on a warm day in the park, you will probably share your bench with a French person on his or her lunch hour having a *piquenique sur l'herbe,* too.

Dinner (*Dîner*)

Dinner is served from 7 or 7:30 P.M. to 10 or 11 P.M., with the last order being taken about fifteen to thirty minutes before closing.

Dinner is a leisurely affair; the lunchtime frenzy is replaced by a quiet, more sedate mood. American tourists usually eat between 7 and 8 P.M., while 8:30 or 9 P.M. is still the most popular Parisian dinner time. Few cafés serve dinner, so your best bet is a brasserie, bistro, or restaurant. If you want a light meal or a rather late one, go to a wine bar.

Fast Food *à la Française* (*Le Snack*)

Not everyone wants to devote a large segment of the day to a long lunch. Sometimes we get hungry at odd hours or have children who plead starvation if they do not have something within minutes. This is where *le snack* comes in.

Fast food *à la française,* or *le snack,* means a crêpe from the corner stand, a sandwich to go (*pour emporter*) from a café, a quiche or small pizza heated at the *boulangerie,* or something from the *charcuterie* or nearby *traiteur.* There are the café standards: a *croque-monsieur* or a *croque-madame.* A *monsieur* is a toasted ham sandwich with cheese on top, and *madame* adds a fried egg over that. *Boulangeries* also sell delicious sandwiches, where the classic ham-and-cheese sandwich becomes a *jambon et gruyère* on a half of a baguette without mustard or mayo, or it is toasted between two slices of *pain de campagne.* Vegetarians can order a *crudités* sandwich, which includes lettuce, hard-boiled eggs, tomatoes, and sometimes mushrooms. *Charcuteries* and *traiteurs* specialize in prepared salads, pâtés, terrines, whole roasted chickens, a variety of cooked dishes, and usually one or two daily hot specials. All items are packed to go, and sometimes you can get a plastic fork or spoon. Most large grocery stores also have a *charcuterie* section where they sell individual slices of cold meat and portions of cheese. Add a fresh baguette, yogurt, a piece or two of fruit, and a cold drink or bottle of *vin ordinaire,* and you have a cheap and filling meal for little outlay of time and money. You can also assemble your feast from the stalls of one of the colorful street *marchés* or *rues commerçants* (see "Food Shopping," page 34). At these, the sky is the limit for tempting gourmet meals on the run.

Types of Food

Cooking is about sharing pleasure. Food is only half of what is on the plate. There is also love and truth.

— *Yves Camdeborde,*
owner/chef of La Réglade

Bourgeoise Cuisine

Nostalgia has never been more "in," declare the culinary pundits in Paris. There is no doubt about it, *bourgeoise cuisine à la grand-mère* continues to enjoy tremendous popularity in Paris, ensuring that cholesterol remains alive and well throughout France. This reassuring, back-burner bistro fare is the traditional cooking on which the French have subsisted for centuries. On thousands of menus, you can expect to see its mainstays: pâté, terrines, *oeuf dur mayonnaise,* duck, rabbit, *cassoulet, pot-au-feu, boeuf bourguignon, blanquette de veau, tarte Tatin,* and *crème caramel.*

Nouvelle Cuisine

Nouvelle cuisine was coined by food critics Henry Gault and Christian Millau in the 1970s and has probably been one of the most widely talked about developments in French cooking in the past fifty years. Nouvelle cuisine scorns the use of rich and heavy sauces. It emphasizes instead a lighter style of classic French cooking with a greater use of vegetables, an imaginative combination of ingredients, and a stylish and colorful presentation of very small servings . . . all undercooked just a little. Over time, most people have decided that many of the dishes are contrived and result in unsatisfying dining adventures. As a result, the popularity of nouvelle cuisine has waned.

Regional Cuisine

Solid regional cooking from the provinces, once snubbed by food lovers as parochial and unsophisticated, has made a remarkable comeback as the French get closer to their roots and bring back old favorites. You can travel gastronomically throughout France and never leave the Paris city limits. The finest regional cooking is to be found in the capital, and it represents some of the best food you will ever eat.

The big brasseries feature German-influenced Alsatian specialties of steaming platters of sauerkraut, sausages, and bacon; German Riesling wines; and mugs of frosty beer. If a restaurant features food from the Savoy region, near the Swiss-Alpine border, look for a bounty of cheeses, fondues, and *raclettes.* Food from the southwest Basque area is spicy, influenced by its Spanish neighbor. Superb seafood comes from Brittany in the north and from Nice in the south. Food from Provence is heavy with herbs, garlic, olive oil, and tomatoes. You can sample bouillabaisse, *pistou* (a pungent paste of fresh basil, cheese, garlic, and olive oil), *salade niçoise,* and ratatouille made from eggplant, zucchini, garlic, sweet peppers, and tomatoes. Veal and lamb are gifts from Normandy, and hearty *cassoulets* and huge helpings of *l'aligot*—a blend of puréed potatoes, garlic, and melted cheese—signify the robust cooking of the Auvergne. If the dish is *à la Lyonnaise,* it will be cooked with sautéed onions and wine, while the food from Burgundy reflects this wine-growing region in lusty stews flavored with mushrooms, bacon, and onions.

Bread

Bread is one of the great charms of our civilization.
—*Jacques Chirac,*
former prime minister of France

Bread is definitely the staff of life in France, and it is served with every meal. Because a baguette contains no fat, it gets stale quickly. That is why no French person would ever consider buying bread in the morning to eat with dinner. As a result, statistics show that the average Parisian makes at least three trips to the *boulangerie* per day. In the morning, a baguette is split, spread with sweet butter, and eaten with, or dunked in, a big cup of *café crème.* For lunch and dinner, it is served freshly cut, without butter, and is nibbled on throughout the meal and used at the end to wipe up the last few drops of juice on the plate. A fresh basket of bread is also usually served with the cheese course. French bread etiquette holds that you do not put your bread on your plate. It stays on the table next to your plate until you have finished it and are ready for the next piece.

In January 1997, the French government took drastic steps to protect the baguette from mass production and cost-cutting methods, such as using frozen dough. Aimed at safeguarding baker-artisans, a new law is in force that now restricts the name "bakery" (*boulangerie*) only to those shops where the bakers bake their own bread on the premises. This has required an estimated five thousand shops selling bread from factory-frozen dough to remove their *boulangerie* signs.

When looking for a *boulangerie,* watch for those with long lines. You can be sure the neighborhood knows where to go for the best bread and patronizes those bakers who make their own dough and bake it on the premises. There are hundreds of types of bread available. The following list just hits the high spots.

baguette	a loaf legally weighing eight ounces, this is the long, crisp bread served most often in restaurants; it contains no fat
bâtard	similar to a baguette, but with a softer crust
ficelle	a very thin, crusty baguette
pain complet	a whole-grain loaf that comes in various shapes and sizes

pain de campagne	a blend made with whole wheat, rye, and bran that is heavier in texture and comes in all sizes and shapes; it can also be a large white loaf dusted with flour
pain grillé	toasted bread
pain au noix	rye or wheat bread with nuts
pain au son	with bran
pain d'épices	gingerbread
pain de seigle	rye bread
pain Poilâne	Poilâne is the most famous bakery in Paris, with outlets in Japan and mail orders sent to the United States. It is famous for its dark sourdough blend baked in a wood-burning oven. Though *pain Poilâne* can be found elsewhere and is served in many restaurants, the main source is at the Poilâne bakery in the sixth arrondissement (see page 141 for details).

Cheese

The French will only be united under the threat of danger. No one can simply bring together a country that has over 265 kinds of cheese.
—*Charles de Gaulle*

Actually, France produces more than four hundred varieties of cheese, and the average Frenchperson consumes between forty and fifty pounds of it per year. When dining in France, you will quickly recognize that cheese is a vital ingredient in any meal. Cheese is served after the main course, never before dinner with cocktails or a glass of wine as it is in the United States. When you are presented the cheese tray, don't be afraid to branch out and select a variety you have never tasted. And don't worry if you see some mold around the edges. For the French, runny, moldy, smelly cheeses are the best. If a cheese does not mold a little, it is too pasteurized to be worth anything. After you return home, you may wonder why the chèvre in your market does not compare to that in your favorite Parisian bistro. The answer is simple: exported cheese must be sterilized, which kills the bacteria that give it taste. The following list of cheese types should help you when the cheese tray appears after a meal, or when you are trying to decide which cheese to buy at the *marché*.

mild	*beaufort, beaumont, belle étoile, boursin,* brie, *cantal, comté, petit-suisse, port-salut, reblochon, saint-paulin, tomme*
sharp	*bleu de Bresse, brousse,* camembert, *livarot, maroilles,* muenster, *pont-l'évêque,* roquefort, *vacherin*
goat's milk	*bûcheron, cabécou, crottin de Chavignol, rocamadour, st-marcellin*
Swiss cheese	*emmental,* gruyère

Meat

The French cook their meat much less than we do. Witness the popularity of steak tartare, a reoccuring specialty in many of the best restaurants in Paris. Pink chicken is the norm, and *bleu* beef (blue, or blood raw to most Americans) is considered the height of good eating. *Saignant* (rare) is only slightly better done, but *à point* (medium rare) approaches the edible. *Bien cuit* (well done) may still be dripping blood, but it is at least hot and most of it will be cooked. Some meats simply do not taste good when they are well cooked, and the waiter will tell you, "It cannot be done." Trust him or her and order something else.

To help you answer the inevitable question, *Quelle cuisson?* ("How do you want that cooked?"), here is a list of responses:

cru	raw
bleu	almost raw
saignant	rare, still bleeding
rosé	pink
à point	medium rare
bien cuit	well done
très bien cuit	very well done

Pâtisseries

French pastries, like French women, are put together with precision.
—Anonymous

The Gallic passion for *pâtisserie* is a national obsession, arousing cravings unknown to most foreigners. Paris pastry lovers think nothing of traveling across the city in search of the perfect *éclair au café, charlotte au chocolat, forêt-noire* (a rich fudge cake with a cherry topping), or a *millefeuille* (layers of thin, buttery, flaky pastry holding cream, custard, and/or fruit). American brownies, chocolate chip cookies, and layer cakes pale by comparison . . . if you would even think of comparing them. Fine *pâtisserie* is a creation using the best ingredients, made fresh each day, that's meant to be eaten immediately, if not sooner. There are *pâtisseries* all over Paris, all offering an Ali Baba's cave of tempting treats. Your waistline is the only barometer of how much you will consume and enjoy. In this book, I have included a few Parisian *pâtisseries* that I particularly like, but there are literally hundreds more. Those mentioned here should at least get you started in the limitless world of Parisian pastries.

Unusual Foods

There is nothing discreet about French food. Remnants that are discarded in the United States, or animals not normally eaten, are here transformed into gastronomical delicacies. You will encounter *rognons* (kidneys), *cervelles* (brains), *ris de veau* (veal sweetbreads), *mouton* (mutton), *lapin* (rabbit), *andouillettes* (chitterling sausages), *langue de boeuf* or *agneau* (beef or lamb tongue), and the head, ears, toes, lips, cheeks, and tails of many other animals. There are butchers selling only horse meat. You can recognize them by the golden horse head hanging over their shops. Depending on the season, you will also find *pintade* (guinea fowl), *sanglier* (wild boar), *chevreuil* (young deer), and *civet de lièvre* (wild hare stew). Blood is often used to thicken sauces, especially in *civet de lièvre*. Blood is also used to make sausage, as in the *boudin noir* (pork blood sausages). All of these dishes can be delicious, and the French excel in their preparation. They represent dining experiences you must try—at least once.

Vegetarian

A *végétarien(ne)* in Paris need not starve. Gone are the days when one had to settle for boring meals or a plate of crudités and a cup of lukewarm tea at the corner café. While vegetarianism in France is not what it is in the United States, it is gaining ground in Paris. Those who eat some cheese and fish will have the easiest time, but there are also havens for those who eat no animal or dairy products. Most serve a wider range of dishes that are guaranteed to please every dedicated veggie lover as well as their carnivorous friends who don't mind hitching a ride on the green bandwagon, if only for one or two meals. I have noted a number of my favorites in this book.

Very often, if you call ahead to better restaurants and ask if the chef can prepare something for a vegetarian, your request will be met with pleasure. This is the best way to handle the situation, rather than arriving and not giving the chef any advance notice. If the kitchen is busy, your dish may not be very inspired, or you may have to make do with a large order of the vegetable of the day and a side of rich potatoes.

Drinks

Apéritifs, Between-Meal Drinks, and *Digestifs*

The French prefer not to anesthetize their taste buds with American-style cocktails before a meal. If you usually order a dry martini or double scotch on the rocks before dinner, try one of the mildly alcoholic wine apéritifs such as a kir or kir royale. A kir is made from crème de cassis and chilled white wine. A kir royale substitutes champagne for the wine. The slightly bitter Campari and soda or a Pernod, an anise-flavored drink, are two other good choices.

If you are hot and thirsty in the afternoon, try a Vittel menthe: a shot of crème de menthe diluted with Vittel mineral water and served icy cold. It is one of the cheapest and most refreshing between-meal drinks. For a nonalcoholic beverage, a good choice is *l'orange pressé* (fresh orange juice) or *le citron pressé* (lemonade). Coca-Cola (Coka) and Orangina, a carbonated orange drink, are popular soft drinks, as are any of the mineral waters served with a twist of lemon or lime. An important tip for Coke lovers . . . don't order a Coke with your meal. The French consider this absolutely unacceptable.

France is not known for beer, but if you do want a beer, don't say so. There is a French product, *Byrrh,* that sounds the same but is a bitter quinine-based wine apéritif, and this is what you are likely to get if you order "a beer." If you want a draft beer, ask for *un demi* or *une bière à la pression.* They come in three sizes: *demi* (eight ounces), *sérieux* (sixteen ounces), and *formidable* (one quart). Remember, it is pronounced "be-air," not "beer." If you ask simply for *une bière,* you will be asked what kind because you will have ordered a bottle of beer. The best, and usually the cheapest, bottled beer in France is Kronenbourg.

After-dinner drinks (*digestifs*) are popular in Paris. The most common are cognac and various distilled fruit brandies: Calvados (apple), *kirsch* (cherry), *marc* (grape), and *quetsch* (plum). Measures are generous, but they are generally not bargains.

Coffee

Good coffee should be black like the devil, hot like hell, and sweet like a kiss.

—*Hungarian proverb*

If you order *un café s'il vous plaît* ("a coffee, please"), you will be served a small cup of very strong espresso with lumps or packets of sugar on the side. The French consider it barbaric to drink coffee with a meal. Coffee is drunk after a meal or by itself in a café, but never *with* the meal and, after dinner, certainly not with milk or cream. You may order an espresso with dessert, but you will receive an arched eyebrow from the waiter and be considered a rank tourist if you insist on it. Your after-dinner coffee is meant to arrive after dessert, not with it.

French coffee is wonderful. It comes in various bewildering forms, all of which are stronger and more flavorful than American coffee. All coffee is served by the cup, and there are no free refills. The following glossary of coffees should help you get what you want.

Café express, or *café noir,* is espresso made by forcing hot steam through freshly ground beans. If you prefer it weaker, ask for *café allongé,* and you will be given a small pitcher of hot water to dilute it.

Café crème is espresso made with steamed milk, and *café au lait* is espresso with warmed milk. Neither of these is ordered after dinner, and only seldom after lunch. They are strictly breakfast or between-meal *boissons.*

Café filtre is filtered coffee that is the closest to American in taste, but it is often available only in more expensive restaurants, and very seldom in a basic café.

Déca or *café décaféiné* is decaffeinated espresso. It bears the same resemblance to the tasteless U.S. version as a Rolls-Royce does to a bicycle.

Double and *grand* are terms used to request a double-size cup of any of the above.

Tea

Tea is considered a breakfast or between-meal beverage, not a drink to have with a meal or after it. Outside a fancy tearoom, you will usually be served the tea-bag variety, and the water will often be tepid. *Tisanes* or *infusions* are the terms used for herb teas. Every café serves them. They are very nice to order when you have overeaten or feel stressed. The most common infusions are *verveine* (verbena), *menthe* (mint), chamomile, and *tileul* (linden). Iced tea is almost unheard of.

Water

You could almost die of thirst before getting a simple glass of water in Paris, let alone a glass of ice water. You will not automatically be served water the minute you sit down. If you want water, you must ask for it. If you are a purist, order bottled water, which is very popular and available everywhere. You will, however, be just as well off and money ahead by ordering tap water (*une carafe d'eau* or *l'eau ordinaire*), which is one of the few free things you will get in Paris. Favorite bottled mineral waters are Evian and Vittel, which are noncarbonated (*plat* or *non-gazeuse*), and Badoit and Perrier, which are sparkling (*gazeuse*). Perrier is always a between-meal drink because the French consider it too gaseous to be drunk with meals. If you want ice cubes, ask for *glaçons,* but don't always expect to get them.

Wine

Ask any well-fed French person and he or she will tell you that a meal without wine is like a kiss without the squeeze. Wine (*vin*) is drunk at almost every meal, including before breakfast for some. Red is *rouge,* white is *blanc,* and rose is *rosé.* In a bar, you will get the cheapest glass if you ask for *un verre de rouge* or *un ballon de vin rouge* (a glass of red wine) or *un verre de blanc* or *un blanc sec* (a glass of white or dry white wine). The basic wine terms are *brut,* very dry; *sec,* dry; *demi-sec,* semisweet; *doux,* very sweet; and *champagne* is champagne. There are many grape varieties, and the endless complexities of that subject could fill a library's-worth of books. It is beyond the scope of *Great Eats Paris* to attempt a thorough discussion of French wines or to provide a formula for selecting the perfect wine for every meal. However, one change has made it easier: The old rule that red was drunk only with red meat and white with chicken or fish is out—order what you want, and no one will look twice.

If you are interested in saving money, order the house wine (*vin de la maison*) or a pitcher of table wine (*un pichet du vin ordinaire*) or a bottle from the patron's own cave (*cuvée du patron*). Any of these will be perfectly drinkable and usually quite reasonably priced. The wine *carte* can be a budget killer, as most bottled vintages tend to drive up the cost of the meal inordinately. Unless you are a true wine connoisseur, it seems foolish to spend twice as much on the wine as on the food. You can bet that the Frenchperson sitting next to you won't be doing it. If you do decide to branch out and yet find the wine list perplexing, don't be afraid to ask questions, state your budget, or take advice.

The following should take some of the confusion out of reading a French wine label.

AOC *appelation contrôlée*	highest quality, most expensive wine
cépage	grape variety
cru	superior
mis en bouteilles à la château	made at the wine-producing estate
mis en bouteilles par	bottled by
mousseux	sparkling
vin de pays	local wine, less quality control than AOC wines
vin de table	varying quality, usually acceptable
vin ordinaire	means the same as *vin de table,* usually acceptable

French Dining Manners

This is the latest trend. Waiters are becoming *nice!*

—*An alarmed French friend in Paris*

Crowding

When judging a restaurant, don't be put off by location, appearance, or decor. A better gauge is how crowded it is with local French, since as everyone knows, a full house is always a good sign. Crowded restaurants are an accepted fact of dining life in Paris, with the distance between tables often only one thin person wide, if that. You can't fight this phenomenon, and besides, being comfortably wedged in along a banquette leads to some mighty interesting benchmates and conversations, both shared and overheard.

Doggie Bags + Splitting an Order = Two No-Nos

The French have more dogs per capita than any other people on earth. Short of being given the vote, dogs have many rights in Paris, not the least of which is dining out with their owners. While you will seldom see anyone under eighteen in a restaurant, you will always see well-behaved dogs, especially in cafés, sitting on the seat next to their master or quietly lying at his or her feet. You would think this enormous dog population would create a demand for doggie bags, at least for the stay-at-home canines. Wrong. Half of France is on some kind of *régime* (diet), and leaving food on your plate is acceptable. Asking for a doggie bag, whether for Fido or yourself, is not.

Considered just as gauche and unacceptable as the doggie bag is asking to split dishes. Despite the number of courses in a typical French meal, portions are smaller than most Americans are used to, thus diners are expected to order accordingly and do the best they can.

Mind Your Manners and Dress for Success

Good manners don't show, bad ones always do.
—*Neva C. Abernethy*

Wear black, make it tight, accessorize . . . you'll look Parisian.
—*Sandra Busby*

Good manners are international, and *la politesse* is central to all transactions in France. The French are also more formal than we are. They don't call people by their first names, and they preface statements with *Pardon, Monsieur, S'il vous plaît, Madame,* or *Excusez-moi, Mademoiselle.* They will consider you to be rude if you do not do the same, or if you omit the words *monsieur, madame,* or *mademoiselle* when you speak to them. If you want good service, a *Bonjour, Monsieur,* or *Merci, Mademoiselle,* along with lots of *s'il vous plaîts* and *merci beaucoups* thrown in, will go a long way toward making your dining experience better.

To get the waiter's attention, don't shout *Garçon!* Contrary to most Americans, the French consider all restaurant work to be a profession, not a filler-job while waiting for something better to come along. For best results, always refer to the waiter as *monsieur* and the waitress as *mademoiselle,* regardless of age or marital status.

It is considered very rude to eat your *frites* (french fries), chicken, or any other food, for that matter, with your fingers. It is not uncommon to see diners peeling a pear or other piece of fruit with a knife and fork, and eating it with a fork.

The French can spot Americans in any dining establishment without looking: they are the ones with the loud, booming voices that seem to carry out into the street. If you want to blend in and not look like a green tourist, keep your voice down.

Dressing well is part of a French person's makeup, especially in Paris. While men do not always need to wear a coat and tie and women are not always required to dress to the nines, a little conservative good judgment is in order. The French have limited tolerance for the concept of sacrificing fashion for comfort. This is especially true when it comes to footwear. While a woman could not be expected to negotiate the tourist trails in high heels, white athletic shoes are definitely *out* for all adults. Yes, wear a good pair of walking shoes . . . but be sure they are a dark color. In addition, short shorts, halter tops, T-shirts with insignias, and baseball caps in restaurants are frowned on; they will immediately brand you as a tacky tourist.

French etiquette demands that both hands be kept above the table while eating, not in the lap. And, finally, if you are full, don't look up "full" in your French dictionary and say, *Je suis plein.* This is a phrase used for cows, meaning they are pregnant. Say instead, if you do not want anymore to eat, *Je n'ai plus faim* ("I am not hungry any longer").

Food Shopping
Markets (*Marchés*)

The French shop for the meal, not for the week, and they measure the freshness of their food in minutes, not days. If you ask the fruit merchant if the pears are ripe, he or she will ask you when that day you will eat them, and often at what time, and then select just the right ones. It's customary at the smaller corner markets for the clerk to serve you; at larger *marchés,* they may or may not pick your fruits and vegetables for you, and if not, they will hand you a metal pan or basket to put your selections in. Even though indoor *supermarchés* are all over Paris, every neighborhood *quartier* has its own *rue commerçante* (shopping street) or *marché volant* (roving market), each with its own special character and offering an inspiring selection of food. These *marchés* offer an endless source of interest and insight into the hearts and minds of ordinary Parisians, and visiting one of them is a cultural experience you should not miss. Go in the morning and gather the ingredients for a picnic lunch or supper; admire the rows of produce arranged with the same care and precision as fine jewelry displays. In seeking out the best stalls, look for the sign *producteur,* which means these merchants are selling food they grow or produce themselves. Take your camera and a string bag, don't mind the crowds, watch your wallet, and enjoy these lively alternatives to galleries, monuments, churches, and other must-see stops on every visitor's list. When dining out, order the food you have seen in the market. You can bet the chef was there long before you were to select perfectly ripe strawberries, fat spears of asparagus, the freshest fish, and the ripest cheeses, all for that day's menu.

Roving Markets (*Marchés Volantes*)

Roving markets move from one neighborhood to another on specific days. They are open from 8 A.M. to 1 P.M. only on the days listed.

Carnes, 5th, place Maubert, Métro: Maubert-Mutualité; Tues, Thur, and Sat.

Monge, 5th, place Monge, Métro: Monge; Wed, Fri, and Sat.

Port-Royal, 5th, in front of l'hôpital du val de Grâce at rue St-Jacques, Métro: Port-Royal; Tues, Thur, and Sat.

Raspail, 6th, boulevard Raspail between rue de Cherche-Midi and rue de Rennes, Métro: Rennes or Sèvres-Babylone; Tues and Fri. On Sunday this is a *marché biologique* (organic market).

Saxe-Breteuil, 7th, avenue de Saxe from avenue de Ségur to place Breteuil, Métro: Segur; Thur and Sat. This is one of the most beautiful, where you can see the Eiffel Tower in the distance between the rows of food and flower stalls.

Bastille, 11th, boulevard Richard-Lenoir at rue Amelot, Métro: Bastille; Thur and Sun.

Boulevard de Belleville, 11th/20th, Métro: Belleville, Couronnes; Tues and Fri. Low prices, ethnic foods.

Cour de Vincennes, 12th, Métro: Nation; Wed and Sat.

Boulevard de Grenelle, 15th, between rue Lourmel and rue du Commerce, Métro: Dupleix or La Motte-Picquet; Wed and Sun.

Cours de la Reine-Marché Président Wilson, 16th, between rue Debrousse and Place Iéna, Métro: Alma Marceau or Iéna; Wed and Sat.

Organic Markets (*Marchés Bio or Biologique*)

Raspail, 6th, boulevard Raspail between rue de Cherche-Midi and rue de Rennes, Métro: Rennes or Sèvres-Babylone; Sun 8:30 A.M.–1 P.M.

Batignolles, 17th, boulevard de Batignolles between rue de Rome and place de Clichy, Métro: Place de Clichy, Sat 9 A.M.–1:30 P.M.

Shopping Streets (*Rue Commerçants*)

These permanent shopping streets are usually open from 8:30 or 9 A.M. to 1 P.M. and from 4 to 7 P.M. Tuesday through Saturday. Sunday they are open only in the morning. During holidays and in July and August not all merchants are open.

Rue Montorgueil, 2nd, Métro: Sentier or Étienne Marcel.

Rue Mouffetard, 5th, Métro: Monge.

Rue de Buci, 6th, Métro: Odéon.

Rue Cler, 7th, Métro: École-Militaire.

Rues des Martyres, 9th, Métro: Notre Dame-de-Lorette.

Aligré, 12th, place d'Aligré, Métro: Ledru-Rollin; Tues through Sun, mornings only (best on Sun).

Rue Daguerre, 14th, Métro: Denfert-Rochereau; the market begins at the southern end of the street.

Rue de l'Annonciation, 16th, Métro: La Muette; the market begins at place de Passy and rue de l'Annonciation.

Rue de Levis, 17th, Métro: Villiers; the market begins at boulevard des Batignolles.

Rue Poncelet, 17th, Métro: Ternes; the market begins at avenue des Ternes.

Rue Lepic, 18th, Métro: Abbesses.

Supermarkets (*Supermarchés*)

In Paris you won't find huge supermarket chains offering weekly specials and double coupons. Food shopping requires a different line of attack. Paris department stores are home to some of the most magnificently stocked supermarkets you will ever see. Fauchon, on place de la Madeleine (see page 172), is the standard-bearer for gourmet grocery shopping. Lafayette Gourmet on the first floor of Galeries Lafayette (see page 182) and La Grande Épicerie de Paris at Bon Marché (see page 153) are the two most luxurious. Marks & Spencer (see below) stocks British goodies along with French comestibles. Most Monoprix stores have a basement grocery selling everything from bread and cheese to wine, beer, and frozen products. One of the best Monoprix grocery locations is on rue de Rennes, Métro: St-Germain-des-Prés. Grocery chains such as Shopi, Codec, and le Marché Franprix sell all the canned, bottled, and packaged basics. Then there are the little stores, open every day and until late at night, selling wilted veggies and bruised fruit in front . . . but if you only need a bottle of mineral water or a box of tissues, they are ports in a storm.

Marks & Spencer has two Paris locations:

35, boulevard Haussmann, 8th, Métro: Chaussée-d'Antin-La Fayette
88, rue de Rivoli, 1st, Métro: Châtelet
Open: Mon, Wed–Sat 9:30 A.M.–7 P.M., Tues 10 A.M.–7 P.M.
Closed: Sun
Credit Cards: MC, V

Cooking Classes

Promenades Gourmande

Not only did I learn a lot about cooking, but I had the opportunity to meet a wonderful person!

—*George Brooks, attorney-at-law*

It doesn't matter who you are—everyone from gourmet chefs to fledging novices will learn something from the dynamic Parisian chef Paule Caillat, whose love of cooking and culinary heritage transform everything she touches. Paule, who was born and raised in Paris and college-educated in the States, gives private and group cooking lessons in Paris, but I can assure you they are a quantum leap from the ordinary, stilted classes I have often attended. Menus are selected according to the season, student preferences, and a careful eye for product availability once you have returned home. Cooking with Paule means hands-on from the get-go: shopping at the market right through enjoying what you have prepared and cleaning up afterward. On the trip to the outdoor market, you will learn how to recognize the best ingredients, discern the different types of bread and cheese, detect a French apricot from one imported from Israel and know which one to buy, select the perfect meats and fish, and avoid anything that is not absolutely fresh. Through her knowledge of food you will also be able to place the products you buy into their historical and geographical context in France. After lunch (if you have signed up for a full-day session) Paule will take you on another Promenade Gourmande (gourmet walking tour) to visit famous bakeries, kitchens of well-known restaurants, the bistros of rising young chefs, landmark kitchen equipment emporiums, saffron producers, and much more.

Cooking lessons are not the half of Paule and her enthusiasm about food. She also leads small groups on excursions to areas in France that are specifically known for their exceptional food products. The trips include train travel, all meals and accommodations, and visits to points of interest.

Paule is a delightful, dynamic, knowledgeable woman. If you love food and cooking, please treat yourself to one of her cooking lessons or trips. You won't regret it for a minute. As one very happy participant said, "This was the best day I have ever spent in Paris, and the highlight of my entire trip!" I agree, and so does everyone lucky enough to spend time with Paule.

Note: No classes or tours are held in August.

Paule Caillat—Promenades Gourmande

187, rue du Temple, 75003

Telephone: 01-48-04-56-84

Fax: 01-42-78-59-77

Email: paule.caillat@wanadoo.fr

Credit Cards: None, cash only

Prices: Half day: market visit, cooking class, and lunch, $200; two half days, $360; full day: market visit, class, lunch, gourmet walking tour, $290; two full days, $560.

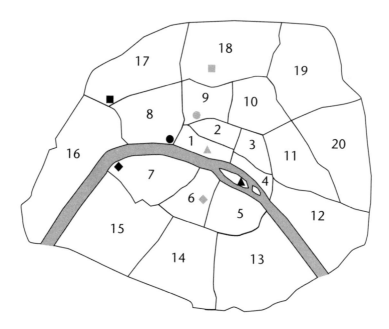

● Place de la Concorde
■ Arc de Triomphe
▲ Notre Dame
◆ Tour Eiffel

● Opéra
■ Sacré Cœur
▲ Louvre
◆ Jardin du Luxembourg

RESTAURANTS IN PARIS
BY ARRONDISSEMENT

Paris is divided into twenty districts, or zones, known as *arrondissements.* Knowing which arrondissement is which is the key to understanding Paris and quickly finding your way around. Starting with the first arrondissement, which is the district around the Louvre, the numbering goes clockwise in a snail-like spiral. The postal code, or zip code, for Paris is 750, followed by the number of the arrondissement. Thus, 75001 refers to the first arrondissement, 75004 to the fourth, and 75016 means the location is in the expensive sixteenth.

An arrondissement has its own special character and feeling, so that Paris, when you get to know it, is a city of twenty neighborhood villages. Each has its own mayor, central post office, police station, and town hall, where marriages can be performed and deaths recorded. It takes a few afternoons of what the French call *flânerie*—unhurried, aimless wandering—to truly appreciate some of the more intriguing neighborhoods. When you go out, prepare to be sidetracked, diverted, and happily lost discovering all sorts of wonderful places and things.

The maps in this book are meant to help you locate the restaurants and the major landmarks, not to negotiate the city. I highly recommend you purchase a copy of the *Plan de Paris par Arrondissement* if you are going to be in Paris for more than one or two days. See also "Maps," page 12.

First Arrondissement

The Île de la Cité is the historic heart of Paris. It was on this island in the middle of the Seine that a Celtic tribe of fishermen called the Parisii settled in the third century B.C. and where the Gallo-Romans later built the city they called Lutetia in the first century A.D.

The history of Les Halles parallels the growth of Paris itself over the last twenty-five or thirty years. For decades Les Halles was the central wholesale food market in Paris. Nicknamed "the belly of Paris," it was an early-morning place of meat markets, fishmongers, fruit and vegetable sellers, and cheese merchants. In 1969, the market was moved to Rungis, on the outskirts of Paris, and in its place was built the Forum des Halles, a tremendous, multilevel indoor shopping complex, housing shops and the biggest métro station in the world. It is claimed you can walk here for hours and never see daylight. The area around the Forum des Halles now teems night and day with an inexhaustible supply of people of every size, shape, and style, providing the observer with an eye-opening look at the fashion crazes of the moment. While here, you can watch a fire-eating act, a sword swallower, an ascetic lying on a bed of nails, listen to all sorts of street-corner music, buy far-out fashions, observe the French *clochards* (bums) relaxing in doorways, get your hair colored or spiked, see an X-rated film, fill up on fast food, or sit in a café and almost literally watch the world parade by.

RIGHT BANK
Conciergeri (where Marie Antoinette was beheaded), Île de la Cité, Ste-Chapelle (with fifteen hundred square yards of blue and red stained glass), Palais de Justice, Louvre, Jardin des Tuileries, Pont Neuf (the oldest bridge in Paris), place Vendôme, Les Halles, Palais Royal, Comédie Française, and Quai de la Mégisserie (bird, flower, and animal market)

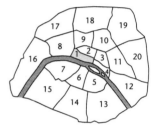

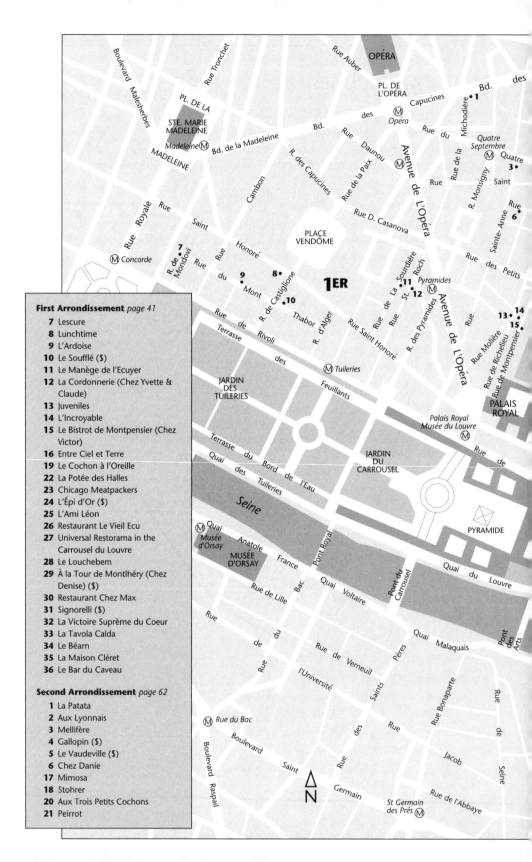

First and Second Arrondissements

FIRST ARRONDISSEMENT RESTAURANTS

($) indicates a Big Splurge

À LA TOUR DE MONTLHÉRY (CHEZ DENISE) ($, 29)
5, rue des Prouvaires
Métro: Châtelet–Les Halles, Louvre-Rivoli

"It's not good, it's wonderful!" That is what the man seated one elbow away told me the first time I ate here. And he knew what he was talking about: he had eaten here every day for years, as have scores of other robust French. If you are looking for a colorful and authentic Les Halles bistro that has not changed in a hundred years, À la Tour de Montlhéry, or Chez Denise to the regulars, is a must if you are willing to spend a little more. The classic spot is busy twenty-four hours a day with a colorful mixture of artists, businesspeople, and writers, all served by surefooted, white-aproned career waiters who keep running, flirting, and smiling despite the crunch. The small tables are always jam-packed, and the din of happy diners creating a blue haze of Gauloise smoke is typically French.

Eternity stands behind the almost indecipherable chalkboard menu, and no dieters need apply: this is hearty food with portions that some might consider lethal. To start, order the snails in garlic butter or the *salade frisée* with crisp homemade croutons. Follow this with *tripes au Calvados, haricot de mouton,* tender rabbit in grainy mustard sauce, or the wonderful stuffed cabbage. Complement your meal with a bottle of Brouilly, the house wine. The desserts can be ignored if you insist, but I always try to save room to sample the generous cheese tray or a piece of the *gâteau Marguerite,* laden with fresh strawberries and cream.

TELEPHONE
01-42-36-21-82

OPEN
Mon–Sat: 7 A.M.–7 A.M., 24 hours a day, continuous service

CLOSED
Sat (after 7 A.M.)–Sun; holidays, July 14–Aug 15

RESERVATIONS
Essential

CREDIT CARDS
V

À LA CARTE
250–270F (38.11–41.16€), BC

PRIX FIXE
None

ENGLISH SPOKEN
Enough

CHICAGO MEATPACKERS (23)
8, rue Coquillière
Métro: Les Halles

The Midwestern twang of the Chicago WJMK radio disc jockey announces that it is 5:30 P.M. in Chicago and the commute is, as usual, gridlocked, then he introduces Frank Sinatra crooning, "Chicago is my kinda town." If Chicago is your kind of town, then the Chicago Meatpackers in Les Halles is your kind of restaurant. Big, bright, and fast moving, it lets you know from the minute you enter that you are in for a good time.

The American food and drinks have rapidly won the hearts and stomachs of Parisians, who come to feast on baby back ribs, prime steaks, eight gourmet hamburgers (including the Big Bopper, an enormous thirteen ounces), buffalo wings, stuffed potato skins, corn on the

TELEPHONE
01-40-28-02-33

INTERNET
www.chicagomeatpackers.com

OPEN
Daily: 11:30 A.M.–1 A.M., continuous service; children's shows Wed, Sat, Sun 1 and 2 P.M.

CLOSED
Dec 24, NAC

RESERVATIONS
Needed only for parties of 6 or more; not accepted for Sat night or for the children's shows

CREDIT CARDS
AE, MC, V (100F, 15.24€, minimum)

À LA CARTE
100–170F (15.24–25.92€), BNC

PRIX FIXE
Lunch Mon–Fri (11:30 A.M.– 4 P.M.): 60F (9.15€), 75F (11.43€), 2 courses, BC or dessert; dinner Mon–Fri (from 6 P.M.) and lunch Sat–Sun: 135F (20.58€), 3 courses, BC; children's menu (served continuously): 65F (9.91€), BC

ENGLISH SPOKEN
Yes

cob, an onion loaf, garlic bread, taco salad, five-way chili, New York cheesecake, rich mud pie, and apple pie à la mode. At the huge mirror-lined bar, the friendly bartender dispenses fifty brands of whiskey, makes one of the driest martinis in town, mixes a lethal Singapore sling, and pours their own brew—Chicago Old Gold Beer—into ice-cold mugs. Children love the bibs, badges, and balloons; their own special menu; the clowns performing half-hour magic shows on Wednesday, Saturday, and Sunday; and the model Chicago & Pacific train running and tooting overhead.

Can't finish your onion hamburger, chili cheeseburger, or Meatpackers chicken platter? Then ask for a doggie bag, probably the only one you will see in Paris. The waiters and waitresses all speak English, the restaurant is open every day, and it makes for a great taste of home. Don't miss it.

NOTE: There is a nonsmoking section.

ENTRE CIEL ET TERRE (16)
5, rue Hérold
Métro: Bourse, Les Halles

What do H. G. Wells, Gandhi, Leonardo da Vinci, Tolstoy, Buddha, Voltaire, Einstein, Socrates, and Paul McCartney have in common? They are, or were, all vegetarians, and you can join their healthy ranks by eating at this attractive restaurant not far from the Paris Bourse (stock exchange). The interior is painted with a cloud theme, highlighting angels, stars, and the moon, and it is further enhanced by changing art exhibits.

TELEPHONE
01-45-08-49-84

OPEN
Mon–Fri: lunch noon–3 P.M., dinner 7–10 P.M., tea 3–6 P.M.

CLOSED
Sat–Sun; major holidays, Aug

RESERVATIONS
Advised

CREDIT CARDS
MC, V

À LA CARTE
120F (18.29€), BC

PRIX FIXE
Lunch: 75F (11.43€), 2 courses, 99F (15.09€), 3 courses, both BNC; dinner: 110F (16.77€), 3 courses, BNC

ENGLISH SPOKEN
Yes

The food here is not only good but good for you, and it's served in a 100 percent smoke-free environment, yet another reason to put it on your best-value dining map of Paris. Owner and chef Guillaume Botté takes his work seriously and turns out daily fare that appeals to both hard-core vegetarians and freewheeling omnivores. *Entrées* include onion or vegetable soup, avocado mousse served with toasted brioche, tapenade, and always a *plat du jour*. I would avoid the *pâté végétariale* because it is not *maison* (made here). Savory *tartes,* vegetable pancakes, lasagne, omelettes, and gratins round out the main courses. Botté's desserts are showcased on a large buffet. If it's here, the pear and chocolate chip cake is memorable, but if you are looking for a lighter ending, have the lemon cake with raspberry sauce. If you are not in the neighborhood for either lunch or dinner, stop by for tea, coffee, or hot chocolate, which is served between 3 and

6 P.M., and enjoy a *tartinette* served with vegetable pâté or a piece of rich quiche garnished with crudités, always remembering to save room for one of the special desserts.

NOTE: No smoking is allowed.

JUVENILES (13)
47, rue de Richelieu
Métro: Pyramides, Palais-Royal

Juveniles is a smart address to remember if you want a light meal at any time of the afternoon or evening, accompanied by a glass or two of a little-known but superb Spanish, French, or Australian wine. It is also a good place for those who enjoy malt whiskey or sour mash straight bourbon.

Mark Williamson of Willi's Wine Bar fame and Tim Johnston opened Juveniles a decade ago. It was an instant hit, and remains popular today. Now run exclusively by Tim, it was voted one of the best places to drink wine in Paris and is especially popular with readers of *Great Eats Paris*. In addition to wines and spirits, sold by the glass, bottle, or case, Juveniles excels in serving tapas—small plates of food that can be ordered individually or as part of a prix fixe formula. Your meal might include a *tortilla d'Espagna* (a thick Spanish omelette) or warm basil-spiked ratatouille, followed by a duck filet, a simply grilled piece of fresh seasonal fish, and tiramisu with amaretto or the famous Donald's chocolate cake for dessert. Cheese lovers will revel in a chunk of English cheddar or Stilton blue cheese accompanied by a glass of East Indian sherry.

While you are here, be sure to notice the children's drawings hung behind the bar and in the back room. They are all by Tim's daughters.

TELEPHONE
01-42-97-46-49

OPEN
Mon–Sat: noon–11 P.M., continuous service

CLOSED
Sun; NAC

RESERVATIONS
Suggested for Fri and Sat

CREDIT CARDS
AE, MC, V

À LA CARTE
75–150F (11.43–22.87€), BNC

PRIX FIXE
Lunch and dinner: 105F (16.01€), 2 courses, 150F (22.87€), 3 courses, both BC

ENGLISH SPOKEN
Yes

LA CORDONNERIE (CHEZ YVETTE & CLAUDE) (12)
20, rue St-Roch
Métro: Pyramides

La Cordonnerie is a little restaurant with two dining rooms that seat just twenty-four people. One room is dominated by an open kitchen with an enviable collection of copper pots, pans, and molds; the other has a tiny bar, an antique icebox, a vintage cash register, and five tables with fresh flowers and matching red tablecloths and napkins. The restaurant was opened over thirty years ago by Claude and Yvette, with Claude in the kitchen turning out his renditions of soothing, old-fashioned French food, and Yvette acting as charming hostess and

TELEPHONE
01-42-60-17-42

OPEN
Mon–Fri: lunch noon–2:30 P.M., dinner 7:15–10 P.M.

CLOSED
Sat–Sun; holidays, Aug

RESERVATIONS
Advised

CREDIT CARDS
MC, V

À LA CARTE
160–200F (24.39–30.49€), BC

PRIX FIXE
Lunch and dinner: 150F
(22.87€), 3 courses, BNC
ENGLISH SPOKEN
Yes

helper. The cooking is now done by their son, Hugo, and the hostess duties are shared by his wife, Valerie, during the evening and by Yvette during lunch. Hugo does the shopping at Rungis, the huge wholesale food market outside Paris, and he prepares everything here, including the ice creams and sorbets.

I like to start my meal with a plate of well-dressed crudités or the *terrine de foie de volaille maison,* a creamy chicken liver pâté. For my main course I always pay attention to Hugo's *plat du jour,* or whatever fresh fish he offers. For dessert, there is usually *tarte au citron* with a meringue topping, one of his father's specialties, or my other favorite, *fondant au chocolate,* made with whipped cream and dark chocolate. It is warm on the outside, cool inside, and decadently wonderful to the last bite.

LA MAISON CLÉRET (35)
4, rue des Lavandières Ste-Opportune, at rue Jean Lantier
Métro: Châtelet

TELEPHONE
01-42-33-82-68
OPEN
Tues–Sat: 7 A.M.–8 P.M.,
continuous service for pastries;
lunch noon–2 P.M.
CLOSED
Mon, Sun; major holidays, July
or Aug (call to check)
RESERVATIONS
Not accepted
CREDIT CARDS
None
À LA CARTE
20–70F (3.05–10.67€), BNC
PRIX FIXE
None
ENGLISH SPOKEN
Limited

In my opinion, the area around Châtelet is a dining desert, populated by impersonal corner brasseries, fast-food franchises, and here-today, gone-tomorrow greasy spoons. The one star-studded exception is this *pâtisserie* and *salon de thé* where, for nearly two decades, four women have been working nonstop from 7 A.M. to 8 P.M. Tuesday to Saturday selling the best breads, pastries, and hot lunches in the *quartier.* I lived just around the corner and observed them and their never-ending stream of customers, including restaurant chefs, who bought them out on a daily basis.

It's not a fancy place, but there are stand-up tables in the bakery itself, sit-down tables in the back (it's an extra 3F, .46€, to be served here and worth it), and a few tables scattered on the sidewalk when the weather permits. Your window of opportunity to indulge is large. You can start your day with a *café au lait* and a powdered sugar–dusted *croissant aux amandes,* a *pain aux raisins,* or a fruit-studded *viennoiserie* (Danish). For lunch, order one of the *plats du jour* and a fresh fruit *tarte.* In the afternoon, sip a cup of tea and treat yourself to an assortment of their cakes and pastries; later on, pick up a loaf or two of their delicious bread and a box of their own chocolates. If you are a camera buff, on Saturday mornings the shelves are lined with picture-perfect goodies . . . don't miss your chance to capture it all on film.

L'AMI LÉON (25)
11, rue Jean-Jacques Rousseau
Métro: Louvre-Rivoli, Palais-Royal

What is the magic quality that makes discriminating diners zero in on a little place and stick with it for years? Whatever it is, L'Ami Léon has it, the perfect setting and the kind of meal one hopes to find in Paris. The interior reminds me of a country restaurant somewhere in the south of France. The nicely laid tables, with their own lamps and tiny bouquets of flowers, are placed far enough apart to ensure a peacefully intimate evening.

The prix fixe menu changes monthly, and the à la carte seasonally. The choices are a bit limited, but they are nonetheless studded with treasures, all made by owner-chef Jean-Marie Léon Martin. Everything is always reliable, from the bowl of nuts placed on the table while you peruse the menu to the last drop of *café express* and the chocolates that accompany it. The restaurant's many regulars know that the velvety chicken liver terrine will always be available as an appetizer. Main courses, designed to please meat-and-potato fans, might include tender pieces of lamb in coriander, succulent rabbit with sage, or pork sautéed with olives and fresh turnips. All are garnished with fresh vegetables and roasted potatoes. The desserts are overwhelmingly tempting, especially the flaky springtime rhubarb and strawberry *tarte,* or the winter favorite: caramelized apples, flambéed with Calvados, and topped with ice cream.

NOTE: There is a special nonsmoking section.

TELEPHONE
01-42-33-06-20

OPEN
Mon–Fri: lunch noon–2 P.M., dinner 8–10 P.M.; Sat: dinner 8–10 P.M.

CLOSED
Sat lunch, Sun; holidays, mid-July to mid-Aug

RESERVATIONS
Advised

CREDIT CARDS
V

À LA CARTE
190F (28.97€), BNC

PRIX FIXE
Lunch and dinner: 100F (15.24€), 3 courses, BNC

ENGLISH SPOKEN
Enough to order

LA POTÉE DES HALLES (22)
3, rue Étienne Marcel
Métro: Étienne Marcel

Book ahead . . . you won't be the only one eager to dine in this haven of Paris nostalgia, which began as a café in 1906. Classified by the French government as a national historic monument, the restaurant, with ornate hand-painted tile walls portraying the goddesses of beer and coffee, still has its original chairs, whose brass plaques bear the names of Les Halles workers who ate here every day when the wholesale food market of Paris dominated the area. Even today, some of these chairs are occupied daily by their seventy- and eighty-year-old "owners."

New owners and a new chef have breathed new life into this neighborhood institution, but the hearty food remains the same and still packs in wall-to-wall diners.

TELEPHONE
01-40-41-98-15

OPEN
Tues–Fri: lunch noon–2:15 P.M., dinner 7:30 P.M.–midnight; Sat–Sun: dinner 7:30 P.M.–midnight

CLOSED
Sat–Sun lunch, Mon; major holidays, Aug

RESERVATIONS
Essential

CREDIT CARDS
AE, DC, MC, V

À LA CARTE
190F (28.97€), BNC

PRIX FIXE
Lunch: 80F (12.20€), 2 courses, BNC; dinner: 100F (15.24€), 2 courses, BNC

ENGLISH SPOKEN
Yes

Unless you are ravenous, order a light *entrée* before your *plat* and plan to go easy on dessert or skip it altogether. Instead, pay serious attention to the Auvergne specialty of the house, *potée-Georgette*. It comes in a big pot with white beans, cabbage, carrots, salt pork, ribs, smoked sausage, garlic butter, and cream. Other specialties include a rich *confit de canard, boeuf bourguignon* with steamed potatoes, and always the *plat du jour*. At the end of this *grand bouffe,* you will probably stagger away a little heavier, but definitely well satisfied.

L'ARDOISE (9)
28, rue du Mont-Thabor
Métro: Concorde, Tuileries

TELEPHONE
01-42-96-28-18

OPEN
Tues–Fri, Sun: lunch noon–2 P.M., dinner 7:30–11 P.M.; Sat: dinner 7:30–11 P.M.

CLOSED
Sat lunch, Mon; 3 weeks in Aug, few days in May and Dec

RESERVATIONS
Essential

CREDIT CARDS
MC, V

À LA CARTE
None

PRIX FIXE
Lunch and dinner: 170F (25.92€), 3 courses, BNC

ENGLISH SPOKEN
Yes

Small, tightly packed, brightly lit bistros offering a set menu for two or three courses now dot the Parisian dining landscape. At L'Ardoise, chef Pierre Jay—who honed his skills at several top Parisian dining cathedrals, including La Tour d'Argent—has energized the already flourishing dining scene in the first arrondissement. The frenetic lunch service, somehow carried out by two racing waitresses, is predominantly composed of businessfolk. Dinner, which is almost as rushed, draws a stylish crowd in dark suits or fashionable casual attire who are served with dispatch in order to turn the tables at least twice, hopefully more. Bare tables are dressed with linen napkins and tumblers for the wine.

As soon as you are seated, a basket of dark bread and a dish of *fromage frais* laced with fresh herbs arrives. The blackboard lists a selection of ten *entrées* and *plats,* plus a final cheese course or one of six desserts, all featuring market-fresh ingredients simply prepared. Depending on the season and the mood of the chef, you might start with a tomato *tarte* dressed with an eggplant confit, fresh anchovies with a terrine of tapenade, or a salad with two warm hearts of artichoke filled with potato purée sitting on a bed of warm endives and *pissenlits* (dandelion greens). Follow this with lamb *tournedos,* fresh fish, or a perfectly roasted pigeon—all nicely garnished with at least one vegetable or potatoes. End the meal with a light *baba au rhum,* or a light *feuillantine au citron*—a flaky pastry layered with tangy lemon cream and dusted with sugar. Despite the hustle of the service, the food is wonderful, the price is right, and the experience very Parisian.

LA TAVOLA CALDA (33)
38, rue des Bourdonnais
Métro: Châtelet

They say good things come in small packages, and this is certainly true about the wood-fired pizzas and good pastas turned out by this little Italian eatery near Les Halles. Blink twice and you will have passed the minuscule ground-floor dining room, with its brick pizza oven and its crowd of contented diners, who consist of students, neighborhood regulars, and a varied set of budget-minded international vagabonds. The thin-crusted pizzas are terrific, and all are made here. There's a good choice of the usual toppings, such as four cheeses, mushrooms, anchovies, tomatoes, and the requisite sausages. Not to be overlooked are the filling pastas, various meat dishes, and the puffed calzone, which is loaded with eggs, cheese, tomato, and ham. Desserts? Not an issue of importance here . . . unless you like tiramisu.

TELEPHONE
01-45-08-94-66

OPEN
Mon–Sat: lunch noon–2:30 P.M., dinner 7–10:30 P.M.

CLOSED
Sun; a few days at Christmas, Aug

RESERVATIONS
Not necessary

CREDIT CARDS
MC, V

À LA CARTE
75–95F (11.43–14.48€), BNC

PRIX FIXE
None

ENGLISH SPOKEN
Yes

LA VICTOIRE SUPRÈME DU COEUR (32)
41, rue des Bourdonnais
Métro: Châtelet

La Victoire Suprème du Coeur is a serious vegetarian restaurant that focuses the mind on what's on the plate—simple food that's nicely presented and, above all, good for you. The busiest time is at lunch, when health-conscious office workers in the neighborhood around La Samaritaine department store fill every seat. The set-price lunch menus, as well as the à la carte offerings, parade a list of vegetarian standbys with a few modern twists. Of course, tofu is presented every way imaginable, from fresh to smoked and sautéed, and there are grains, veggies (both cooked and raw and served in terrines), salads, soups, daily pastries, and simple fruit desserts, along with ciders, fresh pressed juices, and assorted *cocktails maison*. From the simple *cocktail maison* made with apple, carrot, and soy milk to the all-out *cocktail du marathonien*—featuring a mélange of raspberry, blueberry, banana, apple, and orange juices doused with soy protein—you are guaranteed to have a clear head for the afternoon and no hangover tomorrow.

From Monday through Saturday, regulars can count on a specific *plat du jour* that rings in for under $10. On Monday, it is couscous, *choucroute,* and paella; Tuesday, an Italian offering; Wednesday, something potato based; Thursday, Indian; Friday and Saturday, a dish *à la française.* If you plan to be a regular and eat here ten

TELEPHONE
01-40-41-93-95

OPEN
Mon–Sat: lunch noon–2:30 P.M., dinner 6:30–10 P.M.

CLOSED
Sun; NAC

RESERVATIONS
Not necessary

CREDIT CARDS
AE, MC, V

À LA CARTE
50–100F (7.62–15.24€), BNC

PRIX FIXE
Lunch Mon–Fri: 55–65F (8.38–9.91€), 2 courses, BNC

ENGLISH SPOKEN
Yes

times within thirty days, ask for a *Carte de Fidelite,* which will entitle you to a free *plat du jour* after the tenth meal. Even better for the dedicated patron: if you eat here four times in one week, you get one *plat du jour* on the house, and if you can make it only three times in one week, you save 50 percent on your fourth *plat du jour.*

LE BAR DU CAVEAU (36)
17, place Dauphine
Métro: Pont-Neuf

TELEPHONE
01-43-54-45-95

OPEN
Mon–Fri: 8 A.M.–6:30 P.M., continuous service; Sat in summer only: 10 A.M.–7 P.M.

CLOSED
Sat in winter, Sun; Dec 15–31, major holidays, 15 days in Aug (varies)

RESERVATIONS
Not accepted

CREDIT CARDS
None

À LA CARTE
45–60F (6.86–9.15€), BNC

PRIX FIXE
None

ENGLISH SPOKEN
Limited

Le Bar du Caveau occupies a prime spot on the charming place Dauphine, which is at the tip of Île de la Cité, just after you cross the Pont-Neuf bridge. Relatively undiscovered by tourists, this lovely little square was home to Yves Montand and Simone Signoret, and it boasts a half dozen or so restaurants and a famous bargain hotel in Paris, the Hotel Henri IV (see *Great Sleeps Paris*). Featuring sandwiches on *pain Poilâne, croques-monsieur* or *-madame,* salads, egg dishes, cheese and *charcuterie* plates, and a mix of Bordeaux and other wines by the glass, *pot* (pitcher), and bottle, Le Bar du Caveau appeals to upscale regulars who arrive early and stay late, idling away a lazy Paris afternoon over wine and fellowship.

NOTE: Be sure you go to the bar, not to its sister restaurant next door, which is not designed for the budgets of most value-conscious diners in Paris.

LE BÉARN (34)
2, place Ste-Opportune
Métro: Châtelet (exit place Ste-Opportune)

TELEPHONE
01-42-36-93-35

OPEN
Mon–Sat: bar 8 A.M.–11 P.M., lunch noon–3:30 P.M., dinner 7–8 P.M.

CLOSED
Sun; holidays, NAC

RESERVATIONS
Not accepted

CREDIT CARDS
MC, V

À LA CARTE
50–110F (7.62–16.77€), BC

PRIX FIXE
None

ENGLISH SPOKEN
Some

In addition to being an earthy good deal, Le Béarn is a great place to hone your people-watching skills. In the morning, you are likely to find red-cheeked workers standing at the bar, lingering over what is obviously not their first glass of *vin rouge* of the day. A predominantly young crowd of every conceivable orientation and dress pours in at lunchtime to take advantage of the low-priced *plats du jour,* which come in pre-*nouvelle*-size portions. These are usually overflowing plates of no-nonsense meats, accompanied by equally serious portions of homemade *frites.* Regulars know to avoid all veggies here—they are frozen. They also know that the *huitres* (oyster) stand in front is one of the cheapest and best in the *quartier.* Unless it is raining or freezing cold, the outside tables on the place Ste-Opportune are the place to sit, serving as front-row vantage points for watching Les Halles fashion victims preen and prance and the surging crowds emerging from the métro stop next to it.

LE BISTROT DE MONTPENSIER (CHEZ VICTOR) (15)
37 bis, rue de Montpensier
Métro: Palais-Royal, Pyramides

Le Bistrot de Montpensier is the latest enterprise of the energetic, unstoppable Victor Orsenne, who with his delightful wife, Maria (and their dog Faust), owns the Hôtel Latour-Maubourg, a firm favorite for discerning travelers in the seventh arrondissement (see *Great Sleeps Paris*).

All his life, Victor has had a love affair with cooking, so it is no surprise to those who know him to see him wearing a chef's hat and turning out robust meals of red meat, potatoes, noodles, and creamy desserts in his little bistro located not far away from the Palais Royal. The three set-lunch menus are impressive bargains for sure. Consider his 95F three-course menu, which starts with a *pâté de campagne* or daily soup, moves on to grilled beef or the *plat du jour,* both served with his homemade french fries or fresh noodles, and ends with a pudding for dessert and coffee. Lighter appetites can go for two courses or have only a main course. Early diners, who for whatever reason want to eat before 7:30 P.M., are rewarded with a two- or three-course menu highlighting grilled beef and tarragon chicken (again with his own *frites* or noodles), a small salad, and chestnut cream or *fromage blanc* with a fresh fruit sauce. Coffee is included. The gourmet menu, served either for lunch or dinner, features duck foie gras on a toasted brioche, filet of venison with a cream sauce, and crêpes filled with vanilla ice cream and topped with orange sauce. There is no coffee with this menu, and with all three wine is extra. However, lusty red wines to go with your meat feast are fairly priced from around 85F to 225F (12.96–34.30€).

NOTE: There is a nonsmoking section.

TELEPHONE
01-40-20-03-02

EMAIL
gourmet@latour-maubourg.fr

INTERNET
www.latour-maubourg.fr/gourmet

OPEN
Tues–Sat: lunch noon–3 P.M., dinner 6:30–9 P.M.

CLOSED
Mon, Sun; NAC

RESERVATIONS
Preferred

CREDIT CARDS
MC, V

À LA CARTE
None

PRIX FIXE
Lunch: 65F (9.91€), main course; 85F (12.96€), 2 courses; 95F (14.48€), 3 courses, all with coffee; early dinner (until 7:30 P.M.): 95F (14.48€), 2 courses, 115F (17.53€), 3 courses, both with coffee; lunch and dinner: 125F (19.06€), any 2 courses; 145F (22.11€), any 3 courses; gourmet menu 165F (25.15€), 3 courses, all BNC

ENGLISH SPOKEN
Yes

LE COCHON À L'OREILLE (19)
15, rue Montmartre
Métro: Les Halles

The business hours of this tiny bar in Les Halles give you a hint of its clientele: at 8 A.M., the place is alive with local workers and red-faced tradesmen in blue coveralls drinking their early-morning cognac and coffee. Lunchtime is the same, when they flock in for the daily specials

TELEPHONE
01-42-36-07-56

OPEN
Mon–Sat: bar 8 A.M.–6 P.M., continuous service for cold food; hot lunch noon–3 P.M.

CLOSED
Sun; holidays, NAC

RESERVATIONS
Not necessary

CREDIT CARDS
None

À LA CARTE
70–100F (10.67–15.24€), BC

PRIX FIXE
None

ENGLISH SPOKEN
The waitress told me, "I speak English with my hands. Everyone understands."

and a bottle of red or a hefty sandwich on a crispy baguette and a tall beer. If getting up early or rubbing elbows with the locals at lunch doesn't appeal to you, do stop by for a coffee, a drink, or a homemade pastry and admire one of the most beautiful small working-class haunts still intact in Paris. It has its original zinc bar and a superbly detailed faience mural depicting Les Halles market at the turn of the twentieth century.

LE LOUCHEBEM (28)
31, rue Berger, angle rue des Prouvaires
Métro: Les Halles, Châtelet–Les Halles

TELEPHONE
01-42-33-12-99

OPEN
Mon–Sat: lunch noon–2:30 P.M., dinner 7–11:30 P.M.

CLOSED
Sun; NAC

RESERVATIONS
Advised, especially on Fri and Sat

CREDIT CARDS
AE, DC, MC, V

À LA CARTE
190–200F (28.97–30.49€), BNC

PRIX FIXE
Lunch and dinner (until 9 P.M.): 95F (14.48€), 3 courses, BNC

ENGLISH SPOKEN
Yes

The red interior goes well with your beef and so do the many pictures of animals that line the walls at Le Louchebem, a temple of tradition in Les Halles. Despite its tourist-trap location near the Forum des Halles, it is largely unknown to outsiders. Featuring red meat in huge and satisfying portions, it has outlived dining and dietary crazes and continues to please a largely French audience that is serious about eating and drinking well.

If you go early and sit upstairs by a picture window overlooking the ornate Église St-Eustache, you will be captivated even before your waiter appears with bowls of olives and pieces of ham and beef to dip into a caper sauce. When ordering your meal, throw caution, calories, and cholesterol to the wind and dig into he-man servings of steak tartare, leg of lamb, côte de boeuf, os en t— a plate-size T-bone steak, or the daunting all-you-can-eat assiette du rotisseur—a mixed grill of beef, leg of lamb, and roast ham accompanied by three sauces. The salads are best forgotten, but not the desserts. If you can manage it by the end, go for the warm tarte Tatin or one of the ice cream or sorbet creations, such as the Coupe de Lochebém (apple sorbet topped with Calvados) or the Coupe General, a dish of pistachio ice cream covered with whiskey. The wine list is limited but well priced. If you are dining with a friend, separate checks are possible without the waiter scowling, and if they forget to give you the prix fixe menu, ask for it!

NOTE: There is a nonsmoking section.

LE MANÈGE DE L'ECUYER (11)
6, rue de La Sourdière
Métro: Tuileries, Pyramides

When I first walked by this place, everyone inside was smiling, but at the restaurant next door, the people were all scowling and talking on their cellular telephones. This was just enough for me to try Jeannine and Géorge's Le Manège de l'Ecuyer. It was a winner then . . . and it still is.

Jeannine, with her bright smile and warm welcome, has created a place to return to time and again. The regulars thrive on Géorge's changing prix fixe blackboard menu, which features all the well-loved standbys: seasonally fresh asparagus vinaigrette, a lusty *terrine maison,* or the ever popular onion soup gratinée to start, followed by leg of lamb, fresh salmon, or for the more adventursome diner, *rognon de veau* (veal kidneys). The desserts never fail to please and include a fresh fruit *tarte,* crême brûlée, and a delicate *île flottante.* Wines are available by the glass, *pichet,* or bottle, but those by the *pichet* are just fine to complement this exceptional value-packed choice in Paris.

TELEPHONE
01-49-27-00-64

OPEN
Mon–Fri: lunch noon–2:30 P.M., dinner 7:30–10 P.M.

CLOSED
Sat–Sun; holidays, one week at Christmas, July 20–Aug 20

RESERVATIONS
Advised

CREDIT CARDS
MC, V

À LA CARTE
165F (25.15€), BNC

PRIX FIXE
Lunch: 95F (14.48€), 2 courses, 135F (20.58€), 3 courses, both BNC; dinner: 150F (22.87€), 3 courses, BNC

ENGLISH SPOKEN
Enough to order, and Jeannine speaks Spanish

L'ÉPI D'OR ($, 24)
25, rue Jean-Jacques Rousseau
Métro: Louvre-Rivoli

L'Épi d'Or typifies what eating in Paris is all about: waiters in black pants and long aprons serving traditional food in oversize portions to a diversified legion of habitués, who dine here regularly and until very, very late. The decor is cluttered, the place is crowded, the seats hard, and the one toilet is an antique from Turkey, but the food and atmosphere are oh, so French.

For the best experience of L'Épi d'Or, reserve for an 8:30 dinner and be on time, or your reservation might be given away. The best value is definitely the prix fixe menu, which is served only until 9 P.M.; the only drawback is that the *plats du jour* are not on it. You can order one of the filling servings of *jambonneau à la lyonnaise* (cured pork), *foie de veau* (liver), the *entrecôte bordelaise avec moelle,* or the popular steak tartare *de l'Épi d'Or.* Wines of the month always feature selections from Bordeaux or the Loire Valley. Finish your feast with a slice of double-chocolate walnut cake surrounded by a rich *crème anglaise* or a piece of their famous *tarte Tatin au Calvados,* a five-kilogram wonder that looks like a giant soufflé. If you are not up to one of these finales, at least sample a

TELEPHONE
01-42-36-38-12

OPEN
Mon–Fri: lunch noon–3 P.M., dinner 7:30 P.M.–midnight; Sat: dinner 7:30 P.M.–midnight

CLOSED
Sat lunch, Sun; holidays, Aug

RESERVATIONS
Advised, especially after 8:30 P.M. Fri and Sat nights

CREDIT CARDS
MC, V

À LA CARTE
250F (38.11€), BNC

PRIX FIXE
Lunch and dinner, Mon–Fri (until 9 P.M.): 105F (16.01€), 3 courses, BNC

ENGLISH SPOKEN
Yes

selection of the Berthillon ice cream or sorbet. A meal here is guaranteed to fill you to your toes, and you will leave happy and satisfied, probably swearing never to eat again.

LESCURE (7)
7, rue de Mondovi
Métro: Concorde

TELEPHONE
01-42-60-18-91

OPEN
Mon–Fri: lunch noon–2:15 P.M., dinner 7–10:30 P.M.

CLOSED
Sat–Sun; holidays, Aug, Dec 22–Jan 1

RESERVATIONS
Not necessary

CREDIT CARDS
MC, V

À LA CARTE
150F (22.87€), BNC

PRIX FIXE
Lunch and dinner: 115F (17.53€), 3 courses, BC

ENGLISH SPOKEN
Yes

Located at the end of a short street just around the corner from place de la Concorde, the restaurant was founded in 1919 by Lèon Lescure. Today it is still owned and operated by his family, who serve simple French bourgeoise cooking at very reasonable prices. For both lunch and dinner, diners vie for one of the sidewalk tables or else sit elbow-to-elbow inside beneath ropes of garlic and country sausages dangling from the rafters. The service is friendly and perhaps the fastest in Paris.

If you select a dish that must be prepared that day, or better yet, cooked to order, you will be happy. Otherwise, you may run into some ingredients that are past their prime or have been reheated too much. The poached haddock is always a safe bet, and so is *la poule au riz sauce basquaise*—chicken and rice with a tangy tomato and green pepper sauce (order it on the side). The most popular dessert is the special fruit *tarte*.

NOTE: There is a nonsmoking section.

LE SOUFFLÉ ($, 10)
36, rue du Mont-Thabor
Métro: Tuileries, Concorde (exit rue Cambon)

TELEPHONE
01-42-60-27-19

OPEN
Mon–Sat: lunch noon–2:30 P.M., dinner 7–10:30 P.M.

CLOSED
Sun; holidays, NAC

RESERVATIONS
Essential, several days in advance if possible

CREDIT CARDS
AE, DC, MC, V

À LA CARTE
225–250F (34.30–38.11€), BNC

PRIX FIXE
Lunch and dinner: 170F (25.92€), 3 courses, BNC; 175F (26.68€), 3 courses, all soufflés plus a green salad, BNC; 220F (33.54€), 3 courses, BNC

ENGLISH SPOKEN
Yes, and well

It is unanimous: Everyone loves Le Soufflé.

Many Parisians as well as a host of international visitors know that in this uncertain world Le Soufflé is one restaurant you can always count on for a wonderful meal. After dining here, you will feel like you are in heaven—and know that you are in Paris. The interior glows with soft lighting, pale yellow walls, and fresh flowers in miniature pots. The tables are laid with starched linens, heavy cutlery, beautiful china, and sparkling crystal. The second dining room evokes the spirit of Paris with its fleur-de-lys wall treatment, murals of Parisian gardens, and royal red carpeting. Along with polite service and discreet waiters, Le Soufflé maintains its reputation for memorable dining in Paris. After all, what could be more Parisian than a soufflé? Whether you order a fluffy cheese or spinach soufflé, a delicate smoked salmon soufflé, or a rich chocolate or a classic

Grand Marnier soufflé—or any of the other imaginative offerings—you will enjoy dramatic dining guaranteed to please even the most jaded palate. If you want to avoid the most tourists, however, book your table for after 8:30 P.M.

In addition to the fantasia of soufflés, there are many appealing seasonal appetizers, hearty main courses, and luscious desserts. At the height of the spring season, the fat white asparagus vinaigrette is a definite must. The fresh artichoke heart and mushrooms dressed in a tangy lemon cream sauce is another popular *entrée*, as is the homemade terrine or the duck with green pepper and pistachios. For apple lovers, the *tarte fine aux pommes chaudes* is a dreamy dessert raising this standard French menu item to new heights. Another cloudlike choice is the *crêpe soufflé Rothschild*—a puffed crêpe doused in kirsch. When it arrives, covering the entire plate, you will think you can't finish it, but let me assure you that you will eat every bite and wish for more. Whatever you have at Le Soufflé will be divine and well worth the extra centimes.

NOTE: There is no smoking in the second dining room.

L'INCROYABLE (14)
Passage between 26, rue de Richelieu, and 23, rue de Montpensier
Métro: Palais-Royal

L'Incroyable—"The Incredible"—is aptly named, with its three-course lunch and dinner menus going for less than $20, and its *menu Colette* for under $25. While for some it may not be the rock-bottom bargain meal it once was, and the quality can be spotty, it is still well worth considering. For these prices you can't expect smoked salmon or pheasant under glass served by waiters in tuxedos, but you will get the usual basics of homestyle pâtés, chicken, beef, pork, vegetables, creamed potatoes, simple salads, and unassuming desserts. However, if you stay with the prix fixe menu and the daily specials, you will rarely be disappointed.

Getting to L'Incroyable is half the fun, since it is hidden in a narrow passage running between two streets near the Palais-Royal. Either walk up rue de Richelieu or rue de Montpensier behind the Comédie Française. Once you have found it, settle in to either the flower-filled courtyard adjoining the two-room restaurant or inside one of the cluttered dining rooms and enjoy a good-natured meal in Paris.

TELEPHONE
01-42-96-24-64

OPEN
Mon–Fri: lunch noon–2:30 P.M., dinner 7–9 P.M.

CLOSED
Sat–Sun; 15 days in July or Aug (call to check)

RESERVATIONS
Not necessary

CREDIT CARDS
MC, V

À LA CARTE
140–165F (21.34–25.15€), BNC

PRIX FIXE
Lunch (except holidays): 85F (12.96€), 3 courses, BNC; dinner: 115F (17.53€), 3 courses, BNC; lunch and dinner, *menu Colette:* 140F (21.34€), 3 courses, BNC

ENGLISH SPOKEN
Yes

LUNCHTIME (8)
255, rue St-Honoré
Métro: Tuileries, Concorde

TELEPHONE
01-42-60-80-40
OPEN
Mon–Fri: lunch 11 A.M.–4 P.M.
CLOSED
Sat–Sun; holidays, NAC
RESERVATIONS
Not necessary
CREDIT CARDS
None
À LA CARTE
30–65F (4.57–9.91€), BNC
PRIX FIXE
None
ENGLISH SPOKEN
Limited

Its wide variety of well-stacked sandwiches, fresh salads, and hot soups in winter have made Lunchtime a favorite haunt of secretaries, smart tourists, and cute young things around the fashionable rue St-Honoré. The restaurant is buried at the back of a courtyard off the street, but the inside is spacious and nicely done with murals of Cape Cod and interesting displays of big seashells, sailor's knots, and sailing artifacts.

You have a choice of at least twenty sandwiches served hot or cold on crusty *pain complet, pain de campagne,* or pita bread. The sandwiches are filled with every possible combination of chicken, cheese, egg, fish, turkey, beef, and vegetables. Six or seven salads, a few soups, and some rather mundane desserts complete the dining picture. Everything can be eaten here at comfortable tables or you can have your order packed to go. They also deliver if your order is large enough. If you take your sandwich with you, it will cost a few francs less.

NOTE: There is a nonsmoking section.

RESTAURANT CHEZ MAX (30)
47, rue St-Honoré (1st floor)
Métro: Louvre-Rivoli, Châtelet (exit place Ste-Opportune or Les Halles)

TELEPHONE
01-45-08-80-13
OPEN
Mon–Fri: lunch noon–2 P.M., dinner 8 P.M.–midnight; Sat: dinner 8 P.M.–midnight
CLOSED
Sat lunch, Sun; Aug
RESERVATIONS
Advised
CREDIT CARDS
AE, DC, MC, V
À LA CARTE
170F (25.92€), BNC
PRIX FIXE
Lunch: 65F (9.91€), 120F (18.29€), both 3 courses, BC; dinner: 85F (12.96€), 135F (20.58€), both 3 courses, BC
ENGLISH SPOKEN
Yes

Max has been feeding loyal patrons in his first-floor dining room for more than two decades. If you can look past the bright pink walls and the lighted tree branches overhead hung with paper bells and birds, you, too, will do well at Chez Max. The attention-getting deal is his daily changing, *marché*-based 65F (9.91€) three-course lunch menu written on a blackboard. It headlines five choices for your *entrée* and *plat* and includes house pastries or ice cream for dessert. Double your money for lunch and dinner and you get starters of homemade foie gras, escargots, spinach salad, fresh salmon, confit, and *magret de canard,* and a wider dessert choice. *En plus,* Max throws in a carafe of drinkable house red or white wine with all his menus. There's à la carte, too, but what for? Everything is already on one of the value-packed set menus.

RESTAURANT LE VIEIL ECU (26)
166, rue St-Honoré
Métro: Palais-Royal

Rustic and generous are the bywords at Le Vieil Ecu, which serves mountains of basic French fare to scores of thrift-minded patrons every day except Sunday. At lunchtime, it seems to be the favorite canteen for sturdy office workers who appreciate meat and potatoes served in trucker-size portions.

On the main floor, tables are squished together under a beamed ceiling hung with copper pots, farm utensils, and lace-covered lights. Upstairs, the tone is quieter, prettier, and much less congested. The catch is that the upstairs is open only when the downstairs room is packed full. Smart lunchers know to order the 59F (8.99€) two-course menu, which offers either a choice from the *entrées* and the *plats du jour* or the salad and *plat du jour* plus dessert. At dinner, the two prix fixe menus are a bit more upscale, offering escargots, salmon, *confit de canard,* and even a vegetarian plate. Fine pastries and opulent desserts are not the forte here, so opt for the sorbet or a fruit *tarte* if it looks fresh. À la carte is available only in the evening, but I can't imagine going this route unless you want only a main course and nothing else. House wine is the screw-cap variety, so you may want to upgrade a notch or two.

TELEPHONE
01-42-60-20-14

OPEN
Mon–Sat: lunch noon–3 P.M., dinner 7–10:30 P.M.

CLOSED
Sun; NAC

RESERVATIONS
Not necessary

CREDIT CARDS
MC, V

À LA CARTE
140F (21.34€), BNC

PRIX FIXE
Lunch: 59F (8.99€), 2 courses, BNC; 69F (10.52€), 99F (15.09€), both 3 courses, BNC; dinner: 75F (11.43€), 110F (16.77€), both 3 courses, BNC; children's menu, lunch only: 50F (7.62€), 2 courses, 100F (15.24€), 3 courses

ENGLISH SPOKEN
Yes, with English menu

SIGNORELLI ($, 31)
35, rue St-Honoré
Métro: Louvre-Rivoli, Châtelet

The sophisticated, sun-kissed Italian food served at Signorelli is a welcome oasis in the sea of tourist traps in this corner of Les Halles. Located almost at the end of rue St-Honoré, Nunzio Porrometo's restaurant has been welcoming Parisians for more than two decades with wonderful dishes based on simple, long-standing Italian recipes and fine ingredients, the essentials at the heart of any good Italian cooking. Properly set tables are nicely positioned in an upstairs dining room that is graced with beams and the traditional pink hues found in so many Italian restaurants. What first drew me here was the fairly priced set menu, which features two courses and is available for both lunch and dinner. *Entrées* include carpaccio, warm bruschetta with tomatoes and mozzarella, and a plate of assorted salami and cold meats. Your main course will be a pasta: macaroni with four cheeses, spaghetti carbonara, penne with a spicy tomato

TELEPHONE
01-40-13-91-41

OPEN
Mon–Sat: lunch noon–2 P.M, dinner 7:30–10:30 P.M.

CLOSED
Sun; Aug 1–18

RESERVATIONS
Preferred

CREDIT CARDS
AE, MC, V

À LA CARTE
215–225F (32.78–34.30€), BNC

PRIX FIXE
Lunch and dinner: 80F (12.20€), 2 courses, BNC

ENGLISH SPOKEN
Yes, and Italian

sauce, or tagliatelle with fresh salmon. Diners enjoying this bargain meal receive the same gracious service by the courtly Italian-speaking waiters as those who are going all out with four courses and fine wines to accompany each dish.

Should you decide to splash out a bit and forgo the set menu, you will not be disappointed with anything on the à la carte side. Start with the antipasto misto and feast on artichokes, cèpes, sun-dried tomatoes, peppers, eggplant, ham, and fresh mozzarella. Something lighter would be the *isola di ponza,* slices of *mozzarella di buffala* layered with ripe red tomatoes, drizzled with olive oil, and topped with sprigs of fresh basil. The pasta is *à la casa* . . . and all are recommendable, especially the *pappardelle ai tartufi* (ribbons of pasta tossed in a black truffle sauce) and the gnocchi with gorgonzola cheese. Meat dishes lean toward veal and there's a grilled mixed fish plate. Desserts are worth forty more minutes on the treadmill, especially their tiramisu and the *zabajone.* If you order coffee, the limits of your appetite will be further tested by the plate of biscotti and macaroons—which gild the lily on this well-recommended alternative to a French dining experience.

UNIVERSAL RESTORAMA IN THE CARROUSEL DU LOUVRE (27)
Passage du Carrousel, under the Louvre (entrance through 99, rue de Rivoli)
Métro: Palais-Royal

TELEPHONE
01-40-20-53-17
OPEN
Daily: 10 A.M.–8 P.M., continuous service
CLOSED
Major holidays, NAC
RESERVATIONS
Not accepted
CREDIT CARDS
Depends on the stand, but generally MC, V
À LA CARTE
35–120F (5.34–18.29€), BC
PRIX FIXE
None
ENGLISH SPOKEN
Depends on the stand

When the Carrousel du Louvre underground shopping mall opened in November 1993, the first North American–style food court opened alongside it, serving *le fast food à la française.* The self-service food stands are set on the mezzanine of the mall, just off I. M. Pei's majestic pyramid. The food certainly is not three-star gourmet, but it is filling, fresh, and inexpensive, especially when you consider the million-dollar surroundings. Judging by the crowds during lunch, the self-service concept is an unqualified hit. The best battle plan is to walk around, survey the stands, and then decide what looks best. The food stands come and go, so it is impossible to guarantee that your favorite stall will be in business the next time around. However, the round-the-world choices available during my last visit included Asian, Libyan, Tex-Mex, Italian pizza and pasta, French crêpes, a health bar (with fresh fruits, veggie plates, and juices), hamburgers and fries, Hector le Poulet (serving rotisserie chicken), Spanish tapas, Boulangerie Paul (serving quiches, salads, sandwiches, and irresistible pastries), and a coffee stand dispensing muffins and cookies to munch with your *café au lait* or to buy for later indulging. In the late afternoon, it is relaxing to stop by the cheese bar, which offers a selection of French cheeses and wines, and then take your glass of wine to one of the tables along the edge and watch the throngs surging below.

NOTE: *Avoid* the Café du Louvre, which is near the food court and serves premade wrapped sandwiches.

Second Arrondissement

RIGHT BANK
Bibliothèque Nationale, Bourse, Cognacq-Jay Museum, *passages,* place des Victoires, rue Montorgueil shopping street

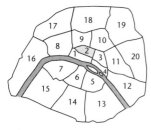

The second arrondissement can hardly be called a tourist hub in comparison to some others. It is the home of the stock market (Bourse) and some big banks. It is also dotted with *passages:* those shopping malls of the early 1900s, relics of the time before department stores. (See *Great Sleeps Paris,* "Shopping," for a listing of the most interesting *passages.*)

SECOND ARRONDISSEMENT RESTAURANTS (see map page 42)

($) indicates a Big Splurge

AUX LYONNAIS (2)
32, rue St-Marc
Métro: Bourse, Richelieu-Drouot

What more can anyone ask of a bistro? Pretty surroundings, interesting people, reliable food, a pleasant owner and staff, honest prices . . . Aux Lyonnais has them all. At lunch it hums with the voices of office workers and stockbrokers from the Bourse and of waitresses in black rushing to serve them. In the evening, the pace slows and the service and mood become more relaxed and refined.

The menu offers dishes that have been served here and in bistros like it for generations. The first-rate fare is well prepared and all made here, including the pâtés, and there are no unpleasant surprises. You start with a basket of crispy baguettes to be spread with sweet butter. *Entrées* include a salad with warm sausage or chicken livers, a trio of spicy sausage patties covered in herbs and lightly sautéed, and a fish terrine. Chicken fixed several ways, lamb chops with fresh spinach, *confit de canard,* and a tender rabbit covered in shallots, all served with *gratin dauphinois* (potatoes baked in cream), highlight the main courses. The dessert not to miss is the *oeufs à la neige*—floating island served in a large sundae dish and topped with caramel glaze.

TELEPHONE
01-42-96-65-04

OPEN
Mon–Fri: lunch noon–2:30 P.M., dinner 7–11:30 P.M.; Sat: dinner 7–11:30 P.M.

CLOSED
Sat lunch, Sun; holidays during May–Sept, mid-July–mid-Aug

RESERVATIONS
Advised

CREDIT CARDS
AE, DC, MC, V

À LA CARTE
160F (24.39€), BNC

PRIX FIXE
Lunch: 95F (14.48€), 2 courses, BNC

ENGLISH SPOKEN
Yes

AUX TROIS PETITS COCHONS (20)
31, rue Tiquetonne
Métro: Étienne Marcel

Aux Trois Petits Cochons ("the three little pigs") stands for the original three very slim and slight friends who joined together to open this outstanding good-value restaurant in Paris. Open only for dinner, the place comes into its own around 9:30 P.M. when it fills with a glossy, artistic mix of patrons both straight and otherwise.

These dedicated returnees know a bargain in delicious dining when they find it, and they always book at least a day ahead to be assured a table. The prix fixe menu offers a choice of two or three courses of up-to-date food that is imaginatively prepared and artistically presented. The service is always polite, the linen and crystal table settings correct, the flowers perfect, and the candles glowing. Most importantly, you are in the hands of an exceptionally talented chef. Your dining pleasures might include a springtime salad of warm white asparagus from Landes topped with virgin olive oil and fresh chives,

TELEPHONE
01-42-33-39-69

INTERNET
www.auxtroispetitscochons.com

OPEN
Daily: dinner 8 P.M.–midnight

CLOSED
Aug

RESERVATIONS
Essential

CREDIT CARDS
AE, MC, V

À LA CARTE
None

PRIX FIXE
Dinner: 135F (20.58€), 2 courses, 159F (24.24€), 3 courses, both BNC

ENGLISH SPOKEN
Yes, and English menu

lentilles du Puy served with Lyonnaise sausage, shallots, and herbs, or a mound of *roquette* dressed with roast pancetta and a light lemon vinaigrette and capped with fresh parmesan cheese. Recent springtime *plats* were a roast guinea fowl with *pleurote* mushrooms accented with fresh asparagus and preserved potatoes; mullet in a fennel cream sauce served with spinach, broccoli, and a fondue of leeks; and roast lamb chops with braised, stuffed artichokes and a potato marmalade seasoned with garlic. Desserts keep up the pace with an almond-flavored cookie basket housing a trio of fresh sorbets, a puff pastry of gingerbread filled with coconut sorbet and covered with chocolate sauce, and the crisp apple tart studded with raisins and almonds and served with vanilla ice cream and a Calvados sauce. Mmmm . . . good!

CHEZ DANIE (6)
5, rue de Louvois
Métro: 4-Septembre

TELEPHONE
01-42-96-64-05

OPEN
Mon–Fri: lunch noon–2:45 P.M.

CLOSED
Sat–Sun; holidays, 2 weeks in Aug

RESERVATIONS
Not necessary

CREDIT CARDS
MC, V

À LA CARTE
65F (9.91€), BNC

PRIX FIXE
Lunch: 50–58F (7.62–8.84€), 3 courses, BNC

ENGLISH SPOKEN
Some

You don't have to be down and out in Paris to eat here, but it is a good place to come if you are. It is also a useful bargain destination if one of you wants only a large salad and the other is ready to tackle something more substantial. The tiny cream-colored room is casual, to say the least. There are only a few tables, and the menu is scribbled on a blackboard over the window of the Lilliputian kitchen in the back. You can order the regionally inspired *plat du jour*—maybe a beef and carrot stew—or a quiche and a side salad, and for dessert, splurge on a slice of *tarte Tatin* or a plate of Danie's *beignets de poire, figue, clementine,* or *ananas* . . . deep-fried sweet fritters that literally melt in your mouth as if they were fresh from the cauldron. Danie does all the cooking herself, and she is assisted out front by one waitress and occasionally her dog, Carbonne. By 12:30 or 1 P.M., every seat is taken, while next door it is half empty. This tells you the locals know something, and value hounds should pay attention.

GALLOPIN ($, 4)
40, rue Notre-Dame-des-Victoires
Métro: Bourse

TELEPHONE
01-42-36-45-38

OPEN
Mon–Sat: noon–midnight, continuous service;

CLOSED
Sun; NAC

Since opening its doors in 1876, Gallopin has continually been one of the most popular brasseries around the Bourse (stock market). The interior showcases magnificent Art Nouveau painted windows, Delft tiles, massive mirrors, and brass hat and coat racks behind long banquette seating. Waiters are clad in traditional black with long aprons dusting the tops of their shoes.

The three menu choices, for both lunch and dinner, have great value and offer enough choices to allow most diners to ignore the à la carte suggestions altogether. The food consists of well-executed brasserie classics: fresh oysters, bricks of foie gras, terrines, the venerable *oeufs dur mayonnaise*, and a mound of crisply tender baby green beans in vinaigrette, served with fresh mushrooms and bits of cashews. *Plats* run the gamut from a delicate sole *meunière* surrounded by parsleyed potatoes to grills, *andouillette* (certified "A.A.A.A."; see Au Gourmet de l'Île, page 82, for more on this designation), and their signature dish—*choucroute Gallopin,* made up of *confit de canard,* sausages, and grilled bacon served with piquant cabbage and potatoes. Desserts that make a stellar endings are flaming crêpes Suzette, a *baba au rhum,* and their own crème brûlée spiked with bourbon.

RESERVATIONS
Suggested at lunch and weekends for dinner

CREDIT CARDS
AE, DC, MC, V

À LA CARTE
185–250F (27.44–38.11€), BNC

PRIX FIXE
Lunch and dinner: 135F (20.58€), 2 courses, BNC; 165F (25.15€), 3 courses, BNC; 195F (29.73€), 3 courses, BC

ENGLISH SPOKEN
Yes

LA PATATA (1)
25, boulevard des Italiens
Métro: Opéra

For more food than you can probably eat in one sitting, drop in anytime at La Patata and order a giant baked potato topped with a variety of delicious ingredients and served on platters garnished with salad and fresh fruit. There is something for every taste and appetite. Starting with a *Patata Tradition* (topped with chicken gizzards and sour cream), you can move on to the *Patata Sportive* (cucumbers, corn, tomatoes, carrots, and chive sauce), or the *Patata Californienne* (hamburger, ketchup, onions, and corn slathered with cheese fondue). Mushroom fans can order *Patata Champignons,* filled with diced ham, a mélange of mushrooms, and covered with bubbly cheese. If you want to lower both your guilt and fat gram intake, order one of the main dish salads: the *Salade Grecque* (lettuce, potatoes, tomatoes, cucumbers, onions, peppers, black olives, and feta cheese), the *Baltique* (white cabbage, cucumbers, shrimp, and tomatoes), and the *Parisienne* (lettuce and potatoes tossed with green beans, gouda cheese, ham, hard-boiled eggs, tomatoes, and a sprinkling of nuts). For those budgeteers in the mood for a light snack, there is a tapas menu, where for under 20F (3.05€) you can order a potato tortilla, guacamole, marinated red peppers, or a plate of sausage, all washed down with a glass or a pitcher of sangria. Tipping the dessert scales are huge sundaes, the

TELEPHONE
01-42-68-16-66

OPEN
Daily: 11 A.M.–midnight, continuous service

CLOSED
Christmas day, NAC

RESERVATIONS
Not necessary

CREDIT CARDS
V

À LA CARTE
50–90F (7.62–13.72€), BNC

PRIX FIXE
Eight menus: 65–115F (9.91–17.53€), 2 courses, all BC (except for least expensive menu)

ENGLISH SPOKEN
Limited

amazing *Coupe Patata* (a big dish overflowing with vanilla ice cream, caramel sauce, nuts, and whipped cream), and the chocolate blowout—*Toute Chocolate,* a chocolate cookie covered in chocolate mousse and topped with chocolate sauce.

NOTE: If you are in Paris long enough, join the *Patata Club.* Members who eat ten potato dishes in three months or less get the eleventh one free.

LE VAUDEVILLE ($, 5)
29, rue Vivienne
Métro: Bourse

TELEPHONE
01-40-20-04-62
OPEN
Daily: lunch noon–3:30 P.M., dinner 7 P.M.–2 A.M.
CLOSED
Dec 24 for dinner, NAC
RESERVATIONS
Advised, especially for dinner and on weekends
CREDIT CARDS
AE, DC, MC, V
À LA CARTE
190–225F (28.97–34.30€), BNC
PRIX FIXE
Lunch: 138F (21.04€), 2 courses, BC; dinner: 190F (28.97€), 3 courses, BC; dinner only after 10 P.M.: 140F (21.34€), 2 courses, BC; children's menu (under 12): 60F (9.15€), 2 courses, BC
ENGLISH SPOKEN
Yes

A polished crowd of locals and out-of-towners drifts into Jean-Paul Bucher's 1920s-style brasserie for the pleasure of meeting and eating. At lunch, you will share your meal with stockbrokers and commodity traders from the nearby Bourse. Late in the evening, the sophisticated set arrives in anything from black tie and satin to pastel pullovers and athletic shoes to take advantage of the two-course menu deal available *only* after 10 P.M. Formally clad waiters serve during the peak hours without keeping anyone waiting too long or appearing overworked.

On a warm day, the coveted terrace tables are a great place to sit and soak up the street scene as you delve into familiar dishes from the vast daily changing menu. A good-value, two-course prix fixe lunch option includes not only wine but a *café.* The dinner menu includes three courses, a kir to start, and wine or mineral water with the meal. Even more of a bargain is the late dining menu available after 10 P.M. This includes both wine and coffee along with a choice of any two courses on the menu. Children generally do not fare well in French restaurants, but here, those under twelve have their own two-course menu accompanied by fruit juice or a soda.

MELLIFÈRE (3)
8, rue de Monsigny
Métro: 4-Septembre

TELEPHONE
01-42-61-21-71
OPEN
Mon–Fri: lunch noon–2:30 P.M., dinner 7:15–11 P.M.; Sat: dinner 7:15–11 P.M.
CLOSED
Sat lunch, Sun; NAC
RESERVATIONS
Essential

For Paris restaurateurs still in the grip of the economic crisis, maintaining *le business* is what counts. At Mellifère, *le business* is booming, and after eating here just once it is easy to see why locals create an SRO situation for both lunch and dinner. The food stands out not only for its quality and value but for its preparation. There are two *formules* offering various selections for either a two- or three-course meal. Wine is extra, but the house pitcher is good. When reserving, ask for a table along the mirrored wall of banquettes. Try to avoid those close to the bar and the upright piano or you will be watching the kitchen action and sitting in the line of fire of the amazing waiter. If I ever open a restaurant, I am going to hire this young man, whose hair stands on end . . . and no wonder. He *never* stops moving. My dinner companion equated him to a ballet dancer as he glided through the traditional room never missing a step, ignoring a table, or failing to negotiate a sharp turn.

Your meal will get off to a good start with one of the vegetable terrines, the lentil salad with chopped bacon and onions, or the tomato *tarte* served with a salad topped with parmesan cheese. Noteworthy seasonal main courses include fresh cod, *coquilles St-Jacques,* poached turbot with hollandaise, and a sensational honey-roasted tender pink rack of lamb served with a tomato-zucchini gratin. Dessert classics tempt with crème brûlée, a fruit crumble with crème fraîche, and my very favorite . . . profiteroles blanketed with rich, warm chocolate sauce.

CREDIT CARDS
AE, MC, V

À LA CARTE
None

PRIX FIXE
Lunch and dinner: 130F (19.82€), any 2 courses, 150F (22.87€), any 3 courses, both BNC

ENGLISH SPOKEN
Yes, and menu in English

MIMOSA (17)
44, rue d'Argout
Métro: Sentier, Étienne Marcel

You can go with a slim wallet and a big appetite to Cédric Ung's Mimosa, a pocket-size, low-cost choice buried on a side street near the main post office on rue du Louvre. This is a place where it pays to arrive early because once one of his savory rich *tartes* or homespun *plats du jour* sells out . . . that's it. But also, if you arrive ahead of the crowd, you'll get to watch him cooking in his minuscule kitchen in the back section. Seating inside is at wooden tables, there are pavement tables outside on a sunny day, and you can have your meal wrapped and packaged to go.

In addition to his delicious daily changing hot dishes, which always include fish on Friday, you can order one of chef Ung's regional platters. My favorite is the *Perigord,* made up of *jambon de Bayonne,* smoked duck, foie gras, terrine, and artichoke hearts. He also makes fresh sandwiches, picture-perfect salads, and three or four mouthwatering desserts, including apple, lemon, or chocolate *tartes,* chocolate mousse, and crème caramel.

NOTE: Mimosa has later summer hours from June through mid-August, when it is open for both lunch and

TELEPHONE
01-40-28-15-75

OPEN
Mon–Sat: lunch 11:30 A.M.–6 P.M.; summer (June–mid-Aug), Mon–Sat: lunch and dinner 11:30 A.M.–9 P.M.

CLOSED
Sun; Aug 15–Sept 1

RESERVATIONS
Not necessary

CREDIT CARDS
MC, V

À LA CARTE
40–80F (6.10–12.20€)

PRIX FIXE
Lunch: 70F (10.67€), 2 courses, BC

ENGLISH SPOKEN
Yes

dinner, but call to check, since the dinner hours may change. The rest of the year, it is open only for lunch.

PEIRROT (21)
18, rue Étienne Marcel
Métro: Étienne Marcel

TELEPHONE
01-45-08-00-10

OPEN
Mon–Fri: lunch noon–2 P.M.,
dinner 7–11 P.M.; Sat: dinner
7–11 P.M.

CLOSED
Sat lunch, Sun; holidays, Aug

RESERVATIONS
Essential

CREDIT CARDS
AE, DC, MC, V

À LA CARTE
200F (30.49€), BNC

PRIX FIXE
Lunch: 92F (14.03€), 2 courses,
BNC

ENGLISH SPOKEN
Yes

The modern bistro Pierrot draws a well-heeled yet price-conscious food-loving crowd twice a day. At lunch, workers, models, and their bosses from the surrounding garment district pour in for the two-course menu. In the evening a young, fashionable local audience fills every table and delves into the blackboard menu of *plats* featuring rack of lamb and sautéed potatoes, succulent roast chicken, duck, and rare steaks sauced several ways. *Entrées* are remarkably imaginative and generous, especially the duo of fresh tomatoes stuffed with fresh chèvre, garlic, and chives; the *roquette* salad piled high with creamy white mushrooms and shaved parmesan cheese; and the plate of *haricort verts* holding a slice of rich foie gras. Everyone seems to have room for dessert . . . and who wouldn't when the choices are ice cream–filled profiteroles covered in dark chocolate sauce, a generous slice of chocolate or lemon *tarte,* and crème brûlée with a sugary-browned top crust. The only drawback I found was the initial attitude of the flip waiter, who was hell-bent to practice his English on us and reluctant to discuss the house wine. However, as the night wore on, he reverted to French and it was smooth sailing right through dessert and the bracing espresso.

STOHRER (18)
51, rue Montorgueil
Métro: Étienne Marcel, Sentier

TELEPHONE
01-42-33-38-20

OPEN
Daily: 7:30 A.M.–8:30 P.M.,
continuous service

CLOSED
First 3 weeks of Aug

RESERVATIONS
Not taken

CREDIT CARDS
MC, V (100F, 15.24€,
minimum)

À LA CARTE
15–90F (2.29–13.72€), BNC

PRIX FIXE
None

ENGLISH SPOKEN
Some

Parisian pastry lovers think nothing of crossing the city in search of the perfect croissant, the richest chocolate mousse cake, or the best lemon *tarte.* At Stohrer's they come for the *puits d'amour* (wells of love)—individual, cream-filled, flaky puff pastries lightly caramelized with a hot iron. Others come for the famous seven-fruit tart made up of picture-perfect raspberries, strawberries, tangerines, peaches, kiwi fruit, rose figs, and white pears set in almond paste in a *sablé* crust. I like to go when the doors open and buy a bag of their buttery croissants, or to go by at lunchtime and take out a picnic *extraordinaire* made up of quiche, pâtés, fresh salads, and of course, several divine desserts. In the afternoon, schoolchildren line up outside by the cart selling homemade ice creams and sorbet.

The shop has a long and interesting history. It was opened in 1730 by one of Louis XV's pastry chefs and named for Marie Antoinette's private *pâtissier*. It is now classified as a historic monument. Inside, the beautiful painted walls and ceiling depicting nymphs holding trays of pastries were painted by Paul Baudry, who is famous for his paintings on the Opéra.

Third Arrondissement

RIGHT BANK
Carnavalet Museum (the museum of the city of Paris), French National Archives, part of the Marais, Picasso Museum, the wholesale garment district, and the stunning, newly renovated Musée des Arts et Métiers in the medieval abbey of St-Martin-les-Champs.

Marais means "swamp" in French, and this area was just that until the fourteenth century, when it became a royal park. Today, a walk through this area is a lesson in the history of French domestic architecture. The area has been redeveloped with panache, and many of the seventeenth- and eighteenth-century buildings have been made into museums or returned to their former glory as sumptuous apartments. This heaven for walkers and wanderers of all types is full of shops, boutiques, appealing restaurants, and fascinating history.

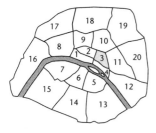

THIRD ARRONDISSEMENT RESTAURANTS

($) indicates a Big Splurge

A 2 PAS DU DOS (8)
101, rue Vieille du Temple
Métro: Arts et Métiers, St-Sébastien–Froissart

For a complete description, please see Le Dos de la Baleine, page 91. All other information is the same, though there are some minor menu variations in both the food and prices. This one is close to the Picasso Museum. It should be noted that reservations are taken by an answering machine, which always leaves some doubt in my mind if I really *do* have a table.

TELEPHONE
01-42-77-10-52

OPEN
Tues–Fri: lunch noon–
2:30 P.M., dinner 8–11 P.M.;
Sat–Sun dinner 8–11 P.M. (till
midnight on Sat)

CLOSED
Sat–Sun lunch, Mon; 2 weeks
in Aug (dates vary)

AU BASCOU ($, 2)
38, rue de Réaumur
Métro: Arts et Métiers

If you can't go to the Basque region of France, Jean-Guy Loustau's Au Bascou will at least put you in a southwestern frame of mind with its modern Basque food and sensibly priced wines. The 1930s bistro, which won the Bistro of the Year award in 1995, is not near the usual tourist track. The area is full of wholesale clothing merchants and cheap Chinese restaurants and frequented by older Parisians carrying little dogs and feeding the ravenous pigeons. Don't let this slice of local color discourage you. The restaurant is less than a two-minute walk from the métro, and remember, you are here for the food, which is not only rich and full-flavored but also extremely well made and presented.

The menu is seasonally based, but there are some standards that always appear. Count on starters of duck terrine, *piperade basquaise* (sweet peppers and tomatoes flavored with onion and garlic and served with scrambled eggs and cured ham), and their own foie gras. *Morue* (salted codfish) is the steady fish staple, but if you love abundance, order the roast leg of milk-fed lamb from the Pyrenees, which is served with fresh vegetables. Desserts and cheeses do not quite measure up to the rest of the meal. I would skip the small and dry cheese offerings and order instead the *duo de gâteaux basques* or the *béret basque,* a rich, dark chocolate cake.

TELEPHONE
01-42-72-69-25

OPEN
Mon, Sat: dinner 8–11 P.M.;
Tues–Fri: lunch noon–2 P.M.,
dinner 8–11 P.M.

CLOSED
Mon and Sat lunch, Sun;
holidays, 1 week between
Christmas and New Year's,
Aug

RESERVATIONS
Essential

CREDIT CARDS
AE, MC

À LA CARTE
180–225F (27.44–34.30€),
BNC

PRIX FIXE
Lunch: 95F (14.48€), 2 courses,
BNC

ENGLISH SPOKEN
Yes

Third and Fourth Arrondissements

Strasbourg Ⓜ St. Denis

Boulevard

Rue

Rue

Rue Réaumur

Sébastopol

R. Sal. de Caus

St. Martin

R. Montgolfier

Rue

Rue du Louvre

Réaumur Ⓜ Sebastopol

Boulevard de

Rue

Arts et Métiers Ⓜ

• 2 Rue Réaumur

Montmartre

Étienne

Étienne Marcel Ⓜ

de

Turbigo

Rue

Martin

des Gravilliers

Rue

Marcel

Rue

St.

Rue du Grenier-St.-Lazare

• 5

Beaubourg

3E

Les Halles Ⓜ

Rue Rambuteau

Rue

Imp. Berthaud

• 6

Temple

R. de

Rue Berger

FORUM DES HALLES

Châtelet Les Halles

Rue

Sébastopol

Rambuteau Ⓜ

Rue

Archives

CENTRE GEORGES POMPIDOU

du

Rambuteau

Pont Neuf

Châtelet Ⓜ

R. des Halles

R. des

de

R. des Blancs

Manteaux

Rue

• 9

Rue

du

de

Rivoli

Boulevard

Lombards

R. N. Flam.

R. de la

• 10

de

Renard

R. Ste. Croix de la Bret.

• 11

R. des

Vieille

• 12

• 14

Quai de la Mégisserie

Avenue

PL. DU CHÂTELET

TOUR ST. JACQUES

Rue

Verrerie

R. Bourg-Tibourg

• 13

Rue

Voie

Châtelet

Victoria

Hôtel de Ville Ⓜ

Rue

G. Pompidou

Seine

Quai de l'Horloge

Quai

de

l'Horloge

Quai de Gesvres

HÔTEL DE VILLE

Rue de Roi

de

PLACE DAUPHINE

CONCIERGERIE

P. au Change

Pont Notre Dame

4E

Rue

des

Écouffer

PALAIS DE JUSTICE

Quai

Quai de l'Hôtel de Ville

Rue

Fr.

R. des

Miro

STE CHAPELLE

Bd. du Palais

Cité Ⓜ

de la Corse

P. d' Arcole

R. Pt.-L. Philippe

• 26

ÎLE DE LA CITÉ

HÔTEL DIEU DE CITÉ

Rue d'Arcole

Seine

R. Pt.-L. Philippe

• 27

St. Michel Ⓜ

Quai St. Michel

Rue de la Cité

Quai

aux

P.-L. Philippe

Voie

Pont Marie

St. Michel

Saint Michel

Q. de

NOTRE DAME

Fleurs

• 37

Pont Marie Georges

Saint Jacques

Montebello

Pont St. Louis

Q. de Bourbon

• 38 ÎLE ST. LOUIS

Q. d'Anjou

Bd.

Cluny La Sorbonne Ⓜ

Rue

St. Germain

Q. de

d'Orleans

• 39

Rue

• 40

St. Louis en l'île

• 41

ST. LOUIS

R. des Deux Ponts

Q. de Bethune

△ N

500 meters

Ⓜ Métro Station

CAFÉ DES MUSÉES (21)
49, rue de Turenne
Métro: Chemin Vert

TELEPHONE
01-42-72-96-17,
01-44-59-86-16

OPEN
Daily: bar 7 A.M.–2 A.M.,
lunch noon–3 P.M., dinner 7–
10:30 P.M.; Sun continuous food
service noon–11 P.M.

CLOSED
Holidays, Aug

RESERVATIONS
Not accepted

CREDIT CARDS
None

À LA CARTE
160–200F (24.39–30.49€),
BNC

PRIX FIXE
None

ENGLISH SPOKEN
Some

Café des Musées is a well-worn corner café that plays to a packed house of contented regulars. For lunch, it is best to go early to nab one of the prized tables on the sidewalk; otherwise you will be crowded inside, where it can get hot and smoky, not to mention very noisy with the din of the happy crowd. Don't come here for fancy garnishes or the latest food fad. Instead, bring your appetite and expect a satisfying meal quickly served by hardworking waitresses. Check the blackboard specials, and if the duck foie gras with port, *chèvre chaud* atop a bed of greens, steak tartare, or veal liver with sautéed potatoes don't speak to you, perhaps a warm lentil salad or a soothing *pot-au-feu* will. The *patron* bottles his own Côtes de Lyonnais house wine and features a wide selection of beers. Desserts? You can safely save the guilt for someplace else.

CAMILLE (19)
24, rue des Francs-Bourgeois
Métro: St-Paul

TELEPHONE
01-42-72-20-59

OPEN
Daily: bar 8 A.M.–11:30 P.M.,
food service noon–11:30 P.M.

CLOSED
Dec 24 and 25, New Year's
Eve, NAC

RESERVATIONS
Suggested for dinner after 9 P.M.

CREDIT CARDS
AE, DC, MC, V

À LA CARTE
170F (25.92€), BNC

PRIX FIXE
Lunch: 90F (13.72€), 2 courses,
BNC

ENGLISH SPOKEN
Yes, and menu in English (but
no prices)

Camille is a useful address to remember if you are looking for a place that is child-friendly, or if you want to eat dinner before 8 P.M. The corner location on one of the most interesting shopping streets in the Marais draws a diverse crowd. Tourists pack in for lunch and early dinners, and the French arrive for lunch and for dinner after 9 P.M. The kitchen turns out all the seasonal bistro classics with few misses. In the winter, look for *entrées* of sausage with warm potato salad, leeks vinaigrette, green beans dotted with bits of foie gras, and just-cooked scrambled eggs with smoked salmon. *Salade niçoise* is added to the list in the summer. *Plats* destined to please include *blanquette de veau, confit de canard* with crispy sautéed potatoes, *petit sale aux lentilles, entrecôte,* veal kidneys, and liver. Desserts are not made here, but the *tarte aux poires* is certainly far better than the runny *tarte aux pommes.*

CHEZ JENNY (1)
39, boulevard du Temple
Métro: République

TELEPHONE
01-42-74-75-75

OPEN
Daily: 11:30 A.M.–1 A.M.,
continuous service

Chez Jenny celebrates the food and wine of Alsace, which is served in a magnificent old brasserie full of fabulous regional artwork. Rosy-cheeked waitresses wearing starched headdresses and dirndls serve the brimming plates with speed and, unfortunately, very little good cheer. However, if you are looking for some of the best *choucroute* in Paris, look no further. For the uninitiated, *choucroute* is a steaming platter of smoked slab bacon, bratwurst, plump white veal sausages, lean smoked pork loin, and savory sauerkraut and potatoes; a stein of golden beer is the perfect accompaniment. For a lighter supper, order the assorted *charcuterie* of mild Alsatian sausages or a *plat* of iced oysters and shellfish with a glass of chilled Reisling wine. Warning: The fish *choucroute* makes for a strange combination.

The cavernous interior is as impressive as the food: it's decorated with carved wall plaques, life-size wooden figures in native Alsatian dress, and lovely murals depicting life in this colorful region along the German border. For the best overall atmosphere, reserve a table on the ground floor.

CLOSED
Never

RESERVATIONS
Advised

CREDIT CARDS
AE, DC, MC, V

À LA CARTE
200F (30.49€), BNC

PRIX FIXE
Lunch *express menu* (Mon–Fri only): 70F (10.67€), BNC; lunch: 89F (13.57€), garnished main course, BNC; lunch and dinner: 155F (23.63€), 2 courses, 185F (28.20€), 3 courses, both BC; *Petit Génie* (children under 12): 50F (7.62€), 2 courses, BC; all orders placed before noon receive a 10 percent discount

ENGLISH SPOKEN
Yes

CHEZ OMAR (4)
47, rue de Bretagne
Métro: Arts et Métiers

Diners at Chez Omar arrive in droves to tackle monumental portions of some of the best couscous in Paris. This traditional Parisian café, which has not changed in fifty years, buzzes for both lunch and dinner with a trendy-by-association crowd that swears by Omar's six varieties of couscous. There are other choices on the menu, ranging from grilled fish to plates of red meat, but when you are at Chez Omar, think only lamb, beef, *merguez* (spicy sausage), chicken, or vegetable couscous. You simply cannot go wrong.

TELEPHONE
01-42-72-36-26

OPEN
Mon–Sat: lunch noon–2:30 P.M., dinner 7 P.M.–midnight; Sun: lunch noon–2:30 P.M.

CLOSED
Sun dinner; major holidays, NAC

RESERVATIONS
Essential after 8 P.M. and on weekends

CREDIT CARDS
None

À LA CARTE
125–150F (19.06–22.87€), BNC

PRIX FIXE
None

ENGLISH SPOKEN
Yes

L'AMBASSADE D'AUVERGNE ($, 5)
22, rue du Grenier-St-Lazare
Métro: Rambuteau (rue du Grenier-St-Lazare exit)

The long-standing owners of L'Ambassade d'Auvergne regard themselves as culinary representatives of their native region. Throughout the years, their restaurant has remained true to its heritage and is today one of the finest regional restaurants in Paris. I have eaten here

TELEPHONE
01-42-72-31-22

INTERNET
www.ambassade-auvergne.com

OPEN
Daily: lunch noon–2 P.M., dinner 7:30–11 P.M.

CLOSED
Never

RESERVATIONS
Essential

CREDIT CARDS
AE, MC, V

À LA CARTE
225–250F (34.30–38.11€),
BNC

PRIX FIXE
Lunch and dinner: 170F
(25.92€), 3 courses, BNC

ENGLISH SPOKEN
Yes

many times, and I always find all of the restaurant's elements working together to create a satisfying dining experience. Its six dining rooms are always filled, and its clientele includes prominent political figures. For the most authentic and beautiful atmosphere, reserve a table downstairs, which has massive beams from which hang hundreds of Auvergne hams. If you are eating alone, ask for a place at the *table d'hôte,* where you will be seated with other solo diners who probably won't be strangers by the end of the meal.

Country abundance is evident in every delicious dish, from the specials that remain the same each day of the week to the monthly and seasonal offerings. A variety of excellent, little-known regional wines are available to accompany your feast. Wonderful *entrées* anytime are the cabbage soup—with white beans, ham chunks, potatoes, carrots, and roquefort cheese—and the warm *lentilles du puy* salad. Tempting main dishes include the spicy blood sausage with chestnuts, thyme-roasted leg of lamb, a *potée de porc,* a winter stew made with chunks of pork and root vegetables, and for the adventurous, the *tripous à l'estragon* (tripe). An absolute must with whatever you order is *l'aligot,* a masterful blend of garlic-infused puréed potatoes and *tomme* cheese whipped at your table and served from copper pans. Trying to save room for dessert is next to impossible, but if you can, the creamy chocolate mousse served nonstop from a crystal bowl is worth the overload. If you can't do dessert, consider ordering one of their ten prune *digestifs* as a *grand finale.*

LA MULE DU PAPE (22)
8, rue du Pas de la Mule
Métro: Chemin Vert

TELEPHONE
01-42-74-55-80

INTERNET
www.adx.fr/la-mule-du-pape/

OPEN
Mon–Fri: lunch 11 A.M.–4 P.M.,
dinner 7–10:30 P.M.;
Sat: 11 A.M.–11 P.M., continuous service; Sun: 11 A.M.–7 P.M.,
continuous service

CLOSED
Sun dinner; weekend of Aug
15, 3 days at Christmas, Easter,
NAC

RESERVATIONS
Suggested

CREDIT CARDS
AE, MC, V

La Mule du Pape has everything a choice, real value in Paris should: comfortable flower-filled surroundings, good food, fair prices, and an adorable pooch. Ursule, a long-haired dachshund, comes for lunch each day with her owner, Mme. André, who runs the restaurant along with her son, Alexis. The menu offers enticing choices that make dining here a pleasure worth repeating. The emphasis is on light lunches, dinners, weekend afternoon tea, and Sunday brunch. Beautiful main-dish salads are served with a basket of fresh toast. Habit-forming egg creations include *oeufs florentine* (eggs resting on a bed of creamed spinach topped with parmesan), scrambled eggs with smoked salmon, and a cheese, bacon, and chive omelette garnished with a side salad and toast. For dinner, you might try poached haddock, pork medallions with an onion confiture, or a roast veal with sautéed cumin-spiked carrots. All the lovely desserts are displayed for your selection. The fruit crumbles are always popular and so is the chocolate *tarte* served with a pistachio ice cream. If you are visiting the Picasso Museum or the place des Vosges just down the street, this is definitely one to remember.

À LA CARTE
90–140F (13.72–21.34€), BNC

PRIX FIXE
Sun brunch: 140F (21.34€), BC

ENGLISH SPOKEN
Yes

LE HANGAR (6)
12, impasse Berthaud
Métro: Rambuteau

Le Hangar, on a hidden *impasse* just steps from the Beaubourg, Forum des Halles, and the little-known Musée de la Poupée (doll musem), attracts a knowing clientele who value the chef's sophisticated interpretations of familiar favorites and the smiling welcome extended by any one of the four owners. On a warm day, it is very pleasant to sit on the covered terrace, which is free from dust, birds, dirt, and automobile fumes. The mood inside is rather stark, with linens, crystal, green plants, and an efficient waitstaff changing the silver and crumbing the tables between courses. The prices are as attractive as the setting, with imaginative choices for each course and appropriate wines from small producers that enhance the dishes.

TELEPHONE
01-42-74-55-44

OPEN
Mon–Sat: lunch noon–3 P.M., dinner 7:30 P.M.–midnight

CLOSED
Sun; holidays, Aug

RESERVATIONS
Advised

CREDIT CARDS
None

À LA CARTE
130–170F (19.82–25.92€), BNC

PRIX FIXE
None

ENGLISH SPOKEN
Yes

As you decide your order, you are served a rich olive tapenade and toast. Depending on the season, cold *entrées* may feature a salmon tartare, barely cooked green beans drizzled with olive oil, artichokes served in a balsamic vinaigrette, or a lusty lentil soup flavored with pieces of duck liver. If you love *chèvre chaud,* it comes in three roasted mounds resting on a bed of designer greens. Another delicious hot *entrée* is the ravioli in an eggplant cream sauce. Carnivores will love the meaty servings of *blanquette de veau,* the beef filet with *morille* sauce, and the mouthwatering pan-fried fois gras served with creamy, olive oil–flavored mashed potatoes. Depending on the season, fish fanciers can look for *daurade* (white sea bream) with steamed potatoes or scallops in a parsley cream sauce. Save room for dessert, especially the orange crêpes with Grand Marnier sauce, fresh fruit *clafoutis* cooked to order, or the chocolate creation filled with warm chocolate sauce that melts over two little scoops of vanilla ice cream. A plate of their own cookies and an espresso is an ideal end to this truly wonderful meal.

WEB BAR (3)
32, rue de Picardie
Métro: Filles du Calvaire

TELEPHONE
01-42-72-66-55

FAX
01-42-72-66-75

EMAIL
webbar@webbar.fr

INTERNET
www.webbar.fr

OPEN
Mon–Fri: 8:30 A.M.–2 A.M.;
Sat–Sun: 11 A.M.–2 A.M.

CLOSED
Aug 1–15

RESERVATIONS
Not necesssary

CREDIT CARDS
MC, V

À LA CARTE
60–100F (90–15.24€)

PRIX FIXE
Lunch and dinner: 70F
(10.67€), 2 courses, 85F
(12.96€), 3 courses, both BNC

INTERNET PRICES
1F (0.15€) per minute, 25F
(3.81€) per half hour, 40F
(6.10€) per hour; 175F
(26.68€) for 5 hours, 300F
(45.73€) for 10 hours

ENGLISH SPOKEN
Yes

Cyber cafés are popping up all over Paris, and none are more plugged in to cyberspace than this cool hangout, located on a backwater street near the crumbling Marché du Temple. You won't have trouble finding it—just look for the purple exterior with "Web Bar" written in glowing red lights across the top. Inside the cavernous space, downstairs has tables on a gray concrete-slab floor, and the circular mezzanine above is where the computers are positioned. Besides plugging in to the Internet, sending email, and checking your stock portfolio, there is a lot you can do here . . . and it is all free. You can take salsa lessons on Monday, listen to a DJ from Tuesday through Thursday, and watch short movies on Friday. Oh yes, they even serve food: sandwiches, *tartes,* a few hot dishes and salads, five desserts, and a few wines by the glass or bottle.

Fourth Arrondissement

Point zero is a compass rose set in the pavement in front of Notre Dame Cathedral. This is the spot from which all distances are measured in France, but more than that, the cathedral serves as the spiritual and emotional heart of France.

Île St-Louis was developed by Henri IV in the seventeenth century. It has been home to Voltaire, Baudelaire, Colette, and George Sand. Today it is one of the most expensive plots of real estate in Paris. Full of atmosphere, the narrow streets house beautiful *hôtel particulières* (private mansions) occupied by film stars, authors, the Rothschilds, and six thousand other lucky people. In the Marais, the place des Vosges is the oldest and considered the most beautiful and romantic square in Paris. It was an up-and-coming area some years ago—now it has arrived! Young fashion designers fight for shop space and rents are astronomical. The famous fashion houses on the rue de Faubourg St-Honoré and avenue Montaigne are for affluent, stylish French men and women, who shop in the Marais for the last word in clothes. The area is also the center of the Parisian Jewish and gay communities. Take a stroll down rue des Rosiers and discover marvelous kosher delicatessens, bakeries, and restaurants. The gay crowd fills the bars and restaurants on and around rue Vielle du Temple. While you are in the fourth arrondissement, you can visit the museum of modern art, better known as the Centre Georges Pompidou or the Beaubourg. It's now the number-one tourist attraction in Paris, surpassing the Eiffel Tower and the Louvre Museum in its number of visitors per year.

RIGHT BANK
Notre Dame, Île St-Louis, Centre Georges Pompidou (Beaubourg), Hôtel-de-Ville (City Hall), Jewish Quarter, continuation of the Marais, Maison de Victor Hugo, place des Vosges

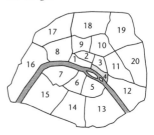

FOURTH ARRONDISSEMENT RESTAURANTS
(see map page 72)

($) indicates a Big Splurge

AQUARIUS (11)
54, rue Ste-Croix-de-la-Bretonnerie
Métro: Hôtel de Ville

For a healthy, low-cost vegetarian lunch or dinner, Parisians head for one of the two Aquarius locations. The choices range from colorful salads, *tartes,* quiches, and homemade soups to large *plats du jour* designed around grains and cooked veggies. Fruit desserts seem to be more popular than the plain yogurt and dishes of prunes. The nondescript decor leans toward the ascetic, as do most of the diners, who seem to be engrossed in books or magazines even when they are sharing a table. A nice feature is that you can order as little or as much as you want and not feel out of place doing so. Keep this one in mind when the budget is in trouble, because you can always have a satisfying, healthy, economical meal here with a glass of organic wine or designer water for under 100F.

NOTE: There is no smoking allowed. The other location is at 40, rue de Gergovie in the fourteenth arrondissement (see page 217).

TELEPHONE
01-48-87-48-71

OPEN
Mon–Sat: noon–10:15 P.M., continuous service

CLOSED
Sun; holidays, Aug (dates vary)

RESERVATIONS
Not necessary

CREDIT CARDS
MC, V (100F, 15.24€, minimum)

À LA CARTE
65–100F (9.91–15.24€), BNC

PRIX FIXE
Lunch: 68F (10.37€), *plat du jour* and dessert, BNC; lunch and dinner: 100F (15.24€), 3 courses, BNC

ENGLISH SPOKEN
Usually

AUBERGE DE JARENTE (24)
7, rue de Jarente
Métro: St-Paul

It is not much from the outside, but what counts is the food, and it is good. This two-room, family-owned *auberge* on the edge of the Marais specializes in filling Basque dishes from southwestern France. If you order any of the prix fixe menus, you will have some difficult dining decisions ahead. Should you start with the *pipérade,* a mixture of sweet red peppers, tomatoes, onions, and garlic mixed with scrambled eggs and topped with spicy sausage? Or would a bowl of fish soup or the Basque *salade Kayola,* with fresh foie gras, figs, chestnuts, and preserved gizzards, be a better beginning? For the main course, will it be the *cassoulet* or the *confit de canard,* both for two people, or the *cailles à la façon du chef,* two highly flavored quail served with sautéed potatoes? The house specialty is *paella valenciana,* which is served for a minimum of two persons and must be ordered twenty-four hours ahead. For dessert, far and away the two best choices are their versions of *gâteau Basque,* a plain cream-filled cake, and the *tourtière au pommes*—apples and raisins cooked in honey and layered in a flaky crust. For the nicest experience of the restaurant, arrive about 9 or 9:30 P.M. when the French do,

TELEPHONE
01-42-77-49-35

OPEN
Tues–Sat: lunch noon–2:30 P.M., dinner 7:30–10:30 P.M.

CLOSED
Mon, Sun; holidays, one week from Aug 15

RESERVATIONS
Advised for lunch and after 9 P.M.

CREDIT CARDS
AE, MC, V

À LA CARTE
190–200F (28.97–30.49€), BNC

PRIX FIXE
Lunch: 80F (12.20€), 3 courses, BC; lunch and dinner: 120F (18.29€), 4 courses, BNC; 140F (21.34€), 3 courses, BC; 190F (27.44€) 4 courses, BC

ENGLISH SPOKEN
Yes

order a bottle of the Madiran red wine, and settle in to a full-flavored meal that will not put a major strain on your budget.

AU BISTROT DE LA PLACE (25)
2, place du Marché Ste-Catherine
Métro: St-Paul

TELEPHONE
01-42-78-21-32
OPEN
Mon–Sat: lunch noon–2 P.M., drinks and afternoon tea, 3–7 P.M., dinner 7–11 P.M.
CLOSED
Sun; call to check in Aug
RESERVATIONS
Suggested for terrace tables on Sat
CREDIT CARDS
MC, V
À LA CARTE
165–180F (25.15–27.44€), BNC
PRIX FIXE
Lunch and dinner: 135F (20.58€), 3 courses, BNC
ENGLISH SPOKEN
Usually

On a warm sunny day or summer evening, it would be hard to imagine a more delightful setting for a meal than this popular spot on the quiet place du Marché Ste-Catherine, a few minutes from place des Vosges. The inside is definitely laid-back. When I was there on Valentine's Day, Christmas decorations were still in place. In addition to anachronistic holiday displays, there are pictures of American film stars from the forties and fifties and a handful of small tapestry-covered tables, which are served by one or two hard-pressed waiters. But never mind the inside; you want a table on the pretty outside terrace, where you can enjoy a typical bistro meal and delight in watching the passing parade of Parisians. The menu is the same for lunch and dinner and offers reliable fare with few surprises. Look for standard-bearers of snails in a light pastry with garlic butter and a green salad, lentil salad with gizzards, and marinated herring and anchovies served with potatoes. Sweet-and-sour duck breast is served with sautéed garlic potatoes, and the chef's specialty—*confit cassoulet*—comes with white beans, duck sausage, and thick bacon. Jugged rabbit with prunes and polenta, guinea fowl on a bed of green cabbage, and a veggie lasagna wrap up the *plats*. For dessert, the tiramisu is a good bet, and so is the ever-present chocolate *fondant* floating in a light custard sauce.

AU GOURMET DE L'ÎLE (41)
42, rue St-Louis-en-l'Île
Métro: Pont-Marie

TELEPHONE
01-43-26-79-27
OPEN
Wed–Sun: lunch noon–2 P.M., dinner 7–10 P.M.
CLOSED
Mon–Tues; Aug
RESERVATIONS
Advised for Sunday lunch and dinner on weekends
CREDIT CARDS
AE, MC, V
À LA CARTE
None

One of the more interesting meals in Paris can be found at this rustic seventeenth-century restaurant on the Île St-Louis, where diners can be assured of finding expert versions of French country classics served in a friendly atmosphere. On Sunday, the lunch crowd is heavy with portly locals who have made this a family tradition. When reserving, especially on Sunday, be sure to request a table on the ground floor, not in the cramped, stuffy subterranean room below.

A warning is in order: The food here is not for the fainthearted or those with tame tastes. In the window is a simple sign reading, "A.A.A.A.A.," which stands for the Amiable Association of Amateurs of the Authentic Andouillette. This presumably voluntary organization makes sure members follow certain guidelines of preparation, and what the notification tells you is that these are the Rolls-Royce of French chitlins. If you would like to but have never tried one of these soul-food sausages (made from the intestines of hogs), now is the time. This is also the place to sample such French standards as *boudin* (blood sausage) and *ris d'agneau* (lamb kidneys).

Those with less adventurous palates will enjoy the other house specialties of grilled guinea hen with lentils and *la charbonnée de l'Île,* a robust, filling pork stew in red wine with bacon, onions, potatoes, and croutons. For the wine accompaniment, try a bottle of Marcillac, a Chinon, or a red Saumur from the Loire Valley.

Everyone will agree on the delicious desserts, especially the *crème limousine,* a caramel custard swimming in warm chocolate sauce, the poached pear in red wine, or the rich profiteroles filled with ice cream.

NOTE: There is a nonsmoking area.

PRIX FIXE
Lunch Wed–Sat: 100F (15.24€), any 2 courses on menu, BC; lunch and dinner: 150F (22.87€), 4 courses, BNC; 190F (28.97€), 4 courses, BC (kir, wine, and coffee)

ENGLISH SPOKEN
Yes, with English menu

AU LYS D'ARGENT (38)
90, rue St-Louis-en-l'Île
Métro: Pont-Marie

Forty varieties of tea, light meals based around quiches, *tartes,* salads, and crêpes, plus homemade pastries keep visitors well fed here when they are on Île St-Louis—an island in the middle of the River Seine that is a picturesque microslice of Paris. On weekends and holidays, the waves of tourists, browsers, and occasional natives can be very discouraging. For those looking for a bit of sustenance, Au Lys d'Argent provides something on its menu for just about everyone. They serve a daily brunch, which includes freshly squeezed orange juice, *fromage blanc* with dried fruits, pancakes and maple syrup, toast with butter and jam, and a choice of four types of eggs and a small green salad. Not to be forgotten are their rich chocolate drinks made to order from melted bars of pure chocolate, whole milk, and cream (allow ten minutes please and don't tell your cardiologist). For a complete chocolate blowout—and why not?—order a slice of their dark chocolate cake to go with your *chocolat à l'ancienne.*

NOTE: In summer, Au Lys d'Argent closes for three hours every afternoon after brunch.

TELEPHONE
01-46-33-65-13

OPEN
Daily: winter hours: noon–9:30 P.M. (till 10:30 P.M. on Fri and Sat); summer hours: noon–3:30 P.M., 6:30–10:30 P.M.; year-round: brunch noon–3:30 P.M.

CLOSED
15 days in Aug (dates vary)

RESERVATIONS
Not necessary

CREDIT CARDS
MC, V (100F, 15.24€, minimum)

À LA CARTE
70–100F (10.67–15.24€), BC

PRIX FIXE
Lunch and dinner: 59F (8.99), 79F (12.04€), 99F (15.09€), all 3 courses and BNC; brunch: 95F (14.48€), BC

ENGLISH SPOKEN
Yes, and English menu

AU PETIT FER À CHEVAL (14)
30, rue Vieille du Temple
Métro: Hôtel de Ville, St-Paul

TELEPHONE
01-42-72-47-47

OPEN
Daily: 9 A.M.–2 A.M.,
continuous service

CLOSED
Never

RESERVATIONS
Not necessary

CREDIT CARDS
MC, V

À LA CARTE
75–130F (11.43–19.82€), BNC

PRIX FIXE
None

ENGLISH SPOKEN
Yes

Cheap, cheerful, and truly French—that's Au Petit Fer à Cheval, a popular meeting place for everyone from shopkeepers and stray tourists to New Wave patrons just in from Pluto.

The slightly seedy Marais landmark has been in operation since 1903 and consists of sidewalk tables and a marble-topped horseshoe (*fer à cheval*) bar in the front room. In back, there is a larger room with booths made from old wooden métro seats. For Flash Gordon and Captain Marvel fans, the stainless-steel WCs are not to be missed. The nice thing about this place is that you can come in anytime for a quick *café* standing at the bar, or you can sit down and consume a home-cooked lunch or dinner. While the food doesn't inspire rave reviews, it is filling and typical native grub consisting of salads, daily *plats,* and the dessert standards of chocolate mousse and floating island.

BARACANE—BISTROT DE L'OULETTE ($, 23)
38, rue des Tournelles
Métro: Bastille

TELEPHONE
01-42-71-43-33

OPEN
Mon–Fri: lunch noon–2:30 P.M.,
dinner 7 P.M.–midnight; Sat:
dinner 7 P.M.–midnight

CLOSED
Sat lunch, Sun; holidays, NAC

RESERVATIONS
Essential

CREDIT CARDS
MC, V

À LA CARTE
225F (34.30€), BNC

PRIX FIXE
Lunch: 55F (8.38€), *plat du jour,* 85F (12.96€), 2 courses, both BC; lunch and dinner: *Menu du Marché,* 140F (21.34€), 3 courses, BNC; *Le Menu-Carte,* 220F (33.54€), 3 courses, BC

ENGLISH SPOKEN
Yes

For one of the best bistro meals going, book a table at Baracane—Bistrot de l'Oulette on the edge of the Marais. Owner and chef Marcel Baudis opened here a few years ago and was an instant hit with his impeccable dishes from Quercy in southwestern France. Now Baudis has moved to a larger location in the Bercy area near the Gare de Lyon (see L'Oulette, page 209), but he still oversees the kitchen, which maintains his standards of excellence in every dish served. His business partner, Alain Fontaine, monitors the business end of the nar-row dining room, which has also lost nothing in the transition.

The real appeal of this bistro lies in its consistently fresh foods complemented by an excellent wine list, with most bottles selling for under 140F (21.34€). The *formule* menus—available for either lunch or dinner—offer a wide selection from the seasonal menu. Some favorites do remain, at the insistence of loyal patrons. For starters, you can count on a bountiful salad bursting with pre-served chicken gizzards or the satiny-smooth duck foie gras spread on pieces of whole-grain bread. For the main course, the *cassoulet, confit de canard* with parsleyed potatoes, and the grilled *magret de canard* are surefire winners.

Seasonal specialties and fresh fish round out the choices. Sweet endings no one wants to miss include an orange-flavored chocolate cake, a refreshing prune ice cream with Armagnac, and the satisfying *croustillant aux pommes,* or apple crumble.

BRASSERIE BOFINGER ($, 30)
5–7, rue de la Bastille
Métro: Bastille

What better way to spend the evening than in the company of friends, enjoying good food and wine in the oldest and most handsome brasserie in Paris, located only a few minutes from the opera house at place de la Bastille? While not the place for a romantic tête-à-tête, you can't help feeling glamorous and festive when dining at Bofinger. The magnificent Belle Epoque decor on two floors, with its maze of mirrors, brass, stained glass, and flowers, provides the perfect backdrop for the see-and-be-seen crowds of fashionable French who flock here every night. Do not even consider arriving without a reservation, and when booking, request a seat under the stained-glass dome, the most beautiful part of the restaurant, which is also the nonsmoking section.

While culinary fireworks are not the order of the day, the food is dependable, and the generous servings cater to healthy, meat-loving appetites. Platters of oysters, traditional *choucroutes,* and grilled meats lead the list of the best dining choices. The house Riesling is a good wine selection. The service by black-tied waiters, who sometimes ferry plates over the heads of diners, is swift and accurate.

NOTE: There is a nonsmoking section. See page 93 for information on Le Petit Bofinger.

TELEPHONE
01-42-72-87-82

OPEN
Mon–Fri: lunch noon–3 P.M., dinner 6:30 P.M.–1 A.M.; Sat–Sun: noon–1 A.M., continuous service

CLOSED
Never

RESERVATIONS
Essential

CREDIT CARDS
AE, DC, MC, V

À LA CARTE
200–250F (30.49–38.11€), BNC

PRIX FIXE
Mon–Fri only: lunch, 120F (18.29€); lunch and dinner, 189F (28.81€), both 3 courses and BC

ENGLISH SPOKEN
Yes

BRASSERIE DE L'ÎLE ST-LOUIS (37)
55, quai de Bourbon
Métro: Pont-Marie

A stroll over the pedestrian bridge behind Notre Dame to Île St-Louis brings you right to the doorstep of this picturesque old *auberge,* which is the favorite watering hole and gathering place for many of the writers, entertainers, and expatriates who live on the island. Its outdoor terrace is prime seating for a lazy afternoon spent with friends, admiring the beautiful people passing by or just celebrating your visit to Paris. Inside, the atmosphere is bustling, colorful, and friendly, making it impossible to feel lonely here for long.

TELEPHONE
01-43-54-02-59

OPEN
Mon–Tues, Fri–Sun: 11 A.M.–2 A.M., continuous service; Thur: 6:30 P.M.–2 A.M.

CLOSED
Thur lunch, Wed; Aug

RESERVATIONS
Not necessary

CREDIT CARDS
MC, V

À LA CARTE
160–180F (24.39–27.44€), BC
PRIX FIXE
None
ENGLISH SPOKEN
Yes

The food . . . well, in all honesty that is not this place's *raison d'etre*. It is the camaraderie that counts; eating is secondary. What to expect? The menu features typical brasserie dishes as well as Alsatian specialties of tripes in Riesling wine, pig's knuckles, omelettes, terrines, pâtés, *cassoulet,* and onion *tartes* served with pitchers of house wine or mugs of frothy beer. Desserts tend to be uninspiring. Instead walk down the center of the island to any one of the ice cream shops—or go straight to the renowned Berthillon itself (31, rue St-Louis-en-l'Île) and treat yourself to several scoops of their famous ice cream or sorbet, with equally famous prices and long queues.

CAFÉ DE LA POSTE (33)
13, rue Castex
Métro: Bastille

TELEPHONE
01-42-72-95-35
OPEN
Mon–Fri: lunch noon–3 P.M.,
dinner 7–10:30 P.M.
CLOSED
Sat–Sun; NAC
RESERVATIONS
Preferred
CREDIT CARDS
AE, MC, V
À LA CARTE
80–115F (12.20–17.53€), BNC
PRIX FIXE
None
ENGLISH SPOKEN
Yes

Don't let the plain exterior or tiny interior deter you from this bargain hunter's command post near the Bastille. Past the doorway framed by green plants, and safely situated at one of the ten or so bare wooden tables on the well-trod, brown tile floor, peruse the blackboard menu for one of the *plats du jour,* which always include a pasta, come with a garnish, and are served for under $9. Equally cheap are the *grandes assiettes*—huge salads that, when paired with a basket of bread, make a light yet satisfying lunch or dinner. Otherwise, you can dig in to a grilled steak served with a roquefort or pepper sauce. A *clafoutis* with red fruit or a *charlotte aux poires* will leave you with a sweet, satisfying ending to another cost-cutting meal in Paris.

CHEZ MARIANNE (15)
2, rue des Hospitalières-St-Gervais
Métro: St-Paul

TELEPHONE
01-42-72-18-86
OPEN
Daily: noon–midnight,
continuous service
CLOSED
Never
RESERVATIONS
Not necessary
CREDIT CARDS
MC, V
À LA CARTE
50–175F (7.62–26.68€), BNC

Chez Marianne is one of the best dining choices in this Jewish corner of Paris. I like it not only for the quality of the food—which is a mix of Eastern European and Middle Eastern cuisines—but for the variety of ways you can enjoy it. If you are in a hurry and need a quick bite on the run, stop by the takeaway window and order a pita sandwich, or make a selection from the deli cases, which house everything from olives, caviar, and pickles to pastrami. Otherwise, take a seat, either in the front deli or at a table in the stone-walled dining room, and order a *plat* with four or five "elements," which are similar to Middle Eastern *mezes*. The selection seems endless: hummus, eggplant caviar, pickled mushrooms, artichokes with fennel, *kefta,* stuffed grape leaves, falafel, tabbouleh, *tzatziki,* blinis, and more. For dessert? Baklava, of course.

PRIX FIXE
Lunch and dinner: 65F (9.91€), 75F (11.43€), 85F (12.96), 105F (16.01€), all 2–3 courses and BNC

ENGLISH SPOKEN
Yes

DE BOUCHE À OREILLE (29)
15, rue des Tournelles
Métro: Bastille

"Everything is for sale, except for me," says Franck Perini, the friendly owner, collector, and chef in this appealing spot in the Marais. At his multifaceted De Bouche à Oreille, you indeed can do more than just eat: you can purchase his homemade jams and preserves, buy a piece of *brocante* gleaned from one of his weekend flea market visits, or bargain for anything you see that you like—and can figure a way to get home—even the oriental rugs and the tables and chairs. Of course, most people come to enjoy a weekend brunch, lunch, afternoon tea, or dinner on Friday and Saturday, and the prix fix menus include all of Franck's specialties: vegetable soup, main course salads (including one with green beans and his homemade duck foie gras), *croque-monsieur* with either chèvre or gruyère cheese and ham on *pain Poilâne,* warm *tartes* served with a lettuce and tomato salad, *cassoulet au confit de canard,* and ten tempting desserts, such as fruit crumbles, crème brûlée, two chocolate delights, and a lemon meringue *tarte.* Soft classical music wafts over it all, making this a nice Marais choice, either alone or with friends.

TELEPHONE
01-44-61-07-02

OPEN
Tues–Thur: lunch noon–4 P.M.; Fri–Sat: lunch noon–3 P.M., dinner 7–10:30 P.M.; Sun (Oct–Mar only): noon–4 P.M.

CLOSED
Sun April–Sept, Mon; 2 weeks in Aug (dates vary)

RESERVATIONS
Not necessary

CREDIT CARDS
MC, V

À LA CARTE
125F (19.06€)

PRIX FIXE
Lunch Tues–Fri (except holidays): 70F (10.67€), 2 courses, coffee; 80F (12.20€), 2 courses, wine and coffee; dinner: 120F (18.29€), 3 courses, BNC; brunch Sat–Sun and holidays: 120F (18.29€), 3 courses, coffee

ENGLISH SPOKEN
Yes

FINKELSZTAJN: FLORENCE AND SACHA

FLORENCE FINKELSZTAJN (18)
24, rue des Écouffes, at 19, rue des Rosiers

SACHA FINKELSZTAJN (16)
27, rue des Rosiers
Métro: St-Paul

The two Finkelsztajn bakery/*traiteur* shops sell treats not to be missed in Paris. For over five decades, they have been household names in the Jewish Quarter of Paris, where they dish out daily supplies of sweet and savory Russian and Eastern European Jewish foods. At Florence's, nicknamed "The Blue Bakery," prepare yourself for authentic recipes of borscht, blini, Polish almond *babkes,* strudels, and a dozen or more homestyle breads,

TELEPHONE
Florence: 01-48-87-92-85
Sacha: 01-42-72-78-91

OPEN
Florence: Mon–Tues, Thur–Sun: 10 A.M.–7 P.M., continuous service
Sacha: Mon, Wed–Thur: 10 A.M.–2 P.M., 3–7 P.M.; Fri–Sun: 10 A.M.–7 P.M.

CLOSED
Florence: Wed; NAC
Sacha: Tues; NAC

either plain or bursting with seeds and dried fruits. Walk into Sacha's yellow location a few doors away on rue des Rosiers and try the traditional Russian cheesecake, along with Linzertort, *pirojkis, tarama,* latkes, cold meats, and herring. At both sites, plan to take your food with you because the corner stools in each are almost always full.

RESERVATIONS
Not taken

CREDIT CARDS
None

À LA CARTE
15–80F (2.29–12.20€), BNC

PRIX FIXE
None

ENGLISH SPOKEN
Yes

LA CASTAFIORE (39)
51, rue St-Louis-en-l'Île
Métro: Pont-Marie

TELEPHONE
01-43-54-78-62

OPEN
Daily: lunch noon–2:30 P.M., dinner 6:30–11 P.M.

CLOSED
Never

RESERVATIONS
Essential, especially for dinner

CREDIT CARDS
AE, DC, MC, V

À LA CARTE
200F (30.49€), BNC

PRIX FIXE
Lunch: 65F (9.91€), 2 courses, BNC; lunch and dinner: 170F (25.92€), 3 courses, BNC; dinner (until 8:30 P.M.): 100F (15.24€), 2 courses, BNC

ENGLISH SPOKEN
Yes

La Castafiore has had many lives. When I lived on Île St-Louis, it was a family-owned bistro and one of my favorite dining destinations. Since then, it has had a series of owners, but nothing seemed to make it until Gerrard and Edward took over and began serving wonderful Italian dishes. There is room for only eleven small, closely packed tables, and to make sure you are sitting at one of them, reservations are essential.

If your budget is tight, remember the 65F, two-course lunch menu, which comes with a bowl of onion soup or mozzarella on toast followed by a plate of gnocchi with basil sauce, turkey marsala, or steak and grilled onions. Desserts are 25F extra, but frankly, the main course portions are so big you won't be able to consider anything extra. The two-course dinner menu allows you to select from any of the *entrées* (except the snails) and any of the pastas on the menu. This bargain meal, good until 8:30 P.M., draws many of the visitors staying in the several charming hotels on the island (see *Great Sleeps Paris*), creating an unfortunately hot, stuffy, sardinelike atmosphere. Later, around 9 P.M., when the rush is over, the mood is much more peaceful and romantic in the candlelit room. When ordering, start with the traditional mozzarella and tomato salad or the lusty stuffed mushrooms, filled with spinach and cream cheese, in a tomato sauce. Eight vegetarian pastas, five or six meat or seafood pastas, meat dishes that win praise from the carnivores among us, flowing house wine, and a wicked tiramisu add up to terrific dining. I wish I still lived in the neighborhood.

LA CHARLOTTE DE L'ÎLE (42)
24, rue St-Louis-en-l'Île
Métro: Pont-Marie, Sully-Morland

Sylvie Langlet is the well-loved owner and mother superior of this quarter-century-old Paris tearoom that specializes in her own rich chocolate pastries and candies, poetry readings, puppet shows, live piano music, and most important, warm, fuzzy good cheer. Just being in her cluttered two-room shop—which is filled with a whimsical collection of baskets, children's drawings, chocolate sculptures of children and animals, old teapots, and painted plates—makes you feel like you are having tea with *grand-mère*. For its regular customers, it obviously is an ideal oasis for meeting friends for a good dose of gossip, mild flirtation, listening to music, or treating a child to sweets before a puppet performance (two shows on Wednesday only). When you go, order a hot chocolate made from melted bars of pure chocolate (thinned with milk, if you must dilute it) or Sylvie's bittersweet *chocolate tarte de tantie,* a baked chocolate mousse with a chocolate glaze. Don't overlook her pure fruit lollipops, which grown men have been known to buy by the bagful. A small handwritten sign in the window says it all: "Here we sell happiness." How true.

TELEPHONE
01-43-54-25-83

INTERNET
www.le_charlotte.fr

OPEN
Thur–Sun: tearoom 2–8 P.M., continuous service;
Wed: puppet shows only at 2:30 and 4 P.M.; live piano music Fri 6–8 P.M.

CLOSED
Mon–Wed; most holidays, July and Aug

RESERVATIONS
Required for puppet shows (minimum 12 children)

CREDIT CARDS
MC, V

À LA CARTE
50–80F (7.62–12.20€), BC

PRIX FIXE
None

ENGLISH SPOKEN
Yes

L'AS DU FALLAFEL (17)
34, rue des Rosiers
Métro: St-Paul

For twenty years Issac and Daisy have sold the best falafel on this food-lined street smack in the heart of the Jewish Quarter. You can't miss their place—it is the one with the shiny green exterior and the line snaked up to the takeout window. For years, that's all there was: you selected your falafel, made to order by a team of swift fry cooks, and then walked down the street eating it as the sauce dripped off your chin. Caving in to demands for tables, they have now added several inside seats as well as a bench out front. A wide audience—including everyone from members of the Rolling Stones to mink-clad matrons toting little dogs in Louis Vuitton carry-cases—arrives nonstop every day but Saturday to order either the falafel *normal,* with shredded cabbage and sesame sauce, or the *spécial,* heaped with fried eggplant and hummus. Whichever you order, wash it down with a glass of their homemade lemonade, and if dessert is on your mind, forget it here and go across the street to either of the Finkelsztajn bakeries (see page 87).

TELEPHONE
01-48-87-63-60

OPEN
Mon–Fri, Sun: 11:30 A.M.–midnight, continuous service

CLOSED
Sat; NAC

RESERVATIONS
Not accepted

CREDIT CARDS
MC, V

À LA CARTE
50–70F (7.62–10.67€), BC

PRIX FIXE
None

ENGLISH SPOKEN
Enough

LA TABLE DES GOURMETS (10)
14, rue des Lombards
Métro: Châtelet, Hôtel de Ville

TELEPHONE
01-40-27-00-87

OPEN
Mon–Sat: lunch noon–
2:30 P.M., dinner 7–11 P.M.

CLOSED
Sun; NAC

RESERVATIONS
Advised for 4 or more

CREDIT CARDS
MC, V

À LA CARTE
195F (29.73€), BNC

PRIX FIXE
Lunch and dinner: 65F (9.91€),
2 courses, BNC; 86F (13.11€),
138F (21.04€), 185F (28.20€),
all 3 courses and BNC

ENGLISH SPOKEN
Some

Ray Lampard, owner of RothRay apartments (see *Great Sleeps Paris*), once said, "Paris is like a treasure box, and when you open it, there is always something wonderful and interesting inside." Though he meant the entire city, he just as easily could have been describing La Table des Gourmets, a hidden find on one of the most touristy trails in Les Halles. From the outside it looks like nothing, and even when you walk inside, the first level is barren with the exception of a plant or two and an aquarium. The surprise comes when you are ushered downstairs to the dining room, which is housed in a twelfth-century chapel, complete with stone arches and pillars. However, though the setting is matchless—with soft lighting, fresh flowers on white linen–covered tables, and solicitous service—the food doesn't quite keep up. Still, it is dependable, there is plenty of it, and most important, it is priced right.

My advice is to ignore the à la carte menu completely and select one of the four prix fixe menus, including a two-course choice for under $10. You could start with two pieces of *chèvre chaud* on a bed of lettuce, onion soup, or endives vinaigrette tossed with ham. Skip the fatty lamb chops as a main course and stick with any fresh fish or the *plat du jour*. With the exception of the crème brûlée, desserts are not the kitchen's forte.

LE BISTROT DU DÔME ($, 31)
2, rue de la Bastille
Métro: Bastille

TELEPHONE
01-48-04-88-44

OPEN
Daily: lunch 12:30–2:30 P.M.,
dinner 7:30–11:30 P.M.

CLOSED
Mon and Sun in Aug

RESERVATIONS
Advised

CREDIT CARDS
AE, MC, V

À LA CARTE
210–225F (32.01–34.30€),
BNC

PRIX FIXE
None

ENGLISH SPOKEN
Yes

Good tips often come from readers, and this is one of them. However, if you do not like fish, move on . . . because fish is the only thing you can order here. The sunny, yellow interiors by noted restaurant designer Philippe Slavik are casually elegant, creating a sleek and contemporary look that gives diners a feeling of space in the uncluttered two-level surroundings.

As everyone knows, fish is never cheap in Paris, whether you buy it at the market or order it in a restaurant. Here, all the fish is guaranteed fresh—nothing is frozen. Prices here are not for budgeteers counting every penny, but they are certainly competitive. Depending on the main course, you may want to vary your starter. The *fricassée de langoustines au curry* (curried prawns), the *soupe de pistou* (fish soup laden with vegetables), or the *palourdes sautées à la fleur de thyme* (cherrystone clams sautéed with shallots and thyme) are hearty and delicious beginnings. Popular *plats* are the *filets de racasse,* white rockfish in a fresh tomato sauce served with garlic-laced mashed potatoes, and the *gigot de lotte braisé aux choux,* monkfish with cabbage. For something un-adorned, try the grilled tuna (*pavé de thon*) or the traditional sole *meunière.* The dessert extravaganza means you must try to save a little space for the *crêpe exotique,* crepes filled with mangoes, coconut, and other fruits and topped with a caramel-and-honey sauce, or the *gratin de poire aux glace cannelle,* warm pears filled with cinnamon ice cream.

NOTE: There is a second location at 1, rue Delambre in the fourteenth arrondissement (see page 225).

LE COUDE FOU (13)
12, rue de Bourg-Tibourg
Métro: Hôtel de Ville, St-Paul

To paraphrase an old saying, "Life is too short to drink bad, boring wine." That will never happen at Le Coude Fou, Patric Segall's appealing *bistro à vins,* which is a nice, enjoyable, safe place to try various wines at a reasonable cost. The food is secondary to the wines, but the locals still indulge in lunchtime plates of sturdy hot meals and return in the evening for French country cheeses and *charcuteries.* Everyone stands around the bar or spills into the two rustic rooms, sitting at the bare tables made from wine casks. The lighthearted mood is enhanced by murals depicting party-goers from ancient times and caricatures of Parisian barflies. As for the wines, try whatever is the special of the month, or perhaps a red Saint-Joseph from the central part of France.

TELEPHONE
01-42-77-15-16

OPEN
Daily: lunch noon–3:15 P.M. (Sun till 4 P.M.); dinner 7:15 P.M.–midnight

CLOSED
Never

RESERVATIONS
Advised on weekends

CREDIT CARDS
AE, MC, V

À LA CARTE
75–150F (11.43–22.87€), BNC

PRIX FIXE
Lunch Mon–Fri: 95F (14.48€), 2 courses, 115F (17.53€), 3 courses, both BC; dinner Mon–Thur: 140F (21.34€), 3 courses, BNC

ENGLISH SPOKEN
Yes

LE DOS DE LA BALEINE (9)
40, rue des Blancs-Manteaux
Métro: Hôtel de Ville, Rambuteau

For imaginative twists on the usual French menu standards with pleasing dishes for every course, book a table at this late-night Marais dining favorite. The stone-arched back room has plank floors dotted with oriental rugs, and the banquettes and settees are positioned amid changing art exhibits. Waiters provide friendly service to the definitely mixed all-French crowd, but sometimes

TELEPHONE
01-42-72-38-98

OPEN
Tues–Fri: lunch noon–2:30 P.M., dinner 8–11 P.M.; Sat–Sun dinner 8–11 P.M. (till midnight on Sat)

CLOSED
Sat–Sun lunch, Mon; 2 weeks in Aug (dates vary)

RESERVATIONS
Advised

CREDIT CARDS
MC, V (100F, 15.24€,
minimum)

À LA CARTE
None

PRIX FIXE
Lunch: 79F (12.04€), 2 courses,
BNC; dinner: 125F (19.06€),
2 courses, 155F (23.63€), 3
courses, both BNC

ENGLISH SPOKEN
Yes

on the weekend as the evening builds, the service and decibel levels can be stretched to their limits.

The monthly changing menu is driven by what is best at the *marché,* but it always includes several salads, fresh fish, two *entrées* and *plats du jour,* and a to-die-for chocolate cake with chocolate sauce hiding a ball of vanilla ice cream—a dish that is aptly named *suicide au chocolat.* On my last winter visit, I enjoyed the salmon salad with eggplant and poached quail eggs, filet of sole baked and served with caramelized endives, and the chestnut ice cream with a robe of chocolate sauce. Red wines of the month dominate the wine card, but there are enough whites to keep everyone happy.

NOTE: Their second restaurant, A 2 Pas du Dos, is near the Picasso Museum. See page 71.

LE GRENIER SUR L'EAU (26)
14, rue du Pont-Louis-Philippe
Métro: Pont-Marie

TELEPHONE
01-42-77-80-96

OPEN
Mon–Fri: lunch noon–2 P.M.,
dinner 8–11:30 P.M.;
Sat: dinner 8–11:30 P.M.

CLOSED
Sat lunch, Sun; holidays,
first 3 weeks in Aug

RESERVATIONS
Advised

CREDIT CARDS
MC, V

À LA CARTE
None

PRIX FIXE
Lunch: 120F (18.29€),
2 courses, BC; dinner: 160F
(24.39€), 3 courses, BNC

ENGLISH SPOKEN
Limited

Bernard Mauget's intimate, two-level interior with starched pink linens, classical music, and masses of Provençal dried-flower arrangements strikes a formal tone for the fashion-conscious matrons and business executives who dine here at lunch. In the evening, couples of all ages are still pouring in at 10 P.M. For a discreet lunch or dinner with someone special, reserve a corner banquette table on the ground floor.

The well-thought-out lunch and dinner *formules* make sense for most prudent diners in Paris, and you can be reassured that whatever you order will reflect well-maintained standards of good food and polite service by the pleasant waitstaff. The menus afford interesting choices for all three courses. To begin, there are four hot or cold *entrées* plus a daily special. Depending on the season, your cold choices could be slices of rabbit atop three little salads or a savory *mille-feuille* of shrimp and tomatoes flavored with basil. Warm beginnings include chèvre ravioli in a flavorful red pepper sauce or a *soupe de moules* (mussels) with a touch of sesame oil. In addition to the *entrée* and *plat du jour,* there are always two or three fresh fish offerings, filet mignon, and perhaps veal liver in a caramelized balsamic vinegar sauce, served with a creamy purée, or *magret de canard* with exotic spices. Desserts try your willpower, but one very nice sweet surrender is the *mousse de fromage blanc au coulis des fruits rouges*—a light cottage cheese mousse with a tangy seasonal red fruit sauce.

LE PETIT BOFINGER (32)
6, rue de la Bastille
Métro: Bastille

The demands of Parisian life make it both unrealistic and unfashionable to spend huge sums of money dining out on a regular basis. People no longer have the time to spend hours over large lunches or drawn-out dinners accompanied by expensive wines and liquors. The trend is toward lighter food, quickly prepared and consumed, all without sacrificing quality. Many two- and three-star restaurants have jumped on the bistro bandwagon and opened less expensive venues. Not to be left behind in the race to attract diners, Brasserie Bofinger, the oldest and most beautiful brasserie in Paris, opened a spin-off called Le Petit Bofinger. There are now at least five in Paris, but my favorite is the first in the small chain, located right across the street from Brasserie Bofinger near the place de la Bastille. The decor is simple by comparison and evokes the old neighborhood of the Bastille with black-and-white photos of the area, an original tiled floor, and a mural along one wall. A non-smoking section demonstrates the management's desire to please the growing number of French who find life very pleasant when not dining in a smoke-induced haze.

The food is not lavish, but it is reasonable and dependable. Pay attention to the daily specials and the two prix fixe menus. Two other features worth remembering are that you can order just one dish at a time and not be subjected to icy stares from a frosty waiter, and today's menu lists tomorrow's specials on both the à la carte and prix fixe menus. Two excellent starters are always the *foie gras de canard maison* and half a dozen Brittany oysters. The kitchen has a sure hand with fish and meat, as demonstrated by the filets of fresh *dorade* (sea bream) and the steak tartare, served with a side of *pommes frites* and a small salad. Popular desserts are the modish crème brûlée spiked with bourbon and the fresh pear poached in red wine and served with an orange marmalade sauce.

NOTE: There is a nonsmoking section. Le Petit Bofinger also has branches in the ninth, fifteenth, and seventeenth arrondissements. See pages 184, 232, 250, and 251.

TELEPHONE
01-42-72-05-23

OPEN
Daily: lunch noon–3 P.M., dinner 7 P.M.–midnight

CLOSED
Never

RESERVATIONS
Advised

CREDIT CARDS
AE, MC, V

À LA CARTE
150–160F (22.87–24.39€), BNC

PRIX FIXE
Lunch Mon–Sat: 100F (15.24€), 2 courses, BC; lunch and dinner: 150F (22.87€), 3 courses, BNC; children's menu (under 12): 45F (6.86€), 3 courses, BC

ENGLISH SPOKEN
Yes

LE PETIT MARCEL (7)
65, rue Rambuteau
Métro: Rambuteau

TELEPHONE
01-48-87-10-20

OPEN
Mon–Sat: 7 A.M.–2 A.M.; Sun:
noon–midnight, continuous
service

CLOSED
Never

RESERVATIONS
Not necessary

CREDIT CARDS
None

À LA CARTE
40–65F (6.10–9.91€), BNC

PRIX FIXE
None

ENGLISH SPOKEN
Yes

The only imitation in this tiny Les Halles bar about a two-minute stroll from the Centre Georges Pompidou is the telephone. Everything else you see is the real thing: the marble bar, the half-tiled mirrored walls, the banquette seating hiding storage bins for coffee, tea, and sugar, the brass hat and coat racks, and the kitchen housed in a space the size of a closet. The young and enthusiastic owners, M. and Mme. Renaudin, are on hand daily serving food, drinks, and good cheer to the regulars, who either stand at the bar for their morning coffee and *tartine* (a half baguette split in two and spread with butter) or sit at the nine round tables inside or at the four tables squeezed along the sidewalk. The 7 to 8 P.M. happy hour finds them sipping a cold draft beer wherever they can. Given the confines of the open kitchen, high gourmet expectations should be left at the door. However, it is amazing that the cook can turn out renditions of *boudin noir* (black blood pudding) and *farci de veau* (stuffed veal) in addition to salads, omelettes, pâtés, and *pain Poilâne* spread with tomatoes, chèvre, and olive oil. Desserts come up a bit short except for the only one made here: the crème brûlée.

LE ROUGE GORGE (35)
8, rue St-Paul
Métro: Sully-Morland, St-Paul

TELEPHONE
01-48-04-75-89

OPEN
Daily: bar noon–11:30 P.M.,
lunch noon–4 P.M., dinner
7:30–11:30 P.M.

CLOSED
Never

RESERVATIONS
Not necessary

CREDIT CARDS
MC, V

À LA CARTE
90–125F (13.72–19.06€), BNC

PRIX FIXE
None

ENGLISH SPOKEN
Limited

After visiting the lovely place des Vosges, I like to browse through the treasure trove of antique shops lining rue St-Paul. Afterward, I always seem to wind up at this friendly wine bar. The nice thing about Le Rouge Gorge is that you can eat and drink as much, or as little, as you like and always feel welcome. If you are alone, take a seat at the bar in front. Otherwise, head for one of the wooden tables in the back, which is decorated with a mishmash of old and semi-old kitsch. Fellow diners and imbibers are serious black-clad students and intellectuals who come to sample a wide selection of wines sold by the glass. On Friday everyone knows to order couscous, at lunch the *plat du jour* is the only dish to consider, and later on in the evening, you might try sample plates of cold meats and cheese, an endive salad loaded with blue cheese and walnuts, chicken on a bed of pasta, or perhaps a spicy *andouillette*.

LES ENFANTS GÂTÉS (20)
43, rue des Francs-Bourgeois
Métro: St-Paul

At Les Enfants Gâtés (The Spoiled Children), a favorite haunt for lunch, afternoon tea, and weekend brunch in the Marais, photos of film stars and assorted posters on the walls, along with a collection of worn tables and comfortable wicker armchairs, comprise the interior. The diners are an interesting collection of Parisian matrons lapping up gooey pastries, whispering young couples sharing a dish of Berthillon ice cream, and international travelers weary from a morning spent wandering around place des Vosges and the Picasso Museum. Weekend brunches are either small, medium, or large: they start with orange juice, eggs, toast, and marmalade and grow to include all of that plus *tarama* (roe), smoked salmon, and dessert. For lunch, tuck in to a salad and a bowl of their comforting soup, but be sure to save room for a brownie, a bowl of apple flan, or the warm *tarte Tatin*. All of the tea served is from Mariage Frères (see page 97).

TELEPHONE
01-42-77-07-63

OPEN
Mon, Wed–Fri: noon–7 P.M.; Sat–Sun: 11 A.M.–8 P.M.

CLOSED
Tues; Aug

RESERVATIONS
Not necessary

CREDIT CARDS
MC, V

À LA CARTE
80–110F (12.20–16.77€)

PRIX FIXE
Weekend brunch: small 95F (14.48€), medium 135F (20.58€), large 150F (22.87€), all BC

ENGLISH SPOKEN
Usually

LES VINS DES PYRÉNÉES (28)
25, rue Beautreillis
Métro: Bastille, St-Paul

In the Marais, not far from place des Vosges, Les Vins des Pyrénées specializes in a changing selection of wines bought directly from small producers throughout France. The decor mirrors the crowd—low-key and casual—and has a certain vintage charm that many newer places never achieve: it's ringed with red banquettes, has choir pew seating in front, and its window is crammed with a dusty collection of themed liquor bottles and old wooden skis and skates. The blackboard menu provides a good mix of bourgeoise comfort food, including a delicious foie gras *maison,* braised kidneys with mustard sauce, *confit de canard* with parsleyed potatoes, beef tartare with fries or a salad, roast lamb, and chicken fricassee served with puréed potatoes with olive oil. For dessert, chocoholics will lap up the *molleux au chocolat*—a creamy chocolate cake served with vanilla ice cream. Otherwise, the choices include apple crumble with raspberry sauce, cinnamon baked apple, or a plate of cheese to enjoy with another glass of interesting wine.

TELEPHONE
01-42-72-64-94

OPEN
Mon–Fri: lunch noon–3 P.M., dinner 7:30–11:30 P.M., bar till 2 A.M.; Sat: dinner 7:30–11:30 P.M., bar till 2 A.M.

CLOSED
Sat lunch, Sun; Aug 15–31

RESERVATIONS
Advised for dinner Fri and Sat

CREDIT CARDS
MC, V

À LA CARTE
145–180F (22.11–27.44€), BNC

PRIX FIXE
Lunch: 80F (12.20€), 2 courses, BNC, or *plat du jour,* wine, and coffee

ENGLISH SPOKEN
Yes

LE TEMPS DES CERISES (36)
31, rue de la Cerisaie
Métro: Sully-Morland, Bastille

TELEPHONE
01-42-72-08-63

OPEN
Mon–Fri: bar 7:30 A.M.–8 P.M.,
continuous service; lunch
11:30 A.M.–2:30 P.M.

CLOSED
Sat–Sun; holidays, Aug

RESERVATIONS
Not taken

CREDIT CARDS
None

À LA CARTE
70–100F (10.67–15.24€), BNC

PRIX FIXE
Lunch: 72F (10.98€), 3 courses,
BNC

ENGLISH SPOKEN
No

Le Temps des Cerises is the place to have a cheap lunch and a beer or two while polishing your fractured French. When you arrive, you won't miss owner Gerard and his handlebar mustache—he's the one standing behind the bar pouring drinks for the regulars and teasing all the women. Lunch is the liveliest time here (and the only hot meal), attracting a neighborhood clientele who accept the crowded conditions as the inevitable price for enjoying the kind of honest home cooking that Mother never has time to make anymore. The blackboard-listed selections read like a café cookbook and include all the basics, from Auvergne sausage and grilled steak with a pile of sinful *frites* to a plain fruit *tarte* for dessert. Before and after the hectic lunch scene, the café is calm and only cold food is served, with old-timers standing at the bar dusting off memories of times gone by. No one speaks much English, and you might have to share a table or elbow your way to a space at the bar, but go ahead, don't be shy. Everyone is friendly, and new faces are welcome.

L'EXCUSE ($, 34)
14, rue Charles V
Métro: St-Paul, Sully-Morland

TELEPHONE
01-42-77-98-97

OPEN
Mon–Sat: lunch noon–2 P.M.,
dinner 7:30–11 P.M.

CLOSED
Sun; holidays, Aug 1-15

RESERVATIONS
Essential

CREDIT CARDS
AE, MC, V

À LA CARTE
300–325F (45.73–49.55€),
BNC

PRIX FIXE
Lunch: 120F (18.29€),
2 courses, 150F (22.87€),
3 courses, both unlimited
choice and BC; dinner: 185F
(28.20€), 3 courses (limited
choice), BNC

ENGLISH SPOKEN
Yes

There is an elegant glow to the small bar and two dining rooms, which are tastefully decorated with soft lighting, fresh flowers, and attractive framed posters. Correctly set, well-spaced tables preserve a sense of intimacy, and the strains of classical music enhance the sophisticated mood, making L'Excuse a perfect choice for *le dîner à deux*.

Owner Jean-Denis Barbet is on hand daily to make sure no details go unnoticed or unattended. Throughout the year, his chef creates four seasonally innovative à la carte menus and weekly prix fixe menus that reflect the best the *marchés* have at the moment. In the winter, the à la carte menu may list such imaginative starters as ravioli filled with wild mushrooms in a creamy tomato sauce, eggs scrambled with fresh sea urchins, or fresh crab cannelloni. Heading the list of worthy main courses might be *filet de mignon de porc aux epinards en croute de pain et tomates confites* (tender pork filets and spinach wrapped in a flaky crust and served with preserved tomatoes), fresh *coquilles St-Jacques,* roasted venison, or a tender *entrecôte* in a red wine sauce served on a bed of fresh pasta. Desserts are all designed to please, especially the two that must be ordered at the start of the meal: a warm, light honey sponge cake topped with caramelized pears, and the rich chocolate cake with an espresso sauce. The warm apple caramel *tarte* with a buttery crust is also exquisite. In the fifteen years it has been open, L'Excuse has developed a dedicated following of *Great Eats* readers, as well as of Parisians, making reservations essential. Whenever you go, you will have an exceptional meal and enjoy impeccable service.

MARIAGE FRÈRES (12)
30–32, rue de Bourg-Tibourg
Métro: Hôtel de Ville, St-Paul

No serious tea lover can afford to miss the Tiffany of tearooms in Paris: Mariage Frères, which for more than 140 years has been dedicated to the art of tea drinking. Over 460 teas from twenty-five countries are prepared in these world-famous shops by master tea makers who still do everything by hand, including carefully cutting and stitching each tea bag out of tissue or muslin.

As the menu states, "Tea is not all in the pot." The ambience is an important part of the experience of drinking tea in this civilized establishment reminiscent of colonial times. Waiters in white present the tea menu, suggesting the appropriate tea to drink with each meal with the seriousness of a sommelier. The tea is prepared with filtered water and served in an insulated pot at the temperature best suited to its taste. Many of the dishes are prepared with tea, from jams and jellies to sauces, ice creams, and sorbets. The food in general is not as remarkable as the teas, but the pastries do keep pace, so plan to go for a lovely pastry and a sublime cup of tea. However, if you arrive outside of afternoon tea hours, you must order a meal. The prices are slightly high and so are the noses of some of the management, but it's all worth it for the experience.

Adjoining each of the tearooms is a wonderful tea shop. The shop at this location uses the original cash box from the first tea shop and houses a small tea museum. There is also a tea boutique across the street where you can buy teas and many of the pastries packaged to go. The other locations do not quite have the wide range of teas and tea accessories as these two shops, but the tearooms, food, and prices are the same.

TELEPHONE
01-42-72-28-11

INTERNET
www.mariagefreres.com/

OPEN
Daily: lunch Mon–Fri noon–6 P.M., brunch Sat–Sun noon–6 P.M.; afternoon tea 3–6:30 P.M.; tea boutique 10:30 A.M.–7:30 P.M.

CLOSED
Major holidays, NAC

RESERVATIONS
Not necessary

CREDIT CARDS
AE, MC, V

À LA CARTE
120–160F (18.29–24.39€), BC

PRIX FIXE
Weekend brunch: 135F (20.58€), 150F (22.87€), 160F (24.39€), 175F (26.68€), all 3–4 courses, juice, and tea

ENGLISH SPOKEN
Yes

NOTE: At all the tearooms, patrons are requested not to smoke. For other locations, see the sixth and eighth arrondissements, pages 140 and 178.

NOS ANCÊTRES LES GAULOIS (40)
39, rue St-Louis-en-l'Île
Métro: Pont-Marie

TELEPHONE
01-46-33-66-07,
01-46-33-66-12

INTERNET
www.nosancetreslesgaulois.com

OPEN
Daily: lunch Sun and holidays noon–2 P.M.; dinner daily, two seatings at 7 P.M. and 10:30 P.M.

CLOSED
Lunch Mon–Sat; NAC

RESERVATIONS
Advised, especially on weekends

CREDIT CARDS
AE, DC, MC, V

À LA CARTE
None

PRIX FIXE
Lunch and dinner: 200F (30.49€), 4 courses (all-you-can-eat), BC

ENGLISH SPOKEN
Yes

"Our Ancestors the Gauls" promises raucous fun and all-you-can-eat farm food in beamed and vaulted rooms with trestle tables, which are set for two to twenty revelers. Up to 330 party animals can be served each night by the tireless, rough-hewn waiters, who coerce guests into making gluttons of themselves. You start by munching on loaves of dark country bread, cold meats, and raw vegetables and helping yourself to the salad buffet while waiting for your chosen main dish, which might be a steak, lamb chops, or shish kebabs grilled over an open fire and accompanied by rice, ratatouille, or green beans. The main course is followed by great platters of cheese, fruit, and a choice of five desserts. As much red wine as you can drink, served from a huge cask at the center of the restaurant, is included in the price of the meal. Strolling guitarists and a singer entertain during the 7 P.M. seating. Although gorging yourself and drinking quantities of barrel wine do not an intimate, romantic evening make, this is a great place to unwind with a group and have a Rabelaisian feast you will long remember.

TRUMILOU (27)
84, quai de l'Hôtel-de-Ville
Métro: Pont-Marie

TELEPHONE
01-42-77-63-98

OPEN
Daily: bar 8 A.M.–1 A.M., lunch noon–3 P.M., dinner 7–11 P.M.

CLOSED
3–4 days at Christmas, NAC

RESERVATIONS
Recommended for larger parties

CREDIT CARDS
MC, V

À LA CARTE
150F (22.87€), BNC

PRIX FIXE
Lunch: 85F (12.96€), 2 courses, BNC; dinner: 105F (16.01€), 3 courses, BNC

ENGLISH SPOKEN
Yes

It's a bar, a bistro, or a restaurant depending on where you sit in this institution of cheap eating. Located in a sixteenth-century building along the Seine and run by the members of the Dumond family, Trumilou has been rewarding artists, writers, students, and many other devotees for years with low tabs, good service, and uninspired but sensible food that has survived the changing times, trends, and food crazes that periodically roll through Paris. The place radiates authenticity. The large main room is crowded with tables for two or four and filled with farm and family memorabilia from the Dumonds' ancestors; the slightly smaller, more intimate dining room has vases of flowers and crystal chandeliers; and then there's the bar (with pinball machine) and the sidewalk terrace. However, it doesn't matter where you eat; the only thing to concern yourself with is the food, which brings diners back time after time. The regulars know enough to go early for both lunch and dinner to avoid the inevitable crowds.

The tried-and-true *plats du jour* change for winter and summer, but the 105F (16.01€) three-course dinner menu changes daily. You may start with a cauliflower *tarte* or *poireaux vinaigrette,* then move on to veal liver or a *magret de canard* with pears, and finish with cheese, crème caramel, or a fruit *tarte.* Naturally, choices widen if you go for the à la carte menu. Look for terrines, a *salade de chèvre chaud,* herring with potatoes, or a dozen escargots. Main dishes include the usual lamb, beef, and veal preparations, plus their house specialties: duck with prunes or veal sweetbreads. Desserts usually fail to get my attention, but if you insist on something sweet, the fruit *tarte* is a safe bet.

Fifth Arrondissement

LEFT BANK
Cluny Museum (art of the Middle Ages and ruins of Roman Baths), Jardin des Plantes, Latin Quarter, rue Mouffetard, Panthéon, place St-Michel, Sorbonne, La Mosquée de Paris, Muséum National d'Histoire Naturelle, Institut du Monde Arabe

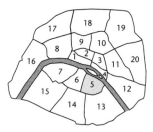

The Latin Quarter is named after the students who came to Paris in the Middle Ages to study at the Sorbonne. Since that time, this area has remained the student quarter of the city. Associated with youth, intellectuals, artists, writers, poets, and a bohemian lifestyle, the area is filled with restaurants, cafés, bars, bookstores, and movie theaters. Many of the eating places are nothing more than greasy spoons, especially along rue de la Harpe and rue de la Huchette. A visit to one of the most colorful outdoor markets in Paris, along rue Mouffetard, is a must. The *marché* is open Tuesday through Sunday from 8 A.M. to 1 P.M. and is overflowing with every kind of food imaginable, plus clothing boutiques, little cafés, and a fascinating parade of people. The nearby Panthéon church is where many famous French are buried, including Rousseau, Voltaire, and Émile Zola. At La Mosquée de Paris, you can take either tea or a Turkish bath, and from the roof of the Institut du Monde Arabe, there is a sensational view of Notre Dame.

FIFTH ARRONDISSEMENT RESTAURANTS

($) indicates a Big Splurge

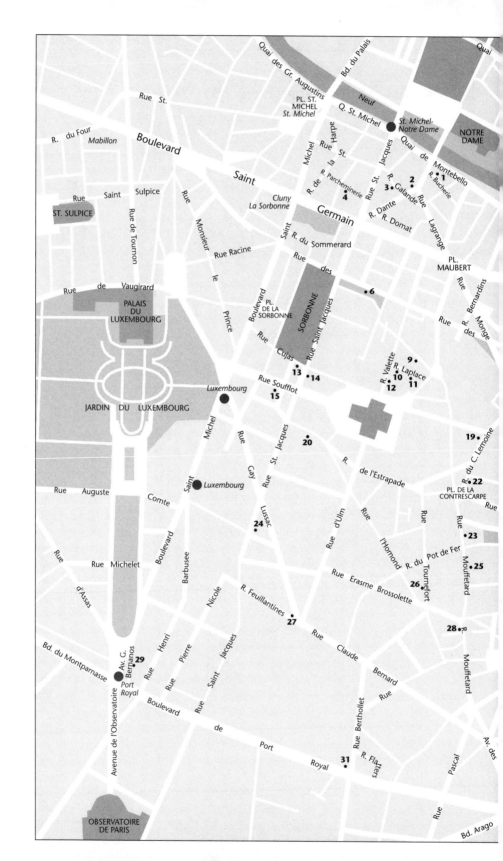

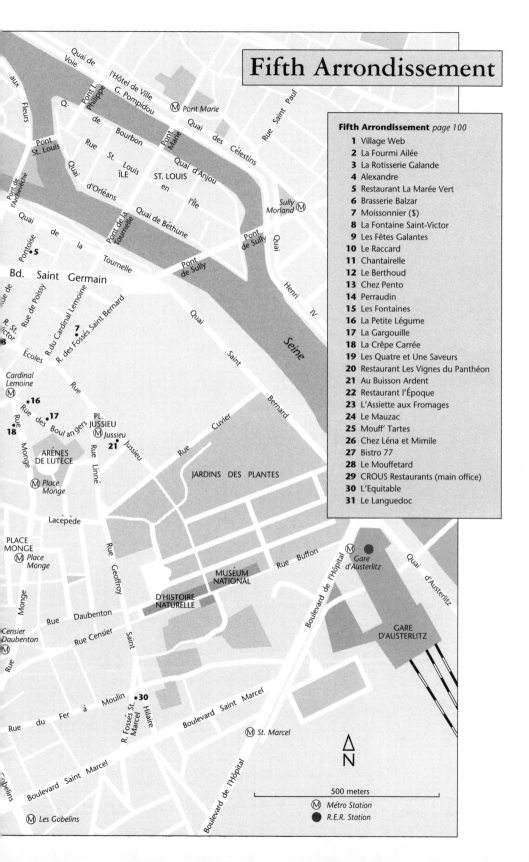

Fifth Arrondissement

500 meters

Ⓜ Métro Station
● R.E.R. Station

ALEXANDRE (4)
24, rue de la Parcheminerie
Métro: St-Michel, Cluny–La Sorbonne

TELEPHONE
01-43-26-49-66

OPEN
Daily: dinner 6–11:30 P.M.,
happy hour 6–8 P.M.

CLOSED
Major holidays, Aug
(dates vary)

RESERVATIONS
Not necessary

CREDIT CARDS
MC, V

À LA CARTE
110F (16.77€), BNC

PRIX FIXE
None

ENGLISH SPOKEN
Yes

Open every night from 6 to 11:30 P.M., Alexandre keeps it short and to the point, serving only three signature dishes from the French Savoy region near the Swiss and Italian borders. The menu is an all-you-can-eat bonanza of either *fondue bourguignonne,* served with sautéed potatoes, a green salad, and various condiments; *fondue savoyard,* bubbling cheese with toasted bread and a salad; or *pierrade,* beef you cook on a hot stone at your table. Desserts? Not here. Wine and coffee? Of course, but they are extra. It is a popular choice on winter evenings when the stone-walled dining room is buzzing with young, happy couples, or on warm evenings at one of the coveted tables on the terrace, which is mercifully free from traffic noise and fumes.

AU BUISSON ARDENT (21)
25, rue Jussieu
Métro: Jussieu

TELEPHONE
01-43-54-93-02

OPEN
Mon–Fri: lunch noon–
2:30 P.M., dinner 7–10 P.M.

CLOSED
Sat–Sun; holidays (call to
check), Aug, week between
Christmas and New Year's

RESERVATIONS
Recommended

CREDIT CARDS
AE, MC, V

À LA CARTE
Entrées 50F (7.62€), *plats* 90F
(13.72€), desserts 40F (6.10€),
BNC

PRIX FIXE
Lunch: 90F (13.72€), 3 courses,
BNC; dinner: 160F (24.39€),
3 courses (unlimited choice),
BNC

ENGLISH SPOKEN
Yes

This restaurant once sparked the beginning of a romance of mine. The romance did not last too long, but my affection for this old Left Bank landmark has never wavered. For years nothing changed: not the drab decor, not the bourgeois menu served in daunting portions, not even the prices enough to speak of, and certainly never the rosy-cheeked, middle-aged waitresses who insisted you clean your plate. Now, things have changed dramatically, and I am happy to say . . . all for the better. The Duclos brothers are the energetic new owners, with Philippe in the kitchen and François in front. The consistently good cooking with a modern twist, the bargain lunch menu, the brightened decor, and the continued warm welcome has kept regulars coming back, and word-of-mouth has brought in many more.

Recent samplings from the changing prix fixe lunch menu included starters of a tangy watercress salad tossed with feta cheese in a balsamic vinaigrette, a sausage *tarte,* and smoked herring with potatoes. The main course offered tender beef stew with carrots, fresh perch with a fennel and tomato compote, and roasted leg of duck served with cabbage. I loved the apple strudel and the rich vanilla *pot-de-crème* but would certainly pass on the leaden lemon *tarte.* However, I would never think of passing on the continually filled basket of Philippe's homemade bread, accompanied by a tub of butter if requested. The selections on the dinner menu are expanded and include such seasonal favorites as white asparagus, duck carpaccio served with Cantal cheese and avocado purée, and a delicate quail salad surrounded by fresh vegetables and tiny grilled pork sausages. The long-baked lamb shank literally fell of the bone, the filet steak served with an aromatic pepper sauce was cooked to pink perfection, and the *magret de canard* served with a pesto risotto received rave reviews. The tiramisu was delicious, and so was the moist chocolate cake. Wines are served by the *pichet* or bottle.

BISTRO 77 (27)
77, rue Claude Bernard
Métro: Port Royal

The Durand family has been greeting, cooking, and serving here for more than a decade, happily assisted by Lola, their Yorkshire terrier, who holds court from her raised perch behind the bar. While hardly in the realm of destination dining, Bistro 77 is a typical neighborhood bar, café, and restaurant where locals head when they don't feel like cooking at home, or when they are lonely and want a bit of camaraderie. The place is open from 7 A.M. until 1 A.M., but hot food is served for only lunch and dinner. The menu lists everyone's favorite standbys: *oeuf dur mayonnaise,* onion soup, *salade niçoise,* homemade pâtés and terrines, *blanquette de veau,* spicy sausages sitting on a bed of lentils, crêpes filled with smoked salmon, *confit de canard,* and steaks with piles of *frites.* All the desserts are made here, so bypass the ice cream concoctions and pick from the chef's *tarte du jour,* or select the *feuilleté aux fruits*—a puff pastry filled with fresh fruit and whipped cream. The wine list highlights wines from small producers, which are available by the glass, pitcher, or bottle.

TELEPHONE
01-43-31-40-45

OPEN
Mon–Sat: bar 7 A.M.–1 A.M.;
Mon–Fri: lunch noon–3:30 P.M.,
dinner 7–11 P.M.; Sat lunch
noon–3:30 P.M.

CLOSED
Sat dinner, Sun; 15 days in Aug
(dates vary)

RESERVATIONS
Not necessary

CREDIT CARDS
MC, V

À LA CARTE
110F (16.77€), BNC

PRIX FIXE
Lunch: 59F (8.99€), 2 courses,
69F (10.52€), 3 courses, both
BNC

ENGLISH SPOKEN
Yes, and menu in English

BRASSERIE BALZAR (6)
49, rue des Écoles
Métro: Cluny–La Sorbonne

You will find sawdust on the floor and waiters in white shirts and black cutaway vests in this genuine old Left Bank brasserie, which was founded in 1890 by the same family who began Brasserie Lipp. In its life, Brasserie Balzar has had several owners, but none have been as controversial as the present ones: Group Flo, an umbrella company that also runs Brasserie Flo and numerous other well-known and respected Parisian brasseries and

TELEPHONE
01-43-54-13-67

OPEN
Daily: 8 A.M.–midnight,
continuous service

CLOSED
Never

RESERVATIONS
Necessary

CREDIT CARDS
AE, MC, V

À LA CARTE
180–200F (27.44–30.49€),
BNC

PRIX FIXE
None

ENGLISH SPOKEN
Yes

restaurants. When Group Flo took over in 1998, Balzar regulars formed the Friends of the Balzar to ensure that nothing would change and that the veteran staff would be treated fairly. To everyone's great relief . . . nothing changed. In fact, I think the food is much better than it was. Located close to the Sorbonne's sprawling campus, it still remains a favorite of Left Bank intellectuals and would-be bohemians of all types. Sartre and Camus were customers, and it is said they had their last argument here. During the day you will find it has a faded charm, one you will quickly learn to appreciate and enjoy as a reflection of the literary and political life of the *quartier.* In the evening the pace picks up, and the clientele is a bright mix of pipe-smoking professors, artists, actors, and pretty young singles, making this one of the liveliest places to be in the Latin Quarter. On Sunday nights, it is considered *de rigueur* for the neighborhood regulars to have dinner here.

When you go, zero in on the succulent *poulet rôti* (roast chicken) and a basket of *pommes frites* made the correct way—with beef suet, not boiling oil. Or try the *gratin dauphinoise* (creamed potatoes) and the *raie au beurre* (skate fish) with a bottle of the house Beaujolais. Top it off with a piece of warm *tarte Tatin,* and you will have had a truly traditional Parisian meal without straining your pocketbook.

CHANTAIRELLE (11)
17, rue de Laplace
Métro: Maubert-Mutualité, Cardinal Lemoine

TELEPHONE
01-46-33-18-59

INTERNET
www.chantairelle.com

OPEN
Mon–Fri: lunch noon–2 P.M.,
dinner 7–11 P.M.; Sat: dinner
7–11 P.M.

CLOSED
Sat lunch, Sun; 15 days in Aug
(dates vary)

RESERVATIONS
Essential

CREDIT CARDS
MC, V

À LA CARTE
180–200F (27.44–30.49€),
BNC

If you cannot get to France's Massif Central and the area of Livradois-Forez located between Clermont-Ferrand and Lyon, then you must promise to treat yourself to a taste of the region by dining at Chantairelle in the heart of Paris. This regionally inspired restaurant offers guests a total experience of the area, one that involves the eyes and ears as well as the palate. Tapes of chirping birds, mooing cows, and ringing church bells from owner/chef Frédéric Bethe's native village of Marsac float through the rustic, beamed dining room, where guests sit on rush-seated, ladder-backed chairs placed around bare wooden tables and look onto a back garden filled with native trees and plants. In front, as you enter, is a boutique overflowing with products from this little Auvergne village.

The food is as authentic as the surroundings and the portions so enormous you might want to share an *entrée* of *lentilles verts de Puy* with *jambon* (ham), the *livradois* (a salad made with country ham, tomato, and Cantal cheese), or the blue cheese and leek *tarte*. *Les plats* feature copious servings of wonderful Auvergne *charcuteries, truffades* (made with ham from Marsac-en-Livradois, thin slices of potatoes, and *cantal* cheese), stuffed cabbage, and sturdy pork *potées* (stews). Dessert—if you have room—should be the *millard aux mirtilles* (blueberry) *tarte* served with a poached pear and cream or the honey-based warm apple *tarte* with prunes in Armagnac ice cream. Apéritifs, wines, and even the mineral water all come from the region, guaranteeing a total immersion in this lovely part of France, if only for a few hours.

NOTE: You can check out Chantairelle's Website to find out the day's *plat du jour*.

PRIX FIXE
Lunch (except holidays): 80F (12.20€), 2 courses, 105F (16.01€), 3 courses, both BC; lunch and dinner, *menu livradois:* 150F (22.87€), 3 courses (with daily specials), BNC

ENGLISH SPOKEN
Yes

CHEZ LÉNA ET MIMILE (26)
32, rue Tournefort
Métro: Place Monge, Censier-Daubenton

The slightly passé pink dining room—with burgundy velvet seats, an odd mixture of mediocre art, and tulip lamps on the tables—opens onto a delightful summer terrace overlooking a leafy square filled with jacaranda trees.

The lunch and dinner one-price menus, which change twice a year, are a study in tried-and-true French cooking. Be sure to bring your appetite. Winter starters include the house terrine, escargots, warm beef salad with shallots, and fish soup. The fish *choucroute,* steak with bearnaise sauce, leg of lamb, and rabbit in a mustard sauce are nothing fancy, but they are still satisfying main courses. Desserts are headlined by pears poached in wine, *oeufs à la neige* (floating island), and the daily pastry. The nougat ice cream is best forgotten. A kir to start, wine poured throughout dinner, and a *café* to end are included with the price of the meal.

TELEPHONE
01-47-07-72-47

OPEN
Mon–Fri: lunch noon–2 P.M., dinner 7:30–11 P.M.; Sat: dinner 7:30–11 P.M.

CLOSED
Sat lunch, Sun; major holidays, one week in Jan or Feb (dates vary)

RESERVATIONS
Advised for dinner

CREDIT CARDS
MC, V

À LA CARTE
None

PRIX FIXE
Lunch: 100F (15.24€), 2 courses, 140F (21.34€), 3 courses, both BNC; lunch and dinner: 190F (28.97€), 3 courses, BC

ENGLISH SPOKEN
Yes

CHEZ PENTO (13)
9, rue Cujas
Métro: Luxembourg

If I lived in this neighborhood near the Panthéon, I could easily become a regular at the always bustling, noisy, and crowded Chez Pento, where a comfortable clientele descends for both lunch and dinner. Bare tables

TELEPHONE
01-43-26-81-54

OPEN
Mon–Fri: lunch noon–2 P.M., dinner 7:30–10:30 P.M.; Sat: dinner 7:30–10:30 P.M.

CLOSED
Sat lunch, Sun; NAC

RESERVATIONS
Advised

CREDIT CARDS
AE, MC, V

À LA CARTE
None

PRIX FIXE
Lunch: 85F (12.96€),
2 courses, 95F (14.48€),
3 courses, both limited choices
and BNC; lunch and dinner:
120F (18.29€), 2 courses,
160F (24.39€) 3 courses, both
unlimited choices and BNC

ENGLISH SPOKEN
Yes

with white paper covers and linen napkins are sandwiched in a properly frayed room ringed with posters and banquettes in need of retying. To one side is another room reserved for nonsmoking patrons, an almost unheard-of courtesy anywhere in Paris.

The menu offers what the French call *qualité prix,* or what we call value for money. For their rations of French comfort food, diners show up on Monday for *blanquette de veau,* on Tuesday for *pot-au-feu,* on Wednesday for *estouffade de boeuf à la bourguigon,* on Thursday for *tête de veau,* and on Friday for *pot-au-feu de la mer.* In addition, there are always three different *entrées* and *plats* along with world-class regulars of *soupe à l'oignon,* herring with warm potato salad, a half dozen oysters, hot goat cheese salad, and escargots. Desserts are familiar servings of chocolate cake, apple *tarte,* crème brûlée, ice creams, and sorbets. Because the service is swift, lingering usually isn't part of the experience at Chez Pento.

NOTE: There is a room reserved for nonsmokers.

LA CRÊPE CARRÉE (18)
42, rue Monge
Métro: Place Monge, Cardinal Lemoine

TELEPHONE
01-43-26-99-98

OPEN
Mon–Sat: lunch noon–3 P.M.,
dinner 6:30–10 P.M.

CLOSED
Sun; holidays, 2 weeks in Aug
(dates vary)

RESERVATIONS
Not accepted

CREDIT CARDS
MC, V (100F, 15.24€,
minimum)

À LA CARTE
35–75F (5.34–11.43€), BNC

PRIX FIXE
None

ENGLISH SPOKEN
Yes

You say a crêpe is a crêpe is a crêpe . . . but not at this little *crêperie,* which is a notch or two above the competition. You can either order yours to go or sit at one of the twenty-eight places inside to enjoy this French fast-food treat. Owner and crêpe maker *par excellence,* M. Combastel is inspired by his worldwide travels, which are chronicled by the interesting display of photos on the walls. He proudly offers over one hundred types of crêpes: from one spread simply with butter to the *Texane,* bursting with ground beef, cheese, onions, and béchamel sauce. To commemorate the year 2000, he created *La Compute 2000,* filled with eggs, potatoes, bacon, onion, cheese, and crème fraîche; *Le Carée,* combining eggs, ground beef, and two cheeses; and finally *La 2000 Lieues,* with tuna, salmon, spinach, and cream. The forty-four dessert selections start with a sugar-filled crêpe and grow to one wrapped around what would otherwise be called a banana split, including the whipped cream and nuts. There are also three new dessert crêpes to celebrate the new millennium: *Le Frisson,* loaded with three fruit sorbets, dark red plum liqueur, and whipped cream; *La Tentation,* with marzipan, vanilla ice cream, and cream; and finally *La Folie 2000,* a simple combination of chestnut purée and ice cream sprinkled with nuts. Cider, wine, and beer are the extent of the drink options, and the prices should meet even the most miserly of budgets.

LA FONTAINE SAINT-VICTOR (8)
Maison de la Mutualité, 24, rue St-Victor (off rue des Écoles)
Métro: Cardinal Lemoine, Maubert-Mutualité

"Who would ever want to eat here?" I thought the first time I arrived at the unimpressive French Social Security building just off rue des Écoles. Things began to pick up as I ascended the expansive Art Deco staircase to the second-floor dining room. And as I finished the last bite of my lemon *tarte,* I knew why this bargain-priced sleeper is so popular with dignified French pensioners, who have been lunching here for half a century.

From the bar you can order a gin and tonic, a dry martini, or a scotch and soda, and a good bottle of wine will be less than 100F (15.24€). To polish off your lunch (the only meal they serve) in grand style, an Armagnac or cognac will set you back less than 45F (6.86€). Along with the inexpensive booze, you will probably want something to eat, and the traditional menu is varied, the food good, and above all, it is well priced, whether you stick to the set menu or go à la carte. I like the four-course, 120F (18.29€) menu because it includes a sampling of cheeses along with everything else. It is a big meal, but you can go easy on dinner. The service by white-jacketed waiters is flawless, the tables are set with linens and fresh flowers, and during your quiet and proper lunch you will be surrounded by sweet, properly dressed *grand-mères* and *grand-pères* who haven't forgotten how to dine well.

TELEPHONE
01-40-46-12-04
OPEN
Daily: lunch 11:45 A.M.–2:30 P.M.
CLOSED
Holidays, Aug
RESERVATIONS
Accepted for groups only
CREDIT CARDS
MC, V
À LA CARTE
Entrées 50F (7.62€), *plats* 79F and 98F (12.04€, 14.94€), cheese 40F (6.10€), desserts 33F (5.03€), BNC
PRIX FIXE
Lunch: 90F (13.72€), 2 courses, BC; 120F (18.29€) and 190F (28.97€), both 4 courses and BNC
ENGLISH SPOKEN
Some

LA FOURMI AILÉE (2)
8, rue du Fouarre
Métro: Maubert-Mutualité, Cluny–La Sorbonne

La Fourmi Ailée, which means "the winged ant," is a comforting tearoom that lends itself to long cozy lunches *à deux,* or if you are *toute seul,* to a pleasant respite with a bracing cup of tea and a slice of one of the chef's specialty *tartes* while plotting the rest of your day in Paris. Inside it reminds me of an absentminded professor's dimly lit home, as it's filled with an odd assortment of furniture, stacks of books, and pots of struggling plants. Menus are hidden in old books, and the food is limited to Sunday brunch, weekly lunches, and pastries. The list of teas goes on forever, and when you finally decide on your

TELEPHONE
01-43-29-40-99
OPEN
Daily: lunch noon–3 P.M. (Sat–Sun till 4 P.M.), tea 3–7 P.M., dinner 7 P.M.–midnight
CLOSED
Never
RESERVATIONS
Not necessary
CREDIT CARDS
None
À LA CARTE
85–120F (12.96–18.29€), BC

particular brew, it will be served in a large pot that stays hot for a long time. All the baking is done here, including the bread.

NOTE: There is a second location in Montmartre near the Sacré Coeur. See L'Ete en Pente Douce, page 261.

LA GARGOUILLE (17)
20, rue des Boulangers
Métro: Cardinal Lemoine

As I stood outside the restaurant studying the menu, a man walked up to me and said, "It's super—good quality for the price. Try it!" I did a few days later and he was right. La Gargouille delivers great eats in Paris at very fair prices. It is a small place, with the usual Left Bank beams, crowded tables, and dripping candles. They need to buy different tablecloths, but the green placemats are passable. So are the pitchers of house red and white wine. During both lunch and dinner, you almost need a shoehorn to wedge yourself in, and no wonder when you can order a full-fledged three-course à la carte meal and a glass or two of the house wine for around 100F (15.24€).

The chef is obviously trying to be as imaginative as possible given the price constraints. *Entrées* on a cold February night included a warming pumpkin soup, *flan de moules,* warm sausage served with potatoes, and a leek *tarte.* The *plats* included a soothing *potée* (meat stew) filled with cabbage, carrots, celery hearts, and fennel; whole fresh trout; and a mutton ragout. The desserts do not make my hit parade . . . especially not the *fondant de chocolat* surrounded by a watery orange sauce. A better choice would be the hot apple *tarte* or even the plebian baked apple.

LA PETITE LÉGUME (16)
36, rue des Boulangers
Métro: Cardinal Lemoine

"Live well, eat sensibly" is the motto at Michel and Patricia's La Petite Légume. And they deliver: A meal here is prepared without refined sugar, salt, added fat, or meat products and is served in a smoke-free atmosphere. For cash-strapped vegetarians or anyone eager to watch what they eat, this is a bargain spot worth noting. For between $8 and $12 you can walk out guilt-free and full of food that's nutritious and satisfying. Every level of vegetarian should find something satisfying on the menu, which lists everything from whole-cereal dishes with seaweed, miso, and tofu to salads, soups, and an overflowing *plat du jour* of *crudités,* rice and grains, vegetables, dried fruit, and nuts. Order a nonalcoholic beer, organic wine, or a tumbler of freshly pressed carrot juice, and indulge in a slice of their nonfat cheesecake or chocolate cake to round out the repast. Don't have time to stop for a meal? They will pack everything to go and even charge a bit less to do so. On your way, take a minute or two to glance through the shop, which sells macrobiotic books and natural products.

NOTE: No smoking is allowed.

À LA CARTE
45–100F (6.86–15.24€), BC

PRIX FIXE
Lunch: 55–70F (8.38–10.67€), 3 courses, BNC; 80F (12.20€), 3 courses, BC

ENGLISH SPOKEN
Yes, and English menu

LA ROTISSERIE GALANDE (3)
57, rue Galande
Métro: Maubert-Mutualité, Cluny–La Sorbonne

All tried-and-true carnivores can satisfy their daily rations here, where the meats come roasted on an open fire, grilled, or baked and served with plenty of potatoes and green beans. Besides the usual cuts of lamb, beef, pork, and veal, you can sample duck, whole roasted pig, and wild game in season. There is a value-packed lunch menu with a half dozen *entrées* to choose from, almost as many desserts, but only three *plats*: a *faux-filet,* roast chicken, or the *plat du jour*. At dinner, or if you are feeling a bit more flush in the afternoon—and very hungry, as the portions are *énorme*—go for either the *Menu Sympa,* starring roast ham or an herb-grilled *entrecôte,* or the *Menu Gourmet,* featuring roast duck, two types of brochettes, or a filet mignon. Ordering à la carte widens the choices even more, but unless you want five-hundred-gram slabs of meat or platters of several cuts, including kidneys, you will probably be satisfied with the set menus.

TELEPHONE
01-46-34-70-96

OPEN
Daily: lunch noon–2:30 P.M., dinner 7–11 P.M.

CLOSED
Never

RESERVATIONS
Suggested on weekends

CREDIT CARDS
AE, DC, MC, V

À LA CARTE
150–200F (22.87–30.49€), BNC

PRIX FIXE
Lunch: 70F (10.67€), 3 courses, BNC; lunch and dinner: 90F (13.72€), 150F (22.87€), both 3 courses and BNC

ENGLISH SPOKEN
Yes

L'ASSIETTE AUX FROMAGES (23)
27, rue Mouffetard
Métro: Place Monge

Smile, say "Cheese," and head for L'Assiette aux Fromages, a great place to go for lunch with a small group, order several different plates of cheese, have a couple bottles of the house red or white wine, and then walk off the consequences in the nearby Jardin des Plantes. Unfortunately, not all of the staff smile when they say *fromage,* and they could stand to brush up their customer service skills.

France reportedly produces over four hundred varieties of cheese, a fact that can be overwhelming to anyone

TELEPHONE
01-45-35-14-21

OPEN
Mon–Tues, Thur–Sun: noon–11 P.M., continuous service; shop 10:30 A.M.–10 P.M.

CLOSED
Wed; one week at Christmas, NAC

RESERVATIONS
Not taken

CREDIT CARDS
MC, V

À LA CARTE
95–145F (14.48–22.11€), BNC

PRIX FIXE
Lunch and dinner: 45F (6.86€),
2 courses, BC

ENGLISH SPOKEN
Limited, with English menu

used to only roquefort, cheddar, and swiss. Now cheese-lovers of all types can sample, eat, and buy over two hundred varieties of French cheese in this bright, modern *fromagerie,* with its garden restaurant, not far from place de la Contrescarpe on the colorful rue Mouffetard. The menu, which is in English and German as well as French, offers many enticing cheese-inspired dishes, from big salads and sandwiches to quiches, *tartes, raclettes,* fondues, and desserts. The smart move here is to order a *salade de saison* and one of the *plateaux des fromages,* which have five regional or specialty cheeses per plate: *doucer* (mild), *saveur* (strong), chèvre (goat), *l'avergnat* (cheese from the Auvergne), and *suspens* (their selection). Or order *personnalisé,* five cheeses of your choice from a list of eleven. All cheese plates are served with pots of sweet butter, crusty baguettes, and *pain Poilâne.*

LE BERTHOUD (12)
1, rue Valette
Métro: Maubert-Mutualité, Cardinal Lemoine

TELEPHONE
01-43-54-38-81

OPEN
Mon–Fri: lunch noon–2 P.M.,
dinner 7:30–10:30 P.M.; Sat:
dinner 7:30–10:30 P.M.

CLOSED
Sat lunch, Sun; NAC

RESERVATIONS
Suggested, especially on
Fri and Sat

CREDIT CARDS
AE, MC, V

À LA CARTE
180F (27.44€), BNC

PRIX FIXE
Lunch: 89F (13.57€), 2 courses,
110F (16.77€), 3 courses, both
BNC; lunch and dinner: 165F
(25.15€), 3 courses, BNC

ENGLISH SPOKEN
Yes, and menu in English

Comfortable seating in two adjoining tapestry-hung rooms, highlighted by a stunning collection of hand-painted glass lamps with beaded fringe shades, creates the atmosphere for dining at Le Berthoud. New owner Axel Moreaux has breathed renewed vigor into the kitchen, which for years was stuck in a morass of butter, cheese, and cream sauces . . . all acceptable before everyone kept track of their cholesterol and fat gram counts on a meal-by-meal basis. The menu now offers deliciously picturesque salads; soups ranging from bouillon to cream of spinach, carrot, and cauliflower; a trio of egg dishes; traditional red meats; and fresh seasonal fish. One holdover from the past I still love is *Le Vivaldi*—a colorful mélange of puréed vegetables under a robe of bubbling cheese. For dessert, I can never decide between the *tarte Tatin* or the moist slice of chocolate *ganache,* served with custard cream and rum-soaked raisins.

LE LANGUEDOC (31)
64, boulevard de Port-Royal, at rue Berthollet
Métro: Port Royal

TELEPHONE
01-47-07-24-47

OPEN
Mon, Thur–Sun: lunch noon–
2 P.M., dinner 7–10 P.M.

CLOSED
Tues–Wed; Dec 21–Jan 5, Aug

Le Languedoc has the relaxed feel of an old-fashioned Parisian restaurant, where its contented regulars enjoy the authentic atmosphere and know to stick to the basics when ordering. Red-checked tie-back curtains, wooden tables covered with yellow linen and white paper overlays, three coat racks, a grandfather clock, assorted copper pots—everything has been in the same position for twenty-plus years . . . and there is no hint of change on the horizon.

There is plenty to choose from on the purple-and-pink, handwritten, stenciled menu and really no need to stray from the bargain-priced prix fixe, which allows a wide choice from the à la carte selections. Start with bowls of herring filets or flavorful terrines brought to the table and left for you to help yourself, or try the artichoke hearts vinaigrette. Follow with a good *cassoulet,* the *confit canard maison,* any *plat du jour,* or the grilled *entrecôte,* which comes with crispy *frites* and a side salad. Seasonal desserts or chocolate mousse are a nice ending to a very well-priced meal in Paris.

NOTE: There is a nonsmoking section.

LE MAUZAC (24)
7, rue de l'Abbé de l'Épée
Métro: Luxembourg

"Oh, you must be joking. We aren't going to have dinner here!" groused my dinner companion. "What could be so special about this Latin Quarter café buried behind the Luxembourg Gardens?"

Admittedly, Le Mauzac looks like just another neighborhood hangout with a nice summer terrace in front; inside, there's a wall of mirrors and a curved bar covered in a frankly hideous tile motif. But after an evening spent enjoying their wine and honest cooking, both my companion and I wished we lived close enough to make this one of our regular stops. People seem to wander in all day long—in the morning for the usual jolt of espresso and later on for lunch to sample owner Jean-Michel Delhoume's hearty food and drink. In the afternoon it serves as the neighborhood meeting place, where people linger over a glass or two of wine while catching up on the latest news and gossip. As evening approaches, it fills with a happy crowd eager to slice into platters of Auvergne *charcuterie* and cheese, steak and *frites,* guinea hen served with sautéed potatoes, or a fat *andouillette.* Desserts are tried-and-true versions of apple crumble, pears poached in wine, and a piece of *fondant au chocolat.*

RESERVATIONS
Advised on weekends

CREDIT CARDS
MC, V (130F, 19.82€, minimum)

À LA CARTE
145F (22.11€), BNC

PRIX FIXE
Lunch and dinner: 110F (16.77€), 3 courses, BC

ENGLISH SPOKEN
Limited

TELEPHONE
01-46-33-75-22

OPEN
Mon–Fri: bar 7 A.M.–2 A.M., lunch noon–2:30 P.M., dinner 8–10:30 P.M.

CLOSED
Sat–Sun; one week at Christmas, Aug

RESERVATIONS
Preferred on Friday night

CREDIT CARDS
MC, V

À LA CARTE
115–130F (17.53–19.82€), BNC

PRIX FIXE
None

ENGLISH SPOKEN
Limited

LE MOUFFETARD (28)
116, rue Mouffetard
Métro: Censier-Daubenton

TELEPHONE
01-43-31-42-50

OPEN
Tues–Sat: 7:30 A.M.–11 P.M.;
Sun: 7:30 A.M.– 9 P.M.;
continuous service

CLOSED
Mon; July, Dec 25–Jan 1

RESERVATIONS
Not taken

CREDIT CARDS
AE (100F, 15.24€, minimum)

À LA CARTE
40–95F (6.10–14.48€), BC

PRIX FIXE
Breakfast: 40–50F (6.10–
7.62€); lunch and dinner:
60F (9.15€), 2 courses,
70F (10.67€), 3 courses,
both BNC

ENGLISH SPOKEN
Yes, and menu in English

In the fifteenth century, rue Mouffetard was known as Hell Raisers' Hill because of the many taverns and brothels in the area. The long steep street, which begins at place de la Contrescarp and winds down to the St-Mediard Church near the Censier-Daubenton métro stop, is still full of greasy spoons and probably a brothel or two if you look hard enough. The best reason to go there today is to wander through the colorful open-air morning street *marché* and the inexpensive clothing shops that line both sides of the street. When you go, be sure to stop in at the down-to-earth café known as Le Mouffetard, which is far and away the best-value choice.

The café has been owned and run by members of the Chartran family for years, and they get up with the chickens to serve locals on their way to work. Arrive a little later in the morning and you can indulge in the house specialties: buttery croissants and rich yeasty brioches made every day by M. Chartran. At lunchtime, try the pork in a tangy mustard sauce or the thickly sliced ham with plum sauce and a side of pasta. With your meal comes a basket of their home-baked *pain de campagne*. Even if you are not up to sharing an eye-opening cognac with the locals at dawn, or you can't make it for lunch or dinner, at least stop by for a coffee and one of their *chaussons aux pommes* or *pruneaux*—flaky apple or prune turnovers—a savory tart made with salmon, spinach, and chèvre, or their homemade bread spread with camembert cheese.

L'EQUITABLE (30)
1, rue des Fossés St-Marcel
Métro: St-Marcel, Censier-Daubenton

TELEPHONE
01-43-31-69-20

OPEN
Tues–Fri: lunch noon–
2:30 P.M., dinner 7:30–11 P.M.;
Sat: dinner 7:30–11 P.M.;
Sun: lunch noon–2:30 P.M.

CLOSED
Sat lunch, Sun dinner, Mon;
Aug (dates vary)

RESERVATIONS
Essential

CREDIT CARDS
AE, V

Up-and-coming chefs who have trained under well-known Michelin star chefs, or at the temples of haute cuisine in Paris, continue to venture out on their own, opening their own bistros in parts of Paris visitors would normally never see. Such is the case with Yves Mutin, who worked at Jules Vern in the Eiffel Tower and Les Bouchons de François Clerc before opening his increasingly popular restaurant in the bottom of the fifth arrondissement.

The exposed stone walls, dark beamed ceiling, and high ladder-back chairs give L'Equitable's two rooms the feel of an old country *auberge*. Formally set tables are well spaced. Service by Mutin's wife and one other waiter is polite and helpful, but often painfully slow between courses. Never mind . . . sip your wine, nibble on the basket of whole-grain sourdough bread served with tomato chutney and a bowl of crème fraîche and chives, and know that each course will be imaginative in both execution and presentation. The exceptionally well priced 168F (25.61€) menu allows you to choose from the entire à la carte menu. One of the most popular *entrées* is poached eggs served with a mushroom cream sauce garnished with toast fingers lightly spread with foie gras. Another wonderful beginning is the lightly cooked foie gras presented on a bed of carmelized onions. The duck filet, garnished with orange-scented couscous and a phyllo-dough flower, is as delicious as it is artistic. Cod is served with *provençal* vegetables, and the steak is gilded with a marrow bone and celery crêpes. Desserts do not fall by the wayside: save room for the slice of dark chocolate pecan cake topped with coffee sauce or the cooked pears on a thin layer of spiced bread with a little ball of vanilla ice cream on the side.

À LA CARTE
195F (29.73€); *entrées* 60F (9.15€), *plats* 95F (14.48€), cheese 30F (4.57€), desserts 40F (6.10€), BNC

PRIX FIXE
Lunch Tues–Fri: 130F (19.82€), 3 courses, BNC; 150F (22.87€), 3 courses, BC (kir, wine, and coffee); lunch and dinner: 168F (25.61€), 3 courses (unlimited choice), BNC

ENGLISH SPOKEN
Yes

LE RACCARD (10)
19, rue Laplace
Métro: Maubert-Mutualité, Cardinal Lemoine

With a group or just one other person, Le Raccard is the place to fill up on the lip-smacking Swiss specialties of fondue and *raclette. Raclette,* for the uninitiated, is bubbling-hot melted cheese served over boiled new potatoes and sometimes accompanied with air-dried meat, but it's always served with tangy *cornichons* (pickles) and tiny pickled onions. I absolutely guarantee that it is as delectable as it is filling and fattening.

The Swiss-style chalet is located not far from the Panthéon, and you may actually be thankful for the short climb from the métro, since you definitely need a good appetite when eating here. Stay with the house specialties and you won't go away unhappy. The desserts, which you will not have room for anyway, are best forgotten. The waiters can be impatient, but when pushed they do speak enough English to suggest appropriate combinations. Before leaving, be sure to notice the authentic hay crib, or *raccard,* in the back, which has been skillfully turned into a little bar.

TELEPHONE
01-43-54-83-75, 01-43-25-27-27

OPEN
Tues–Sun: dinner 7:30 P.M.– 12:30 A.M.

CLOSED
Mon; NAC

RESERVATIONS
Advised on weekends

CREDIT CARDS
AE

À LA CARTE
160–180F (24.39–27.44€), BNC

PRIX FIXE
None

ENGLISH SPOKEN
Limited

LES FÊTES GALANTES (9)
17, rue de l'École Polytechnique
Métro: Maubert-Mutualité, Cardinal Lemoine

TELEPHONE
01-43-26-10-40

OPEN
Mon–Sat: lunch noon–
2:30 P.M., dinner 6:30–
11:30 P.M.

CLOSED
Sun; Christmas day, 2 weeks in
July or Aug (dates vary)

RESERVATIONS
Advised on weekends

CREDIT CARDS
MC, V

À LA CARTE
180–200F (27.44–30.49 €),
BNC

PRIX FIXE
Lunch: 66F (10.06€), 2 courses,
BNC; early dinner (see text for
times): 88F (13.42€),
3 courses, BNC; dinner: 116F
(17.68€), 170F (25.92€), both
3 courses and BNC

ENGLISH SPOKEN
Yes, with English menu

Good things often come in small packages, and this is certainly true at Les Fêtes Galantes. The welcome offered by Bibi, the owner and chef, and his sweet wife, Isabelle, along with the food and, most especially, the appealing prices will make you want to return again. The best bargains are their two-course lunch (66F, 10.06€) and their three-course early dinner menu (88F, 13.42€), which is available only during the fashionably incorrect dining hours of 6:30 to 9:30 P.M. Monday to Thursday and from 6:30 to 8:30 P.M. Friday and Saturday.

A hand-painted forest mural makes a nice backdrop for the twenty-two places on pink-clad tables, each with its own glass-shaded lamp and a bouquet of fresh flowers. Forget the à la carte and zero in on one of the very affordable prix fixe menus. The well-planned presentations revolve around seasonal food. Pâtes, terrines, escargots, hot and cold soups, and salads laden with fresh asparagus, foie gras, and avocados figure among the able starters. Lamb, veal, duck, and fresh fish are featured on the vegetable-garnished *plats*. Desserts delight with a warm apple *tarte* covered with almonds, profiteroles filled with vanilla ice cream and covered in dark, hot chocolate sauce, and seasonal fruit creations.

LES FONTAINES (15)
9, rue Soufflot
Métro: Luxembourg

TELEPHONE
01-43-26-42-80

OPEN
Mon–Sat: bar 8 A.M.–11 P.M.,
lunch noon–3 P.M., snacks and
pastries 3–7 P.M., dinner
7–11 P.M.

CLOSED
Sun; major holidays, NAC

RESERVATIONS
Essential

CREDIT CARDS
MC, V

À LA CARTE
150–180F (22.87–27.44€),
BNC

PRIX FIXE
None

ENGLISH SPOKEN
Yes

You can't judge a book by its cover, and that is certainly true about Les Fontaines. Unless you knew about it ahead of time, you would never go inside on the basis of looks alone. When it comes to cafés in Paris, everyone has his or her favorite. But dogs, children, pensioners, trendies, bespectacled professors, blue-haired matrons, families—everyone comes to this popular spot owned by chef Jean-Marie Plas-Debecker and his wife, Josiane, located in the tourist-intensive area between the Panthéon and the entrance to the Luxembourg Gardens.

No one comes here for polished ambience: the interior is a time warp of plastic, chrome, and bright neon. But the food—ahhh—that is something to return for again and again. The menu will melt the hearts of carnivores with time-honored dishes of *poireaux vinaigrette* (leeks vinaigrette), *filets d'hareng,* foie gras, *rillettes de porc* (a coarse type of pâté), *confit de canard* (duck cooked and preserved in its own fat), *rognons de veau* (veal kidneys) in a mustard sauce, and huge steaks. The meat-based meals arrive on platters, not plates. Fish lovers will have at least seven seasonal selections, including tuna, salmon, and lobster. If you love pears and chocolate (and who doesn't?), request the *feuilleté de poires au chocolat chaud* when you place your order. Otherwise, try the apple *tarte* or crème brûlée. All of this is brought to you with speed and precision by a fleet of fast-footed servers in black pants, white shirts, and snappy ties.

LES QUATRE ET UNE SAVEURS (19)
72, rue du Cardinal Lemoine
Métro: Cardinal Lemoine, Place Monge

Only fresh, natural ingredients that are 100 percent organic are used at this appealing *macrobiotique* vegetarian restaurant near place de la Contrescarpe and rue Mouffetard. The open, airy interior is arranged with glass-topped tables showing four various grains. Changing local art adds interest. Just as important are the winning combinations of food, which go a long way toward promoting your health and happiness while you're in Paris. Owner Sophie Court has incorporated the old Chinese eating philosophy that all meals should include five savors: saltiness, bitterness, pungency, sweetness, and sourness, each one giving special energy to our bodies. Nothing frozen or microwaved is served, and neither are eggs, dairy products, or refined sugars. The daily changing menu starts off with full-bodied miso or vegetable soups and accents one-dish meals of salads or hot vegetables centered around grains, beans, tofu, or fish. Fresh fruit and vegetable juices, herbal teas, organic wine, plus the best sugar-free apple crisp you will ever taste add up to a healthy and delicious dining selection.

NOTE: No smoking is allowed.

TELEPHONE
01-43-26-88-80

OPEN
Tues–Sun: lunch noon–2:30 P.M., dinner 7–10:30 P.M.

CLOSED
Mon; major holidays, Aug

RESERVATIONS
Not necessary

CREDIT CARDS
MC, V

À LA CARTE
80–140F (12.20–21.34€), BNC

PRIX FIXE
Lunch and dinner: vegetarian 140F (21.34€), fish 150F (22.87€), both 3 courses and BC

ENGLISH SPOKEN
Yes

MOISSONNIER ($, 7)
28, rue des Fossés St-Bernard
Métro: Cardinal Lemoine

Moissonnier is a forty-year-old family-owned Left Bank landmark that specializes in Lyonnaise cooking. It is run by a friendly young couple, Philippe and Valérie Mayet. He cooks, and she runs the dining room, making sure that all of her guests are happy and well fed. The best seating in the two-floor restaurant is on the ground

TELEPHONE
01-43-29-87-65

OPEN
Tues–Sat: lunch noon–2 P.M., dinner 7:30–10 P.M.

CLOSED
Mon, Sun; major holidays, Aug

RESERVATIONS
Necessary

CREDIT CARDS
MC, V

À LA CARTE
250–300F (38.11–45.73€),
BNC

PRIX FIXE
Lunch Tues–Fri: 150F
(22.87€), 3 courses, BNC

ENGLISH SPOKEN
Yes, with English menu

floor, with its high ceiling, massive bouquet of fresh flowers, and tiny service bar along one side. The best time to go is for lunch, when they offer a prix fixe menu.

The well-rounded selection of Lyonnaise dishes makes this an excellent dining choice and a good culinary value considering the quality of the food, which is prepared from scratch on the premises every day. Look for the regional and house specialties written in red on the menu. A good *entrée* choice is the *saladier,* a large cart rolled to your table laden with salads, terrines, herring in cream, marinated vegetables, and many other tempting appetizers. But proceed with caution . . . if you don't go easy on the first course, you may not be able to manage the rib-sticking specialties that follow, such as *quenelles de brochet* (light pike dumplings in a smooth tomato sauce), *tablier de sapeur* (fried tripe), veal kidneys in mustard sauce, or a rack of lamb with potatoes au gratin. Complete the meal with an assortment of fine regional cheeses, ethereal *oeufs à la neige* (puffs of egg whites floating in vanilla custard), or a seasonally perfect *tartlette aux fraises* (strawberry tart). House wines are served in *pots,* heavy, thick glass bottles that keep the wine cool.

MOUFF' TARTES (25)
53, rue Mouffetard
Métro: Place Monge

TELEPHONE
01-43-37-21-89

OPEN
Tues–Sun: 11:30 A.M.–
midnight, continuous service

CLOSED
Mon; NAC

RESERVATIONS
Not accepted

CREDIT CARDS
None

À LA CARTE
45–65F (6.86–9.91€), BNC

PRIX FIXE
None

ENGLISH SPOKEN
Yes

When you first arrive, check out the window display of homemade quiches—both savory and sweet—then go in and sit at one of the yellow cloth–covered tables and enjoy a nice repast that's easy on the wallet. All the food is made and served by a husband-and-wife team. A baker's dozen of savory quiches and as many sweet ones comprise the menu, along with salads you can create yourself at 8F (1.22€) per ingredient, or order one of the ten choices from the menu. This is a good pit stop if you have hungry children on your hands or need a filling snack on the run. Also, they will pack any order to go. If you order a slice of their signature quiche, or the popular Athena (made with tomatoes, feta cheese, and olives), the chocolate dessert specialty, and a cup of tea, you will barely be out $10.

NOTE: Everything can be packed to go.

PERRAUDIN (14)
157, rue St-Jacques
Métro: Luxembourg

For decades, Perraudin has demonstrated the glory of substantial French cooking. Possessing a winning combination, it serves homespun, realistically priced food to a packed audience for both lunch and dinner. In addition, some of the wines are exceptional, the atmosphere is authentic, and children are welcome! Sitting at one of the little bistro tables, perusing the classic daily menu, and watching the cast of faithfuls positioned around the room, you will soon get the feeling that nothing has changed here for years—and you will be right.

After polishing off weighty servings of smoked herring with warm potato salad or tangy onion *tartes,* diners tuck in to main courses of *confit de canard,* poached salmon, grilled steaks, and popular daily specials. They top it all off with a slice of the irresistible fruit *tartes,* a *clafoutis maison* (fruit cooked in a pancakelike batter), or a wedge of camembert cheese. Wine can be anything from a glass or pitcher of the house variety to a little-known regional *cru* seldom seen in Paris. Owner Hubert Gloaguen (who also owns Le Bistrot d'André, see page 231) and his sister, Marie-Christine Kvella, who is the manager, are proud of their wine *cave* and its wide-ranging, undiscovered selections in all price ranges.

TELEPHONE
01-46-33-15-75

OPEN
Mon: dinner 7:30–10 P.M.;
Tues–Sat: lunch noon–
2:30 P.M., dinner 7:30–10 P.M.

CLOSED
Mon lunch, Sun; last 15 days in Aug

RESERVATIONS
Not accepted

CREDIT CARDS
None

À LA CARTE
125F (19.06€), BNC

PRIX FIXE
Lunch: 65F (9.91€), 3 courses, BNC; lunch and dinner: *Menu Gourmandise,* 150F (22.87€), 3 courses, BNC

ENGLISH SPOKEN
Yes, with English menu

RESTAURANT LA MARÉE VERT (5)
9, rue de Pointoise
Métro: Maubert-Mutualité

La Marée Vert's green facade hides a maritime theme carried out by a life raft in front of the tiny bar and pictures of sailing ships hanging on the yellow enamel walls. Regulars are warmly greeted with hugs and shown to small, linen-covered tables that are candlelit at night. The service by the owner and his wife is always accommodating and correct. After you sit down, a dish of salmon butter cream to spread on freshly cut bread is brought to the table while you decide what to order. The specialties of the house center around fish, and in fact, the fish-based dishes are the most successful. Disappointing are the chunks of long-cooked lamb that arrive in a pool of gravy. Better main-course choices include the *poêlée de l'océan aux sucs des tomates et pistou* (a trio of scorpion fish, fresh cod, and salmon sautéed in tomatoes and served with pasta) and the roast salmon served with braised cabbage. An *entrée* highlight is the filling *soupe de poissons,*

TELEPHONE
01-43-25-89-41

OPEN
Mon–Sat: lunch noon–
2:30 P.M., dinner 7:30–
10:30 P.M.

CLOSED
Sun; major holidays, Aug (dates vary)

RESERVATIONS
Recommended

CREDIT CARDS
MC, V

À LA CARTE
None

PRIX FIXE
Lunch: 78F (11.89€), 3 courses,
BNC; lunch and dinner: 148F
(22.85€), 168F (25.61€),
2–3 courses (unlimited choices),
both BNC; 198F (30.18€),
3 courses (unlimited choices),
BC

ENGLISH SPOKEN
Yes

which is served in a seemingly endless tureen along with garlicky *aïoli* to spread on croutons you float in the soup and grated cheese to sprinkle on top—not to mention *entrées* of seafood ravioli, deep-fried sardines in a tangy lemon-horseradish vinaigrette, and an interesting fricassee of artichoke hearts and *pleurottes,* accompanied by slices of duck confit. One of the best desserts is the light *oeufs à la neige*—a mountain of meringue floating in a vanilla custard sauce and drizzled with caramel.

RESTAURANT L'ÉPOQUE (22)
81, rue du Cardinal Lemoine
Métro: Place Monge

TELEPHONE
01-46-34-15-84
OPEN
Mon–Sat: lunch noon–
2:30 P.M., dinner 6–11 P.M.
CLOSED
Sun; 3–4 days at Christmas,
Aug
RESERVATIONS
Recommended on Fri–Sat
CREDIT CARDS
MC, V (100F, 15.24€,
minimum)
À LA CARTE
150F (22.87€), BNC
PRIX FIXE
Lunch: 60F (9.15€), 2 courses,
70F (10.67€), 3 courses, both
BNC; dinner: 90–130F
(13.72–19.82€), 3 courses,
170F (25.92€), 4 courses, all
BNC
ENGLISH SPOKEN
Yes

L'Époque is just far enough from the hype along the rue Mouffetard to escape the endless line of touristy restaurants reaching out for your wallet with loud music, gaudy fake decor, windows full of sizzling meats, and sweaty chefs serving poor fare. This is a utilitarian pick that doesn't put on airs with either the decor or the food. The small room's wooden bistro tables are topped with straw placemats and paper napkins. The customer profile shifts with the hour: at lunch it is workers and shopkeepers, and at night, students, couples, and just plain folks.

All pocketbooks are accommodated with a series of well-constructed prix fixe menus for both lunch and dinner. À la carte is also available, but frankly, don't bother: it's not the good-value meal here. Depending on your budget and taste, start with plate of *crudités,* a salad with *chèvre chaud,* onion soup, or herring served with warm potatoes. The main courses for all menus are meat based, costarring heaps of potatoes. Desserts are the usuals: chocolate mousse, *tartes,* floating island, and sorbets.

RESTAURANT LES VIGNES DU PANTHÉON (20)
4, rue Fossés St-Jacques
Métro: Luxembourg

TELEPHONE
01-43-54-80-81
OPEN
Mon–Fri: lunch noon–
2:30 P.M., dinner 7–10:30 P.M.
CLOSED
Sat–Sun; NAC
RESERVATIONS
Recommended
CREDIT CARDS
V

The food at Les Vignes du Panthéon draws an appreciative audience who like the rather sedate yet intimate atmosphere and the wholesome food, adeptly prepared by an able chef and served by his charming wife. The front room houses bar and banquette seating. Further along past the kitchen is another stone-walled dining room that's large enough to accommodate several changing art exhibitions throughout the year. Small table lamps add just the right air of romance.

The prudent dining choice is definitely the bargain-priced lunch menu, which highlights French favorites such as endives with nuts, *pâté en croute,* and ratatouille with ham. Rich, wholesome plates of beef tongue, roast salmon, or steak with bearnaise sauce are next, followed by finales of *tartes, fromage blanc,* or *île flottante.* If you dine here in the evening, there is no question that you will spend more (since there is no prix fixe), but the choices expand and so does the repertoire. The classic Parisian hallmarks of foie gras and *pâtés maison,* filet of sole, steak with marrowbone, and homemade profiteroles with chocolate sauce are all here, along with a good selection of fresh fish, the chef's own *andouillette,* and duck confit.

À LA CARTE
180–200F (27.44–30.49€), BNC

PRIX FIXE
Lunch: 85F (12.96€), 2 courses, BNC

ENGLISH SPOKEN
Yes

VILLAGE WEB (1)
18, rue de la Bûcherie
Métro: St-Michel, Maubert-Mutualité

Antoine Boucalil has two cyber cafés in Paris: this one in the shadow of Notre Dame and the other on the Butte Montmartre close to Sacré Coeur. At either location you can check your email, log on to *le chat,* and surf *le web* on either a PC or Mac (with an English keyboard). You can also scan, send and receive faxes, and make photocopies in black-and-white and color. No food is served, only drinks.

NOTE: In Montmartre, Village Web is at 6, rue Ravignan (18th); Tel: 01-42-64-77-70; Fax: 01-42-64-78-23; Métro: Abbesses.

TELEPHONE
01-44-07-20-15

FAX
01-44-07-20-18

EMAIL
Infos@village-web.net

INTERNET
www.village-web.net

OPEN
Daily: 10 A.M.–10 P.M.

CLOSED
Never

RESERVATIONS
Not taken

CREDIT CARDS
None

INTERNET PRICES
1F (0.15€) per minute, 200F (30.46€) 5 hours, 500F (76.22€) 20 hours; students, 4F (0.61€) 5 minutes, 45F (6.86€) 1 hour

ENGLISH SPOKEN
Yes

Sixth Arrondissement

LEFT BANK
École des Beaux-Arts,
Luxembourg Gardens, Odéon
National Theater, place St-
Michel, St-German-des-Prés
Church (the oldest in Paris), St-
Séverin, St-Sulpice (murals by
Delacroix), Musée Delacroix

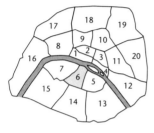

The sixth is a continuation of the Latin Quarter, but *plus chic*. Running from the Seine to the busy boulevard du Montparnasse, the sixth is symbolized by the trendy yet scholarly neighborhood around the church of St-Germain-des-Prés, the oldest church in Paris. The emphasis is on art galleries, antiques, fashion boutiques, and restaurants in all categories. Café society in Paris has always been epitomized by two famous cafés here: Les Deux Magots and Café de Flore. In their glory, they were the prime haunts of the existentialists of the postwar years, notably Sartre, Camus, and Simone de Beauvoir. While their original luster has dimmed, they are still crowded day and night and offer some of the best people-watching in Paris. An hour spent sitting in the Luxembourg Gardens is one of the delights of Paris, especially on a sunny Sunday afternoon when the children are floating their boats in the pond. The Palais du Luxembourg was built for the widow of Henri IV, Marie de' Medici, in the 1620s. The palace now houses the French Senate.

SIXTH ARRONDISSEMENT RESTAURANTS

($) indicates a Big Splurge

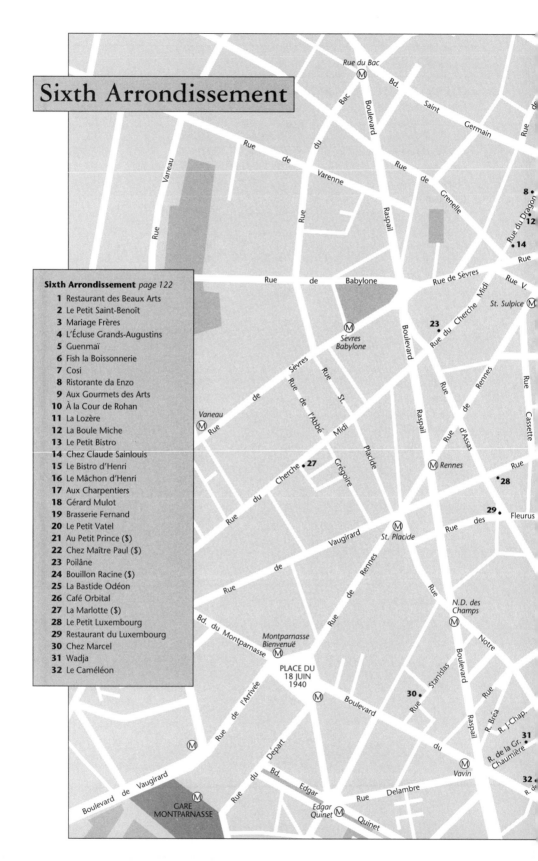

Sixth Arrondissement

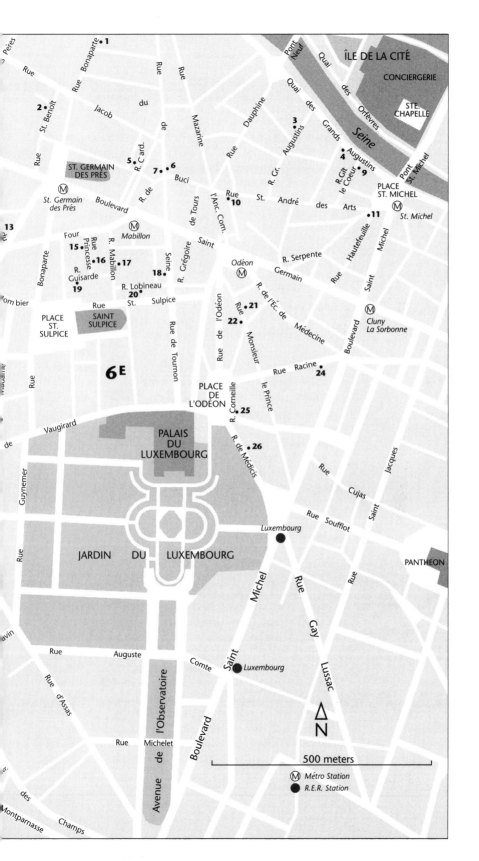

À LA COUR DE ROHAN (10)
59–61, rue St-André-des-Arts (enter through Cour du Commerce St-André)
Métro: Odéon

TELEPHONE
01-43-25-79-67

OPEN
Daily: noon–7:30 P.M.;
lunch and weekend brunch
noon–3 P.M.

CLOSED
July15–Aug 15

RESERVATIONS
Advised for weekends

CREDIT CARDS
MC, V (120F, 18.29€,
minimum)

À LA CARTE
75–125F (11.43–19.06€), BC

PRIX FIXE
Sat–Sun brunch: 110F
(16.77€), 150F (22.87€), 170F
(25.92€), all BC

ENGLISH SPOKEN
Limited

Situated in an eighteenth-century *passage* that runs between boulevard St-Germain and rue St-André-des-Arts, À la Cour de Rohan is a cozy tearoom that has become a Left Bank fixture, and it is *the* place to go with a friend for an intimate afternoon of gossip or romance surrounded by soft classical music. The downstairs room overlooking the *passage* is crowded with tables and a big hutch displaying high-calorie temptations. For a cozier experience, I prefer to sit upstairs, where the frilly chintz curtains and print tablecloths, well-worn English furniture, and aromas of tea remind me of a British maiden auntie's parlor.

Beautiful salads, pastas, creamy eggs dishes, house specialties of ratatouille or *gratins,* and a host of homemade pastries are served on an eclectic collection of flowered china. On Saturdays and Sundays, three types of brunches are served that range in the number of dishes included and the selection, but all come with fruit juice, tea, or coffee. Twenty or more varieties of tea are poured from pretty china teapots into delicate teacups. Nothing quite matches, but that is part of the charm.

NOTE: No smoking is allowed.

AU PETIT PRINCE ($, 21)
3, rue Monsieur-le-Prince
Métro: Odéon

TELEPHONE
01-43-29-74-92

OPEN
Mon: dinner 7:30–11 P.M.;
Tues–Sat: lunch noon–2 P.M.,
dinner 7:30–11 P.M.

CLOSED
Mon lunch, Sun; holidays, Aug

RESERVATIONS
Advised

CREDIT CARDS
AE, MC, V

À LA CARTE
220–240F (33.54–36.59€),
BNC

PRIX FIXE
Lunch: 100F (15.24€),
2 courses, BNC; lunch and
dinner: 145F (22.11€),
3 courses, BNC

ENGLISH SPOKEN
Yes

According to my mail, this continues to be one of the most popular Left Bank listings in *Great Eats Paris.* The tiny, two-level, very Parisian restaurant is decorated in an aviation motif with airplane posters and pictures from Saint-Exupéry's novel *The Little Prince.* The clientele is a predominantly young crowd of businesspeople at lunch and a still young but casually attired group for dinner. Very attentive hosts run the dining room, always making sure every guest is pleased with the meal and service.

Both the lunch and dinner prix fixe menus change weekly and feature whatever caught the chef's fancy that day at the market. The selections are limited but always imaginatively executed and well presented. The à la carte menu offers a wider variety of seasonal dishes that display the same creativity as the daily changing menus. On the à la carte side, I like to start with *salade du Petit Prince,* made with fresh and smoked salmon and haddock on a bed of greens with avocado. *Sole meunière* or the duck confit with sautéed potatoes are sure main course selections, and the *tarte Tatin* with apples and pears or the *moelleux au chocolat noire* (with coffee cream sauce and vanilla ice cream) are only two of the tempting endings. Coffee comes with a plate of tiny cookies . . . the perfect ending to the kind of meal we all hope to find in Paris.

AUX CHARPENTIERS (17)
10, rue Mabillon
Métro: Mabillon

Aux Charpentiers—The Carpenters—is the type of Parisian bistro I hope will never die, with its zinc bar, wooden floors sprinkled with sawdust, and diners straight out of central casting. The name commemorates the important role of the eighteenth-century journeyman carpenter and cabinetmaker's guild in the politics and architecture of France. Next door is a small museum that displays scale models created by guild members in preparation for the construction of the spires and roofs of such famous landmarks as Notre Dame and Ste-Chapelle.

The solid, stick-to-your-ribs fare includes platters of roast duck and olives, beef fillet cooked with bone marrow, pig's feet, veal kidneys, roast Bresse chicken, and blood sausage. If these do not appeal, take advantage of the Monday through Sunday *plats du jour:* veal Marengo, beef with carrots, salt pork and lentils, *pot-au-feu,* cod with garlic sauce, stuffed cabbage, and leg of lamb. While you will not be overwhelmed with delicate or subtle cooking, you will enjoy a typical French meal without spending a fortune.

TELEPHONE
01-43-26-30-05

OPEN
Daily: lunch noon–3 P.M., dinner 7–11:30 P.M.

CLOSED
Never

RESERVATIONS
Advised

CREDIT CARDS
AE, DC, MC, V

À LA CARTE
175–200F (26.68–30.49€), BNC

PRIX FIXE
Lunch Mon–Fri: 125F (19.06€), 2 courses, BC; lunch and dinner daily: 160F (24.39€), 3 courses, BNC

ENGLISH SPOKEN
Yes

AUX GOURMETS DES ARTS (9)
15, rue Gît-le-Coeur
Métro: St-Michel

Put this one on your list for inexpensive, basic food served in nondiet portions when you have meat eating on your mind. The location is in a touristy corner dog-eared with tacky restaurants whose menus are in four or five languages in hopes of snagging one-time diners from the competition next door. The food at Aux Gourmets des Arts is better than most in the vicinity and served in more attractive surroundings. The beamed dining room has the requisite wainscoated, white stuccoed walls, candles at night, and semicomfortable padded seats you will encounter in many such places in Paris. The service is attentive and eager to please.

TELEPHONE
01-43-26-29-44

OPEN
Mon–Sat in winter: lunch noon–2 P.M., dinner 7–11 P.M.; open daily in summer, same hours

CLOSED
Sun in winter; NAC

RESERVATIONS
Not necessary

CREDIT CARDS
MC, V

À LA CARTE
Not recommended

When consulting the menu, don't pause by the à la carte selections or the long wine list. Go right to the prix fixe menus and order a big *pichet* of the house red or white wine to sip throughout your meal. The prix fixe menus are smart choices, especially when you can have salad with smoked duck or *chèvre chaud aux amandes, confit de canard,* herb-grilled lamb chops, or steak with roquefort sauce, and for dessert, profiteroles, *tarte Tatin,* or zabaglione. Spring for the top price and you will be eating salads with homemade foie gras, shrimps flambéed in whiskey, *coquilles St-Jacques à la provençale* (scallops in a spicy tomato sauce), or *tournedos* with mushrooms. At night, cheese or beef fondues are served along with a green salad and dessert.

BOUILLON RACINE ($, 24)
3, rue Racine
Métro: Cluny–La Sorbonne

The focus is on Belgian food and drink at this classified Art Nouveau restaurant near the Sorbonne. In another life, it served as a canteen for students at the Sorbonne and local workers. Now completely redone and restored down to the last painted leaf and tiny tile in the mosaic floor, the restaurant's two magnificent floors serve as reminders of a gilded past. The downstairs is nice for lunch or tea, but for dinner, I like the upstairs with its lovely iris stained-glass windows and pretty banquette seating. On Monday and Thursday nights, live jazz adds yet another reason to sample the wide variety of Belgian cuisine, which, at Bouillon Racine, is much more than mussels, *frites,* and beer.

At lunch there are two express menus that make bargain sense for great eaters in Paris. The first one (around 80F, 12.20€) includes the *entrée* and *plat du jour,* plus one or two other choices for each course. If you go for the slightly higher priced lunch menu, you get dessert as well. The most expensive menu, which is available for either lunch or dinner, lets you select any starter, a fish or meat dish, and a dessert. On a cool winter day you could start with a fish soup steeped with Duvel beer and served with grilled chunks of garlic bread and grated cheese. Or try the pork pâté marinated in Gueuze beer from Brussels and served with chestnut chutney and toasted bread. For the next course, try the salmon and rolled, stuffed sole simmered with white beans in a Duvel beer sauce, or the famous Belgian *waterzooi,* made with poached sole, salmon, and cod cooked in a light cream sauce with braised vegetables. Meat eaters will revel in the rooster, slowly cooked in beer and served with potatoes, wild mushrooms, and Belgian mustard spread on toast, or the caramelized duck in an orange-quince beer sauce. For dessert, I look no further than the Belgian version of profiteroles—*le chou géant du Bouillon*—a huge puff-pastry filled with vanilla ice cream and covered with a cherry beer and dark chocolate sauce.

BRASSERIE FERNAND (19)
13, rue Guissarde
Métro: Mabillon

Brasserie Fernand is fun and typically Parisian, but I recommend it with a few cautionary warnings first. To begin, it is busy all the time, but most especially on Friday and Saturday nights. Avoid these evenings unless you can contend with tables packed so tightly you need the skills of a contortionist to wedge into a banquette seat. On the other hand, some might appreciate the crowd-created din loud enough to mask a struggling French accent. Then again, if you are here for an early seating, such as around 8 or 8:30 P.M., don't expect to linger over a coffee. Instead, expect the bum's rush if you see waiting hoards, as management is usually intent on turning the tables again two or three times. Finally, if you are with a group, forget separate checks. Appoint a designated mathematician to keep track of each order; otherwise you will have an impossible task on your hands trying to decipher the lumped-together bill.

Throughout the meal, the overextended staff does their best, running relays between the kitchen and tables and serving well-cooked, substantial fare that holds few surprises. The blackboard menu lists simple dishes: green beans with foie gras, salads, grilled fish, red meat, *cassoulet, tarte Tatin,* two chocolate desserts, and fruit crumble.

TELEPHONE
01-43-54-61-47

OPEN
Mon–Sat: lunch noon–
2:30 P.M., dinner 7–11:30 P.M.

CLOSED
Sun; 3 weeks Aug (dates vary)

RESERVATIONS
Essential

CREDIT CARDS
MC, V

À LA CARTE
200F (30.49€), BNC

PRIX FIXE
None

ENGLISH SPOKEN
Generally

CAFÉ ORBITAL (26)
13, rue de Médicis
Métro: Odéon, Luxembourg

At this cyber way station you can do just about anything, from sending Mom an email to designing your own Website. Café Orbital is across from the Luxembourg Gardens, and there are tables outside where drinks are served, but don't count on food, unless you

TELEPHONE
01-43-25-76-77

EMAIL
info@orbital.fr

INTERNET
www.onetwork.net (English);
www.orbital.fr (French)

buy a candy bar from the machine inside. They are open every day, and someone who speaks English is always around.

CHEZ CLAUDE SAINLOUIS (14)
27, rue du Dragon
Métro: St-Germain-des-Prés, St-Sulpice

With a set formula he has followed for more than thirty-eight years, Claude Sainlouis promises no surprises, just good food and plenty of it. For under $25 you will get a three-course lunch or dinner that includes salad, a bowl of dark chocolate mousse, and only four choices for your main dish: grilled salmon with a basil butter sauce, steak plain or *à la crème,* lamb chops with thyme, or steak or salmon tartare *maison,* all garnished with hot potato puffs or spinach. There is also a daily special that includes salad and cheese or dessert. In all cases, drinks are extra.

That's it: good, dependable, well-cooked food served by red-shirted waiters. The congenial room is accented with bright red linen tablecloths and napkins, and it attracts scores of hungry French diners eager to enjoy the well-priced meals.

CHEZ MAÎTRE PAUL ($, 22)
12, rue Monsieur-le-Prince
Métro: Odéon

Upscale patrons continue to fill this refined, comfortable restaurant presided over by Jean François Debert. The nicely spaced tables are formally set with starched linens, fresh flowers, and sparkling crystal in a soft gray room with subdued lighting and attractive artwork on the walls.

The decidedly rich, full-flavored cuisine features specialties from the Franche–Comté region in eastern France. Among the *entrées* you will find a *terrine maison* made with chicken livers, a plate of garlicky sausages served warm with tiny potatoes, and in the spring, fat white asparagus in warm vinaigrette. A main course must is the *poulet au vin jaune*—tender chicken in a tomato, mushroom, and wine sauce. Two other award-winning chicken dishes are the *poulet sauté au vin rouge d'Arbois* and the *poulette à la crème gratinée* (chicken in a cream and cheese sauce). Most of the other main course dishes are served with Jura wine sauces that are perfect for mopping up with crusty baguettes. If you can still think about dessert, the crème brûlée or the thin, warm cinnamon-apple *tarte* are both definitely worthwhile, and the local cheeses are interesting.

CLOSED
July–Aug: Mon lunch, Sun; May 1, Dec 25, Jan 1, NAC

RESERVATIONS
Advised

CREDIT CARDS
AE, DC, MC, V

À LA CARTE
190–225F (28.97–34.30€), BNC

PRIX FIXE
Lunch and dinner: 170F (25.92€), 3 courses, BNC; 200F (30.49€), 3 courses, BC

ENGLISH SPOKEN
Yes

CHEZ MARCEL (30)
7, rue Stanislas
Métro: Notre-Dame-des-Champs, Vavin

In this area of Paris, where you are likely to see more baseball caps than berets, it is hard to find an authentic neighborhood restaurant. Chez Marcel is just that—a local pick, nothing fancy or worth a taxi ride across town, but definitely worth consideration if you are nearby. It is a reliable place, the sort we all go to when we don't feel like cooking. The place could double as a set on the back lot of a Hollywood film studio: old walls hung with curling posters, two original 1936 chandeliers, an antique buffet displaying desserts, fresh flowers in a pretty vase, a table or two on the sidewalk, and a gentle owner, M. Daumail, who has been here almost fifteen years . . . plenty of time to know all of his customers by name.

The Lyonnaise food is served à la carte for lunch and dinner, and there is a bargain lunch *formule*. The food choices run from A to almost Z, beginning with artichokes vinaigrette, escargots, and pâtés to Lyonnaise sausages, lamb, beef, and veal. The *tarte au chocolat* is my dessert of choice, though a scoop or two of Berthillon ice cream on a warm summer day is always welcome, and it's the only dessert not made here.

TELEPHONE
01-45-48-29-94

OPEN
Mon–Fri: lunch noon–2 P.M., dinner 7:30–10:30 P.M.

CLOSED
Sat–Sun; holidays, 2 weeks in Aug

RESERVATIONS
Preferred

CREDIT CARDS
MC, V

À LA CARTE
190F (28.97€), BNC

PRIX FIXE
Lunch: 80F (12.20€), 2 courses, BNC

ENGLISH SPOKEN
Yes

COSI (7)
54, rue de Seine
Métro: Odéon, Mabillon

TELEPHONE
01-46-33-35-36
OPEN
Daily: noon–midnight,
continuous service
CLOSED
Dec 24–Jan 2, NAC
RESERVATIONS
Not taken
CREDIT CARDS
None
À LA CARTE
Sandwiches 25–50F (3.81–
7.62€), soups and salads 15–
30F (2.29–4.57€), desserts 25–
30F (3.81–4.57), BNC
PRIX FIXE
None
ENGLISH SPOKEN
Yes

Cosi is a chichi gourmet sandwich shop just off rue de Buci. Put together a delicious, hot, made-to-order-while-you-watch sandwich on warm bread, a glass of good wine, and classical opera music and you have Cosi, a fast-food concept in Paris that has caught on big-time, keeping the little spot continually busy and crowded. The idea was developed by a New Zealander who made violins in Italy, learned how to make bread there, then moved to Paris, adapted the bread recipe, and *voila!* It's Cosi. The colorful and tasty sandwiches are made with focaccia-style bread, cooked as you watch in a wood-fired oven, then filled while still hot with an ingenious combination of tasty ingredients. You pay according to the ingredients you select, which could be anything from chèvre and cucumbers to roasted eggplant, guacamole, tomatoes, salmon, chili, cole slaw vinaigrette, tuna, and roast beef. Your order is placed on a tray that you carry to an attractive upstairs dining room, where you eat surrounded by photos of famous opera stars while listening to their famous arias. In addition to the marvelous sandwiches, there are soups and salads served with bread on the side and desserts made with a thousand calories of butter and sugar . . . especially the chocolate treachery, otherwise known as chocolate cake. Slightly less sinful is the Italian gelato.

NOTE: Everything on the menu can be taken out.

FISH LA BOISSONNERIE (6)
69, rue de Seine
Métro: St-Germain-des-Prés, Odéon

TELEPHONE
01-43-54-34-69
OPEN
Tues–Sat: lunch noon–3 P.M.,
dinner 7–11 P.M.; Sun: dinner
7–11 P.M.
CLOSED
Sun lunch, Mon; NAC
RESERVATIONS
Essential
CREDIT CARDS
AE, MC, V
À LA CARTE
165F (25.15€), BNC
PRIX FIXE
None
ENGLISH SPOKEN
Yes

Drew Harré, who owns Cosi across the street (see above), and Juan Sanchez, who runs La Dernièr Goute, a great wine shop nearby (see "Shopping" in *Great Sleeps Paris*), have joined forces and opened Fish la Boissonnerie. You can't miss the building on rue de Seine—it is the one with the colorful mosaic tiles that date from the early twentieth century covering the entire front. The original lettering said *poissonnerie* because it used to be a fish shop, but Drew wanted it to be a place to eat fish *and* drink, so the *p* was changed to a *b*.

You consult the menu while sipping a glass of wine and munching on black radishes dipped in toasted sesame seeds. Naturally, the best order of the day will be one of the fresh fish catches. Otherwise, go for any of the four homemade pastas. I like to start the meal with a salad of bitter *roquette* mixed with dates and parmesan cheese slices or the basil-flavored shrimp. If pasta is your preference, consider the creamy risotto or the linguine with clams. For dessert, order the chocolate *tarte* with a ginger-pear sauce. Wines are all selected by Juan and feature weekly choices available by the glass or *pichet*.

GÉRARD MULOT (18)
76, rue de Seine
Métro: Odéon

A passion for French pastries can be satisfied at this beautiful shop, where a full range of traditional and sublime French sweets and baked goods are made each day with the freshest ingredients. In addition to the almost museum-quality *pâtisseries,* they have a magnificent selection of hot and cold dishes that can be packaged to go, making it a place to remember for a fast-food lunch. Why settle for a plebian ham-and-cheese baguette when you can sample fresh salmon or creamy pâté garnished with crudités, a savory herb quiche filled with chèvre and tomatoes, or wild mushrooms and a salad for just a little more money? The only seating is at a window counter, but on a warm day you can put together *le picnique* and enjoy it sitting on a park chair in the beautiful Luxembourg Gardens, only a few minutes away on foot.

TELEPHONE
01-43-26-85-77,
01-46-33-49-27

OPEN
Mon–Tues, Thur–Sun: 7 A.M.–8 P.M., continuous service

CLOSED
Wed; July 15–Aug 15

RESERVATIONS
Not taken

CREDIT CARDS
None

À LA CARTE
15–100F (2.29–15.24€), BNC

PRIX FIXE
None

ENGLISH SPOKEN
Very little

GUENMAÏ (5)
6, rue Cardinale
Métro: St-Germain-des-Prés, Mabillon

"What are all these fashion models, actors, and other attractive people doing milling around outside with plates of food in their hands?" I wondered the first time I strolled by this natural foods restaurant and shop. When I could get close enough to look in, I could see others sitting on tiny stools balancing plates on their knees, and still more standing behind the shop counter and sitting on the stairway. I knew that Guenmaï had to be offering something very good to attract such a crowd in a neighborhood known for having every type of restaurant imaginable. When I was finally served, my lunch was not only delicious and filling, it was reasonably priced. No one stands on ceremony here, and service can be distracted during the noon mob scene.

The food leans toward the macrobiotic and uses no butter, sugar, milk, or eggs. Limited amounts of fish are

TELEPHONE
01-43-26-03-24

OPEN
Mon–Sat: lunch noon–3:30 P.M.; shop 9 A.M.–8:30 P.M.

CLOSED
Sun; holidays, Aug

RESERVATIONS
Not accepted

CREDIT CARDS
V

À LA CARTE
70–100F (10.67–15.24€), BNC

PRIX FIXE
None

ENGLISH SPOKEN
Yes

served. The entirely à la carte menu features such creations as vegetable spring rolls, croquettes, *tartes,* and *plats du jour* based around grains, tofu, and seaweed. The daily *plat* comes with two proteins, two cereals, crudités, and pickles. There is also a nice array of freshly squeezed juices, *biologique* (organic) wines, and nonalcoholic beers. For the best selection and variety, because they do run out, arrive before the hungry herd . . . by 12:30 P.M. at the latest.

LA BASTIDE ODÉON (25)
7, rue Corneille, off place de l'Odéon
Métro: Odéon, Luxembourg

People always ask me about my favorite restaurants in Paris. I have many, and when La Bastide Odéon first opened a few years ago, it was definitely one of them. A table here put you in the middle of one of Paris' most talked about culinary successes. Unfortunately, time and success have not worn well.

The Provençal cooking from chef Gilles Ajuelos, whose credentials include working under Michel Rostang, is for the most part authentic, interesting, and delicious . . . and in the beginning there were very few misses. In fact, you could once point blindly to anything on the prix fixe menu and be pleased. However, on several recent visits, I found both the food and service to be uneven, and some of the combinations stretched the imagination to the breaking point. The artichoke *gratinée* with chèvre and a honey-lemon vinaigrette was wonderful, and so were the pieces of chunky bread served with foie gras and a warm lentil salad. Not so the raw salmon with an overly fishy anchovy sauce and the weird pumpkin soup that mixed mussels, sour cream, and caramel. What was the chef trying to do? Main dishes didn't raise my level of enthusiasm much further, especially not the greasy bacon and spare ribs sitting on a mound of cabbage and turnips or the lukewarm gnocchi tossed with snails, white beets, and garlic—eek! Desserts were good, but not outstanding. The best of the lot was the hot bitter chocolate cake with vanilla ice cream. Bottom line: If you are willing to take a chance and hope for the best . . . try it, and please let me know. I hope that La Bastide Odéon is soon back on track.

TELEPHONE
01-43-26-03-65
OPEN
Tues–Sat: lunch 12:30–2 P.M., dinner 7:30–10:30 P.M.
CLOSED
Mon, Sun; holidays, July or Aug (call to check)
RESERVATIONS
Essential
CREDIT CARDS
AE, MC, V
À LA CARTE
None
PRIX FIXE
Lunch and dinner: 152F (23.17€), 2 courses, 192F (29.27€), 3 courses, both BNC
ENGLISH SPOKEN
Yes

LA BOULE MICHE (12)
19, rue du Dragon
Métro: St-Germain-des-Prés, St-Sulpice

After you have been in Paris for a day or so, you realize it is almost impossible to walk more than a block without passing one or two *boulangeries* or *pâtisseries*. What is amazing is how they all manage to thrive, given the intense competition. It is clear that La Boule Miche has the formula for success down pat because since 1788 there has been a bakery at this address, and for the last fifty years it has been run by one very hardworking lady who never changes her measured pace or the stoic look on her face. My Paris flat was located around the corner from the bakery, so I had an opportunity to get to know it well. All day long the owner and her helpers serve a constant stream of customers eager for their delicious breads. From Monday to Saturday a special type is featured in addition to a dozen or more of the regular varieties. Bulk bread orders are also handled. Each morning one of the flour-dusted young bakers loads warm baguettes into the bicycle-wagon parked in front and pedals off to make his delivery rounds. It looks like something right out of *Oliver Twist*!

You can either take your purchase with you or eat here, nabbing one of the two mushroom-shaped black-covered perches along the mirror-backed brass bar or sitting on one of the nursery-school-size backless stools poised around two or three little tables, which spill onto the sidewalk in every type of weather except a driving rainstorm. There is a lunch special of a sandwich, pastry, and coffee that is a steal, as well as unusual sweet treats—all made here, of course—filling the front window.

TELEPHONE
01-42-22-77-12

OPEN
Mon–Sat: 7:30 A.M.–8 P.M., continuous service

CLOSED
Sun; major holidays, 15 days in Aug

RESERVATIONS
Not accepted

CREDIT CARDS
None

À LA CARTE
20–45F (3.05–6.86€), BC

PRIX FIXE
Lunch: 40F (6.10€), sandwich, pastry, and coffee

ENGLISH SPOKEN
No

LA LOZÈRE (11)
4, rue Hautefeuille
Métro: St-Michel

The menu is short, highlighting the cuisine from the rugged Lozère region of central France. Sitting at a wooden table extremely close to your neighbor, you will sample popular country hams, sausages, cheeses, omelettes, and hearty regional specialties. Once you are seated, a huge loaf of dark country bread is brought to your table for you to slice as much as you can eat. Go easy, there is much more to come . . . such as *tripoux Lozère* (mutton tripe cooked with white wine and tomatoes) or *La Maoucho* (a soul-food dish of cabbage and

TELEPHONE
01-43-54-26-64

OPEN
Tues–Sat: lunch noon–2 P.M., dinner 7:30–10 P.M.

CLOSED
Mon, Sun; holidays, Christmas week, Aug (dates vary)

RESERVATIONS
Essential

CREDIT CARDS
MC, V

À LA CARTE
140–160F (21.34–24.39€)
BNC

PRIX FIXE
Lunch: 95F (14.48€), 3 courses,
BNC; lunch and dinner: 130F
(19.82€), 160F (24.39€), both
4 courses and BNC

ENGLISH SPOKEN
Some

sausage baked with potatoes). There is also smoked trout and veal roasted with prunes. On Thursday nights, a line forms for La Lozère's potato specialty, *l'aligot,* a dish of creamy mashed potatoes mixed with melted *cantal* cheese and flavored with garlic. It makes heaven out of any meal it accompanies. At Thursday lunch, you can order it ahead if you are having one of the prix fixe menus, though for lunch there is a two-person minimum. Reservations are essential for Thursday night and strongly recommended other times.

NOTE: The restaurant doubles as a tourist bureau for the Lozère region and operates a boutique across the street selling handmade arts and crafts, preserves, and other gift items.

LA MARLOTTE ($, 27)
55, rue du Cherche-Midi
Métro: St-Placide

TELEPHONE
01-45-48-86-79

INTERNET
www.lamarlotte.com

OPEN
Mon–Fri: lunch noon–
2:30 P.M., dinner 8–11 P.M.;
Sat: dinner 8–11 P.M.

CLOSED
Sat lunch, Sun; holidays,
Aug 5–20

RESERVATIONS
Essential

CREDIT CARDS
AE, MC, V

À LA CARTE
185–200F (28.20–30.49€),
BNC

PRIX FIXE
None

ENGLISH SPOKEN
Yes

Dining at La Marlotte, adeptly run by Eric Roset, the owner, and Patrick Duclos, his chef, is a truly pleasurable experience. The setting—especially at night, with its subdued lighting, pretty provincial paintings, and formally clad, candlelit tables—is elegantly romantic and quietly discreet. The stylish guests have every table filled by 9 P.M., making reservations mandatory as far in advance as possible.

The cooking is the best kind: generous, fresh, and resolutely traditional. Regulars come often for the time-honored renditions of *tarte à l'oignon, escalope de foie gras,* a *salade délicieux* made with green beans and foie gras, and in spring, fat white asparagus dressed in a light vinaigrette. *Coq au vin, sole meunière, magret de canard de citron et au miel,* seasonally fresh fish simply grilled or sauced, and an out-of-this-world lemon tart that positively melts in your mouth are other all-time favorites.

LE BISTRO D'HENRI (15)
16, rue Princesse
Métro: Mabillon

TELEPHONE
01-46-33-51-12

OPEN
Mon–Sat: lunch noon–
2:30 P.M., dinner 7:30–
11:30 P.M.

CLOSED
Sun; Christmas, New Year's
Day, NAC

If you like Le Mâchon d'Henri (see page 138), chances are excellent you will like Le Bistro d'Henri, just around the corner and under the same management. The dining room, with its black-and-white tile floor, offers somewhat comfortable leatherette banquette seating, and the open kitchen gives it a larger feeling. Time-honored bistro fare is featured, with daily changing *entrées* and *plats du jour*. There is a formula menu of sorts for both lunch and dinner, with all the starters, main courses, and desserts identically priced. Featured wines of the month are extra, but you will still be able to eat a three-course meal here for a fraction of what it would set you back for three-star splendor. While neither of the Henri restaurants is a temple of gastronomic art, both provide a Parisian dining experience that includes friendly waiters and results in many satisfied guests.

RESERVATIONS
Advised

CREDIT CARDS
MC, V

À LA CARTE
170F (25.92€), BNC

PRIX FIXE
None

ENGLISH SPOKEN
Yes

LE CAMÉLÉON (32)
6, rue de Chevreuse
Métro: Vavin

Le Caméléon is the best kind of Parisian bistro: always noisy and packed, with all kinds of wonderful-smelling platters borne by fast-moving waiters. Another sure sign of quality is the mixed crowd: businesspeople next to rosy-cheeked elderly husbands and wives next to young couples busy falling in love. Everyone sits along banquettes or at marble-topped tables in the center of the room, digging into steaming plates of flavorful food.

The menu changes two or three times a year, but you can always count on *courgettes marinées au citron* (raw, grated zucchini in lemon marinade), a superb *salade des haricots verts et foie gras,* and rich lobster-filled ravioli. For the main course, the *blanquette de veau* is one of my favorites. During the winter the *confit de canard* (preserved duck) and braised beef cheeks in a red wine sauce with onions are dishes the faithful adore. For dessert any time of year, you must try the *fondant au poires,* a pear cake/tart made from a classic recipe, and usually available only for dinner. When it is served, the enormous slice seems too big to finish . . . but miraculously, everyone always finds a way.

TELEPHONE
01-43-20-63-43

OPEN
Mon–Fri: lunch noon–2 P.M., dinner 8–10:30 P.M.; Sat: dinner 8–10:30 P.M.

CLOSED
Sat lunch, Sun; holidays, 3 weeks in Aug (dates vary)

RESERVATIONS
Essential

CREDIT CARDS
AE, MC, V

À LA CARTE
185–200F (28.20–30.49€), BNC

PRIX FIXE
Lunch: 125F (19.06€), 2 courses, BNC

ENGLISH SPOKEN
Yes

L'ÉCLUSE GRANDS-AUGUSTINS (4)
15, quai des Grands-Augustins
Métro: St-Michel

L'Écluse was a trailblazer in popularizing wine bars in Paris, and it is still one of the best and most popular. Offering wines by the glass or the bottle, these trendy spots cater to those seeking food, wine, and uncomplicated meals served in agreeable surroundings by a low-key waitstaff. The final bill ultimately depends on the modesty or the majesty of the vintages you consume—as well as, of course, how much food you order.

TELEPHONE
01-46-33-58-74

OPEN
Daily: noon–1:30 A.M., continuous service

CLOSED
Christmas Eve and Christmas Day, NAC

RESERVATIONS
Not accepted

CREDIT CARDS
AE, DC, MC, V
À LA CARTE
80–165F (12.20–25.15€), BNC
PRIX FIXE
None
ENGLISH SPOKEN
Enough

Specializing in Bordeaux wines, all L'Écluse locations have the same menu right down to an identical *plat du jour,* but each wine bar features a different type of Bordeaux wine. The upmarket clientele drops by from noon until the wee hours to sample wines ranging from 25F for a simple glass to over 250F for a bottle of a *grand cru*. The food is selected to go well with the varieties of Bordeaux served. Featured are house terrines, foie gras, platters of *charcuterie,* beef tartare, grilled meats, assorted cheeses, a hot plate of the day, and their famous diet-destroying chocolate cake.

NOTE: There are other locations in the eighth, eleventh, and seventeenth arrondissements. Please see pages 177, 202, and 250.

LE MÂCHON D'HENRI (16)
8, rue Guisarde
Métro: Mabillon

TELEPHONE
01-43-29-08-70
OPEN
Daily: lunch noon–2:30 P.M., dinner 7–11:30 P.M.
CLOSED
Christmas, New Year's Day, NAC
RESERVATIONS
Essential
CREDIT CARDS
None
À LA CARTE
140–165F (21.34–25.15€), BNC
PRIX FIXE
None
ENGLISH SPOKEN
Yes

Le Mâchon d'Henri is a pocket-size bistro that seats twenty-six people sandwiched around twelve tiny marble-topped tables. It is the sort of place where an up-to-date clientele comes for a good, honest meal carefully prepared with seasonal ingredients.

The menu is written in very tiny lettering on a blackboard. The main courses are filling, so start with the fresh green beans or beets tossed in vinaigrette. If you like liver, it is required ordering here. Cooked to pink perfection, it is served with grilled onions and creamy potatoes. Another good selection is the rich beef stew with carrots. The lamb chops can be avoided with ease. Chocolate fans will relish every bite of the chocolate cake, and traditionalists will love the lemon *tarte* or fruit *clafoutis.* Good wines of the month are reasonably priced.

NOTE: Le Bistro d'Henri, around the corner at 16, rue Princesse (see page 136), is under the same management.

LE PETIT BISTRO (13)
2–3, rue du Sabot
Métro: St-Germain-des-Prés, St-Sulpice

TELEPHONE
01-45-48-16-65
OPEN
Mon–Fri: lunch noon–2:30 P.M., dinner 7–10:30 P.M.; Sat: dinner 7–10:30 P.M.
CLOSED
Sat lunch, Sun; holidays, Aug
RESERVATIONS
Preferred

No, it's hardly the *haute cuisine* of your dreams, but the food served at Le Petit Bistro could be encased in a shrine to everyday French cooking. It's a local spot where a cross section of regulars arrive for a filling feed at prices that allow many repeat visits . . . almost every night for some.

Bypass the à la carte and go for one of the weekly changing menus, which list almost everything on the à la carte menu anyway. The solid grandmotherly food starts you off with well-recognized dishes of terrines, warm goat cheese salad, oysters, fish soup, and escargots. Moving along, you will find *sole meunière,* lamb steaks, grilled beef . . . all garnished with *frites* unless you ask for a change of potatoes. If the omelette *Bretagne,* one of the house *plats du jour,* is listed, it is a real tour de force—a three-egg omelette filled with mushrooms, potatoes, tomatoes, and peppers and coupled with a salad, which is probably all you will manage. The desserts are not the restaurant's strong suit, especially not the glass of four lonely prunes soaking in some sort of liqueur. If you must, go for one of the red fruit gratins or the rum raisin ice cream. Drinkable house red or white wines come by the glass and in various sizes of pitchers.

CREDIT CARDS
MC, V

À LA CARTE
150F (22.87€), BNC

PRIX FIXE
Lunch and dinner: 70F (10.67€), 2 courses, BNC; 105F (16.01€), 3 courses, BC

ENGLISH SPOKEN
Yes

LE PETIT LUXEMBOURG (28)
29, rue de Vaugirard
Métro: St-Sulpice, St-Placide

It is a restaurant, a wine bar, and above all, a typical neighborhood hangout. Michel, the colorful patron, banters with the ageless, animated regulars and assorted café lizards lined up at the bar. His wife, Nicole, oversees the dining room while minding everyone's business and serving good wines with homey dishes that have been staples in French kitchens for years. The crunch is really on during the lunch hour, when it assumes its role as the neighborhood rendezvous.

The menu is wide-ranging and tries to cover too many bases. Forget the frills and stick with the specialties of the house: a tartine made on toasted *pain Poilâne, poulet Luxembourg* (chicken with rice and vegetables), *confit de canard,* and on Friday, *brandade de morue,* a flavorful dish that is better than it sounds. It's made with salt cod, garlic, and potatoes simmered in hot milk and cream and then puréed. There is quite a list of desserts, but only three should catch your attention: a slice of either the rich chocolate or orange cake or the *tarte Tatin,* if it is available.

TELEPHONE
01-42-22-12-22

OPEN
Mon–Sat: bar 10 A.M.–midnight, lunch 11 A.M.–2 P.M., dinner 7:30–11:30 P.M.

CLOSED
Sun; holidays, one week at Christmas, Aug

RESERVATIONS
Recommended, especially for lunch

CREDIT CARDS
MC, V

À LA CARTE
110–160F (16.77–24.39€), BNC

PRIX FIXE
None

ENGLISH SPOKEN
Generally

LE PETIT SAINT-BENOÎT (2)
4, rue St-Benoît
Métro: St-Germain-des-Prés

Le Petit Saint-Benoît is a marvelous bistro sitting smack in the heart of St-Germain-des-Prés that will celebrate its centennial in 2001. The interior is vintage Paris: brown walls aged by years of heavy cigarette

TELEPHONE
01-42-60-27-92

OPEN
Mon–Sat: lunch noon–2 P.M., dinner 7–10:30 P.M.

CLOSED
Sun; NAC

RESERVATIONS
Accepted for 4 or more

CREDIT CARDS
None

À LA CARTE
110–125F (16.77–19.06€),
BNC

PRIX FIXE
None

ENGLISH SPOKEN
Yes

smoke, brass hat racks, fresh white paper covering red tablecloths, and at times, a big, lazy dog crowding the busiest aisle. Outside, several hotly contested sidewalk tables offer front row seating for the passing parade. Motherly waitresses serve a cross section of intellectuals, BCBGs (*bon chic bon genre:* French yuppies), artists, and portly gentlemen with young companions.

The handwritten, mimeographed daily menu lists low-priced basics that are cooked to a T and served in portions worthy of lumberjacks. Start with a soothing vegetable soup, a plate of crisp radishes and sweet butter, or an avocado vinaigrette, and go on to a nourishing serving of roast chicken and mashed potatoes, liver with a bacon cream sauce, *petit salé* (salt pork with cabbage), or cold salmon. Top it all off with a pitcher of the house wine and a bowl of chocolate mousse. Lingering over a *café express,* you will no doubt begin to seriously consider moving to Paris.

LE PETIT VATEL (20)
5, rue Lobineau
Métro: Mabillon, Odéon

TELEPHONE
01-43-54-28-49

OPEN
Mon–Sat: lunch noon–3 P.M.,
dinner 7 P.M.–midnight

CLOSED
Sun; holidays, Aug (dates vary)

RESERVATIONS
Not necessary

CREDIT CARDS
MC, V

À LA CARTE
90–115F (13.72–17.53€), BNC

PRIX FIXE
Lunch: 75F (11.43€), 2 courses,
BC

ENGLISH SPOKEN
Yes

Le Petit Vatel continues to be a good choice for hardcore budgeteers. Everyone sits close together on rush-seated chairs or on stools at tables set with colorful plastics (from Ikea). The Mediterranean-influenced menu includes seasonal hot and cold soups, homemade terrines, a *plat du jour* that changes several times a week, and a vegetarian plate. Always available is the chef's own *pamboli,* which started out as an *entrée* but is now his most popular main course. It is two pieces of toasted whole-grain bread spread with olive oil and then covered with spiced tomatoes, spinach, ham, and a mound of melted cheese. It is a filling meal in itself and costs around 50F (7.62€). For dessert there is a choice of chocolate cake, fruit, ice cream, or *tomme crayeuse de Savoie,* a very special chalky cheese sent specially to Le Petit Vatel's owner, M. Sixte. Wines and ciders are sold by the glass, *pichet,* or bottle, with nothing costing over 100F (15.24€).

MARIAGE FRÈRES (3)
13, rue des Grands-Augustins
Métro: St-Michel

For a complete description, see Mariage Frères, page 97. All other information is the same.
TELEPHONE: 01-40-51-82-50

POILÂNE (23)
8, rue du Cherche-Midi
Métro: Sèvres-Babylone, St-Sulpice

With only slight exaggeration, if any at all, Poilâne says in its brochure, "In the memory of every Parisian diner, there is a slice of Poilâne bread. Its dense texture and rich taste make an event out of every meal."

But about the following, there is no question: *pain Poilâne* is synonymous with the finest bread Paris has to offer; in fact, it is considered France's most celebrated bread. In addition to this bakery, the famous bread is served in countless restaurants and available in many markets, by the slice and by the quarter, half, and whole loaf. The four-pound, round, thick-crusted sourdough country loaf is handmade from whole grain and stone-milled wheat flour that is seasoned with sea salt and raised without yeast or preservatives. Huge oak-fired ovens in the basement can bake up to forty-five loaves at once. The entire process from start to finish takes five hours, including three steps to raise the bread and one hour to bake it. In addition to the famous sourdough bread, a variety of other whole-grain loaves and melt-in-your-mouth butter cookies, called *punitions,* are sold daily in this bakery, which has a perpetual line winding out the door and down the street.

Thanks to modern computer technology and Federal Express, you do not need to be in Paris to have *pain Poilâne* on your dining table. It can be flown to the United States and delivered directly to your door, but brace yourself for the price . . . almost $40 per loaf! But if you slice it thinly, a loaf can last up to ten days, and if you are a Poilâne fan, it might be worth it to have it in your own kitchen, whether toasted with peanut butter, spread with pâté, or topped with your favorite ham and melted cheese. For details on shipping, send a fax or check the Website.

NOTE: There is a second location in the 15th arrondissement at 49, boulevard de Grenelle.

TELEPHONE
01-45-48-42-59,
01-44-39-20-94

FAX
01-45-44-99-80

EMAIL
commerce@poilane.fr

INTERNET
www.poilane.com/

OPEN
Mon–Sat: 7:15 A.M.–8:15 P.M.

CLOSED
Sun; NAC

RESERVATIONS
Not accepted

CREDIT CARDS
None

À LA CARTE
15–100F (2.29–15.24€), BNC

PRIX FIXE
None

ENGLISH SPOKEN
Yes

RESTAURANT DES BEAUX ARTS (1)
11, rue Bonaparte
Métro: St-Germain-des-Prés

If you want to know what student life used to be like in Paris, eat at Restaurant des Beaux Arts, one of the most famous canteens when the neighborhood was filled with starving artists, struggling students, and bohemian intellectuals. The dining rooms are busy and cramped

TELEPHONE
01-43-26-92-64

OPEN
Daily: lunch noon–2 P.M.,
dinner 7–10:45 P.M.

CLOSED
Christmas day, NAC

RESERVATIONS
Preferred

CREDIT CARDS
MC, V

À LA CARTE
150–170F (22.87–25.92€),
BNC

PRIX FIXE
Lunch: 75F (11.43€), 2 courses,
BNC; lunch and dinner: 105F
(16.01€), 3 courses, BNC;
children's menu: 55F (8.38€),
main course and dessert

ENGLISH SPOKEN
Yes

but not enough to discourage the faithful, who are more interested in filling rather than gourmet food. The best seating is on the main floor, where you get a view of the steaming pots in the open kitchen and of the murals painted by students from l'École Nationale des Beaux-Arts across the street. It is also air-conditioned, which should help diffuse the fog of cigarette smoke. Upstairs the mood is more relaxed but definitely not as much fun. Although not the cheap thrill it once was, the prix fixe menu is a decent buy considering the size of the portions. With a pitcher of wine or a mug of beer, you will probably get away with spending around 130F (19.82€). The à la carte offers little of interest to those determined to eat cheaply in Paris.

RESTAURANT DU LUXEMBOURG (29)
44, rue d'Assas, at rue de Fleurus
Métro: Notre-Dame-des-Champs, St-Placide

TELEPHONE
01-45-48-90-22

OPEN
Mon–Fri: lunch noon–2 P.M.,
dinner 7–9:30 P.M.; Sat: lunch
noon–2 P.M.

CLOSED
Sat dinner, Sun; holidays, Aug

RESERVATIONS
Advised

CREDIT CARDS
MC, V

À LA CARTE
145F (22.11€), BNC

PRIX FIXE
Lunch: 55–80F (8.38–12.20F),
garnished *plat du jour,* BNC

ENGLISH SPOKEN
Very little

The regulars who live in the neighborhood consider the Luxembourg to be an extension of their own homes, a place where they can always go for a dependable variety of fresh food at affordable prices. The friendly *patron,* Sylvain Pommerau, meets and greets everyone with warmth and good cheer. Unless you arrive right when they open, be prepared to wait up to an hour if you are without reservations, especially at lunch. The service is personable, even when it gets hectic. The decor is classic: walls covered with antique and reproduction posters, ceiling fans, the original tiled floors, and a bar to the right as you enter. For most visitors, it is a window on the day-to-day dining of middle-class Parisians.

The food is just as time-honored as the clientele. Snails, foie gras, terrines, salads, and smoked fish lead the way to prime portions of *confit de canard, bavette aux échalottes* (skirt steak with shallots), and *escalope de veau normande* (veal in cream sauce), all liberally garnished with *pommes frites.* Desserts aimed to please are centered around homemade *tartes,* fresh fruit, *île flottante* (puffs of egg whites floating in custard), and the usual ice creams and sorbets. The wine list is satisfying, with some pleasant alternatives to the basic house variety.

RISTORANTE DA ENZO (8)
12, rue du Dragon
Métro: St-Germain-des-Prés

Somehow this one has slipped by the other guidebooks, probably because it is buried in a sea of Left Bank gastronomic tourist traps. In all honesty, the inside of Ristorante da Enzo does look "touristy," especially the streetside dining room: beaded lights hang over tables set with bright orange table linens, which clash with the dated, velvet chair and banquette coverings. Even though it is windowless, the intimate room downstairs, with a painted arched ceiling, is more appealing. Wherever you sit, however, it won't change what arrives on your plate, and let me assure you that it will be good—wholesome Italian favorites that the Di Renzo family have been cooking and serving for years.

The pastas are rich and filling, never overpowered by heavy red sauces and gooey creams. All the required regulars we know and love make appearances: pasta with pesto, shrimp and garlic, lasagna, rigatoni, tortellini, and eggplant parmesan. Veal is the meat headliner, prepared with herbs, cheese, lemon, or tomatoes. All main courses are garnished with zucchini or pasta, or both if you can handle it. Just as in many *ristorantes* in Italy, gnocchi is always the Thursday special and you can count on fresh fish on Friday. Tiramisu and the chef's special hot apple *tarte* are the best dessert considerations. Inexpensive pitchers of Italian wine will complement any order.

TELEPHONE
01-42-22-84-87

OPEN
Mon–Sat: lunch noon–
2:30 P.M., dinner 7–11 P.M.

CLOSED
Sun; NAC

RESERVATIONS
Advised for dinner

CREDIT CARDS
MC, V

À LA CARTE
125–150F (19.06–22.87€),
BNC

PRIX FIXE
None

ENGLISH SPOKEN
Limited

WADJA (31)
10, rue de la Grande-Chaumière
Métro: Vavin

Wadja has an interesting history. From the thirties, during World War II, and for thirty-plus years afterward, it was called Chez Wadja and was run by two brothers and their sister. Very little ever changed, including the poignant collection of photos of the soldiers who ate here, the beat-up bistro tables in the dingy dining room, and the faded curtains at the window and on the door. The food stayed about the same, and so did the prices, which encouraged a loyal band of cheap-eating followers from all walks of life. Then in the early 1990s Chez Wadja shut its doors. Several owners tried to make a go of it, including one bizarre attempt at a Mexican restaurant. All failed until Denise Leguay took

TELEPHONE
01-46-33-02-02

OPEN
Mon: dinner 7:30–11 P.M.;
Tues–Sat: lunch noon–
2:30 P.M., dinner 7:30–11 P.M.

CLOSED
Mon lunch, Sun

RESERVATIONS
Essential

CREDIT CARDS
MC, V

À LA CARTE
200F (30.49€), BNC

PRIX FIXE
Lunch Tues–Fri: 89F (13.57€),
3 courses, BNC

charge, and now, with her talented chef, Didier Panisset, she has turned this into one of the favorite bistros in the area, not only for the food but for the warm and friendly atmosphere.

The interior retains its 1930s look, with closely spaced tables and the original tiled floor. The food consists of French specialties prepared with a light, modern touch. A simple green salad, a vegetable aspic with a watercress and roquefort dressing, or the leek pancakes served with a piece of thick grilled bacon are perfect beginnings for the filling plates to come. If you like slow-cooked lamb shanks, order the *gigot de sept heures,* which is served with tasty fried potatoes. The swordfish in a lime sauce is a more delicate choice. A more adventurous dish is the veal kidneys flavored with fresh basil. Desserts qualify as works of art . . . particularily the flaky macaroon and pastry shell filled with chocolate and a nutmeg-flavored mousse, or the flavorful poached pear surrounded by nougat ice cream.

Seventh Arrondissement

The right Paris zip code is 007, as it has been since the early 1700s when blue-blooded families fled Versailles and settled in this part of Paris. A sense of good living and a feeling of luxury pervade the streets of this *beau-quartier,* where fashionable people live and pay high rents and young chic meets old guard. The handsome tree-shaded avenues are lined with government offices, foreign embassies, beautiful shops, and lovely, small hotels. The seventh is also one of the most food-conscious, with outstanding restaurants and some of the city's best bakeries, *charcuteries, traiteurs, fromageries, pâtisseries,* and confectioners.

LEFT BANK
Champ-de-Mars, École Militaire, Eiffel Tower, Invalides (Napoléon's final resting place), Musée d'Orsay, Palais Bourbon (seat of the Assemblée Nationale), Rodin Museum, UNESCO

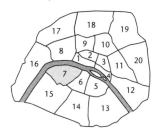

SEVENTH ARRONDISSEMENT RESTAURANTS

($) indicates a Big Splurge

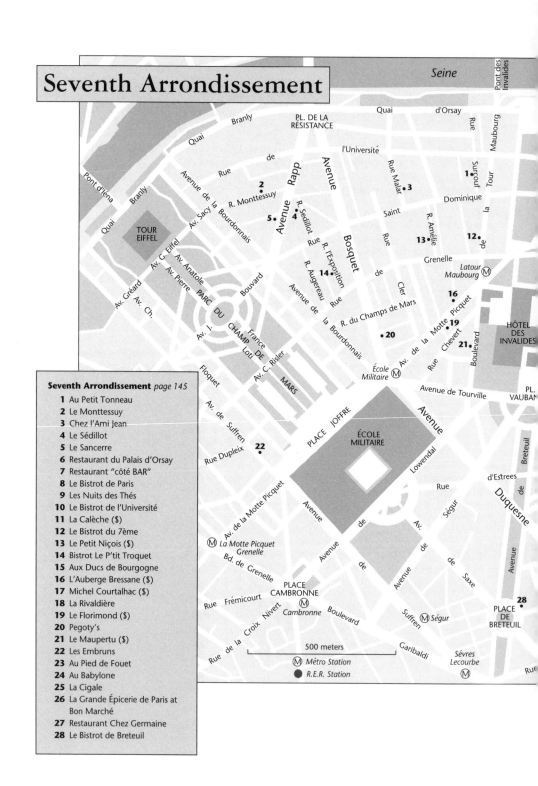

Seventh Arrondissement

AU BABYLONE (24)
13, rue de Babylone
Métro: Sèvres-Babylone

TELEPHONE
01-45-48-72-13

OPEN
Mon–Sat: lunch 11:30 A.M.–
2:30 P.M.

CLOSED
Sun; holidays, Aug

RESERVATIONS
Advised

CREDIT CARDS
None

À LA CARTE
110–120F (16.77–18.29€),
BNC

PRIX FIXE
100F (15.24€), 2 courses, BC

ENGLISH SPOKEN
Yes, ask for Marisa

It is easy to spot Au Babylone's dining habitués: they are the ones using red linen napkins; you will be using white paper ones. When the linen napkins are not in use, they are stored in their own numbered pigeon-hole cupboard at the back of the restaurant.

Time has left its mark on this nostalgic old bistro not far from the Bon Marché department store. Owner Mme. Garavana has been presiding over her flock for five decades and shows no sign of slowing down or changing anything in her yellow-walled establishment, still hung with the same mirrors, plates, and paintings as the day she opened. Serving only lunch, she sets seventy-six places, and they are always filled with a cross section of Parisians enjoying her *bonne maman* cuisine. These predictable standards are served in amazing portions: pâté and simple salads of grated carrots, cooked beets, or sliced cucumbers paired with dishes of roast veal, lamb, chicken, *andouillettes,* and roast chicken, with potato purée and a vegetable as the garnishes. Fish is served only on Friday. If it is on the menu on Saturday, *île flottante* is the dessert specialty everyone orders. Otherwise, order one of the fruit *tartes* or a slab of chocolate cake.

AU PETIT TONNEAU (1)
20, rue Surcouf
Métro: La-Tour-Maubourg

TELEPHONE
01-47-05-09-01

OPEN
Daily: lunch noon–3 P.M.,
dinner 7–11:30 P.M.

CLOSED
Aug, Christmas Eve

RESERVATIONS
Advised, especially for dinner

CREDIT CARDS
AE, DC, MC, V

À LA CARTE
200F (30.49€), BNC

PRIX FIXE
Lunch and dinner: 120F
(18.29€), 3 courses, BNC

ENGLISH SPOKEN
Yes

Ginette Boyer's Au Petit Tonneau is a true gem, and it should be a required stop for anyone who wants to scratch the surface of local life. Service is slow-paced, but the regulars don't mind, since time waiting is well-spent over another bottle of their favorite wine while getting caught up on the neighborhood news. The dining room is small and typical, with smoky walls, an old tile floor, mirrored bar, and assorted paintings. Service and linen-covered tables are correct.

Ginette, a natural-born cook, was taught the basics by her grandmother. Her wonderful food is a lesson in superb simplicity, using only the best fresh ingredients, which she personally selects and buys. How do I know? Because I was lucky enough to go with her several times, along with her dog, Wattie, before the crack of dawn to Rungis, the wholesale food market on the edge of Paris. What a trip! It is not for the squeamish or those who blanch at the thought of enormous warehouses filled with row upon row of hanging animal parts, skinned heads, bins of toes, tails, and tongues, icy-cold fowl storage halls, or pungent fish pavilions—all viewed way before breakfast. However, the food enthusiast will be rewarded with a peek at the largest, most all-encompassing food market in Europe. It is a visit you will never forget, if you are lucky enough to have the opportunity to go. Unfortunately, this food mecca is open only to people in the trade or by special arrangement.

What to order at Au Petit Tonneau? Find out what is fresh from the market and have that. Ginette has a way with fresh fish (especially Scottish salmon), turns out a perfect *blanquette de veau*, prepares the creamiest omelette you will eat in Paris, and creates a chicken liver terrine and velvety foie gras to remember. Her *tarte Tatin* (caramelized apple tart) ignores any dietary constraints, especially when you pile on the crème fraîche served on the side. Or, if you prefer a fresh fruit *clafoutis*, hers is heavenly.

Eating a meal here makes you feel you have entered a house of plenty, not only for the food we usually only dream of, but for the friendly atmosphere and genuine welcome extended to everyone by Ginette, her daughter, AnneMarie, and Odile, her dedicated and pleasant helper. Before you leave, Ginette, wearing her tall chef's hat and white coat, will come out of her tiny kitchen into the dining room to meet you. She is modest yet generous, with a heart of gold. She likes nothing better than to share her food with an appreciative audience. When you go, don't forget to say hello for me, and please check on Wattie, her big black cat Noee, and the newest member of her animal menagerie, Titou, a stray white cat who Ginette says is "amusing, but completely crazy," but who obviously had enough good sense to stop at Ginette's door.

AU PIED DE FOUET (23)
45, rue de Babylone
Métro: Sèvres-Babylone, Vaneau

This noisy, crowded neighborhood gathering spot draws colorful regulars week in and week out for its belt-popping meals. The restaurant is two hundred years old, and believe me, not much has been done to it in that time. The walls are peeling artfully, the coat hooks could use some polishing, and the minuscule kitchen is an

TELEPHONE
01-47-05-12-27

OPEN
Mon–Fri: lunch noon–2:30 P.M., dinner 7–9:30 P.M.; Sat: lunch noon–2:30 P.M.

CLOSED
Sat dinner, Sun; holidays, Aug, Dec 25–Jan 1

RESERVATIONS
Not taken
CREDIT CARDS
None
À LA CARTE
85–100F (12.96–15.24€), BNC
PRIX FIXE
None
ENGLISH SPOKEN
Yes

original. You definitely want to sit downstairs at one of the tables covered with red-and-white-checked bistro cloths. Upstairs is perilous quarters for anyone over five feet tall.

Lunch and dinner offer routine sustenance: grated carrot or cabbage salad, the time-worn *entrée oeuf dur mayonnaise, confit de canard* with mashed spuds, and a daily changing *plat du jour* and fresh fish. If you are committed to desserts, pick the orange meringue tart, or as my dining neighbor wisely confided to me, "anything made by Monique." Coffee is only served standing at the zinc bar, so that they can free the tables faster for the next diners.

AUX DUCS DE BOURGOGNE (15)
30, rue de Bourgogne
Métro: Varenne

TELEPHONE
01-45-51-32-48
OPEN
Mon–Fri: lunch 11 A.M.–
3:30 P.M.
CLOSED
Sat–Sun; holidays, Aug
RESERVATIONS
Not taken
CREDIT CARDS
MC, V (100F, 15.24€,
minimum)
À LA CARTE
95–120F (14.48–18.29€), BNC
PRIX FIXE
60F (9.15€), 3 courses, BC
ENGLISH SPOKEN
Yes, with English menu

There is a new name and new owner, but the smells are still tantalizing and the servings generous at this handkerchief-size *crêperie,* with its cozy kitchen and converted-parlor atmosphere. Open only during the week for lunch, it fills up quickly with people from the nearby French ministries and the Musée d'Orsay, often leaving some waiting outside for a seat.

The menu lists large salads and every mouthwatering buckwheat crêpe you can think of—and probably some you never imagined. The selections are divided into two categories: *Les Classiques* and *Les Spécialties.* I recommend bypassing the run-of-the mill *Classiques* and heading straight for any of the twenty-one *Spécialités* or the *crêpe du semaine.* Depending on your level of hunger and sense of adventure, you can have everything from the *Touraine* (filled with salad, *chèvre chaud,* and olives), the *Popeye* (spinach, eggs, and emmental and cream cheese), and the *Assemblée* (filled with chitterlings, potatoes, crème fraîche, and strong mustard) to the *Paysanne* (a mixture of eggs, bacon, onions, melted cheese, and cream). Saving room for a sweet ending is not difficult when you know the dessert crêpes include the *Mendiante* (with chocolate, almonds, raisins, and walnuts) and the *Flambée*—with Grand Marnier, rum, or Calvados.

NOTE: Orders can be packed to go and receive a 10 percent discount.

BISTROT LE P'TIT TROQUET (14)
28, rue de l'Exposition
Métro: École-Militaire

Bistrot Le P'tit Troquet continually makes my short list of favorite restaurants not to miss whenever I am in Paris. Judging from what many readers have written to me—including such compliments as, "Every course was a treat for the palate and the eyes," and "We should have saved the best for last . . . dining here has spoiled us for all that followed"—everyone seems to agree.

Inside, marble-topped bistro tables with linen cloths and vases of dried flowers fill two small rooms imaginatively decorated with assorted paintings, posters, fringed lamps, and flea-market memorabilia from the 1930s. The entire effect is one of comfortable and quiet intimacy. The food is all purchased and prepared by Patrick Vessière and nicely served by his delightful wife, Dominique. Patrick insists on smoking his own duck and salmon, making his own confits, pâtés, and terrines, baking all the breads, and churning his own ice creams. When you consider the fine quality his food represents, the price tags are low. Depending on the time of year, you might start with a cold avocado and chicken liver pâté surrounded by fresh tomato sauce or a colorful summer salad filled with a mélange of fruits and vegetables. Patrick's *côte de veau, lapin à la moutarde, confit de canard,* and perfectly pink lamb are just a few of the possibilities awaiting you. Of course, no self-respecting diner would forget dessert, and you should not pass up this opportunity to indulge in his expertly prepared crème brûlée, nougat ice cream, or fine pastries filled with the best fruits from the market. The wine list is as wonderful as the food. It features wines from small wineries throughout France and small *crus* from vintage years. After dinner, coffee arrives with a plate of tiny meringue cookies, winding up a leisurely Parisian meal you will long remember.

TELEPHONE
01-47-05-80-39

OPEN
Mon: dinner 7–10:30 P.M.;
Tues–Sat: lunch noon–2 P.M.,
dinner 7–10:30 P.M.

CLOSED
Mon lunch, Sun; holidays, first 3 weeks of Aug, week between Christmas and New Year's

RESERVATIONS
Essential

CREDIT CARDS
MC, V

À LA CARTE
Entrées 44F (6.71€), *plats* 95F (14.48€), desserts 39F (5.95€)

PRIX FIXE
Lunch and dinner: 165F (25.15€), 3 courses, BNC

ENGLISH SPOKEN
Yes

CHEZ L'AMI JEAN (3)
27, rue Malar
Métro: La-Tour-Maubourg

TELEPHONE
01-47-05-86-89
OPEN
Mon–Sat: lunch noon–3 P.M.,
dinner 7–10:30 P.M.
CLOSED
Sun; NAC
RESERVATIONS
Suggested
CREDIT CARDS
MC, V
À LA CARTE
180–200F (27.44–30.49€),
BNC
PRIX FIXE
Lunch and dinner (until 8 P.M.):
100F (15.24€), 3 courses, BNC
ENGLISH SPOKEN
Sometimes

There has been a Basque restaurant on this site since 1931. The current owner, M. Pagueguy, has been running the place for thirty years and represents the third generation of owners, all from the same Basque village. True to its origins, it has a rough-and-tumble, sports atmosphere, catering to burly, red-faced regulars who belly up to the bar in the sawdust-strewn entry. For them, Chez l'Ami Jean is a symbol of their Basque roots, a place where all is right in the world . . . no matter what may be going on in the rest of it. Most of them look like they eat here every day, filling up on overflowing plates of liver and bacon, *poulet basquaise,* sausage and potatoes, or the chef's own *coq au vin.* Don't worry . . . there are lots of other more dietetically correct choices, starting with a quartet of salads, a handful of omelettes, trout fixed two ways, lamb, steak, and several duck dishes. But there is no question about the ending: *gâteau Basque* should be your dessert of choice.

LA CALÈCHE ($, 11)
8, rue de Lille, at rue des Saints-Pères
Métro: Rue du Bac

TELEPHONE
01-42-60-24-76
OPEN
Mon–Fri: lunch noon–
2:30 P.M., dinner 7–10:30 P.M.
CLOSED
Sat–Sun; holidays, Dec 24–Jan
4, last 3 weeks in Aug
RESERVATIONS
Advised
CREDIT CARDS
AE, MC, V
À LA CARTE
225F (34.30€), BNC
PRIX FIXE
Lunch: 89F (13.57€), *plat du
jour* and wine; lunch and
dinner: 100F (15.24€), 130F
(19.82€), and 175F (26.68€),
all 3 courses and BNC
ENGLISH SPOKEN
Yes

Dignified ambience and excellent quality-to-value food are two good reasons to book a table at La Calèche, which has been owned for over a quarter century by M. and Mme. Pouget. The neighborhood bespeaks old money and position and the regulars mirror that image. As you enter the restaurant, look to your left to see framed pictures of several *calèches,* or carriages.

The prix fixe menus and the à la carte menu are designed to please a variety of tastes and inspire repeat visits. Fresh bread, sweet butter, and olives in a little bowl arrive as soon as you are seated. I like to begin with the *salade des gourmets,* which is artichoke hearts, fresh green beans, and foie gras on a bed of perfectly dressed greens. The salmon crêpes, served bubbling hot in their own dish, is another study in simple elegance. Depending on the season, you might find veal served with wild mushrooms, noisettes of lamb flavored with tarragon, or fresh pasta tossed with *morilles* and ham. Desserts are a must, especially the chocolate *charlotte* and the *feuillantine aux poire et chocolat.*

LA CIGALE (25)
11 bis, rue Chomel
Métro: Sèvres-Babylone

Arrive early and you will miss the French experience—when the faithful arrive amid a shower of hugs and kisses, even from the chef, Gérard Idoux, who learned his way around the kitchen while working at Ledoyen. The blackboard menu lists a balanced selection of daily specials, which of course you should pay attention to, but please, not at the cost of missing one of Idoux's wonderful monthly changing savory and sweet soufflés. While you may not want a three-course dinner featuring only soufflés, do consider devoting at least one course to these ethereal clouds. On a recent visit, I enjoyed the asparagus and chive soufflé as my main course, with an interesting dish of vegetable ravioli to start. For dessert, I succumbed to the *soufflé aux fruits rouges,* which tasted the way beautiful roses smell. If you are going to be in Paris for a while, be sure to check the back of the menu to see what the special soufflés will be for the following month.

TELEPHONE
01-45-48-87-87

OPEN
Mon–Fri: lunch noon–2:30 P.M., dinner 7:30–11:30 P.M.; Sat: dinner 7:30–11:30 P.M.

CLOSED
Sat lunch, Sun; NAC

RESERVATIONS
Essential

CREDIT CARDS
MC, V

À LA CARTE
180F (27.44€), BNC

PRIX FIXE
None

ENGLISH SPOKEN
Yes

LA GRANDE ÉPICERIE DE PARIS
AT BON MARCHÉ (26)
38, rue de Sèvres (main floor)
Métro: Sèvres-Babylone

Close your eyes and think of a supermarket in heaven; open them, and you will be in La Grande Épicerie de Paris . . . the Left Bank's answer to Fauchon (see page 172). Even if you have no intention of buying anything, a visit to this Paris market (situated inside the Bon Marché department store) is an interesting break from the usual, almost mandatory, sightseeing and museum-going. Take a few minutes and wander up and down the aisles admiring the magnificent produce, cheeses, and wines, the *pâtisserie* and *boucherie* counters, and every kind of canned, bottled, or packaged food on the planet. There is even an American section if you are suffering withdrawal pangs. If you are planning to put together a picnic, this is the perfect place to create one for the record books.

TELEPHONE
01-44-39-80-00; customer service: 01-44-39-82-80

OPEN
Mon–Sat: 8:30 A.M.–9 P.M.

CLOSED
Sun; major holidays, NAC

CREDIT CARDS
MC, V

ENGLISH SPOKEN
Depends on who serves you

LA RIVALDIÈRE (18)
1, rue St-Simon
Métro: Rue du Bac

TELEPHONE
01-45-48-53-96

OPEN
Mon–Fri: lunch noon–
2:30 P.M., dinner 7:15–
10:30 P.M.; Sat: dinner
7:15–10:30 P.M.

CLOSED
Sat lunch, Sun; NAC

RESERVATIONS
Advised

CREDIT CARDS
MC, V

À LA CARTE
185F (28.20€), BNC

PRIX FIXE
Lunch and dinner: 120F
(18.29€), 3 courses, BNC

ENGLISH SPOKEN
Yes

The two satisfied Parisian diners sitting next to me said, "This is great. We eat here all the time." After just one meal, I knew why and returned as often as possible.

The set menu is hard to beat. For both lunch and dinner, this daily changing menu offers three courses for under $20, which is cheaper than a sandwich, beer, and coffee would be in an expensive brasserie along some of the more well-known Parisian tourist beats. In addition to traditional bistro food, which is prepared with care, and above-average wines, including monthly featured vintages, there are several other things to like about La Rivaldière. First, the yellow walls bordered with grapes remind you that the owner is serious about his wines. The red velvet banquettes promote comfort, and the photo and trophies of Gaspar, the owner's prize-winning long-haired weimaraner dog, add just the right Gallic touch. (Because Gaspar is both a French and German champion dog, he must adhere to a special diet, which doesn't include table tidbits, so you won't see him in the restaurant until about 3 P.M., when most of the lunch crowd is gone.) I also like the cast of businesspeople at lunch and the prim, frugal diners at dinner, who tuck in to such classics as chicken liver terrine, haddock salad, creamy winter soups, liver in a strawberry vinegar sauce, duck *à l'orange*, veal with *gratin dauphinois* (creamy potatoes), and *fromage blanc* or smooth chocolate pudding for dessert.

L'AUBERGE BRESSANE ($, 16)
16, avenue de la Motte-Picquet
Métro: La-Tour-Maubourg

TELEPHONE
01-47-05-98-37

OPEN
Mon–Fri, Sun: lunch noon–
2:30 P.M., dinner 8–11 P.M.;
Sat dinner 8–11 P.M.

CLOSED
Sat lunch; Aug 5–22

RESERVATIONS
Essential

CREDIT CARDS
AE, MC, V

À LA CARTE
200–225F (30.49–34.30€),
BNC

If it's a restaurant with a Parisian atmosphere you are after, they don't come any better or more packed than the wood-paneled L'Auberge Bressane, which a well-heeled crowd has made their own. At lunchtime, men in suits and women in black skirts predominate. In the evening, the dinner trade attracts a more jovial group, who come for a night of eating and drinking and smoking—not just cigarettes but cigars as well. To avoid the brunt of the haze, request a booth toward the front, or if it is warm enough, on the small protected terrace in front.

The loyalists know to base their meal around at least one of the ethereal soufflés, which literally melt in your mouth, especially the deep dark chocolate puff that tastes like a bar of Belgian chocolate. Beautifully presented, pleasing servings of salads piled high with fresh green beans and mushrooms, marinated raw salmon served with herring and warm potatoes, roast chèvre cheese resting atop roasted red peppers, chicken in creamy morel mushroom sauce or cooked in wine, and meaty versions of kidneys and veal liver and seasonal fresh fish are only a few of the rich dishes awaiting you at this wonderful dining address near Les Invalides.

PRIX FIXE
Lunch: 99F (15.09€), 1 course, 130F (19.82€), 2 courses, 150F (22.87€) 3 courses, all BC

ENGLISH SPOKEN
Yes

LE BISTROT DE BRETEUIL (28)
3, place de Breteuil
Métro: Duroc

Le Bistrot de Breteuil has what it takes to keep the respect of discriminating Parisian diners: great atmosphere, attentive service, reasonable prices, and reliable food . . . every time. Located not too far from Les Invalides (the final resting place of Napoléon), the restaurant has one of the most beautiful dining terraces in Paris. Wrapped around an entire corner of the place de Breteuil, and in almost full view of the Eiffel Tower, the open and airy glassed-in site hosts a *branché* crowd who make elegance look easy. The tables are beautifully set with heavy white linens and fresh flowers, and patrons are served with precision and aplomb by teams of traditionally outfitted waiters.

TELEPHONE
01-45-67-07-27

OPEN
Daily: lunch noon–2:30 P.M., dinner 7:15–10:30 P.M.

CLOSED
Never

RESERVATIONS
Advised

CREDIT CARDS
AE, MC, V

À LA CARTE
None

PRIX FIXE
Lunch and dinner: 182F (27.75€), 3 courses, kir, wine, and coffee

ENGLISH SPOKEN
Yes

There is only a prix fixe menu, which includes a kir served with a bowl of olives and at least eight seasonal choices for the *entrée, plat,* and dessert. A half bottle of house wine and after-dinner coffee is included for each person. Good *entrée* bets are the dozen Burgundy snails in garlic butter, fresh oysters, duck foie gras, and smoked Norwegian salmon. For the main course, I love the tender rack of lamb, *magret de canard,* or the veal kidneys with morel mushroom sauce and fresh pasta. For dessert, who wouldn't relish either the flaming crêpes Grand Marnier, the warm apple tart spiked with Calvados, or the dark chocolate fondant surrounded by a coffee custard sauce? By Paris standards, Le Bistot de Breteuil is on the A list, so plan accordingly and don't consider arriving without reservations.

NOTE: There is a nonsmoking section. If you go for Saturday lunch, allow time before you eat to walk through the street *marché* along avenue de Breteuil. It's one of the best.

LE BISTROT DE L'UNIVERSITÉ (10)

TELEPHONE
01-42-61-26-64

OPEN
Mon–Fri: lunch noon–
2:30 P.M., dinner 8–10:30 P.M.

CLOSED
Sat–Sun; holidays, Aug

RESERVATIONS
Advised, especially at lunch

CREDIT CARDS
MC, V

À LA CARTE
150–170F (22.87–25.92€),
BNC

PRIX FIXE
Lunch: 72–82F (10.98–
12.50€), *plat du jour,* BNC

ENGLISH SPOKEN
Limited

40, rue de l'Université (between rue de Beaune and rue du Bac)
Métro: Rue du Bac

As you walk down rue de l'Université between rue de Beaune and rue du Bac, look for No. 40 with its bright red exterior and a chalkboard hanging in the window listing the daily menu. At noon, the narrow, orange room is packed solid and rings with the satisfied buzz of people eating well. The simple, warming fare might start off with a lentil soup, a green salad dressed in a lemon herb vinaigrette, or *oeufs en meurette* (poached eggs in a bacon-and-onion-flavored red wine sauce). Dishes piled with roast chicken, sausage served with sautéed potatoes, and a bowl of *fromage blanc* with raspberry sauce pay homage to the classic bistro cooking we all love.

LE BISTROT DE PARIS (8)

TELEPHONE
01-42-61-16-83,
01-42-61-15-84

INTERNET
www.le-bistrot-de-paris.fr

OPEN
Daily: lunch noon–2:30 P.M.,
dinner 7–11 P.M.

CLOSED
Never

RESERVATIONS
Advised

CREDIT CARDS
AE, MC, V

À LA CARTE
None

PRIX FIXE
Lunch: 95F (14.48€), salad and
any main course, BC; lunch and
dinner: 169F (25.76€), 3
courses, BC

ENGLISH SPOKEN
Yes, and English menu

33, rue de Lille
Métro: Rue du Bac

The sleek bistro decor by Slavic, a well-known interior designer, surrounds the smartly dressed diners with mirrors, brass globe lights, a bar along the back, and starched white linen–covered tables. Busy during the week for lunch, it smooths out in the evening, and the cast changes from suits and ties to turtlenecks and slacks. Service is polite and helpful, and the food holds no unpleasant surprises. Both the seasonally correct two-course lunch menu and the three-course lunch and dinner menu provide eight or nine selections. On a cold winter day, start with the vegetable soup flavored with country bacon or the crab-and-cauliflower flan. Next, there could be plates of sweet-and-sour pork spare ribs, a casserole of slow-cooked lamb and kidney beans, or a veal chop with macaroni and cheese. If chocolate is your passion . . . go for the dark chocolate torte with a pistachio and caramel sauce. Otherwise, the *tarte Tatin* piled with crème fraîche is hard to beat.

LE BISTROT DU 7ÈME (12)

TELEPHONE
01-45-51-93-08

OPEN
Mon–Fri: lunch noon–
2:30 P.M., dinner 7–11 P.M.;
Sat–Sun: dinner 7–11 P.M.

56, boulevard de La-Tour-Maubourg
Métro: La-Tour-Maubourg

"This meal is worth the price of your book!" exclaimed my dining companions. Indeed, M. and Mme. Beauvellet's restaurant is always consistent, and above all, it offers great value for your money. For under $14 for a three-course lunch and less than $20 for dinner, your choices include pâtés; smoked salmon; tomato, basil, and mozzarella salad; herring fillets with warm potatoes; and salads topped with chicken livers. Main courses tempt with *confit de canard,* veal in a mushroom cream sauce, grilled sausage, fresh salmon, poached haddock, and the daily special. Ice cream and sorbets dominate the desserts. Reasonable wines allow you to stay happy during the dinner service, which can be somewhat slow when it gets busy.

CLOSED
Sat–Sun lunch; one week at Christmas, 15 days in Aug (dates vary)

RESERVATIONS
Essential

CREDIT CARDS
MC, V

À LA CARTE
135–165F (20.58–25.15€), BNC

PRIX FIXE
Lunch: 70F (10.67€), 2 courses, 80F (12.20€), 3 courses, both BNC; dinner: 100F (15.24€), 3 courses, BNC

ENGLISH SPOKEN
Yes, and menu in English

LE FLORIMOND ($, 19)
19, avenue de la Motte-Picquet
Métro: Ècole-Militaire

White linens in a burgundy interior set off by lacy window curtains and a small sidewalk terrace form the background for enjoyable dining at Le Florimond, Pascal Guillaumin's twenty-eight-seat restaurant not too far from the Eiffel Tower. People in the neighborhood eat here, hotels listed in *Great Sleeps Paris* recommend it, and after one meal, you, too, are bound to become a fan. It is the perfect choice if you are looking for something geared for a little romance or some serious conversation.

Le Florimond has both seasonal and daily changing menus of delicious pleasures derived from creatively updated humble ingredients. In addition, there are some dishes you can always count on, such as the lobster ravioli to start, followed by a fresh fish, a *plat du jour,* or Guillaumin's grandmother's recipe for slow-cooked cabbage stuffed with pork, onions, and herbs. Desserts will leave you with sweet memories, especially the brown-sugar-crusted crème brûlée or the vanilla *mille-feuille.* Since all these dishes are available on the 168F (25.61€) lunch and dinner prix fixe menu, there is no need to stray into the higher priced à la carte territory.

TELEPHONE
01-45-55-40-38

OPEN
Mon–Fri: lunch noon–2:30 P.M., dinner 7–10 P.M.; Sat: dinner 7–10 P.M.

CLOSED
Sat lunch, Sun; major holidays, Aug, several days at Christmas

RESERVATIONS
Advised

CREDIT CARDS
MC, V

À LA CARTE
200–210F (30.49–32.01€), BNC

PRIX FIXE
Lunch Mon–Fri and dinner Mon–Thurs: 110F (16.77€), 2 courses, BNC; lunch and dinner daily: 168F (25.61€), 3 courses, BNC

ENGLISH SPOKEN
Yes

LE MAUPERTU ($, 21)
94, boulevard de La-Tour-Maubourg
Métro: La-Tour-Maubourg, Ècole-Militaire

At another restaurant not too far away, I knew even before the arrival of my main course that it was destined for the pile of rejects. Then as I spoke to two diners

TELEPHONE
01-45-51-37-96

OPEN
Mon–Fri: lunch noon–2:30 P.M., dinner 7–10 P.M.

CLOSED
Sat–Sun; Aug 10–31

RESERVATIONS
Advised

CREDIT CARDS
MC, V

À LA CARTE
225–250F (34.30–38.11€),
BNC

PRIX FIXE
Lunch and dinner Mon–Fri
and holidays: 150F (22.87€),
3 courses, BNC

ENGLISH SPOKEN
Yes, and menu in English

sitting next to me, they asked if I had been to Le Maupertu, not far away. "Sophie Canton and Alain Deguest know how to keep their customers happily returning on a regular basis. Alain does it with the food . . . Sophie with her affable, charming attention to each guest," they said. Of course, I had to try it, and as a result, I can now recommend Le Maupertu to you. I hope you will be as pleased with it as I continually have been.

The setting, especially at night, couldn't be more beautiful, with floor-length windows and a small terrace overlooking the beautifully lighted dome of Les Invalides. By all means, reserve one of these window tables under the glass roof and you will know what I mean. The presentation of the remarkable, weekly changing prix fixe menu is exceptional, and the portions are balanced to allow you to enjoy three courses without feeling stuffed. The food is all seasonal, and in the early spring, you may see such starters as a *feuilleté de petits légumes au coriandre* (a flaky pastry layered with coriander-scented vegetables), warm sausage with potatoes and celery heart, or ratatouille with a poached egg. The veal scallops surrounded by pasta lightly dressed with tomatoes and the beef in red wine sauce are even more winning food combinations. At the end, a generous cheese board is brought to your table, or you can order a velvety chocolate mousse, *baba au rhum* with whipped cream, or an assortment of ice creams or sorbets served with a Florentine cookie. The monthly featured wines are good buys and are available by the glass, pitcher, or bottle.

LE MONTTESSUY (2)
4, rue de Monttessuy
Métro: Pont de l'Alma

Lacy window curtains, red-and-white-checked tablecloths and napkins, and rather rustic surroundings set the theme for this friendly pick in the tony seventh. If you can snag a table on the narrow pavement, you will feel you can almost reach out and touch the Eiffel Tower.

Always be sure to arrive with a good appetite because the Lyonnaise food is far from dainty in portions or structure. The set menu covers all the bases, starting with a salad filled with bacon and croutons and a poached egg on top, warm herbed pork pâté, and snails served with mushrooms in a flaky pastry. The size and heartiness of these *entrées* raises the question of which main course should follow, especially when your choices include fat Lyonnaise sausages served with lightly sautéed

TELEPHONE
01-45-55-01-90

OPEN
Mon–Fri: lunch noon–
2:30 P.M., dinner 7–10:30 P.M.;
Sat: dinner 7–10:30 P.M.

CLOSED
Sat lunch, Sun; Aug (dates vary)

RESERVATIONS
Suggested

CREDIT CARDS
MC, V

À LA CARTE
190F (28.97€), BNC

potatoes (and plenty of them), calf's liver cooked in garlic and parsley butter and served with a potato gratin, rack of lamb with long-cooked beans, and a steak covered in cheese sauce and served with mashed potatoes. Desserts? I have never had room to even consider them. Thank goodness they all seem dull.

LE PETIT NIÇOIS ($, 13)
10, rue Amélie
Métro: La-Tour-Maubourg

Le Petit Niçois is a tiny, two-level restaurant that is filled to the brim with a noisy, mixed crowd. If you want meat, delicate soufflés, or nouvelle cuisine, look elsewhere. The specialty here is fish, fish, and more fish. Come here for perfectly grilled jumbo shrimp or sardines, fresh lobster, an exquisitely poached piece of turbot, bouillabaisse, and paella (the last two require thirty minutes). To start, there are several tempting appetizers, but the hands-down winner is the *beignets aubergines* (eggplant fritters). The desserts always look good, but after the gargantuan main course and starter, no one has much room for anything more than a cool sorbet.

PRIX FIXE
Lunch: 79F (12.04€), 2 courses, 97F (14.79€), 3 courses, both BNC; dinner: 160F (24.39€), 3 courses, BNC

ENGLISH SPOKEN
Yes

TELEPHONE
01-45-51-83-65

OPEN
Daily: lunch noon–2:30 P.M., dinner 7–10:30 P.M.

CLOSED
Aug

RESERVATIONS
Advised on weekends

CREDIT CARDS
AE, MC, V

À LA CARTE
225–250F (34.30–38.11€), BNC

PRIX FIXE
Lunch Mon–Sat: 100F (15.24€), 2 courses, BNC; lunch and dinner daily: 168F (25.61), 3 courses (includes bouillabaisse and paella), BNC

ENGLISH SPOKEN
Yes, with English menu

LE SANCERRE (5)
22, avenue Rapp
Métro: Pont de l'Alma, École-Militaire

The only thing that has changed since the first time I ate here in 1977 is that the back room, with a real fireplace that is lit during the winter, is now designated for nonsmokers. Other than that, this venerable Parisian wine bar has not really changed at all in the almost fifty years it has been in operation.

The menu is short, but the food and wine always rate an A+ with the regulars, who flow in nonstop and have made Le Sancerre one of the most popular lunch spots in this part of the seventh arrondissement. Past the somber exterior is a pleasant, rustic interior filled with the comforting sounds and smells of the busy kitchen. This is the place for a creamy herb or cheese omelette with a side of golden pan-fried potatoes and a crisp green salad, or for the more adventurous, a spicy *andouillette* made with Sancerre wine. A light choice is to order a *crotin de*

TELEPHONE
01-45-51-75-91

OPEN
Mon–Fri: 8 A.M.–9:30 P.M.; Sat: 8 A.M.–4:30 P.M.; continuous service

CLOSED
Sun; holidays, Aug 15–Sept 1

RESERVATIONS
Suggested for lunch

CREDIT CARDS
MC, V

À LA CARTE
85–115F (12.96–17.53), BNC

PRIX FIXE
None

ENGLISH SPOKEN
Some

Chavignol, a sharp goat cheese that goes perfectly with a glass or two of Sancerre. While waiting for your meal, baskets of Poilâne bread and crocks of sweet butter are brought to the table. Your wine, of course, will be Sancerre, and your dessert should be a piece of the gorgeous *tarte Tatin.* Ask to have it heated.

NOTE: There is a nonsmoking section. Also, if you appreciate Art Nouveau architecture, check out the facade of the building directly across the street at 29, avenue Rapp, constructed in 1901 by the architect Lavirotle. Then turn right and walk to the post office at No. 37. At the end of the dead-end street by the post office you will see more lovely doorways and latticework.

LE SÉDILLOT (4)
2, rue Sédillot
Métro: Pont de l'Alma

TELEPHONE
01-45-51-95-82

OPEN
Mon–Fri: lunch noon–2:30 P.M., dinner 7:30–10 P.M.

CLOSED
Sat–Sun; 2 weeks in Aug (dates vary)

RESERVATIONS
Not necessary

CREDIT CARDS
AE, DC, MC, V

À LA CARTE
None

PRIX FIXE
Lunch and dinner: 110F (16.77€), 2 courses, 145F (22.11€), 3 courses, both BNC

ENGLISH SPOKEN
Yes

On my research trips, some of the best recommendations I get for new restaurant listings come from owners of some of my favorite hotels. That is the case with Le Sédillot, which is on a backwater street almost in the shade of the Eiffel Tower. The Art Nouveau dining room has etched-glass windows, vases of flowers, red velvet seating, and tables set with Villeroy and Boch china and candles in the evening. On warm days, more tables and chairs are set up on the quiet sidewalk in front.

The two democratically priced menus are available for both lunch and dinner, and they leave the competition behind in both the variety and quality of products used. To start, the 110F (16.77€) menu includes several salad choices (such as endives with roquefort or lentils with bacon), a cheese and basil tart, herrings with warm potatoes, or leeks in a chive cream sauce. Main courses star roasted chicken with sautéed potatoes, a juicy grilled *andouillette,* beef tartare, a thick piece of tuna in a pepper sauce, and flank steak smothered in shallots. However, if you want to spring for foie gras, escargots, sole *meunière,* or *magret de canard,* it will cost at least half again as much, which hardly makes budget dining sense. Desserts are also extra for this menu . . . and not worth the outlay. Instead, spend the money you save on one of the patron's fairly priced *vins du propriétaire.*

LES EMBRUNS (22)
73, avenue de Suffren
Métro: La Motte-Picquet–Grenelle

Les embruns means the mist that blows from the sea, which should give you a hint about what is served at this brasserie, which is devoted to everything from *la mer*. Very often fresh fish can cost dearly, putting it out of the range of frugal diners in Paris, but that is not so here, where two amazingly priced menus offer the entire seashore, plus dessert and wine. Yes, they serve lamb, foie gras, and steak, but remember the old saying, "When in Rome . . ." In this case, at Les Embruns, order *only* fish. The less expensive menu starts with a baker's dozen choices for your starter, beginning with six oysters and ending with a *cassolette* of curried mussels. Next you will be faced with almost as many fish choices for your main course, including the *plat du jour,* salmon served grilled with herb butter and tagliatelle or served raw with ratatouille on the side, cod in a cream sauce, and grilled shrimp. Splashing out a bit more means platters of *coquilles St-Jacques,* sole *meunière,* and either *lotte* (monkfish) or *bar* (sea bass) served with leeks or a fennel fondue. In both cases, you will finish with desserts based on ice cream, sorbet, and fresh fruit.

TELEPHONE
01-47-34-90-56

OPEN
Daily: lunch noon–2:30 P.M.,dinner 7–11 P.M.

CLOSED
Aug

RESERVATIONS
Only for parties of 6 or more

CREDIT CARDS
AE, MC, V

À LA CARTE
160–190F (24.39–28.97€), BNC

PRIX FIXE
Lunch and dinner: 119.50F (18.22€), 145F (22.11€), both 3 courses and BC

ENGLISH SPOKEN
Yes

LES NUITS DES THÉS (9)
22, rue de Beaune
Métro: Rue du Bac

Paris tearooms are usually stylishly decorated places where you can relax for an hour or so over a light meal, a pastry, and a cup of good tea. Jacqueline Cédelle's tearoom near the Musée d'Orsay is just such a pleasing refuge for a quiet break from the rigors of museumgoing or wandering the antique and art galleries that define this part of Paris. Her interesting collection of teapots and cups are displayed in the window and in a lighted cupboard near the back. A buffet along one wall is filled with all of her homemade temptations. Everything is fresh and made here, including the jam you spread on your scones and buttery croissants. Lunch leans heavily on salads, cold plates, and egg creations; brunch is a filling multicourse affair starting with juice and tea or coffee, scones or pancakes, eggs fixed several ways, and ending with a choice of four desserts, including chocolate brownies with cream. If you are just going for tea, the lemon meringue and chocolate *tartes* are wonderful, and so are the macaroon cake and the chestnut *tarte.*

TELEPHONE
01-47-03-92-07

OPEN
Daily: 11:30 A.M.–7 P.M., continuous service

CLOSED
Aug

RESERVATIONS
Not necessary

CREDIT CARDS
V

À LA CARTE
120–135F (18.29–20.58€), BNC

PRIX FIXE
Brunch Sat–Sun: 150F (22.87€), BC

ENGLISH SPOKEN
Yes

MICHEL COURTALHAC ($, 17)
47, rue de Bourgogne
Métro: Varenne

TELEPHONE
01-45-55-15-35

OPEN
Mon: dinner 7:45–10 P.M.;
Tues–Fri: lunch 12:30–2 P.M.,
dinner 7:45–10 P.M.; Sat:
dinner 7:45–10 P.M.

CLOSED
Mon and Sat lunch, Sun; week
between Christmas and New
Year's, first week of May, Aug

RESERVATIONS
Essential

CREDIT CARDS
AE, MC, V

À LA CARTE
240–275F (36.59–41.92€),
BNC

PRIX FIXE
None

ENGLISH SPOKEN
Yes

The dining room is small, with a round table by the front window, a few tables along a banquette, and a handful of tables in the back just beyond the open kitchen. The settings are formal, and the welcome by Nadine Courtalhac is always warm, whether you are a first-time diner here or one of her many regulars. Her fashionable food-loving patrons have long recognized that Michel Courtalhac is one of the best unsung chefs cooking in Paris today. These diners, who include high-powered officials and politicians from the nearby prime minister's office, journalists, and residents of some of the most expensive real estate in Paris, could eat anywhere, but they come back again and again to sample Michel's excellent cooking, which is full of spontaneity and imagination.

Each month the short menu changes to reflect the highest quality foods of the season. The list of choices is short, but even so, it is almost impossible to find a disappointment. In the fall, you might start with a simple salad of fresh beets, *mâche,* and a soft-cooked egg or with eggs lightly scrambled with sorrel. The *plats* are textbook examples of their kind, and might include roast guinea hen with assorted vegetables, leg of lamb cooked with honey and pepper sauce, or a perfectly poached piece of *sandre* with a butter sauce. For dessert, the *tarte Tatin* or the rich chocolate ganache with coffee sauce will leave you with wonderful memories of a quintessential Parisian dining experience.

PEGOTY'S (20)
79, avenue Bosquet
Métro: École-Militaire

TELEPHONE
01-45-55-84-50

OPEN
Daily: 9 A.M.–7 P.M. (Sun from
10 A.M.), continuous service

CLOSED
Never

RESERVATIONS
Not necessary

CREDIT CARDS
MC, V

À LA CARTE
100–125F (15.24–19.06€),
BNC

Every French neighborhood has its share of tearooms, those gentle places that nourish the body and soothe the soul, providing a peaceful place to while away an hour or two over a quiet meal or a pot of tea and dessert. Pegoty's, which is close to the Eiffel Tower, Invalides, and École Militaire, will charm you. The tearoom actually consists of several rooms; the stone-lined front room has a picture window overlooking the street and a sofa-style banquette facing the buffet of sweets. Beyond are a series of comfortable little rooms that are ideal places for an intimate afternoon with someone special or for getting away from it all and catching up on your reading or correspondence.

All the beautiful cakes and *tartes* you see lined up under the three brass lights are made here and served on gold-trimmed white china by the pretty owner and hostess, Veronique. Tea and sweet temptations are not the only delightful possibilities she offers. There are two breakfasts, ranging from a simple continental (juice, toast, and crumpets or scones) to the American, which fills you with bacon, sausage, eggs, toast, and tomato. On the weekend and holidays, a large brunch is available that includes champagne. Otherwise there are several omelettes, a daily *tarte,* salads, a *plat du jour,* and assorted cold meat plates. Your tea will be from Mariage Frères (see page 97).

PRIX FIXE
Breakfast: 65–95F (9.91–14.48€), BC; weekend and holiday brunch: 120F (18.29€), BC

ENGLISH SPOKEN
Yes

RESTAURANT CHEZ GERMAINE (27)
30, rue Pierre Leroux
Métro: Vaneau

I first learned about Germaine's from a fellow passenger while we were stranded in the Jakarta airport waiting for a monsoon to let up. Naturally, the minute I got to Paris, I could not wait to try it, and when I did, it lived up to all of its advanced billing: Germaine's is an unsung place that serves homespun food at almost philanthropic prices, especially if you stick to one of the set menus. In all the years I have been seeking cheap, good-value eats in Paris, I have found myself hard-pressed to recommend a better neighborhood restaurant with more local color than this seven-table spot near the Bon Marché department store. The interior, like the food, is simple. It consists of ocher-yellow walls, hanging green plants, and some strange, anthropomorphic pictures of vegetables and fruits. The tables, which are shared, are waited on by two clucking-hen-type waitresses, who shout the orders to the chef through a window in the kitchen door.

From Monday through Saturday, the timeless dishes bring diners back for their own special favorites of thick soups, pâtés, lentils or leeks vinaigrette, kidneys in cream, rabbit with potato purée, roast beef, salmon, and *petit salé* (salt pork). The warm *pomme clafoutis* with thick cream or the homemade chocolate cake swimming in *crème anglaise* are enough to keep me coming back every night. Weight Watchers it is not! It is, however, *the*

TELEPHONE
01-42-73-28-34

OPEN
Mon–Fri: lunch noon–2:30 P.M., dinner 7–9:30 P.M.; Sat: lunch noon–2:30 P.M.

CLOSED
Sat dinner, Sun; holidays, Aug

RESERVATIONS
Recommended for dinner for 4 or more

CREDIT CARDS
None

À LA CARTE
85–100F (12.96–15.24€), BNC

PRIX FIXE
Lunch, *formule rapide* (only noon–12:30 P.M.): 50F (7.62€), 3 courses, BNC; lunch and dinner: 65F (9.91€), 3 courses, BNC

ENGLISH SPOKEN
Yes

destination if you are looking for something truly authentic, not to mention good . . . and cheap.

NOTE: No smoking is allowed.

RESTAURANT "CÔTÉ BAR" (7)
20, rue de Bellechasse
Métro: Solférino

TELEPHONE
01-47-05-48-77

OPEN
Mon–Sat: lunch noon–2 P.M.,
dinner 7:30–10:30 P.M.

CLOSED
Sun; holidays, Aug

RESERVATIONS
Advised

CREDIT CARDS
MC, V

À LA CARTE
185F (28.20€), BNC

PRIX FIXE
Lunch: 94F (14.33€), 2 courses,
BNC; lunch and dinner: 145F
(22.11€), 3 courses, BNC

ENGLISH SPOKEN
Yes

Edith and her husband, Claude, sold Au Petits Oignons (a fixture in my Paris restaurant guide for years), and moved next door to larger, more convenient quarters. As Edith said, "Running up and down the steep, winding staircase in the old location just became too difficult for all of us. Now we are not as tired . . . and so much happier." I agree: the new, two-room ground-floor location is much better for all concerned. More important, this remains the same popular spot everyone has known and loved, where good manners and gentility are as much at home as the local regulars, who have made this bistro a fixture in the *quartier.* They quickly fill all the tables in the dining room, which is simply decorated with tiny floral prints draped over white tablecloths and an amusing collection of framed prints of Ronald Searle's humorous drawings. Trays of Claude's *pâtisserie* and homemade preserves are on display near the entrance, and the house dog, a beautiful Lab named Cashmere, will often be there to greet you along with Edith.

There are two excellent prix fixe menus and an imaginative à la carte section. On the à la carte side, you have a choice of ten cold and six hot *entrées.* For a cold *entrée,* I like to begin with the salade *Bonne Mine,* which combines crudités and fresh mushrooms on lettuce, or the *salade bretonne,* with shrimp and artichokes. My favorite hot beginning is the *délice,* an eggplant and foie gras cake. These light starters leave room for either of the two house specialties: *magret de canard à la confiture de petits oignons* (duck breast with onion jam) or the *foie de veau aux avocats* (veal liver with avocados). On Thursday, order the *pot au feu os à moëlle* (marrow bone) in the winter or *aïoli provençal* (garlic sauce) in the summer. A final word of advice: Leave enough space for the famed chocolate cake or *la tarte au citron d'Edith.* If these are too much, try her other specialty, Irish coffee.

NOTE: There is a nonsmoking section.

RESTAURANT DU PALAIS D'ORSAY (6)
1, rue de Bellechasse (museum entrance)
Métro: Solférino

As everyone knows, cuisine and culture are uppermost in life to the French, so it is not surprising that most major museums in Paris have some sort of restaurant. The best of these by far is the Palais d'Orsay, situated in the Musée d'Orsay, which was built for the 1900 World's Fair and served as the city's most ornate train station. Today, diners can sit in wide wicker armchairs in a massive Belle Epoque dining room with magnificent frescoed ceilings by the nineteenth-century painter Gabriel Ferrier. Marble statues, gilt-framed mirrors, sparkling chandeliers, and sprays of fresh flowers complete the spectacular setting, which is on the second level, overlooking the Seine.

Fortunately, the food is as impressive as the decor. At first glance, you might think the prices would be, too, but they are not, especially *le buffet*. This bargain meal features a beautiful cold buffet with a variety of salads, vegetables, cold meats, and fish followed by a choice of desserts. Also available is a children's menu, a two-course menu, and à la carte. Tea is served in the afternoons, but not on Thursday. That is the only night of the week the restaurant stays open for dinner, since the museum is also open late. On Friday and Saturday nights when the museum is closed, private parties are held. If you are planning an intimate dinner for a hundred or more of your closest Parisian friends, contact the catering department.

NOTE: There is a nonsmoking area.

TELEPHONE
01-45-49-42-03

OPEN
Tues–Wed, Fri–Sun: lunch 11:30 A.M.–2:30 P.M., tea 3:30–5:30 P.M.; Thur: lunch 11:30 A.M.–2:30 P.M., dinner 7–9:30 P.M.

CLOSED
Mon; any holiday the museum is closed, NAC

RESERVATIONS
For large groups

CREDIT CARDS
MC, V

À LA CARTE
100–160F (15.24–24.39€), BNC

PRIX FIXE
Lunch and dinner: 89F (13.57€), daily special and dessert, BNC; cold buffet (no main courses): 100F (15.24€), BNC; children (under 10): 55F (8.38€), BC; tea and pastry: 50F (7.62€)

ENGLISH SPOKEN
Yes, with English menu

Eighth Arrondissement

RIGHT BANK
American Embassy, Arc de Triomphe and l'Étoile, Champs-Élysées, elegant shopping, Madeleine Church, Petit and Grand Palais (built for the 1900 World Exhibition), place de la Concorde

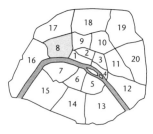

The eighth arrondissement is an area of splendor, elegance, money, and classic Parisian images, especially the sweeping view of the Champs-Élysées from the Arc de Triomphe to the place de la Concorde. The Arc de Triomphe, commemorating Napoléon's reign, is the centerpoint for twelve avenues that radiate in the shape of a star (or l'Étoile). The Madeleine Church was built in 1806 by Napoléon and dedicated to his army. The giant colonnades along the front mirror those of the Assemblée Nationale directly across the Seine. Shoppers with impressive bank balances ply the *haute couture* luxury shops along the avenues Marceau and Montaigne and on the rue de Faubourg St-Honoré. Gourmets and gourmands make pilgrimages to Fauchon, the world's most famous grocery store, and tourists dine at Maxim's, the onetime shrine where the beautiful people congregated in Paris. This part of the eighth is alive and bustling during the weekdays, but on holidays and weekends, it is deserted.

The Champs-Élysées is the gathering place of France. In 1998, the largest crowd since the World War II Liberation congregated here. On New Year's Eve, July 14 (Bastille Day), and for the final stretch of the Tour de France, the avenue is lined top to bottom with celebrants. However, the lovely Champs-Élysées, with its myriad sidewalk cafés filled with pretty young men and women, is very deceptive. No true Parisian would ever seriously dine here, any more than a true New Yorker would head to Times Square for a fine meal. Of course, walking along what the French rightfully term "the most beautiful avenue in the world" and stopping at a café for a drink *is* part of being in Paris. But for a real increase in value and quality, walk one or two blocks on either side of the avenue. A final word: Watch for pickpockets. This is fertile picking grounds for them, and they can do a number on you faster than you can say, "Stop, thief!"

EIGHTH ARRONDISSEMENT RESTAURANTS

($) indicates a Big Splurge

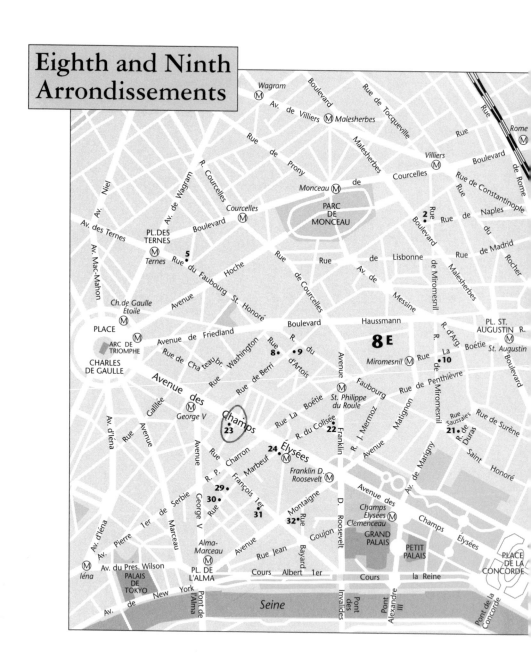

Eighth and Ninth Arrondissements

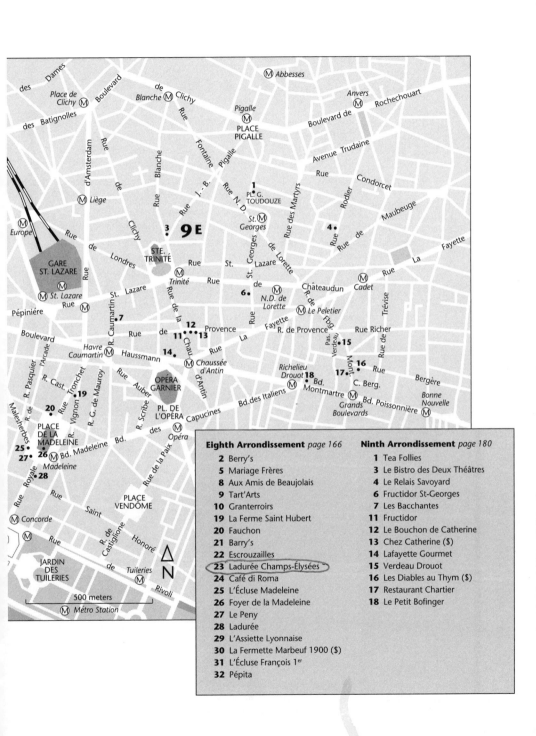

AUX AMIS DE BEAUJOLAIS (8)
28, rue d'Artois
Métro: St-Philippe-du-Roule

TELEPHONE
01-45-63-92-21,
01-45-63-58-64

OPEN
Mon–Fri: lunch noon–3 P.M.,
dinner 6:30–9 P.M.; Sat Sept–
Easter: lunch noon–3 P.M.

CLOSED
Sat Easter–Sept, Sun;
Aug 4–21, week between
Christmas and New Year's

RESERVATIONS
Suggested for lunch

CREDIT CARDS
AE, MC, V

À LA CARTE
130–145F (19.82–22.11€),
BNC

PRIX FIXE
Lunch: 120F (18.29€),
3 courses, BNC

ENGLISH SPOKEN
Limited

You will know you have found Aux Amis de Beaujolais by the crowds: at lunchtime every bar stool and dining room table is filled with local businesspeople, and during dinner all the seats are again fully occupied by smart, value-minded Parisians and clued-in visitors. Bernard Picolet's family has been greeting and feeding their devoted regulars since 1921. His son now works with him in the kitchen, and his wife runs the front. Their food is full bodied and satisfying—and no doubt ruinous for our cholesterol count and arteries—but the down-to-earth cooking and generous portions make me a regular whenever I am lucky enough to be in Paris. Here is the place to try homespun dishes of *céleri rémoulade, pâte de campagne,* cucumbers in cream, or *fromage blanc* showered with fresh herbs. The fish changes every day, but in the meat department you can always count on *magret de canard,* beef tartare with *frites* or a salad, and grilled steaks; beef tongue, sautéed lamb with fat white beans, and an *andouillette* sausage also often make appearances. The suitably soothing desserts are all made here. I love the creamy rice pudding, any of the fruit *tartes,* or the satiny chocolate mousse.

BARRY'S (21)
9, rue de Duras
Métro: Champs-Élysées–Clemenceau

TELEPHONE
01-40-06-02-27

OPEN
Mon–Fri: lunch noon–4 P.M.

CLOSED
Sat–Sun; NAC

RESERVATIONS
Not accepted

CREDIT CARDS
None

À LA CARTE
35–95F (5.34–14.48€), BNC

PRIX FIXE
51F (7.77€), sandwich or
panini, dessert, water or soda

ENGLISH SPOKEN
Usually

Fast lunches served in a little room with equally small prices sum up the offerings at Barry's. The staff at the Ministry of Interior just around the corner have staked it out as a handy pit stop for a handcrafted sandwich on the run, a quick salad, or a one-plate hot or cold meal. You can eat your food here at one of the four high square tables with metal chairs, or you can have your order packaged to go and walk a block or so to the park that lines the Champs-Élysées.

BERRY'S (2)
46, rue de Naples
Métro: Villiers

Berry's is owned by chef Patrick Cirotte, who also runs Le Grenadin, the successful, expensive restaurant next door. The atmosphere at Berry's is laid-back and casual, with eleven red-and-white tables downstairs and a few more upstairs on the mezzanine. Pictures of sports teams and their jerseys hang about and an antique Adidas football sits in the window facing the street. The menu is limited, featuring dishes from Cirotte's native Berry region in France. You will find *andouillette* and macaroni, *jambon de Sancerre,* veal with cabbage, and for dessert, either *chanciau aux pommes* (a thick apple fritter in light egg custard) or a *poirat berrichon,* which is a twist on a chocolate pear *tarte.*

TELEPHONE
01-40-75-01-56

OPEN
Mon: dinner 7 P.M.–1 A.M.;
Tues–Fri: lunch noon–4 P.M.,
dinner 7 P.M.–1 A.M.; Sat dinner
7 P.M.–1 A.M.

CLOSED
Mon and Sat lunch, Sun; July
14–17, Aug 15–20

RESERVATIONS
Advised

CREDIT CARDS
V

À LA CARTE
150–180F (22.87–27.44€),
BNC

PRIX FIXE
Lunch and dinner: 100F
(15.24€), 2 courses, BNC

ENGLISH SPOKEN
Limited

CAFÉ DI ROMA (24)
35, avenue des Champs-Élysées
Métro: Franklin-D-Roosevelt

Where to eat before or after seeing a film along the Champs-Élysées? Finding an acceptable place along this famous avenue has always been a discouraging uphill project. No longer—not if you know about Café di Roma, which is on the corner of rue de Marignan and the Champs-Élysées. I will admit that I had walked right by it for years, never giving it a second thought. It took a Paris pal to point it out to me after a movie one night and insist that we try it. While certainly not destination dining, it is a port in a storm with decent Italian staples served at affordable prices. The later you go, the more authentic it gets as it fills up with Italians of various ages in assorted garbs and guises. If you go for a pizza or a bowl of pasta, you will be happy. Scratch the desserts . . . instead walk a block or two toward place de la Concorde and duck into Häagen-Dazs for a double or triple scoop of their super ice cream.

TELEPHONE
01-53-89-65-60

OPEN
Mon–Fri: 8 A.M.–1:30 A.M.;
Sat–Sun: 11:30 A.M.–1:30 A.M.;
continuous service

CLOSED
Never

RESERVATIONS
Not necessary

CREDIT CARDS
AE, MC, V

À LA CARTE
90–115F (13.72–17.53€), BNC

PRIX FIXE
Lunch and dinner: 59F (8.99€),
pasta and wine; 86F (13.11€),
2 courses, BNC; 109F (16.62€),
3 courses, BNC; children
(under 12): 49F (7.47€),
2 courses, BC

ENGLISH SPOKEN
Limited

ESCROUZAILLES (22)
36, rue du Colisée
Métro: St-Philippe-de-Roule, Franklin-D-Roosevelt

TELEPHONE
01-45-62-94-00
OPEN
Daily: lunch noon–2:30 P.M.,
dinner 7–11 P.M.
CLOSED
Never
RESERVATIONS
Essential
CREDIT CARDS
AE, MC, V
À LA CARTE
None
PRIX FIXE
Lunch: 100F (15.24€), 2
courses, BC; dinner: 134F
(20.43€), 3 courses, BNC
ENGLISH SPOKEN
Can be limited

Budget food stamped with style is the name of the game at any of these three bastions of heavenly southwestern French cooking. On rue Colisée, the two sunny yellow rooms are attractively set with linen napkins on well-spaced tables, which feature an assortment of products that are also for sale. At lunchtime it is packed and can be rushed, but no wonder when you can have a choice of anything on the menu for your *entrée* and *plat,* or a *plat* and dessert, for a mere 100F (15.24€). In the evening, everyone seems to calm down and settle in for a leisurely dinner with plenty of good wine. Decisions, decisions, decisions . . . everything looks appealing in this land of foie gras, including puff pastry layered with curried mussels, strawlike green beans tossed with gizzards, *magret de canard* sauced with truffles, goose *cassoulet,* and a raisin *baba au rhum* or a pear *tarte Tatin* for dessert.

NOTE: There are two other locations in Paris: one at 83, avenue de Ségur (15th), Tel: 01-40-65-99-10; and one at 97, avenue de Villiers (17th), Tel: 01-44-40-45-10.

FAUCHON (20)
26, place de la Madeleine
Métro: Madeleine

TELEPHONE
01-47-42-60-11
OPEN
Mon–Sat: 8:30 A.M.–6:30 P.M.
CLOSED
Sun; major holidays, NAC
CREDIT CARDS
AE, DC, MC, V
ENGLISH SPOKEN
Yes

In 1886 August Fauchon opened his *épicerie fine* on place de la Madeleine. The rest is history. Today, a visit to Fauchon, the most famous gourmet grocery store in the world, is one of the must-dos in Paris. With its magnificent museum-quality window displays and its mind-boggling selection of more than thirty thousand gastronomic goodies, Fauchon is the ultimate gourmet mecca. Its image has been polished even further by the addition of a three-level building next door containing a *pâtisserie* and candy shop and an expanded grocery section, which carries the entire line of Fauchon groceries, spices, teas, and coffees.

FOYER DE LA MADELEINE (26)
place de la Madeleine, underneath the Madeleine Church on the right side
Métro: Madeleine

TELEPHONE
01-47-42-39-84
OPEN
Mon–Fri: lunch
11:45 A.M.–2 P.M.

For the cheapest lunch in Paris, proceed directly to the basement canteen in the Madeleine Church. Not only is the three-course meal breathtakingly affordable, but it is philanthropic to boot, since all proceeds go to the work done by the church. Seating is at shared tables in a massive cafeteria that seems to go on forever. The menu changes daily, and fish is often included on Friday. When you sit down, a row of *entrées* is already on the table. When I was there it was a choice between crudités on a bed of *mâche*, pieces of tuna and tomatoes, or a couple of slices of dried sausage. That is followed by a choice of two hot dishes, which are served by a fleet of very gentle, properly attired ladies who volunteer their services. I had the roast lamb rather than the chicken brochette and the puréed potatoes instead of the mixed beans. Dessert is either fresh fruit, yogurt, pudding, or cheese. Wine would have set me back another 30F, but the bottle of mineral water was only 3F (0.46€) extra. Coffee is not part of the package. When you arrive, and before you sit down, you will pay the cashier and be asked if you would like to contribute an additional 3F or 4F (0.46–0.61€) to help cover the people the church feeds for free. *Mais oui!*

NOTE: There is an 18F (2.74€) yearly membership fee each diner must pay once.

GRANTERROIRS (10)
30, rue de Miromesnil
Metro: Miromesnil

Granterroirs is the lunchtime embodiment of a food lover's dream in this business neighborhood of Paris. The attractive gourmet food shop, deli, and restaurant is open Monday to Friday from morning to evening, but the only meal served is lunch. Everyone sits on benches at one long communal table in the back. Don't worry if your French is not quite up to par; everyone is friendly, and for the regulars it is their adopted home for lunch, a place they gather on a daily basis for simple food served without fanfare. These are people who know and appreciate the quality regional products served and prepared in a straightforward manner by owner Jean-François Ramirez and staff. The selection features soups in the winter, salads in the summer, and *tartines,* a daily *plat,* organic bread, and always homemade desserts and ice cream. When I was there a variety of organically grown tomatoes were highlighting the menu, along with a chocolate *tarte* that everyone adored. If you like what you're eating, you can buy the products and create the dish yourself. Also for sale are wonderful French olive

CLOSED
Sat–Sun; holidays, July 15–Aug 31

RESERVATIONS
Not taken

CREDIT CARDS
None

À LA CARTE
None

PRIX FIXE
45F (6.86€), 3 courses, BNC

ENGLISH SPOKEN
Very little

TELEPHONE
01-47-42-18-18

FAX
01-47-42-18-00

OPEN
Mon–Fri: gourmet grocery and deli, 8:30 A.M.–8 P.M.; lunch noon–2:30 P.M.

CLOSED
Sat–Sun; holidays, 10–15 days mid-Aug

RESERVATIONS
Not accepted

CREDIT CARDS
MC, V

À LA CARTE
80–140F (12.20–21.34€), BNC

PRIX FIXE
None

ENGLISH SPOKEN
Yes

oils, jams, jellies, sauces, and gourmet gift baskets to warm the heart of any Parisian foodie.

NOTE: No smoking is allowed.

LADURÉE (28)
16, rue Royale
Métro: Madeleine, Concorde

TELEPHONE
01-42-60-21-79

EMAIL
laduree@wanadoo.fr

INTERNET
www.laduree.fr

OPEN
Mon–Sat: 8:30 A.M.–7 P.M., lunch 11:30 A.M.–3:30 P.M.; Sun: 10 A.M.–7 P.M., brunch 11:30 A.M.–3:30 P.M.

CLOSED
Christmas Day and New Year's Day

RESERVATIONS
Recommended for lunch and Sun brunch

CREDIT CARDS
AE, V

À LA CARTE
50–165F (7.62–25.15€), BNC

PRIX FIXE
Sun brunch: 150–160F (22.87–24.39€), 3 courses, BC

ENGLISH SPOKEN
Sometimes

It all began in 1862 when Louis Ernest Ladurée, a miller from the southwest, opened the doors of his bakery at 16, rue Royale. In 1871, Jules Chéret, a famous *fin-de-siècle* painter, was commissioned to decorate the shop. He drew his inspiration for the painting you see today from the pictorial techniques used on the Sistine Chapel ceiling and the Garnier Opera house. As cafés developed during the period of the Second Empire, Jeanne Souchard, the wife of Ernest Ladurée, decided to combine the pastry shop with tea service, and thus began what is still one of the finest tearooms in Paris. It is also a superb choice for a proper lunch, Sunday brunch, or a cup of the best *café au lait* or hot chocolate along with one of their famed pastries. Blue ribbons in the dessert category go to their *royals*, almond-flavored macaroon cookie sandwiches filled with chocolate, mocha, vanilla, lemon, pistachio, strawberry, or vanilla cream. Do not miss treating yourself to one . . . if you can stop at just one, because once sampled, they are habit-forming and unforgettable. Just to show how popular these bites from heaven are, it has been calculated that one is sold every twenty-five seconds throughout the day!

At the rue Royal location, downstairs seating is around postage-stamp-size tables arranged under a pastel ceiling mural of chubby cherubs performing all sorts of heavenly baking duties. Here you can watch the hustle and bustle of the well-dressed crowds standing ten-deep at the pastry counter. For lunch or brunch it is much more comfortable to reserve a table upstairs, where the atmosphere is rather solemn, but the scene less hectic, and there is no smoking allowed.

NOTE: There is a nonsmoking section upstairs. There is also a tearoom at Au Printemps department store, 62, boulevard Haussmann (Tel: 01-42-82-40-10; Métro: Chausée-d'Antin-La Fayette), but the ambience and spirit are not the same.

LADURÉE CHAMPS-ÉLYSÉES (23)
75, avenue des Champs-Élysées
Métro: Franklin-D-Roosevelt, George V

In September 1997, Ladurée opened this spectacular restaurant, tearoom, and *pâtisserie* on the most beautiful avenue in the world, the Champs-Élysées. The elegant two-level setting looks as though it has been here forever, but that is not so. For a long time, Japanese Air Lines occupied the site, then Ladurée took over and spent one year creating the magnificent setting you now see, which evokes the refined atmosphere of the Second Empire.

When you go, be sure to sit in one of the five individually decorated adjoining rooms on the first floor. The Salon Mathilde, named after Princess Mathilde, who helped Napoléon III ascend the throne, is furnished in rich wall hangings, wing chairs, and deep sofas. The Salon Castiglione, named after the willful, cunning Countess of Castiglione, who was Napoléon III's mistress, is done in blue and gold with a marble fireplace along one wall. In the center near the wide staircase is the Salon Paeva, named after a famous courtesan. The Chocolaterie, or "chocolate room"—with its wainscoting, antique lamps, ebony marquetry, and gilded mirrors—has the atmosphere of Vienna's most beautiful cafés. And finally there is the intimate book-lined Bibliotheque, which is a cozy re-creation of a small library. Every day forty-five pastry chefs and forty cooks prepare the beautiful food, which is inspired by the regions of France and the cuisines of the world. It is served continuously from breakfast through late supper by a dining room staff of forty-five and six *maîtres d'hôtel*. Even if you don't eat here, you owe it to yourself to stroll by the downstairs pastry counter and order one of their fabulous creations to take with you.

TELEPHONE
01-40-75-08-75

INTERNET
www.laduree.fr

OPEN
Daily: 8 A.M.–midnight, continuous service

CLOSED
Never

RESERVATIONS
Essential for lunch and dinner

CREDIT CARDS
AE, DC, MC, V

À LA CARTE
150–200F (22.87–30.49€), BNC

PRIX FIXE
Dinner: 195F (29.73€) 3 courses, BNC

ENGLISH SPOKEN
Yes

LA FERME SAINT HUBERT (19)
21, rue Vignon
Métro: Madeleine

The cheese shop next door, run by *maître fromager* Henry Voy, has long been recognized as one of the best *fromageries* in Paris. From this treasure-trove of cheeses comes the first-class ingredients for the fondues, *raclettes,* cheese platters, and other cheese-based dishes served in the restaurant. The small room has banquette seating, orange paper table covers and napkins, and a large wall covering depicting cows. The location is around the

TELEPHONE
01-47-42-79-20

OPEN
Mon–Sat: lunch noon–3:30 P.M., dinner 7–11 P.M.

CLOSED
Sun; major holidays, NAC

RESERVATIONS
Essential

CREDIT CARDS
AE, MC, V

À LA CARTE
150–175F (22.87–26.68€);
raclette or fondue, 110–185F
(16.77–28.20€) per person,
BNC

PRIX FIXE
None

ENGLISH SPOKEN
Yes, with English menu

corner from Fauchon and near many offices and shops, so it is swamped at lunch, and if you don't have a reservation, forget it. One of the most popular orders is the *dégustation* platter of seven varieties of cheese. Huge salads, rich cheese-based tarts, and hot dishes, along with evening meals of *raclette* and fondue (two-person minimum), make up the rest of the menu. Pots of white goat's milk butter are served with Poilâne bread.

NOTE: A second cheese shop is located at 14, rue des Sablons in the Galerie St-Didier (16th); Tel: 01-45-53-15-77.

LA FERMETTE MARBEUF 1900 ($, 30)
5, rue Marbeuf
Métro: Franklin-D-Roosevelt

TELEPHONE
01-53-23-08-00

INTERNET
www.blanc.net

OPEN
Daily: lunch noon–3 P.M.,
dinner 7:30–11:30 P.M.

CLOSED
Dec 24, NAC

RESERVATIONS
Recommended

CREDIT CARDS
AE, DC, MC, V

À LA CARTE
285–330F (43.45–50.31€),
BNC

PRIX FIXE
Lunch: 148F (22.56€), 2
courses, BC; lunch and dinner:
185F (28.20€), 3 courses, BNC

ENGLISH SPOKEN
Yes, and English menu

Of the many Art Nouveau restaurants flourishing in Paris today, this one is exceptional. For the best experience of it, reserve a table in the *jardin d'hiver,* a spectacular glass-roofed winter garden with Art Nouveau grillwork, five thousand elaborate *faïence* tiles, and beautiful lead-glass windows with intricate floral designs. The room was purchased in total from the Maisons-Lafitte and installed as the *première salle* at La Fermette Marbeuf. The restaurant was declared a national historic monument in 1983.

Fortunately, the breathtaking decor does not overshadow the food, where the culinary cornerstones of beef tartare prepared to order, leg of lamb, and innovative fish preparations, plus a host of artistic desserts, highlight the lengthy menu. The best dining value is the three-course lunch or dinner menu; it has a choice of four starters, including a *terrine des foies de volaille* (chicken liver terrine) and a choice of four *plats,* followed by either a cheese course or dessert. Of the sweet choices, the *délice chocolat mandarine,* a decadently rich fudge cake flavored with tangerines, is the odds-on favorite.

There is no music, and the rooms are too large and brightly lit to be ideal for an intimate dinner, but La Fermette is close to the Champs-Élysées and is a very pleasing formal dining experience, especially on Sunday or holidays when many other restaurants are closed.

L'ASSIETTE LYONNAISE (29)
21, rue Marbeuf
Métro: Franklin-D-Roosevelt

The prices are too cheap to ignore, the red-and-white interior is adorable, and the restaurant has the advantage of being open on Sunday for both lunch and dinner and nightly until midnight. However, the menu is limited to the Lyonnaise specialties of *andouillettes* (chitterling sausages), tripe, blood sausage, and *plats du jour* featuring heavy-duty pork, *bavettes,* and fish on Friday. It is heaven for carnivores, but for the vegetarian or light eater, unless you order a mushroom omelette or one of their *grandes salades* (*végétarienne, saumon fumé, niçoise,* and *Italienne*), better luck next time. This is not to say that the food at L'Assiette Lyonnaise is not delicious, because it is—just be geared for mountains of hearty meats and fat-infused potatoes. The desserts follow suit with rich selections of *tarte Tatin, fondant au chocolat,* and profiteroles.

TELEPHONE
01-47-20-94-80

OPEN
Daily: lunch noon–3 P.M., dinner 7 P.M.–midnight

CLOSED
Never

RESERVATIONS
Not necessary

CREDIT CARDS
MC, V

À LA CARTE
150–170F (22.87–25.92€), BNC

PRIX FIXE
None

ENGLISH SPOKEN
Yes

L'ÉCLUSE FRANÇOIS 1ᴱᴿ (31)
64, rue François 1ᵉʳ
Métro: Franklin-D-Roosevelt

For a complete description, see L'Écluse, page 137. All other information is the same.
TELEPHONE: 01-47-20-77-09

L'ÉCLUSE MADELEINE (25)
15, place de la Madeleine
Métro: Madeleine

For a complete description, see L'Écluse, page 137. All other information is the same.
TELEPHONE: 01-42-65-34-69

LE PENY (27)
3, place de la Madeleine
Métro: Madeleine

In a neighborhood known for restaurants serving 500F and 600F lunches, Le Peny is a plush but reasonable alternative. If you have spent the morning hoofing it around the Tuileries Gardens, Jeu de Paume, and La Madeleine, or visiting the boutiques that line rue du Faubourg St-Honoré, this is a good place to freshen up and relax, either inside or outside under the shade of umbrellas and sycamore trees, while enjoying a great view of Parisian life. The food is reliable, provided you order correctly, and the interior is clean, comfortable, and filled every day with an attractively stylish crowd.

TELEPHONE
01-42-65-06-75

OPEN
Daily: 7:30 A.M.–10 P.M., continuous service

CLOSED
Christmas, NAC

RESERVATIONS
Not necessary

CREDIT CARDS
MC, V

À LA CARTE
100–150F (15.24–22.87€), BC

PRIX FIXE
Lunch and dinner: 69F
(10.52€), roast chicken and
fries, 139F (21.19€), *plat du jour*
and dessert or cheese, both BC

ENGLISH SPOKEN
Yes, with English menu

The chairs and tables on the sidewalk terrace offer some of the best spots for serious people-watching in this corner of Paris.

A wide variety of café food is offered, and some dishes are better than others. One long-standing favorite is the *poulet à la crème* (boned chicken breast on toast smothered with a delicate cream sauce). It is also a good place for a *croque-monsieur*—a toasted cheese and ham sandwich with béchamel sauce—or a *croque-madame,* which adds an egg on top. For years, the *only* dessert to consider was the *gâteau à la noix de coco* (a feathery light coconut cake), which for some inexplicable reason has been dropped from the menu. However, I was told it would be back, and let's hope so . . . as the alternatives are not exciting.

MARIAGE FRÈRES (5)
260, rue du Faubourg St-Honoré
Métro: Ternes

For a complete description, see Mariage Frères, page 97. All other information is the same.

TELEPHONE: 01-46-22-18-54
OPEN: Daily: 10:30 A.M.–7:30 P.M., continuous service
CLOSED: Major holidays, NAC

PÉPITA (32)
21, rue Bayard
Métro: Franklin-D-Roosevelt

TELEPHONE
01-40-70-06-26

OPEN
Mon–Sat: breakfast 8–11 A.M.,
lunch noon–2:30 P.M., dinner
7–11:30 P.M.

CLOSED
Sun; major holidays, NAC

RESERVATIONS
Essential

CREDIT CARDS
AE, MC, V

À LA CARTE
200F (30.49€), BNC

PRIX FIXE
Lunch: 140F (21.34€), 2
courses, BNC

ENGLISH SPOKEN
Yes

The neighborhood is filled with all the designer-name boutiques we know (and wish we could afford to shop in) and with five-star deluxe hotels, including the newly redone Four Seasons–George V and the Plaza Athénée. Where do travelers and regular Parisians find an affordable meal in this barren landscape for economy eats? Head to Pépita, where the atmosphere is like a theater vignette with a constantly changing cast of characters. In the morning, you will rub elbows with smartly tailored, handsome French professionals gulping down a strong espresso on their way to their nearby offices. VIPs, svelte fashion models, and clusters of ladies in Chanel suits carrying Yorkshire terriers arrive for lunch. Free tables pop up once in a blue moon, if you forget to book at this busy time. Things mellow out in the evening, with a cool, professional crowd clad in designer black draped on the velvet aubergine–covered chairs.

If you are a card-carrying fiscal conservative in Paris, target the two-course, daily changing lunch listed on the blackboard. The choices are limited, but not the quality, and possibilities include rabbit pâté, mussel soup, steak with béchamel sauce, and a pear *tarte* or strawberry soup for dessert. At night, everything is à la carte, but no one seems to mind spending around $30 for a three-course meal of satisfying comfort food. You will see serious servings of *chèvre chaud en salade,* snails in buttery garlic sauce, and chunks of foie gras spread on toast, followed by haddock with mashed potatoes, *blanquette de veau,* blood-rare steaks, and mountains of *frites.* Desserts promise even more calories—with a soft, dark chocolate cake in a custard sauce, *crêpes Suzette,* or crème brûlée.

NOTE: There is a second location in the seventeenth arrondissement called Félix at 99, rue Jouffroy d'Abbans (see page 248).

TART'ARTS (9)
36, rue de Berri
Métro: St-Philippe-du-Roule, George V

For assured seating, be here at the stroke of noon. After that a fashionable mix of all ages and types pours in, making it a full house by 12:30 P.M., with no letup in sight. What is the big draw? Artistic hot and cold salads, the *tarte* and winter dish or summer salad of the day, and calories-be-damned desserts. Cold salads include the *Alexandria,* designer greens topped with chèvre, raisins, carrots, and apples. The *Riveria* is a mix of tomatoes, feta cheese, potatoes, onions, olives, eggs, and anchovies in a basil-flavored vinaigrette dressing. If you would like a gratin of chicken, mushrooms, and potatoes on a bed of lettuce, order the *Paysanne.* Fish fanciers will want to order *La Marée,* a gratin of mussels and pasta flavored with oregano. The list of daily *tartes* is long . . . you could probably go every day for three weeks and never have the same one twice. Desserts stay about the same, so I am always assured of the lemon or orange *tartes,* fresh fruit *charlotte* in the summer, and chestnut cake in the winter.

TELEPHONE
01-42-25-02-76

OPEN
Mon–Fri: lunch noon–2:30 P.M.

CLOSED
Sat–Sun; holidays, NAC

RESERVATIONS
Not accepted

CREDIT CARDS
MC, V

À LA CARTE
65–110F (9.91–16.77€), BNC

PRIX FIXE
None

ENGLISH SPOKEN
Yes

Ninth Arrondissement

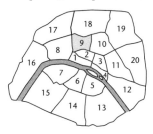

The ninth is predominantly a business area, with many banks, corporate headquarters, law firms, and insurance companies. The Grands Boulevards, laid out by Baron Haussmann, are those wide thoroughfares that lead from the Opéra Garnier (with a Chagall ceiling) to place de la République. The smart end is at the Opéra, the center of Paris during the Belle Epoque, that period of elegance and gaiety characterizing Parisian life from the mid-nineteenth century to World War I.

NINTH ARRONDISSEMENT RESTAURANTS
(see map page 168)

($) indicates a Big Splurge

CHEZ CATHERINE ($, 13)
65, rue de Provence
Métro: Chausée d'Antin–La Fayette

Talented chef Catherine Guerraz has a hit on her hands with her excellent contemporary southwestern-based cooking, which is available both here and next door at her bistro spin-off, Le Bouchon de Catherine (see page 183). Both restaurants stand side by side on a dreary street not far from the Galeries Lafayette and Au Printemps department stores, but please do not let this offbeat location deter you. The food is definitely worth the detour. At Chez Catherine, the 1930s decor has been perfectly preserved in the small banquette-lined room right down to the cigarette-browned walls, the potted palms, and even the clock quietly ticking away. The French atmosphere prevails as the tables become filled with a mixture of families, young and middle-age couples at dinner, and predominantly businessfolk at lunch.

Catherine and her husband, Frederic, along with their longtime waiter (who has worked in this restaurant for twenty-five years and survived five previous owners) offer friendly and helpful advice about the food and the wines. Classics like *feuilleté aux pleurottes, chanterelles et escargots,* lamb served with a truffle-accented macaroni gratin, *confit de canard,* and scallops garnished with a light leek fondue are enhanced by meticulous cooking and well-considered presentation. The cheese assortment is good, but if your taste buds call for a sweeter ending, you won't be disappointed with the apricot or banana mousse or the crème brûlée with pistachios and caramelized pears.

TELEPHONE
01-45-26-72-88

OPEN
Mon: lunch noon–2 P.M.; Tues–Fri: lunch noon–2 P.M., dinner 7:45–10 P.M.

CLOSED
Mon dinner, Sat–Sun; major holidays, Aug

RESERVATIONS
Essential

CREDIT CARDS
MC, V

À LA CARTE
250F (38.11€), BNC

PRIX FIXE
None

ENGLISH SPOKEN
Yes

FRUCTIDOR (11)
67, rue de Provence
Métro: Chausée d'Antin–La Fayette

A dozen or more teas and some of the best sweet and savory tarts served anywhere are prepared here (and at its sibling restaurant) daily for a standing-room-only lunchtime crowd. If you are shopping at Galeries Lafayette, Au Printemps, or Marks & Spencer, try this little hole in the wall for a nutritious lunch that will leave plenty of money in your wallet for serious afternoon buying. Order a fresh vegetable cocktail with a tomato, carrot, or apple base by the glass or carafe. Try a slice of a savory tart, maybe the *alsacienne* (onions and bacon), the *chèvre oseille* (goat cheese and sorrel), or the *forestière* (mush-

TELEPHONE
01-48-74-53-46

OPEN
Mon–Sat: lunch 11 A.M.–3 P.M.

CLOSED
Sun; holidays, NAC

RESERVATIONS
Not taken

CREDIT CARDS
None

À LA CARTE
70–110F (10.67–16.77€), BNC

PRIX FIXE
None

rooms and Auvergne blue cheese), all of which come with a green salad. There are also large one-meal salads, and for dessert . . . more tarts. Choose from fresh fruit, cheese, or chocolate.

At both locations, the tarts are available to go, either whole or by the slice. From Wednesday through Saturday at the rue de Provence location, chicken tandoori is the specialty prepared by the chef, Roland, from a recipe given to him by the owner, Sathi, who is Indian. The changing art you see hanging on the walls has been done by local artists and is for sale.

ENGLISH SPOKEN
Yes

FRUCTIDOR ST-GEORGES (6)
46, rue St-Georges
Métro: Notre-Dame-de-Lorette

See preceding entry for description. All other information is the same.

TELEPHONE: 01-49-95-02-10
OPEN: Mon–Fri: lunch 11 A.M.–3 P.M.
CLOSED: Sat–Sun; NAC

LAFAYETTE GOURMET (14)
48, boulevard Haussmann (1st floor)
Métro: Chausée d'Antin–La Fayette

It is Christmas Day and your birthday rolled into one at Lafayette Gourmet, the magnificent food department that is part of Galeries Lafayette on boulevard Haussmann. Food lovers will feel they have hit the jackpot with the multitude of riches on display. Even if you are not shopping for groceries to take with you, you can come to eat at one of the food stations, where salads, fruits, cheeses, wines, coffees, Lenôtre pastries, pasta, grills, and sushi are served all day, every day but Sunday.

TELEPHONE
01-48-74-46-06
INTERNET
www.lafayettegourmet.com
OPEN
Mon–Sat: 9 A.M.–8 P.M. (Thur till 9 P.M.), continuous service
CLOSED
Sun; holidays, NAC
RESERVATIONS
Not accepted
CREDIT CARDS
AE, MC, V
À LA CARTE
25F (3.81€) and up
PRIX FIXE
None
ENGLISH SPOKEN
Yes

LE BISTRO DES DEUX THÉÂTRES (3)
18, rue Blanche
Métro: Trinité

Clichy and Pigalle are hardly bon-ton Paris neighborhoods. These infamous places, at the northern end of the ninth arrondissement, operate around the clock with peep shows, bordellos, and "ladies of the night" standing in doorways beckoning to passersby. Hidden amid all this

TELEPHONE
01-45-26-41-43
OPEN
Daily: lunch noon–2:30 P.M., dinner 7:15 P.M.–midnight
CLOSED
Never

sleaze are little pockets and jewels of respectability. Le Bistro des Deux Théâtres is one such place, a fine *formule* restaurant with a single prix fixe menu that has preserved its good cooking and authenticity despite its setting. This solid bistro manages to fill a variety of needs with its traditional charm, pressed linens, fresh flowers on each table, and its quality of preparation, which you would expect to find in a place charging twice as much.

The choices are excellent, at least ten for each course. Consider lobster ravioli, fresh asparagus in a buttery chervil sauce, artichoke hearts with a beet root vinaigrette, a dozen snails, goat cheese mousse with crayfish, and candied tomaotes and basil. Liver in a creamy bacon sauce, thyme-flavored lamb, or a cider roasted duck served with apples and potatoes are just a few of the possible main courses, which change frequently based on market availability and the season.

This is a good place to save room for dessert—indulge in flaming Grand Marnier crêpes, baked Alaska, hot apple tart with Calvados, dark chocolate cake, or a dreamy crème brûlée shot with bourbon. Both an apéritif and wine are included in the price, and unlike most restaurants of this type, you have more than one choice for your red, rosé, or white vintages. Dinner ends with a strong espresso.

RESERVATIONS
Advised

CREDIT CARDS
AE, MC, V

À LA CARTE
None

PRIX FIXE
Lunch and dinner: 179F (27.29€), 3 courses, BC

ENGLISH SPOKEN
Yes

LE BOUCHON DE CATHERINE (12)
63, rue de Provence
Métro: Chausée d'Antin–La Fayette

Chez Catherine is a Big Splurge, and a very good one (see page 181), but Le Bouchon de Catherine, the stylish sister bistro next door, is a good place to sample Catherine Guerraz's cooking without entirely abandoning your budget. Seating is on two floors at uncovered tables with rolled dish towels as napkins. The short, simple blackboard menu, for lunch only, centers on a *cuisine du marché* that changes every day. There is always a *plat du jour,* followed by a steak, fresh fish, and a pork or lamb dish. Crème caramel, pears in wine sauce, and chocolate cake are only a few of the rotating finales. The short list of wines is available by the glass, pitcher, or bottle.

TELEPHONE
01-48-78-67-00

OPEN
Mon–Fri: lunch noon–2:30 P.M.

CLOSED
Sat–Sun; holidays, July

RESERVATIONS
Essential

CREDIT CARDS
MC, V

À LA CARTE
145F (22.11€), BNC

PRIX FIXE
None

ENGLISH SPOKEN
Yes

LE PETIT BOFINGER (18)
20, boulevard Montmartre
Métro: Richelieu-Drouot

For a complete description, see Le Petit Bofinger, page 93. All other information is the same.

TELEPHONE: 01-47-70-91-35

LE RELAIS SAVOYARD (4)

TELEPHONE
01-45-26-17-48

OPEN
Mon–Sat: bar 8:30 A.M.–
10 P.M., lunch noon–2:30 P.M.,
dinner 7:30–10 P.M.

CLOSED
Sun; holidays, 10 days in
winter, a few days in May, Aug

RESERVATIONS
Accepted for 4 or more

CREDIT CARDS
V

À LA CARTE
130–150F (19.82–22.87€),
BNC

PRIX FIXE
Lunch and dinner: 85F
(12.96€), 125F (19.06€), both
3 courses and BC

ENGLISH SPOKEN
Limited

13, rue Rodier
Métro: Notre-Dame-de-Lorette

Le Relais Savoyard is a good example of the traditional French bistro, where the middle-aged *patron* and his wife have run things from behind the bar forever and the loyal, long-term waitresses have no intention of leaving. Overall, it is not sophisticated, but for a working-class atmosphere and a decent meal at the right price, it is just the ticket.

The timeless menu is a collection of homey dishes from the Savoy region of France. On a wintry evening it is nice to sit in the wood-paneled room in back, which is lined with the owners' collection of antique coffee and fondue pots, sauce dishes, and a stuffed boar's head. Order the *côte de veau maison,* a rich combination of veal, ham, mushrooms, and cheese, topped with Mornay sauce and flambéed. If you go with several other diners, either of the fondue specialties makes a satisfying choice. Desserts tend to be an afterthought on the part of the chef, so it is better to concentrate on the rest of the meal. If you are ordering white wine, ask for a bottle of Vin de Savoie Apremont.

LES BACCHANTES (7)

TELEPHONE
01-42-65-25-35

OPEN
Mon–Sat: 11:30 A.M.–
12:30 A.M., continuous service

CLOSED
Sun; NAC

RESERVATIONS
Not necessary

CREDIT CARDS
AE, MC, V

À LA CARTE
50–140F (7.62–21.34€), BNC

PRIX FIXE
None

ENGLISH SPOKEN
Limited

21, rue Caumartin
Métro: Havre-Caumartin

You can't order a beer or a cola, and *l'eau municipale est sur demande* (tap water is by request). You can, however, order fine wines by the glass or bottle at Raymond Pocous's popular wine bar. He stocks over forty international vintages, along with the best France has to offer, and he features different bottles weekly. Okay, the wine is good, but is there anything decent to eat? Absolutely . . . you can have plates of cheese or *charcuterie* (cold meats), *tartines* (open-faced sandwiches), their own foie gras and pâté, omelettes, daily specials, salads, and homemade desserts. Besides the good wine and food, the atmosphere is fun and friendly and the prices great for most value-seekers in Paris.

LES DIABLES AU THYM ($, 16)
35, rue Bergère
Métro: Grands Boulevards

If I could, I would return to Serge and Patricia Uriot's Les Diables au Thym every night. Whenever you are fortunate enough to be in Paris, you can always come here for an exquisite meal and impeccable service. Being here makes me feel I am a guest in a good friend's small, intimate dining room. Fresh flowers and hurricane candles grace the linen-covered tables, the china is Villeroy and Boch, and the seating on banquettes and padded chairs is comfortable. One waiter and Patricia serve the entire room, which has tables filled by 8:30 P.M. and people still arriving at 10:30 P.M., just before the kitchen closes.

The à la carte menu is seasonal, but the prix fixe selections change every few weeks. No matter what you order, every beautifully prepared and presented dish seems to be a winner, especially the terrine of foie gras you liberally spread on toast, the real French onion soup (with plenty of simmered onions and a top hat of crusty cheese), and the colorful assortment of fresh vegetables with a soft poached egg on top. Next, consider lamb *tournedos* flavored with tarragon, medallions of veal with asparagus, or the tender rabbit in a broccoli and mustard cream sauce.

For dessert bliss, look no further than these two dishes: the *croquette au chocolat praliné,* a voluptuous creation that oozes bittersweet chocolate with every bite, and the *mille-feuille caramelise aux pommes et son sorbet,* caramelized apples layered with flaky pastry and accented by cool apple sorbet. Coffee comes with a plate of homemade cookies and pieces of white and dark chocolate.

NOTE: There is a nonsmoking section.

TELEPHONE
01-47-70-77-09

OPEN
Mon–Fri: lunch noon–2:30 P.M., dinner 7–10:30 P.M.; Sat: dinner 7–10:30 P.M.

CLOSED
Sat lunch, Sun; Aug

RESERVATIONS
Essential

CREDIT CARDS
AE, MC, V

À LA CARTE
225–240F (34.30–36.59€), BNC

PRIX FIXE
Lunch: 123F (18.75€), 2 courses, BNC; lunch and dinner: 148F (22.56€), 3 courses, BNC

ENGLISH SPOKEN
Yes

RESTAURANT CHARTIER (17)
7, rue du Faubourg Montmartre
Métro: Grands Boulevards

You can trust the French to know a good food bargain when they smell it, and for decades penny-wise Parisians have made Restaurant Chartier a major destination. Not much has changed over the years in this authentic Parisian soup kitchen with its *fin-de-siècle* decor, squads of brusque white-aproned waiters, and basic "no parsley" food. There is no glamour or tinsel here. Big, noisy, barnlike, and always crowded, it is the blue-collar

TELEPHONE
01-47-70-86-29

OPEN
Daily: lunch 11 A.M.–3 P.M., dinner 6–9:30 P.M.

CLOSED
Never

RESERVATIONS
Not necessary

CREDIT CARDS
MC, V (100F, 15.24€, minimum)

À LA CARTE
80–100F (12.20–15.24€), BNC

PRIX FIXE
Lunch and dinner: 110F (16.77€), 3 courses, BC

ENGLISH SPOKEN
Limited

worker's Maxim's, and they and many others eat here in droves every day of the year.

The menu, which changes daily, is long, but if you select carefully, you will have a satisfying and cheap meal. Select the dishes that have to be made to order and save the fancier ones for another place. You could start with a beet or tomato salad, hard-boiled egg and mayonnaise, or a plate of ham. Order a jug of the house wine to go with your main coarse of roast chicken, fish, or grilled beef, along with potatoes that have been fried or boiled. All garnishes are extra, even the ketchup and mayonnaise, but they are not much. If it is listed, the most reliable dessert is a fruit *tarte*.

TEA FOLLIES (1)
6, place Gustave Toudouze
Métro: St-Georges

TELEPHONE
01-42-80-08-44

OPEN
Mon, Sun: 10 A.M.–7 P.M.; Tues–Sat: 10 A.M.–11 P.M.; continuous service (no hot food 4–7 P.M.)

CLOSED
Christmas and New Year's Day, NAC

RESERVATIONS
Recommended for Sun brunch

CREDIT CARDS
AE, MC, V (100F, 15.24€, minimum)

À LA CARTE
90–150F (13.72–22.87€), BNC

PRIX FIXE
Mon–Sat blackboard menu: 69F (10.52€), 2 courses, BNC; Sun brunch: 100F (15.24€), 155F (23.63€), both BNC

ENGLISH SPOKEN
Yes

Many first-time visitors to Paris do not stray far from the beaten track. This is too bad because they miss some of the most interesting places that way. Not too far from Montmartre, and near a number of small theaters, is Tea Follies, a welcome place to relax after looking through the antique shops and funky clothing boutiques around place St-Georges.

When I go, I order the tangy lemon-curd *tarte* or the *archedois,* a fattening delight made with chocolate and chestnuts, and spend a lazy hour leafing through the English and French periodicals stacked about. On warm afternoons, the cobblestone terrace is the place to sit and order a beautiful salad lunch or one of the specialties of the chef: either the Bombay chicken, the cheese ravioli, or the salmon tagliatelle. On Sunday, filling brunches are offered and include buttery scones, light soufflés, and a Bloody Mary to really get you going for the day. Bonuses for many are the special nonsmoking section and the changing art exhibits featuring work by local artists.

NOTE: There is a nonsmoking section.

VERDEAU DROUOT (15)
25, passage Verdeau (across from 6, rue de la Grange Batelière)
Métro: Richelieu-Drouot

TELEPHONE
01-45-23-15-96

OPEN
Mon–Fri: lunch noon–3 P.M., tea 3–4 P.M.

CLOSED
Sat–Sun; holidays, Aug 15–30

Just because a French person goes to an office every day does not mean he or she is going to sacrifice having a proper lunch or, worse yet, brown bag it. On the other hand, French office workers, like those around the world, usually have only an hour to eat, and they don't want to spend big money on a wine-infused, expensive meal. Enter Verdeau Drouot, which brings a touch of class to *la cuisine rapide*. The restaurant is in the passage Verdeau Drouot, a nineteenth-century shopping arcade, which houses small shops selling old books, cameras, early rock-and-roll records, and other collectibles.

Verdeau Drouot offers full meals on a single plate, called *assiettes gourmandes froides* (cold) or *chaudes* (hot). Each has been given a catchy name, such as *Petrouchka* (smoked salmon, *tarama,* salad, dark bread, and fresh fruit), *Safari Tartes* (assorted warm *tartes* with a green salad), *Némèa* (chicken curry on basmati rice with a mixed salad), and *Winnipeg* (cold roast beef with fresh vegetables, potatoes, salad, and fruit). While these *assiettes gourmandes* are well priced, the sage values here are the two prix fixe menus. For example, *la formule gourmande* includes any *assiette gourmande* and dessert, one glass of wine, and coffee. *Le verdeau express* offers the *plat du jour* and a dessert. All desserts are made here. The most popular are the Norwegian apple and cinnamon cake (adapted from a recipe of the owner's mother's) and the house specialty, *gâteau noix* (nut cake). No matter how you order, it will be a filling meal that is much more interesting and French than a burger and fries someplace else.

RESERVATIONS
Not necessary

CREDIT CARDS
MC, V (100F, 15.24€, minimum)

À LA CARTE
100–130F (15.24–19.82€), BNC

PRIX FIXE
La formule gourmande: 106–133F (16.16–20.28€), 2 courses, BC; *verdeau express:* 78F (11.89€), 2 courses, BNC

ENGLISH SPOKEN
Yes

Tenth Arrondissement

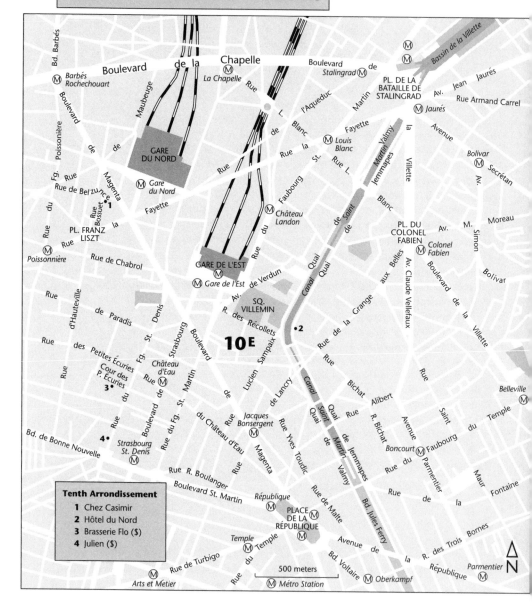

Tenth Arrondissement

1 Chez Casimir
2 Hôtel du Nord
3 Brasserie Flo ($)
4 Julien ($)

Bd. Barbés

Barbés Rochechouart Ⓜ

Boulevard

Boulevard de la Chapelle Ⓜ

de la

Chapelle

La Chapelle

Rue

Boulevard de Stalingrad Ⓜ

PL. DE LA BATAILLE DE STALINGRAD

Bassin de la Villette

Av. Jean Jaurés

Rue Armand Carrel

Ⓜ Jaurés

Boulevard

Poissonière

Maubeuge

l'Aqueduc

Martin

L.

de Blanc

Fayette

Ⓜ Louis Blanc

Valmy

Martin

Jemmapes

la

Villette

Avenue

Bolivar

Ⓜ Secrétan

Av.

de

de

GARE DU NORD

Rue

la

Rue

St.

Rue L.

du Fg. Rue

Rue de Bel zu n ce 1

Magenta

la

Ⓜ Gare du Nord

Rue Bossuet

Fayette

Rue

Rue

Faubourg

de

de Saint

de

Blanc

PL. DU COLONEL FABIEN

M. Moreau

Simon

PL. FRANZ LISZT

Ⓜ Château Landon

Quai

Av. aux Belles

Colonel Ⓜ Fabien

Av. Claude Velefaux

Bolivar

Ⓜ Poissonnière

Rue de Chabrol

GARE DE L'EST

Ⓜ Gare de l'Est de Verdun

Quai

Boulevard de la Villette

Rue

d'Hauteville

Denis

Av.

SQ. VILLEMIN

R. des Récollets

Quai

•2

Rue de la Grange

Rue

de Paradis

St.

Strasbourg

Boulevard

10E

Sampaix

Rue

Bichat

Alibert

Belleville Ⓜ

Rue

des Petites Écuries

Château d'Eau

Rue de

St. Martin

Lucien

Canal

Saint

Rue

R. Bichat

Saint

du Temple

Cour des P. Écuries

3•

Rue du

de

de

Jacques Bonsergent Ⓜ

Quai

de

Avenue

Ⓜ Faubourg

Bd. de Bonne Nouvelle

4•

Strasbourg St. Denis Ⓜ

Rue du Fg. St. Martin

Rue

du Château d'Eau

Rue Yves Toudic

Magenta

Martin

Boncourt Ⓜ du Parmentier

Maur

Fontaine

Rue R. Boulanger

Boulevard St. Martin

République Ⓜ

PLACE DE LA RÉPUBLIQUE Ⓜ

Rue de Malte

Valmy

Bd. Jules Ferry

Rue

de

la

Bornes

Temple Ⓜ du Temple

Rue de Turbigo

Bd. Voltaire

Avenue de

la

République

R. des Trois

Parmentier Ⓜ

Arts et Metier Ⓜ

Rue

du

500 meters

Ⓜ Métro Station

Ⓜ Oberkampf

N

Tenth Arrondissement

Although most visitors to Paris only pass through the tenth arrondissement when they take a train from either the Gare du Nord or the Gare de l'Est, there is another good reason to venture into this *quartier populaire,* or traditional working-class neighborhood: to shop for china and crystal along rue de Paradis and visit the famous Baccarat crystal museum and store about half-way down the same street. For bargains, if you consider anything in Baccarat to be that, look for the red dots on items displayed on the back tables.

RIGHT BANK
Canal St-Martin, place de la République, rue de Paradis, Gare du Nord, and Gare de l'Est

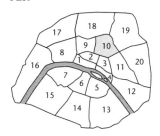

TENTH ARRONDISSEMENT RESTAURANTS

($) indicates a Big Splurge

BRASSERIE FLO ($, 3)
7, cour des Petites-Écuries
Métro: Château d'Eau, Strasbourg–St-Denis

TELEPHONE
01-47-70-13-59

OPEN
Daily: lunch noon–3 P.M.,
dinner 7 P.M.–1 A.M.

CLOSED
Never

RESERVATIONS
Advised, definitely on
weekends

CREDIT CARDS
AE, DC, MC, V

À LA CARTE
225–260F (34.30–39.64€),
BNC

PRIX FIXE
Lunch: 140F (21.34€),
2 courses, 180F (27.44€)
3 courses, both BC; dinner:
190F (28.97€), 3 courses, BC;
dinner after 10 P.M.: 140F
(21.34€), 2 courses, BC

ENGLISH SPOKEN
Yes

Brasserie Flo is another star in the crown of Jean-Paul Bucher's resurrected Art Nouveau brasseries, and if you are shopping along rue de Paradis (see *Great Sleeps Paris,* "Shopping"), this is a great lunch stop. To say that this one is not easy to find is an understatement if there ever was one. The first time I went, I was sure the taxi driver was taking me on a wild goose chase, and when he left me off at the opening of a dark alley in a questionable neighborhood, I was positive of it. Once inside, however, the approach was completely forgotten. Seated along a banquette in one of the two long rooms—with their dark wood walls, zinc bar, and waiters with long aprons serving a dressed-to-the-teeth crowd—you will feel truly Parisian.

Every day of the year Brasserie Flo is a great place to go for platters of oysters, Alsatian *choucroutes* (their specialty), onion soup, foie gras, and grilled meat. Late-nighters and lunch patrons have special menus in addition to the versatile à la carte.

NOTE: Cour des Petites-Écuries is a small alley between rue de Foubourg-St-Denis and passage des Petites-Écuries. Since the neighborhood is questionable, I would advise taking a taxi at night.

CHEZ CASIMIR (1)
6, rue de Belzunce, at rue Bossuet
Métro: Gare du Nord

TELEPHONE
01-48-78-28-80

OPEN
Mon–Fri: lunch noon–2 P.M.,
dinner 7–11:30 P.M.;
Sat: dinner 7–11:30 P.M.

CLOSED
Sat lunch, Sun; Aug, one week
in Dec or Jan

RESERVATIONS
Essential

CREDIT CARDS
None

À LA CARTE
140–160F (21.34–24.39€)

PRIX FIXE
None

ENGLISH SPOKEN
Limited

Chez Casimir is the bare-bones bistro spin-off of Thierry Breton, whose Chez Michel a few doors away has been filled from the first day with Parisian diners eager to encourage talented young chefs to strike out on their own. At Chez Casimir, the prices are reasonable, the mood is simple and relaxed, the atmosphere plain, and the food worth the safari no matter where you are in the city. As with most baby bistros in Paris, the menu is written on a blackboard and reflects the season and the mood of the chef. For either lunch or dinner, you may start with a sardine-and-parmesan-cheese-filled pastry or perhaps a simple salad of bitter greens. You will be thankful the *entrées* are light when next you are faced with strapping dishes of either *petit salé aux lentilles,* roast chicken with mashed potatoes, *boeuf bourguignon* with carrots and garlic confit, or wild game and venison in season. Desserts, including apple bread pudding and stewed pears with caramel ice cream, are mellow reminders of childhood favorites.

HÔTEL DU NORD (2)
102, quai de Jemmapes
Métro: Jacques-Bonsergent

"Being here makes you feel you really know something about Paris," mused my friend as we sat outside overlooking the picturesque Canal St-Martin and the footbridge crossing it. It was a lazy Sunday afternoon, the sun was shining, and spring was just brushing the trees with green. Along with the live music and good, basic café food, it added up to a wonderful Parisian experience. This romantic spot was the site of the 1938 French film classic of the same name, starring Louis Jovet and Arletty. Today, the café has been rediscovered by an eclectic, almost trendy crowd featuring young couples holding hands and grannies peeking into prams.

At midday, stop in and have a drink standing at the original 1930s bar, or sit down with the *plat du jour*. Afterward, walk along the length of the pretty canal. It all has great charm, a worthwhile stop in a part of Paris that has not lost its soul. On Thursday, Friday, and Saturday nights, the café becomes a stage for stand-up comedy (in English) where drinking, smoking, and lots of laughing are on tap, but little in the way food, aside from sandwiches. The lineup of talent is impressive, with the likes of Eddie Izzard, Robert Newman, and Rich Hall having been among the headliners. On Sunday and Monday nights from 8:30 P.M., live music, usually with a singer, keeps everyone in a good mood. Saturday and Sunday daytime openings depend on the weather and mood of the owner, James Arch. For both the comedy and live music performances, always call ahead to book. You can usually count on Hôtel du Nord being open during the day from spring through early autumn, but before you make the trip, it is a good idea to call ahead to check.

NOTE: Cover charge for comedy nights (Thur–Sat) is 100–120F (15.24–18.29€), depending on the act. No cover for live music on Sunday and Monday.

TELEPHONE
01-40-40-78-78 (restaurant reservations),
01-53-19-98-88 (entertainment reservations)

OPEN
Mon–Wed: lunch noon–3 P.M., dinner 8–11:30 P.M.; Thur–Fri: lunch noon–3 P.M.; Thur–Sat stand-up comedy 7:30–10:30 P.M.; Sun, Mon live music 8:30–11:30 P.M.

CLOSED
Sat & Sun during the day in winter, or if the weather is bad; NAC

RESERVATIONS
Recommended for live performances

CREDIT CARDS
AE, DC, MC, V

À LA CARTE
100–150F (15.24–22.87€), BNC

PRIX FIXE
Lunch: 75F (11.43€), 2 courses, 95F (14.48€), 3 courses, both BNC; dinner: 125F (19.06€), 175F (26.68€), both 3 courses and BNC

ENGLISH SPOKEN
Yes

JULIEN ($, 4)
16, rue du Faubourg St-Denis
Métro: Strasbourg–St-Denis

TELEPHONE
01-47-70-12-06

OPEN
Daily: lunch noon–3 P.M.,
dinner 7 P.M.–1:30 A.M.

CLOSED
Never

RESERVATIONS
Essential

CREDIT CARDS
AE, DC, MC, V

À LA CARTE
210–250F (32.01–38.11€),
BNC

PRIX FIXE
Lunch and dinner: 140F
(21.34€), 2 courses, 180F
(27.44€), 3 courses, both BC

ENGLISH SPOKEN
Yes

Leave the shady red-light neighborhood behind as you pass through velvet curtains into this Art Deco wonderland, which encompasses one of the most beautiful brasserie dining rooms in Paris. The stunning decor is an amazing combination of magnificent stained-glass ceiling panels and Mucha-style molten glass, massive globe lights, huge floral displays, and a collection of vintage *chapeaux* hanging from brass hat racks. Even the tiled floor is remarkable. The menu is a standard list of brasserie favorites (without the oyster stand) accompanied by plenty of wine, good cheer, and a formally attired waitstaff serving an audience of fashionable French diners.

NOTE: A taxi is strongly advised at night.

Eleventh Arrondissement

The Bastille was the site of France's most famous prison, which was overrun on July 14, 1789, marking the birth of the French Revolution. All that remains today of the Bastille is a faint outline traced in cobblestones. The latest revolution is the new Bastille opera house, which, upon completion, instantaneously turned this formerly "off-limits" *quartier* into one of the most trendy, must-go, must-see, and must-try parts of Paris. The area mixes back-alley workers and workshops with hip new designers and their boutiques. Don't be surprised to see panhandlers, overflowing garbage cans, and some very seedy restaurants and bars mixed in with the hot spots. Action in the eleventh begins around 10 P.M., when it becomes a meat market and cruising territory for the hipsters who prowl the streets, fill the restaurants, and drink in the bars until the first rays of dawn.

RIGHT BANK
Colonne de Juillet (July Column), Opéra Bastille, rue de Lappe and rue Oberkampf (for nightlife)

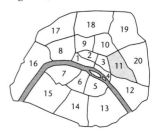

ELEVENTH ARRONDISSEMENT RESTAURANTS

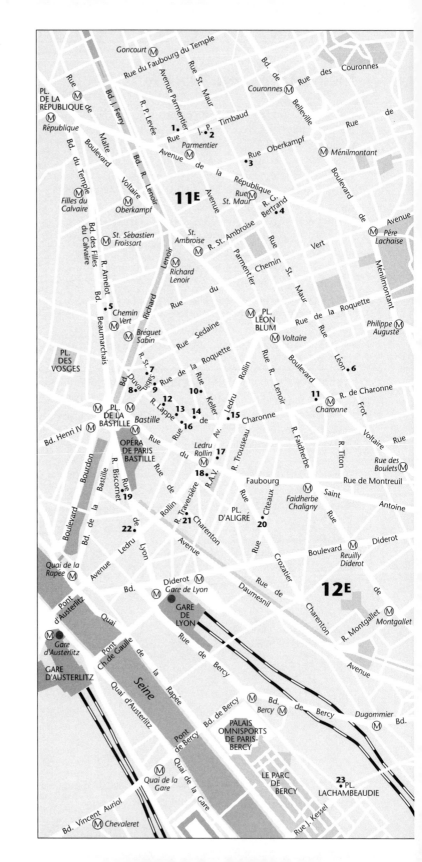

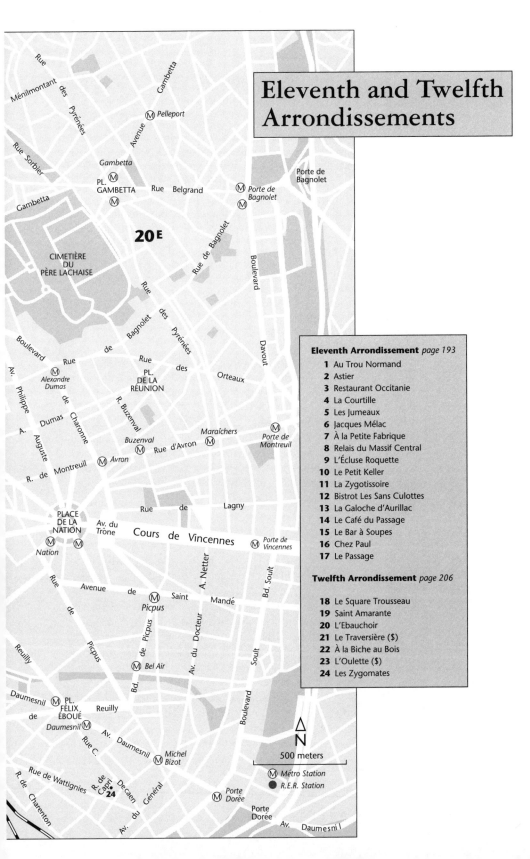

Eleventh and Twelfth Arrondissements

N
500 meters

Ⓜ Métro Station
● R.E.R. Station

À LA PETITE FABRIQUE (7)
12, rue St-Sabin
Métro: Bréguet-Sabin

TELEPHONE
01-43-14-08-82
OPEN
Tues–Sat: 10:30 A.M.–7:30 P.M.
CLOSED
Mon, Sun; 2 weeks in Aug
(dates vary)
CREDIT CARDS
V
PRICES
25F (3.81€) and up
ENGLISH SPOKEN
Limited

Fellow chocoholics are invited to join me at Bruno Cagnazzoli's chocolate factory, where artisinal chocolates are made with only pure ingredients: no preservatives, no vegetable fat, and no cream. Notice I did *not* say "no calories." Ranking among the top ten chocolatiers in the city, Corsican-born Cagnazzoli makes the run-of-the-mill imitations look and taste like axle grease. Just one bite of his cocoa-dusted truffles, his dark chocolate–dipped orange rind, or even a simple bar flecked with nuts will spoil you forever for anything but the best. Not only can you buy his chocolates here, but you can watch them being made in the back.

ASTIER (2)
44, rue Jean-Pierre Timbaud
Métro: Parmentier

TELEPHONE
01-43-57-16-35
OPEN
Mon–Fri: lunch noon–2 P.M.,
dinner 8–11 P.M.
CLOSED
Sat–Sun; holidays, last 2 weeks
in April, last week of July and
all of Aug
RESERVATIONS
Essential as far in advance as
possible
CREDIT CARDS
MC, V
À LA CARTE
None
PRIX FIXE
Lunch: 120F (18.29€),
2 courses, BNC; lunch and
dinner: 145F (22.11€),
4 courses, BNC
ENGLISH SPOKEN
Yes

If Astier did not exist, it would have to be invented because nowhere is everything you have ever heard about Paris dining more in evidence than in this noisy, hot, crowded bistro where everyone looks like a regular. The only thing to admire in the plain interior is the graceful staircase, which is almost lost behind the bar. The seating at tightly packed, smaller-than-usual tables puts you practically on your neighbor's lap, and it causes some ducking if the casually clad waiters swing the plates too low. However, if you speak even a little French, your neighbor's conversations might provide some very thought-provoking eavesdropping.

Abundance is the name of the game for the kitchen and a warning is in order. The prix fixe meal, which is all that's available, includes four *enormous* courses that tend to grow as the meal progresses. The ten-page wine list with over three hundred bottles keeps pace. Be careful when ordering because each course could constitute an entire meal, as my dining companion found out when he ordered the homemade pasta with basil as an *entrée*. When his plate arrived, we both gasped . . . it was enough for both of us, and this was only the beginning. The handwritten (but legible) menu changes constantly, reflecting the seasonal changes at the market. A safe and sane beginning would be one of the salads, which should leave room to do justice to a *blanquette de porc, lapin à la moutard,* or any of the fresh fish dishes the chef loves to prepare. The cheese platter is magnificent and includes at least twenty choices. You are encouraged to help yourself to as much as you can eat. Desserts do not fall behind. There is an impressive array of fruit and sugar creations, which are all made here except for the sorbet. Those going for the calorie jackpot will want the chocolate fudge slice floating in a coffee cream sauce. Those hoping to walk out unassisted will probably go for the fresh fruit or the warm apple gratin.

The food at Astier more than makes up for the crowded conditions, scattered service, and uninspired decor. As my friend said, "You can't eat the decor or the service, but you can certainly pay for it." At Astier, you know that all you are paying for is the food, and it is worth every value-packed bite—as well as the diet you will swear to start tomorrow.

AU TROU NORMAND (1)
9, rue Jean-Pierre Timbaud
Métro: Parmentier

For twenty-six years, Maggie Latrille arrived at 8:30 A.M. and cooked lunch and dinner at Au Trou Normand. She still arrives early but is now stationed behind the bar, pouring the wine into carafes, making the coffee, and handling the cash register. I think she deserves time off from KP; after all, she told me that on her last birthday she turned seventy-six. However, no matter who is cooking, Au Trou Normand is a good, old-time, inexpensive great eat in Paris that promises nothing fancy; it just delivers the basics to students, shirtsleeved merchants, and backpacking tourists on budgets. Everyone sits at tables with yellow tablecloths, and service is by waitresses wearing comfortable shoes and housedresses or tight jeans and tighter T-shirts. The menu hardly transcends the ordinary, but it will satisfy most hunger and budget pangs. A dozen or so *entrées* and *plats* feature hard-boiled eggs in a mayonnaise sauce, *crudités,* anchovies and potatoes, and grated cabbage, carrot, or celery for *entrées*. Main courses include innards, grilled meats, veal, lamb, and pork. To end, look only as far as the banana *tarte*—it's not only the best dessert, but the one nod to originality going.

TELEPHONE
01-48-05-80-23

OPEN
Mon–Fri: lunch noon–
2:30 P.M., dinner 7:30–11 P.M.;
Sat: dinner 7:30–11 P.M.

CLOSED
Sat lunch, Sun; holidays, Aug

RESERVATIONS
Not necessary

CREDIT CARDS
None

À LA CARTE
70–95F (10.67–14.48€), BNC

PRIX FIXE
None

ENGLISH SPOKEN
None

BISTROT LES SANS CULOTTES (12)
27, rue de Lappe
Métro: Bastille

TELEPHONE
01-48-05-42-92

OPEN
Tues–Wed: dinner 7:30 P.M.–
midnight; Thur–Sun: lunch
noon–3 P.M., dinner 7:30 P.M.–
midnight

CLOSED
Tues–Wed lunch, Mon;
holidays, NAC

RESERVATIONS
Advised

CREDIT CARDS
AE, DC, MC, V

À LA CARTE
185F (28.20€), BNC

PRIX FIXE
Lunch: 90F (13.72€), 2 courses,
BC; dinner: 125F (19.06€),
3 courses, BNC

ENGLISH SPOKEN
Yes

Even though the dining establishments in and around the eleventh arrondissement near the modern Opéra Bastille are considered *the* trendy places these days, some of them are old familiar fixtures that have been doing a brisk business for years. Such is Bistrot Les Sans Culottes on the well-trodden rue de Lappe, which cuts through the heart of the district. It began many years ago as a *charcuterie,* and you can still see the old marble counter and colored tiles just to the left of the bar. Now it is a popular place to eat and drink with friends. Seating is downstairs along wooden banquettes or upstairs in a mirrored room with aging yellow walls and an Art Deco mural of the place Vendôme.

Concentrate on the prix fixe meals for either lunch or dinner and the final tab will be well within budget. For lunch you have a choice of any two courses, ranging from the obligatory chicken liver terrine to the interesting bowl of mussels in a balsamic vinaigrette. Mouthwatering main dishes include *blanquette de veau,* chicken with thyme, and a tender *bavette* (skirt steak) smothered in shallots. A choice of substantial desserts—such as *tarte fine chaude aux pommes* (warm apple tart), pistachio crème brûlée with cherries, or a bowl of fresh, seasonal berries—rounds out the meal.

NOTE: There is a nonsmoking section. There is also a hotel in connection with the restaurant, but it is not recommended.

CHEZ PAUL (16)
13, rue Charonne, at rue de Lappe
Métro: Bastille, Ledru-Rollin

TELEPHONE
01-47-00-34-57

OPEN
Daily: lunch noon–3 P.M.,
dinner 7 P.M.–midnight

CLOSED
Never

RESERVATIONS
Essential

CREDIT CARDS
AE, MC, V

À LA CARTE
145–170F (22.11–25.92€),
BNC

A mix of all ages and types know they can afford to be seen at Chez Paul, a virtual mecca for mixing, mingling, and people-watching at the corner of rue de Charonne and rue de Lappe. Beyond the yellowed, flaking walls and perpetual haze of smoke, there is no decor—the atmosphere consists entirely of the people sitting around you, and they will include everyone from construction workers to aging and wanna-be film stars. The purple-inked handwritten menu looks more like hieroglyphics than French, but you will be able to pick out standards of *chèvre en salade, poireaux vinaigrette, filets d'hareng—*

pommes à l'huile (herring with warm potato salad), plates of *charcuterie,* and the house specialty—*soupe de poissons* (fish soup). Meaty dishes of steak, lamb, kidneys, duck, and rabbit are followed by crowd-pleasing desserts of crème caramel, *île flottante,* and *tarte Tatin* with crème fraîche.

PRIX FIXE
None

ENGLISH SPOKEN
Usually

JACQUES MÉLAC (6)
42, rue Léon-Frot
Métro: Charonne

The handwritten sign hanging in this wine bar not too far from the Bastille states, *L'eau est ici reservée pour faire cuire les pommes de terre!*—"Water here is reserved for cooking potatoes!" Started by Jacques's father before World War II, Jacques Mélac is extremely popular, 100 percent authentic, and an absolute must for anyone who loves a good time and good wine. Jacques, with his handlebar mustache and infectious enthusiasm, broadcasts a message of welcome loud and clear to everyone who enters. Don't worry if your high school French is a little rusty; after raising a few glasses at the bar with the rambunctious crowd, your communication skills will improve dramatically. Go with a group or alone and you are bound to be in good company, sampling wines and munching on platters of *charcuterie* or Auvergne cheeses and loaves of chewy Poilâne bread. Jacques also serves hot dishes and fantastic omelettes for both lunch and dinner.

Winner of the 1981 Meilleur Pot (best wine bar in Paris), the wine bar also sells its own wine by the bottle or case. The wine, Domaine des Trois Filles, is a red named for Mélac's three daughters, Marie-Hélène, Laura, and Sara. This is the only wine bar in Paris boasting its own vineyard, with the vines growing on the roof and climbing up the outside walls. In September the grapes are harvested, and usually there is enough for a single barrel of wine, which is always cause for great celebration. Celebration also ensues during the annual arrival of Beaujolais nouveau, which all but flows in the street in late November, as do the patrons. Don't worry, however, if you miss one of these great parties, since as Jacques says, "Here we celebrate wine every day we're open."

TELEPHONE
01-43-70-59-27

OPEN
Mon: bar 9 A.M.–midnight, lunch noon–2:30 P.M.; Tues–Sat: bar 9 A.M.–midnight, lunch noon–2:30 P.M., dinner 7:30–10 P.M.

CLOSED
Mon dinner, Sun; holidays, Aug, one week at Christmas

RESERVATIONS
Not accepted

CREDIT CARDS
MC, V

À LA CARTE
60–85F (9.15–12.96€), BNC

PRIX FIXE
None

ENGLISH SPOKEN
Usually

LA COURTILLE (4)
16, rue Guillaume Bertrand
Métro: St-Maur

TELEPHONE
01-48-06-48-34

OPEN
Mon–Fri: lunch 11:30 A.M.–
2:30 P.M., dinner 7:30–10 P.M.;
Sat: dinner 7:30–10 P.M.

CLOSED
Sat lunch, Sun; major
holidays, Aug

RESERVATIONS
Recommended

CREDIT CARDS
MC, V

À LA CARTE
None

PRIX FIXE
Lunch: 78F (11.89€), 2 courses,
84F (12.81€), 3 courses, both
BNC; dinner: 134F (20.43€),
3 courses, BNC

ENGLISH SPOKEN
Yes

La Courtille is the kind of place you might hear about from someone who knows the quiet, back residential streets in the eleventh arrondissement. I know that everyone I have taken to La Courtille returns . . . even if they are in Paris for only a few days. This is strong testimony to the food served by Yves Millot and Eric Barriol, the congenial new owners of La Courtille. Both men have been friends for more than thirty years, as attested by the group photo hanging behind the bar showing them with the rest of their college class.

The collection of Asian art, the crisp linen table-cloths, and the fresh flowers are welcoming in the small dining room, which is intimate without being crowded. The food is as uncluttered and elegant as the surroundings. The house foie gras on a bed of green beans is always a favorite starter. Whatever fresh fish is offered is worthy of serious consideration, and so is the *magret de canard* or the *escalope courtille*, a chicken cordon bleu. I would never miss the *fondant glacé au chocolat*—a soft dark chocolate cake. However, the rum-soaked *baba* with rum-raisin ice cream on the side has its devoted fans as well.

LA GALOCHE D'AURILLAC (13)
41, rue de Lappe
Métro: Bastille, Ledru-Rollin

TELEPHONE
01-47-00-77-15

OPEN
Tues–Sat: bar 11 A.M.–
11:30 P.M., lunch noon–
2:30 P.M., dinner 7–11:30 P.M.,
charcuterie 10 A.M.–midnight

CLOSED
Mon, Sun; Aug

RESERVATIONS
Advised

CREDIT CARDS
MC, V

À LA CARTE
190–210F (28.97–32.01€),
BNC

PRIX FIXE
Lunch and dinner: 150F
(22.87€), 3 courses, BNC

ENGLISH SPOKEN
Yes

Auvergne food specialties, including regional hams and sausages, are sold until the bewitching hour on the *charcuterie* side of this popular bistro, which is handy to know if someone wants a plate of wonderful sausage at midnight. But if you are eating here, you'll find that the two-level dining section is picturesque, to say the least—all decked out with wooden Auvergne galoshes strung across the ceiling and walls along with hanging hams and sausages. The welcome from owners M. and Mme. Bonnet (who is the cook) and their staff is warm.

The cooking plays tribute to the lusty foods of south-western France and is nonchalantly indifferent to changing trends. The dishes are geared for those indifferent to any sort of diet, who just plain love to eat and relish a satisfying meal. To start, indulge in a plate of Auvergne ham or sausage, a salad filled with lentils, red beans, and goose liver, or a cheese soup whose number of calories could pass for a zip code. Respectable dishes of tripe, roast goose, *confit de canard,* and veal are served daily. On Saturday night, come for the *plate de resistance—chou farci* (baked, stuffed cabbage). Even though you will not be able to consume another bite, desserts do merit serious attention, especially the hot apple tart loaded with Calvados.

LA ZYGOTISSOIRE (11)
101, rue de Charonne
Métro: Charonne

If you like the staple French bistro cooking served at Les Zygomates (see page 208), you will also be enthusiastic about this sister site, which is in a more convenient location from a visitor's point of view. This is simple food in pleasant surroundings, and the specialty is grilled meat, making it a haven for carnivores. If you order either the lunch or dinner prix fixe menu, you can start your meal with a salad, served with a basket of their own bread, and wrap things up with a fruit tart or dish of rice pudding . . . and be out the door for around $15 and change. If you opt for à la carte, which expands your choices almost tenfold, try the juicy duck or the rare *entrecôte* steak in a rich red wine sauce. Still hungry? For dessert, the *assiette gourmande* tempts you with a plate of bite-size samplings of all their desserts.

TELEPHONE
01-40-09-93-03

OPEN
Mon–Fri: lunch noon–2 P.M., dinner 7:30–11 P.M.; Sat: dinner 7:30–11 P.M.

CLOSED
Sat lunch, Sun; 2 weeks in Aug (dates vary)

RESERVATIONS
Recommended

CREDIT CARDS
MC, V

À LA CARTE
180F (27.44€), BNC

PRIX FIXE
Lunch: 85F (12.96€), 3 courses and coffee; dinner: 110F (16.77€), 3 courses, BNC

ENGLISH SPOKEN
Limited

LE BAR À SOUPES (15)
33, rue de Charonne
Métro: Ledru-Rollin

Soups to eat here or take away are Anne Catherine's specialties; she is the proud owner of this sunny yellow soup bar. Every day you can count on at least seven soups, four of which change, to be ladled up with chunks of organic dark bread. Side orders are kept to a minimum: a plate of *charcuterie* or cheese and a dessert or two. Forget all the frills, just order soup. The possibilities are mind-boggling. The *indienne aux lentilles blondes* is flavored with curry, coriander, cumin, tomatoes, onions, and raisins; the tomato cream soup is topped with pieces of ricotta cheese; the *portugaise au haddock* blends in cabbage and chorizo sausage; and the pea soup is flavored with smoky bacon. In the summer, several cold soups join the lineup of one of the best, and certainly the healthiest, meals you will have in Paris.

TELEPHONE
01-43-57-53-79

OPEN
Mon–Sat: lunch noon– 3:30 P.M., dinner 6:30–11 P.M.

CLOSED
Sun; NAC

RESERVATIONS
Not accepted

CREDIT CARDS
None

À LA CARTE
25–35F (3.81–5.34€), soup and bread, BNC; soup to go (no bread): 13–30F (1.98–4.57€)

PRIX FIXE
Lunch: 55F (8.38€), soup, *charcuterie* or cheese, BC

ENGLISH SPOKEN
Yes

LE CAFÉ DU PASSAGE (14)
12, rue de Charonne
Métro: Bastille, Ledru-Rollin

TELEPHONE
01-49-29-97-64

OPEN
Mon–Fri: dinner 6 P.M.–2 A.M.;
Sat: noon–2 A.M., continuous
service

CLOSED
Sun; major holidays, NAC

RESERVATIONS
Not necessary

CREDIT CARDS
MC, V

À LA CARTE
55–95F (8.38–14.48€), BNC

PRIX FIXE
None

ENGLISH SPOKEN
Yes

After the successful opening of Le Passage around the corner (see below), Gerard Pantanacce turned the day-to-day operation over to his wife, and then he directed his attention to this sophisticated nocturnal wine bar, where he specializes in côte du Rhône wines and features an interesting selection of more than threee hundred international wines and single-malt Scotch whiskeys. Seating options range from slatted metal chairs on the sidewalk—providing front-row seats to the passing pageant—and overstuffed armchairs in the intimate, clubby back room to a corner grouping of leopard-cushioned wicker armchairs that overlooks the garden. Food plays second fiddle to the wine, but you can order sandwiches, *le hot dog* (with ketchup and mustard), three or four filling hot dishes, and the usual cheese and *charcuterie* platters.

L'ÉCLUSE ROQUETTE (9)
13, rue de la Roquette
Métro: Bastille

For a description of this wine bar, see L'Écluse, page 137. All other information is the same.
TELEPHONE: 01-48-05-19-12

LE PASSAGE (17)
18, passage de la Bonne-Graine (an alley off rue du Faubourg St-Antoine)
Métro: Ledru-Rollin

TELEPHONE
01-47-00-73-30

OPEN
Mon–Fri: lunch noon–
2:30 P.M., dinner 7:30 P.M.–
midnight

CLOSED
Sat–Sun; Aug

RESERVATIONS
Advised

CREDIT CARDS
AE, MC, V

À LA CARTE
180–190F (27.44–28.97€),
BNC

PRIX FIXE
None

ENGLISH SPOKEN
Yes

Le Passage is an established wine bar with a new outlook and renewed vigor. A few years ago, this area would never have been considered for a smart wine bar . . . but no longer. Even though Le Passage is on a drab, dark street, it is well respected in terms of its fine wines and food.

For the cheapest repast, consult the daily specials written on the blackboard. Every Thursday the boss makes the safari to Rungis and brings back the fixings for dishes of chèvre tossed with apples and bitter endives, a parmesan risotto, or *onglet aux échalots* (flank steak with shallots). Don't overlook the nine varieties of A.A.A.A.A. *andouillettes* (see Au Gourmet de l'Île, page 82, for more on these), including plainly grilled and served with creamed potatoes and fricaseed in a cream and bacon sauce. *Pain perdu* with red fruit or *fondant au chocolat* for dessert keep everyone filled to contentment. So do the wines. There are more than 370 possibilities listed, including a large number of champagnes, many available by the glass. The friendly crew can be counted on to help you decide what wine to order to go best with your meal.

NOTE: Also under the same ownership is Le Café du Passage, page 202.

LE PETIT KELLER (10)
13 bis, rue Keller
Métro: Ledru-Rollin, Bastille

A bar of some sort has been here for fifty years—even the pink pig sitting on the counter has been here that long. Today it's a casual establishment, all done up in yellow and lavender, accented with orange pipes and red-topped bistro tables. No gastronomic fireworks are in store, but the serviceable food provides a quick fix during the noontime rush and is filling sustenance for the struggling artists and financially challenged students who arrive after the sun sets. The two lunch menus are almost giveaways and are great buys given the number of choices. They kick off with spinach and endives tossed with blue cheese, vegetable soup, *terrine de campagne,* and a flan. *Boeuf bourguignon,* the daily quiche, and roast chicken are just three of the five main course possibilities. Apple crumble, chocolate cake, and rice pudding, both with custard sauce or seasonal fruit, sum up the endings.

NOTE: While you are in the neighborhood, allow enough time to browse the up-and-coming artist and fashion boutiques that are sprouting up all over this and the surrounding streets. If you are young and svelte, pay close attention to designer Anne Willi, whose star is definitely rising. She is located next door.

TELEPHONE
01-47-00-12-97

OPEN
Mon–Sat: lunch noon–2:30 P.M., dinner 7:30–11 P.M.

CLOSED
Sun; NAC

RESERVATIONS
Not necessary

CREDIT CARDS
MC, V

À LA CARTE
None

PRIX FIXE
Lunch: 55F (8.38€), 2 courses, BNC; lunch and dinner: 80F (12.20€), 3 courses, BC (except BNC for Fri night and Sat for lunch and dinner)

ENGLISH SPOKEN
Yes

LES JUMEAUX (5)
73, rue Amelot
Métro: Chemin Vert, Bréguet-Sabin

Les Jumeaux is a good address to remember if you are looking for an imaginative take on the mainstream food that is so much a part of French dining. The contemporary room has a simple elegance, and with the right dinner companion, the mood could be quite romantic. The prix fixe menus are market-based, so you never know for sure what treats await. If you see the foie gras, served with warm onion *galette* and a citrus confit, you

TELEPHONE
01-43-14-27-00

OPEN
Mon–Fri: lunch noon–2:30 P.M., dinner 7:30–10:30 P.M.; Sat: dinner 7:30–10:30 P.M.

CLOSED
Sat lunch, Sun; major holidays, Aug

RESERVATIONS
Recommended
CREDIT CARDS
MC, V
À LA CARTE
None
PRIX FIXE
Lunch: 150F (22.87€), 2
courses, BNC; dinner: 185F
(28.20€), 3 courses, BNC
ENGLISH SPOKEN
Yes

are in luck. The camembert, rolled with cumin-seasoned beets, is as lovely to look at as it is to eat, and the raw, marinated sardines that come with an olive tapenade is interesting and certainly different. The tender roast lamb almost melts in your mouth, and the fresh *coquilles St-Jacques* (scallops) are served to perfection here; they are a treat for those who relish this delicacy. The chef, Karl Vandevelde, who spent his formative years in the kitchen at Ledoyen, has an equally inspired hand with desserts, turning the most plebeian ingredients into unexpected taste treats. Try his individual rounds of rich pound cake topped with a chunky prune jam—or anything with chocolate. While Karl is cooking, his twin brother, Erick, is out front taking orders and making sure that all of their guests are taken care of. They both do a superb job.

RELAIS DU MASSIF CENTRAL (8)
16, rue Daval
Métro: Bastille

TELEPHONE
01-47-00-46-55
OPEN
Mon–Sat: lunch noon–3 P.M.,
dinner 7:30 P.M.–1 A.M.
CLOSED
Sun; Aug
RESERVATIONS
Not necessary
CREDIT CARDS
MC, V
À LA CARTE
150F (22.87€), BNC
PRIX FIXE
Lunch and dinner: 70F
(10.67€), 110F (16.77€), and
120F (18.29€), all 3 courses
and BNC; 140F (21.34€), 3
courses, BC (kir and wine)
ENGLISH SPOKEN
Enough to order

Where do the neighborhood workers and local inhabitants go for a hearty feed and inexpensive wines? They step over the German shepherd guarding the doorway and enter Relais du Massif Central, where the emphasis is on nutritionally incorrect, rib-sticking fare that is not recommended for defenders of moderation. They also know to arrive early to nab the best table, which is the one for four by the window. Typical of the kitchen are such starters as hot smoked sausage with potatoes, onion and bacon *tarte* with a small salad, *chèvre chaud* on toast, or slices of Auvergne ham. Main courses feature steak fixed several ways, all with *frites,* duck preserved and cooked in its own fat, or *boeuf bourguignon* with noodles. You can be fiscally conservative with any of the three-course prix fixe menus, or go all out (still for under $25) and add a kir and house wine. Service is honest and kind, and if you need help with the menu, there is usually someone there with enough "menu English" to help.

RESTAURANT OCCITANIE (3)
96, rue Oberkampf
Métro: St-Maur, Parmentier

TELEPHONE
01-48-06-46-98
OPEN
Mon–Fri: lunch noon–2 P.M.,
dinner 7:30–10:30 P.M.; Sat:
. dinner 7:30–10:30 P.M.

By 12:30 P.M., there is not a vacant chair at the rustic Occitanie. Home cooking without pretense sums up the style of the food. Homemade confits, *magrets, cassoulets,* Toulouse sausages, and most of the desserts are created right here in the busy kitchen. The faithful don't worry about consulting the blackboard menu for lunch, scrawled by someone who did not win awards in penmanship. They know to order the 60F (9.15€) lunch menu that includes a choice of two courses—main course and an appetizer or dessert—with wine, beer, or orange juice included. Order this meal in a more tourist-heavy part of Paris and you would pay double. Other bargains include wooden platters heaped with steak, ground beef, chicken, sausage, or ham and served with a salad, a side of fries, and *fromage blanc*. There is an à la carte menu, but with the assortment of prix fixe bargains, who's looking?

CLOSED
Sat lunch, Sun; holidays, July 14–Aug 14

RESERVATIONS
Essential for lunch

CREDIT CARDS
MC, V

À LA CARTE
145F (22.11€), BNC

PRIX FIXE
Lunch: 60F (9.15€), 2 courses, BC; lunch and dinner: 70F (10.76€), 95F (14.48€), and 140F (21.34€), all 3 courses and BNC; 198F (30.18€), 4 courses, BC (kir, wine, and coffee)

ENGLISH SPOKEN
Yes, and à la carte menu in English

Twelfth Arrondissement

Bois de Vincennes, Musée des
Arts d'Afrique et d'Océanie,
place d'Aligré, Viaduc des Arts

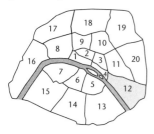

In the past, visitors seldom ventured into the untamed corners of the twelfth, which is situated between the Bastille and Gare de Lyon. A renaissance has taken place, and it is now very *au courant*. The grubby furniture makers have moved on, and people are now discovering its interesting hidden *passages* and courtyards, shopping at the multiethnic street market at place d'Aligré, and filling the new wave of restaurants. The Viaduc des Arts, in a long section of abandoned railway, has had its arched space turned into artist workshops, boutiques, and restaurants. The Promenade Plantée, a walkway with benches, flowers, and a view to flat-fronted buildings that characterize the area, flows along the top.

TWELFTH ARRONDISSEMENT RESTAURANTS (see map page 194)

($) indicates a Big Splurge

À LA BICHE AU BOIS (22)
45, avenue Ledru-Rollin, corner rue de Lyon
Métro: Bastille, Gare de Lyon, Quai de la Rapée

À la Biche au Bois remains one of my all-purpose standbys whenever I want to show a first-time visitor what an untouristy meal in Paris is all about. Inside has about fifty *couverts* (place settings) crowded into a room full of mirrors, starched linens, and contented diners enjoying full-dress fare at medium-range prices. The outdoor terrace is nice if you are here in the evening, when the symphony of squealing tires and screeching brakes calms down.

Go with a big appetite and you will leave with it satisfied. The menu lists a stampede of meats, features fish on Tuesday and Friday, and has wild game in season. From start to finish everything is good, reliable, well served, and enjoyable. The prix fixe, four-course menu is a virtual steal and includes all the favorite dishes. Wines are well priced.

TELEPHONE
01-43-43-34-38

OPEN
Mon–Fri: lunch noon–2 P.M., dinner 7:30–11 P.M.

CLOSED
Sat–Sun; major holidays, mid-July to mid-Aug

RESERVATIONS
Essential

CREDIT CARDS
AE, DC, MC, V

À LA CARTE
150–185F (22.87–28.20€), BNC

PRIX FIXE
Lunch and dinner: 130F (19.82€), 4 courses, BNC

ENGLISH SPOKEN
Yes

L'EBAUCHOIR (20)
45, rue Citeaux
Métro: Faidherbe-Chaligny, Reuilly-Diderot

Lunch is the serious cheap pick at L'Ebauchoir. The cafeterialike room with wooden tables and chairs is devoid of decor, unless you count the messy bookcase by the door or the handful of flowers in a vase on the bar. There are two lunch menus, the cheaper of which is a good deal if you want wine and don't mind that your selection of main courses won't exceed fish, offal, and one offbeat meat dish. The house star dessert, *gâteau de ris* (rice pudding), is part of the package. At dinner only à la carte is available, making this a cut-rate eat *only* for lunch—since all the same food is served at dinner, but at double the lunch prices!

TELEPHONE
01-43-42-49-31

OPEN
Mon–Sat: lunch noon–2:30 P.M., dinner 8–10:30 P.M.

CLOSED
Sun; lunch on holidays, NAC

RESERVATIONS
Not necessary

CREDIT CARDS
MC, V

À LA CARTE
140–150F (21.34–22.87€), BC

PRIX FIXE
Lunch: 70F (10.67€), 90F (13.72€), both 3 courses and BC

ENGLISH SPOKEN
Limited

LE SQUARE TROUSSEAU (18)
1, rue Antoine Vollon
Métro: Ledru-Rollin

The appealingly energetic atmosphere surrounding the Bastille carries right to Le Square Trousseau, where the smart ambience possesses all the bustle you expect in a popular Belle Epoque bistro. Overlooking the leafy Square Trousseau, it has become the *rendezvous-obligé* for a distinctly chic Parisian crowd who want to forget

TELEPHONE
01-43-43-06-00

OPEN
Daily: lunch noon–2:30 P.M., dinner 8–11:30 P.M.

CLOSED
Never

RESERVATIONS
Essential

CREDIT CARDS
AE, MC, V

À LA CARTE
180–200F (27.44–30.49€),
BNC

PRIX FIXE
Lunch Mon–Sat: 115F
(17.53€), 2 courses, 135F
(20.58€), 3 courses, both BNC

ENGLISH SPOKEN
Yes

nouvelle cuisine, chichi settings, tiny portions, snooty maître d's, and overbearing waiters. One glance around the two ocher-colored rooms and the attractive sidewalk terrace, both of which are filled night and day, and you know this is a happening place.

The commitment to quality is evident in the well-thought-out menu, which carries the season's freshest offerings. The à la carte menu changes monthly, and the Monday to Saturday prix fixe lunch menus are new every day. The solid dishes on both are generous yet proportioned sensibly, allowing you to sample a full set of courses. You might start with a springtime *entrée* of asparagus lightly dressed in an olive oil and basil sauce, fresh artichoke hearts and mushrooms with coriander-spiked tomatoes, or the warming cauliflower soup topped with golden croutons and chervil. If you like fish, try any of the daily suggestions and hope one of them is the fresh perch served on a bed of spinach. Meat eaters will be happy with the rabbit and black olives on a bed of courgettes and pasta or the thin slices of roasted duck. Equally tempting desserts include lightly cooked, Calvados-infused apples on a crisp crust or flaky mango pastry. If this isn't enough, you will be served sinfully rich bite-size brownies with your strong after-dinner espresso.

LES ZYGOMATES (24)
7, rue de Capri
Métro: Michel-Bizot, Daumesnil

TELEPHONE
01-40-19-93-04

OPEN
Mon: dinner 7:30–10:30 P.M.;
Tues–Fri: lunch noon–2 P.M.,
dinner 7:30–10:30 P.M.; Sat:
dinner 7:30–10:30 P.M.

CLOSED
Mon and Sat lunch, Sun;
holidays, Aug

RESERVATIONS
Advised

CREDIT CARDS
MC, V

À LA CARTE
175F (26.68€), BNC

PRIX FIXE
Lunch: 80F (12.20€), 3 courses,
BNC; lunch and dinner: 140F
(21.34€), 4 courses, BNC

ENGLISH SPOKEN
Yes

Buried in the depths of the twelfth arrondissement near the Bois de Vincennes is this *quartier* choice that provides luxury dining for less with its two menus. The lunch-only prix fixe changes twice a week on Monday and Thursday; the lunch and dinner menu changes every Wednesday, with choices on both based on what is best in the market. The kitchen gives distinction to the most ordinary ingredients, and it is particularly adept with such starters as cannelloni stuffed with chèvre or a salad filled with smoked salmon. Adventurous eaters will like the pork tongue served with *morille* mushrooms or the beef cheeks in red wine sauce. Conservatives can rely on roasted lamb or a piece of grilled sea bass sprinkled with fennel. Foodies of all persuasions will love the *assiette gourmande des Zygomates,* which gives tiny tastes of every dessert on the menu . . . including the bitter chocolate cake and the bread pudding with honey ice cream.

LE TRAVERSIÈRE ($, 21)
40, rue Traversière, angle 72, rue de Charenton
Métro: Ledru-Rollin, Bastille

Johny Bénaric is the *chef de cuisine,* and his attractive wife, Patricia, is the hostess. Her English is excellent and her welcome gracious. Be sure to tell her you read about them in *Great Eats Paris.* Their restaurant is the kind of place you hope will be a block or two from where you are staying. Unfortunately for most, it is farther than that, but it is absolutely worth the trek. The timbered, stone-walled interior reminds me of a cozy country *auberge,* miles from Paris. It is properly arranged with well-spaced linen-covered tables and fresh flowers, and it continually draws a contented crowd of faithful diners with its emphasis on game in winter, wonderful fresh fish, and a seasonal prix fixe menu that always maintains its high quality.

Your meal might begin with the *salade gourmande au foie gras,* fresh asparagus with smoked salmon, or *le feuilleté d'escargot aux pleurottes,* which is an interesting mixture of snails and mushrooms in a very light pastry. The filet mignon with a macaroni gratin is a wonderful choice, as is the herb-roasted leg of lamb. Fresh fruits star in the artistic desserts. Try the *vacherin maison,* a meringue topped with cherries and cream, or the delectable pear and pink grapefruit gratin. Relax throughout this lovely meal with a bottle of well-priced wine, and be happy you have found this dining jewel in Paris.

TELEPHONE
01-43-44-02-10

OPEN
Tues–Sat: lunch noon–2:30 P.M., dinner 7:30–10:30 P.M.; Sun: lunch noon–2:30 P.M.

CLOSED
Sun dinner, Mon; 3 weeks in Aug

RESERVATIONS
Advised

CREDIT CARDS
AE, DC, MC, V

À LA CARTE
None

PRIX FIXE
Lunch and dinner: 170F (25.92€), 250F (38.11€), both 3 courses and BNC

ENGLISH SPOKEN
Yes

L'OULETTE ($, 23)
15, place Lachambeaudie
Métro: Cour St-Émilion

For a memorable place to celebrate a special occasion or just being with a special person in Paris, L'Oulette is on my very short list of recommendations. From the standpoint of cuisine, service, and ambience, it is almost unbeatable . . . especially if you order the exceptionally good value *menu de saison,* which must be ordered by the entire table. It not only includes a cheese course but a very good bottle of wine.

A few years ago, Chef Marcel Baudis and his wife, Marie-Noëlle, opened a little bistro near place des Vosges—Baracane–Bistrot de l'Oulette (see page 84)—featuring dishes from Baudis's native Montauban in southwestern France. It was soon discovered by *tout le monde* and became the talk of the town. Now they have turned the day-to-day operations of the bistro over to a

TELEPHONE
01-40-02-02-12

OPEN
Mon–Fri: lunch noon–2:15 P.M., dinner 8–10:15 P.M.; Sat: dinner 8–10:15 P.M.

CLOSED
Sat lunch, Sun; Christmas Day, New Year's Day, NAC

RESERVATIONS
Absolutely essential, as far in advance as possible

CREDIT CARDS
AE, DC, MC, V

À LA CARTE
300–325F (45.73–49.55€), BNC

PRIX FIXE

Lunch: 165F (25.15), 3 courses, BNC; lunch and dinner, *menu de saison:* 275F (41.92€), 4 courses, BC

ENGLISH SPOKEN
Yes

young and efficient team and, along with partner Alain Fontaine, moved to the Bercy district in the twelfth arrondissement. This less central location has definitely not deterred savvy French diners. Neither has Baudis lost his inspired touch in the kitchen. Reservations as far in advance as possible are absolutely essential for both lunch and dinner.

The new L'Oulette combines understated elegance in a large room with banquette seating along one wall and floor-to-ceiling windows along another, which overlook an umbrella-shaded dining terrace. The popular maître d', Patrick, has done all of the decoration, and it is stunning. Pots of jam and preserved fruits are whimsically arranged along with dried flowers, creating a southwestern feel that is further enhanced by sunny yellow linens and geometric-patterned fabrics.

While the interior is modern and lean, the dazzling food is anything but. Chef Baudis spends hours preparing his seasonally inspired and meticulously arranged dishes, which are politely presented by a staff of knowledgeable waiters formally clad in black tuxedos. Meals like this cannot be rushed, so plan an evening of sitting back, enjoying a good bottle of wine, and savoring the truly outstanding food. Expect delicate perfection from the chef's talented hands: the innovative dishes include *mille-feuille de ris d'agneau aux feves et jus de truffe*—flaky pastry leaves with tender lamb sweetbreads and broad beans, flavored with truffle juice—or *petits crabes farcis,* baked crab on herbed *roquette.* Old favorites have not been cast aside. The *escabèche de calamars*—squid cooked in olive oil and spices and served with warm potatoes—is still one of the most popular *entrées.* In the summer, miracles are performed with fresh fish. Making dining decisions even more difficult are the wonderful lamb dishes, such as leg of lamb seasoned with garlic and rosemary, and an innovative adaptation of oxtail stew, *queue de boeuf braisée*—slowly cooked beef tail with green cabbage and foie gras. All dishes are served with an assortment of fresh vegetables.

For dessert, the *biscuit chocolat,* layers of rich chocolate filled with dark chocolate mousse in a cocoa sauce, is a required order for chocolate lovers. Lighter choices are the gingerbread pudding with a honey nougat ice cream, or the mascarpone mousse with caramelized nuts. Any fruit dessert creation is bound to be wonderful, especially the *tortière aux pommes et aux mendiants* (flaky apple tart with almonds, figs, nuts, and raisins). There is really nothing more to say, except that if you love and appreciate fine dining, call L'Oulette for reservations the minute you know when you will be in Paris.

NOTE: The new métro line 14 (stop: Cour St-Émilion) has made getting to L'Oulette much easier, but on a cold winter night, I would still vote for a taxi.

SAINT AMARANTE (19)
4, rue Biscornet
Métro: Bastille

Saint Amarante looks like hundreds of other cafés *du quartier* in Paris, and you certainly would not be drawn to it by location or esthetics. However, the plain exterior and the easy-to-describe decor—there isn't any—belie the riches inside. The food is absolutely unbeatable in its category, and everyone who has eaten here agrees. It is located a New York minute away from the new Opéra at the Bastille. By 12:15 P.M. it is full for lunch, and there is not an empty seat in the place for dinner at 9 P.M. Disciples bring their dogs, children, and mothers-in-law to feast on the uncomplicated fare, the type you want to return for again and again.

The menu, written on an old blackboard with dull chalk, takes some work to decode. The choices favor fish, but don't overlook the chef's light versions of lamb and veal standards, such as the melt-in-your-mouth *blanquette de veau* adorned with a light cream sauce and fresh peas on the side. The flavorful *pot-au-feu* and the kidneys cooked with mushrooms will convert you to these dishes if you are not already a believer. Desserts are just as good as they look and sound. Cherries jubilee pours warm cherries over a delicate pistachio *fondant,* and the white chocolate cake with wild strawberries is a new twist on black forest cake.

A final note: There is just one thing you must never forget to do at Saint Amarante . . . make reservations. Without them you will be waiting a long time or, worse, will not be seated at all.

TELEPHONE
01-43-43-00-08

OPEN
Tues–Fri: lunch noon–2:45 P.M., dinner 8–10:30 P.M.; Sat: dinner 8–10:30 P.M.

CLOSED
Sat lunch, Mon, Sun; holidays, last week in July, first 3 weeks of Aug, one week between Christmas and New Year's

RESERVATIONS
Absolutely essential

CREDIT CARDS
MC, V

À LA CARTE
175–190F (26.68–28.97€), BNC

PRIX FIXE
None

ENGLISH SPOKEN
Limited

Thirteenth Arrondissement

Thirteenth Arrondissement
1 Le Terroir ($)
2 L'Auberge Etchegorry ($)

R. Censier

R.

Geoffrey St. Hilaire

Poliveau

Rue

Rue du Fer à Moulin

Marcel

St. Marcel Ⓜ

Avenue

Boulevard Saint

Rue Pascal

R. Jeanne d'Arc

Bd. de Port Royal

Les Gobelins

•1 R. des Gobelins Ⓜ

R. Berbier

Le Brun

Glacière

Arago

Rue

Rue du Banquier

l'Hôpital

Campo Formio Ⓜ

Boulevard

la

Cordelières

des

du Mets

Gobelins

Rue

de

Rue Pinel

Rue Pascal

Rue

des

Rue

Boulevard

Av. S. Pichon

de

Rue

SQ. RENE LE GALL

Croulebarbe

•2

Hovelacque

Rue du Champ de l'Alouette

Corvisart

Rue des

Reculettes

Av. de la S. Rosalie

Ⓜ

Glacière Ⓜ

Rue

Abel

PLACE D'ITALIE

Bd. Vincent Auriol

Ⓜ

13ᴱ

Ⓜ Place d'Italie

Bd. Auguste Blanqui

Ⓜ Bd. Auguste Blanqui

Avenue

Av.

Edison

Corvisart

Rue Bobillot

d'Italie

Avenue

de Choisy

Glacière

Rue Vergniaud

Barrault

R. de la Butte aux Cailles

Rue

PARC DE CHOISY

Rue de la

Rue Daviel

Rue

Rue

Vandrezanne

Wurtz

Rue M. Bernard

Rue du Moulinet

Rue de Tolbiac

Rue

Rue

de

Tolbiac

Ⓜ Tolbiac

Rue

Vergniaud

Rue Bobillot

Rue C. Fourier

Rue de Tolbiac

Avenue

Boussingault

R. H. Pape

d'Italie

Rue

Rue Barrault

Rue de la Colonie

PL. DE L'ABBÉ G. HENOCQUE

△ N

500 meters

Ⓜ Métro Station

Thirteenth Arrondissement

The thirteenth is hardly impressive from a visitor's standpoint. One side is lined with railroad yards and tracks, and most of the rest seems to be a no-man's-land. The one bright star is the area called Butte-aux-Cailles, a pocket of neighborhood charm where the clock stopped ticking fifty years ago.

LEFT BANK
Butte-aux-Cailles, Chinatown, Gare d'Austerlitz, Gobelins Tapestry Factory, place d'Italie

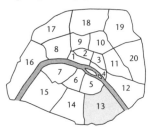

THIRTEENTH ARRONDISSEMENT RESTAURANTS

L'Auberge Etchegorry ($)   **214**
Le Terroir ($)   **214**

($) indicates a Big Splurge

L'AUBERGE ETCHEGORRY ($, 2)
41, rue Croulebarbe
Métro: Gobelins, Corvisart

TELEPHONE
01-44-08-83-51

OPEN
Mon–Sat: lunch noon–3 P.M.,
dinner 7:30–10:30 P.M.

CLOSED
Sun; NAC

RESERVATIONS
Advised

CREDIT CARDS
AE, DC, MC, V

À LA CARTE
225–250F (34.40–38.11€),
BNC

PRIX FIXE
Lunch and dinner: 145F
(22.11€), 170F (25.92€), both
3 courses and BNC

ENGLISH SPOKEN
Yes

Remember how we used to eat before a buffed, toned bod became *de rigueur* and the AMA began publishing their stringent, calorie- and cholesterol-reducing food guidelines? Well, the food at this bastion of Basque cuisine turns back the clock and tips the scales by serving earthy portions of regional dishes all flowing with delicious buttery fat; it will send your calorie count, if you keep track, off the charts. Despite the fact that it is two blocks past Mars for most Paris visitors, this restaurant is in a pretty neighborhood across the street from a lovely green park where *mamans* take their children to play and sweet old couples walk their dogs.

The restaurant resembles a regional country inn, loaded with charm and filled with a sense of happy camaraderie. It is the type of place where sturdy French people go when they want to indulge in soul-warming comfort food. It is clearly a popular destination . . . every time I have been there it has been filled, while the dreary place next door stands almost empty. The interior is as robust as the food, with hanging hams and sausages, braids of garlic and onions, and a time-warped collection of knick-knacks, indicating that nothing has changed, or will, for decades.

If you order à la carte, you will be in Big Splurge territory, but if you order from one of the generous prix fixe menus, you will be fine. When ordering, remember to pace yourself. You will need plenty of room to do justice to the meat-inspired *entrées* and main courses, which are music to the ears of carnivores. Accompany your feast with plenty of red wine and finish it all off with a slice of *le gâteau Basque* for a culinary journey back to a time when we ate with abandon.

NOTE: The owners, M. and Mme. Laborde, also run a very nice hotel, Le Vert Galant, next door to this restaurant. For a description, see *Great Sleeps Paris*.

LE TERROIR ($, 1)
11, boulevard Arago
Métro: Gobelins

TELEPHONE
01-47-07-36-99

OPEN
Mon–Fri: lunch noon–2 P.M.,
dinner 7:45–10:45 P.M.; Sat:
dinner 7:45–10:45 P.M.

If you are looking for a hearty Parisian crowd who value good food—and plenty of it—you will be happy at Michel Chavanon's La Terroir. His robust food celebrates the classic French staples, which remain unchanged by any food or health trend. To get the meal off to a rousing start, big bowls of herring or mackerel are brought to the table from which you can help yourself. Foie gras on a mound of crisp green beans and fat spears of white spring asparagus are just two of the *entrée* possibilities. Then let your belt out a notch or two to get ready for the house *magret de canard* or rich *boeuf bourguignon*. Desserts are not the order of the day here, but you probably won't mind after polishing off the last piece of roast leg of lamb or *steak au poivre*. However, a bowl of ripe red strawberries or the fruit *tarte* of the day do put a nice ending on this authentic bistro meal. Please remember to book ahead . . . the locals always do.

CLOSED
Sat lunch, Sun; Easter, first 3 weeks in Aug, Dec 23–Jan 5

RESERVATIONS
Recommended

CREDIT CARDS
MC, V

À LA CARTE
225F (34.30€), BNC

PRIX FIXE
None

ENGLISH SPOKEN
Limited

Fourteenth Arrondissement

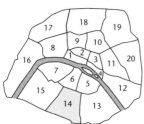

This artistic haven of the 1920s and 1930s is now modernized and for the most part ugly, the unfortunate victim of urban development without much taste or regard for history. The famous cafés—La Coupole, Le Select, Le Dôme, and La Rotunde—were the center of literary and artistic life in Paris between the two World Wars. They are still here, but they lack the soul of their collective past. The area was also home to dancer Isadora Duncan, and singer Edith Piaf performed often at the Bobino Music Hall.

FOURTEENTH ARRONDISSEMENT RESTAURANTS

($) indicates a Big Splurge

AQUARIUS (18)
40, rue de Gergovie
Métro: Pernety, Plaisance

Aquarius has another location near the Marais in the fourth arrondissement (see page 81). While that one is more centrally located, this one has more zip in that the interior does not remind me of a utilitarian cafeteria. At the fourteenth arrondissement location, vegetarian food is served in three small rooms with either pine- or marble-topped tables sensibly set with red placemats and yellow napkins. There is also a shelf littered with yoga flyers, assorted announcements about New Age meetings and classes, and other notices about alternative lifestyles.

The politically and nutritionally aware patrons love the food, which is served on oversize white plates. The popular "mixed grill" pairs tofu and cereal sausages with wheat pancakes, brown rice, and veggies in a mushroom sauce. There is also vegetarian chili, lasagna, and a puff pastry loaded with *pleurottes* (mushrooms), snail butter, and loads of garlic that comes with a side of two veggies and a salad. Other healthy options are the big salads, omelettes, and the *plat du jour*. Purists can always order the steamed vegetable plate; sinners will enjoy the chocolate brownie, the chocolate cake, or the cheesecake. Thirst-quenching juices, teas, *biologique* wines, and designer mineral water complete the menu. Admittedly, you must have a certain mind-set to eat here, but if you do, you will be filled with well-executed, wholesome food that won't give you or your budget heartburn.

TELEPHONE
01-45-41-36-88

OPEN
Mon–Sat: lunch noon–2:30 P.M., dinner 7–10:30 P.M.

CLOSED
Sun; holidays, Christmas through New Year's, NAC

RESERVATIONS
Not necessary

CREDIT CARDS
AE, MC, V

À LA CARTE
100–125F (15.24–19.06€), BNC

PRIX FIXE
Lunch: 70F (10.67€), 3 courses, BNC

ENGLISH SPOKEN
Yes

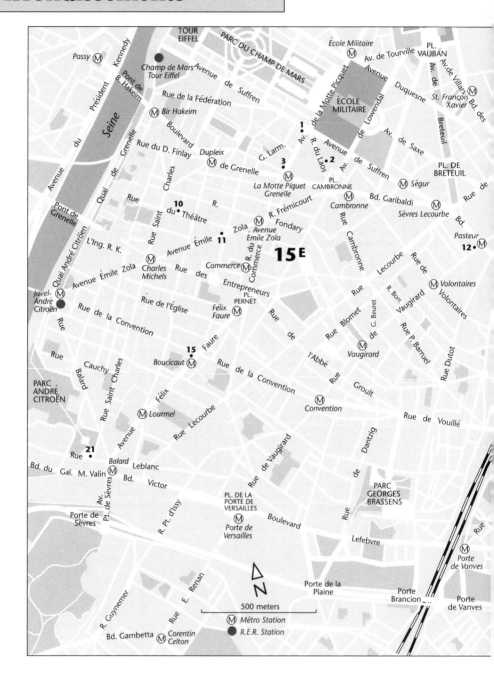

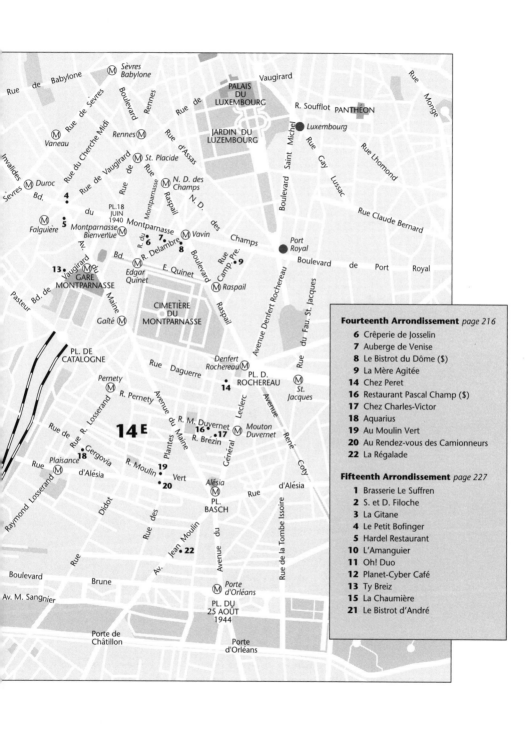

AUBERGE DE VENISE (7)
10, rue Delambre
Métro: Vavin

TELEPHONE
01-43-35-43-09

OPEN
Daily: lunch noon–2:30 P.M.,
dinner 7–11:30 P.M.

CLOSED
Some holidays, Aug (call to
check)

RESERVATIONS
Essential, especially for dinner

CREDIT CARDS
AE, MC, V

À LA CARTE
170–180F (25.92–27.44€),
BNC

PRIX FIXE
Lunch Mon–Sat (except
holidays): 90F (13.72€), 2
courses, BNC; lunch and dinner
daily: 110F (16.77€), 3 courses,
BNC

ENGLISH SPOKEN
Yes, and Italian. There is an
English menu.

Buon appetito and welcome to Auberge de Venise, a taste of *bella Italia* in Paris. The restaurant has been in business almost since time began, and it has served such luminaries as Hemingway, Fitzgerald, and Picasso during their heydays in Paris. Today, it continues to fill to capacity with confirmed regulars, who come back not only for the outstanding food but for the comfortable, homey atmosphere and old-fashioned service.

There is a limited-choice prix fixe menu, but if you love Italian food, treat yourself and order à la carte— some of these wonderful dishes are in many ways better than most you will have in Italy. Any one of the beef carpaccios makes a nice starter, and so does the simply dressed tomato and mozzarella salad. It is easy to get carried away and make a meal on the *entrée*, with several pieces of bread and a good Chianti, but save yourself; there is lots more to come. A rich *tagliatelle al salmone* is a filling main dish, as is the ravioli with either basil or mushrooms. The cream *tortelloni ai 4 fromaggi* throws fat-gram counting into orbit, but just this once won't kill you. The pastas are not garnished, so if you are feeling really hungry, consider an order of green beans liberally tossed with garlic and sautéed in olive oil. Meat eaters will be pleased with the list of veal dishes; try one prepared with lemon, Marsala wine, and tomato sauce or the osso buco.

When it comes time for dessert, you might think it impossible . . . but wait a few minutes and then order the best tiramisu you will find in Paris. Or, if you love profiteroles, their version of these filled cream puffs, seductively covered with a thick chocolate topping and served cold, are *bellissimo!*

AU MOULIN VERT (19)
34 bis, rue des Plantes (at rue du Moulin Vert)
Métro: Alésia

TELEPHONE
01-45-39-31-31

OPEN
Daily: lunch noon–2:30 P.M.,
dinner 7–10:30 P.M.

CLOSED
Sun dinner and Mon in Aug,
NAC

RESERVATIONS
Advised

If you want to treat yourself to a nice meal before or after pounding the pavement along rue d'Alésia in search of the ultimate Parisian bargain (see "Shopping" in *Great Sleeps Paris*), reserve a table at Au Moulin Vert. For my dining expenditure, the restaurant is the best in the area and definitely one of the prettiest dining choices in Paris. It is set in a building with a wraparound glass-walled dining terrace that's surrounded by a serene garden of lush green and blooming plants, giving you the feeling you are miles away from everything. There has been a restaurant on this corner since 1842, and a black-and-white photo of the original hangs by the front door. Fellow diners will be from the neighborhood . . . maybe a large family of three generations celebrating a birthday, a young couple all dressed up on their first or second date, a middle-age couple reliving their first date—and you, watching the drama with pleasure. The later you go the better it gets, especially when the hurricane lights are glowing and the mood says *l'amour*.

The one-price-fits-all dinner menu is far above the usual in terms of the sheer number of choices and the imaginative preparations. The large meal starts with a kir royale and includes a bottle of good wine, a choice of seasonally changing *entrées, plats,* and desserts, and ends with after-dinner coffee. For the most creative choices for each course, look at the the chef's *suggestions du jour*.

CREDIT CARDS
AE, MC, V

À LA CARTE
None

PRIX FIXE
Lunch Mon–Fri: 120F (18.29€), 2 courses, BNC; dinner daily and lunch Sat–Sun: 195F (29.73€), 3 courses, BC

ENGLISH SPOKEN
Yes, and English menu

AU RENDEZ-VOUS DES CAMIONNEURS (20)
34, rue des Plantes
Métro: Alésia

If you have only a little bit to spend on lunch or dinner and want to get away from most of the other tourists in the same boat, head for Monique and Claude's frugal spot tucked away in the bottom of the fourteenth arrondissement, near the rue d'Alésia cheap chic shopping mecca. Au Rendez-vous des Camionneurs is a classic that will be here only until the hardworking couple, who have labored here for more than thirty years, decides to hang up the chef's hat and spatula and retire to the south of France. This restaurant is a dying breed as a result of today's more sophisticated dining demands. What to expect? Think school lunchroom. Interior decor? Not a lot, with a bar along one side of the lime-green room, whose walls are punctuated by pictures and posters. Tables are accessorized with crocks of mustard, salt in the box it comes in, and a pepper grinder.

The cuisine is definitely Mom's kitchen. The typed menu is changed monthly and lists plates of cucumbers, beets, grated carrots, sardines, *saucisson sec,* or sliced terrine to start. Then comes the *bavette* (skirt steak), *cervelle de veau meunière* (veal brains), sautéed lamb with white beans, two *plats du jour,* or fish. If you are ordering from the prix fixe menu, desserts don't get much fancier than a piece of fruit or a bowl of *fromage blanc* with a

TELEPHONE
01-45-40-43-36

OPEN
Mon–Fri: lunch 11:30 A.M.–2:30 P.M., dinner 7:30–9:30 P.M.

CLOSED
Sat–Sun; holidays, Aug

RESERVATIONS
Required

CREDIT CARDS
None

À LA CARTE
105–110F (16.01–16.77€), BNC

PRIX FIXE
Lunch and dinner: 77F (11.74€), 3 courses, BNC

ENGLISH SPOKEN
None

honey or granulated sugar topping. À la carte diners may order the fruit *tarte* or custard. Wines by the *pichet* resemble the Thunderbird screw-cap variety, so spring for a bottle or drink *eau naturel* (tap water) if your budget is extra tight. Though it's not as grim as it may sound, put away any thoughts of gourmet. Arrive desiring only filling and cheap, and you will leave satisfied.

CHEZ CHARLES-VICTOR (17)
8, rue Brézin
Métro: Mouton-Duvernet

TELEPHONE
01-40-44-55-51
OPEN
Mon–Fri: lunch noon–
2:00 P.M., dinner 7:30–
10:30 P.M.; Sat: dinner
7:30–10:30 P.M.
CLOSED
Sat lunch, Sun; NAC
RESERVATIONS
Advised
CREDIT CARDS
MC, V
À LA CARTE
Entrées 35F (5.34€), *plats* 57F
(8.69€), dessert 35F (5.34€)
PRIX FIXE
Lunch and dinner: 79F
(12.04€), 2 courses, 105F
(16.01€), 3 courses, both BNC
ENGLISH SPOKEN
Yes

If *Great Eats Paris* gave "best value" awards, one would go to the two menus offered at this friendly Montparnasse enclave. It is a family affair, with an owner who is on site, speaks English, and loves Americans.

The handwritten (and readable) menu on the green chalkboard entices with the house specialty, *canapés de grand-mère* (a slice of toasted *pain Poilâne* spread with liver terrine and served on a green salad), eggplant caviar, and baked eggs with smoked salmon. For your *plat,* steak tartare and lamb chops are acceptable but ultimately plebeian choices when compared to the house Basque specialty—*axoa,* a hot and spicy affair with sliced chicken, chorizo, tomatoes, onions, and a mixture of red and green peppers and rice. Desserts keep you going with the hot chocolate profiteroles, three-chocolate *fondant,* or a fruit crumble, all of which are made here.

CHEZ PERET (14)
6, rue Daguerre
Métro: Denfert-Rochereau

TELEPHONE
01-43-22-57-05
OPEN
Daily: 7:30 A.M.–11:30 P.M.,
continuous service
CLOSED
Never
RESERVATIONS
Suggested in the evening
CREDIT CARDS
MC,V
À LA CARTE
55–115F (8.38–17.53€), BNC
PRIX FIXE
None
ENGLISH SPOKEN
Yes

For a peek into the life of the average Parisian, walk along rue Daguerre in the fourteenth arrondissement. This is a typical *quartier populaire* (middle-class, working area) and rue Daguerre is the principal market street, with shops selling everything the inhabitants need to keep body and soul together. Chez Peret is right in the middle of it all, and since opening in 1910, it has been an important local watering hole and has been run by the same family. A cross section of regulars comes daily—some to jump-start their day with a shot of espresso, others to trade insults with the bartender later in the day, and most to sit around outdoor café tables into the evening discussing everything . . . and nothing.

Orders are placed for sandwiches on *pain Poilâne,* plates of warm Lyonnaise sausage and potatoes, daily specials, dishes of Berthillon ice cream, and both of the homemade desserts: apple crumble and fruit *tarte.* Beaujolais and burgundy are the wines of choice, and the tables of choice are on the covered terrace, where you may have to resort to pantomime to communicate when it is full, but don't be stressed—instead, enjoy the charm and appeal of being part of the real Paris, even if only for an hour or two. If you like the wine you order here, you can buy it at their wine shop next door.

CRÊPERIE DE JOSSELIN (6)
67, rue du Montparnasse
Métro: Edgar Quinet, Vavin

Montparnasse is known for its Breton *crêperies,* and nowhere in the *quartier* is this more evident than along rue du Montparnasse, where they line both sides of the street. Let me eliminate the guesswork over which one to try: one of the top choices is Crêperie de Josselin, which brings the best of Brittany to Paris with their spectacular crêpes. Plump Breton ladies make the crêpes as fast as they can in the open kitchen, rosy-cheeked waitresses rush from table to table, and the happy crowd loves every bite, knowing the final tally will be reasonable. Lace-covered hanging lamps cast a romantic glow over the wooden booths and tables. Quimper *faïence* plates line the high plate rail, and an old grandfather clock gently ticks in one corner.

Abundant fillings of egg, ham, cheese, vegetables, fish, meat, and fresh herbs are folded into mammoth whole-wheat crêpes. Dessert crêpes are equally overwhelming, filled with wonderful mixtures of honey, nuts, chocolate, fruits, and ice cream and covered with flaming liqueurs. The most authentic drink to order to go with your crêpes is a pitcher of Breton apple cider.

NOTE: Just down the street is Crêperie Le Petit Josselin, the family's second *crêperie,* which is run by a brother-in-law. The room is smaller, and the crêpes and the à la carte prices are about the same, but in addition they have a two-course, 60F (9.15€) prix fixe menu that includes a beverage. The only other advantage to going here is that it is open Monday, when the first store is closed. It's at 59, rue du Montparnasse (Tel: 01-43-22-91-81), and it's open similar hours on Monday to Saturday, closed Sunday.

TELEPHONE
01-43-20-93-50

OPEN
Tues–Fri: lunch noon–3 P.M., dinner 7–11:30 P.M.; Sat–Sun: noon–midnight, continuous service

CLOSED
Mon; sometimes in Aug (call to check)

RESERVATIONS
Not necessary

CREDIT CARDS
None

À LA CARTE
100–150F (15.24–22.87€), BNC

PRIX FIXE
None

ENGLISH SPOKEN
Yes, with English menu

LA MÈRE AGITÉE (9)
21, rue Campagne-Première
Métro: Raspail

TELEPHONE
01-43-35-56-64

OPEN
Tues–Sat: lunch noon–3 P.M.,
dinner 8–11 P.M.

CLOSED
Mon, Sun; holidays, 3 weeks in
Aug (dates vary)

RESERVATIONS
Advised, and required for
special parties of 10 or more on
Sun and Mon

CREDIT CARDS
MC, V

À LA CARTE
Entrées 40F (6.10€), *plats* 75–
80F (11.43–12.20€), cheese
35F (5.34€), desserts 40F
(6.10€), BNC

PRIX FIXE
None

ENGLISH SPOKEN
Yes

La Mère Agitée is about as big as a minute, but the food packs a wallop. Valérie de la Haye and Dominque Decombat are the talented and imaginative cooks, and every day they prepare a different à la carte menu with two choices for each course. There are two things you will know for sure: there is always a soup—hot in winter, cold in summer—and you will always have fish on Friday.

Other than that, it is pot luck, but what good luck you will have. One day you could start with a chilled gazpacho or a cucumber-and-mint soup, then enjoy a fat Lyonnaise sausage, followed by a dish of fresh seasonal berries sprinkled with sugar or a lime mousse. Another day, it could be a slice of pâté, followed by lemon chicken with fat prunes for the garnish, and for the grand finale, a fruit *tarte*. Before your meal, have the house apéritif, and be sure to order one of the Tourene wines to accompany the rest of your meal. When you finish, after complimenting the cooks on a meal well done, you will be checking to see what they're cooking the rest of the time you are in Paris.

NOTE: If you happen to have a party of ten or more, you can make reservations at La Mère Agitée for Sunday or Monday, when they are otherwise closed.

LA RÉGALADE (22)
49, avenue Jean Moulin
Métro: Alésia

TELEPHONE
01-45-45-68-58

OPEN
Tues–Fri: lunch noon–3 P.M.,
dinner 7:30 P.M.–midnight;
Sat: dinner 7:30 P.M.–
midnight

CLOSED
Sat lunch, Mon, Sun; holidays,
Aug, one week at Christmas

RESERVATIONS
Absolutely essential as far in
advance as possible

CREDIT CARDS
MC, V

À LA CARTE
None

Today, lovers of French cuisine are tired of paying wallet-numbing prices, and they are in constant search of good value for their money. As a result, they are branching out and willing to go to the hinterlands, so to speak, if a talented chef is serving food that has flavor, character, and personality.

Parisian gourmets have found what they are looking for at Yves Camdeborde's La Régalade. Camdeborde, a former student of Christian Constant at the Hôtel de Crillon, took a leap of faith and, with his wife, opened this small restaurant in an unimpressive corner of the fourteenth, where he specializes in dishes from his native Béarn in southwestern France. His cooking has an authority that commands attention, and as a result, his are the hottest tables in Paris, making reservations mandatory at least two to three weeks in advance. His food also challenges the notion that good has to be expensive. His one-price, constantly changing seasonal menu covers all three courses. Wines are extra, but if you look at one of the monthly featured wines, or order by the glass, they are well within reason.

To begin, they bring complimentary terrines to your table. Spread a chunk of the spicy mixture on a piece of whole-meal or white bread while you decide what to order. I always hope to find one of my favorite appetizers, the *beignets de légumes* (assorted Provençal vegetables quickly deep fried), served piping hot in a basket with tartar sauce. The barely cooked *coquilles St-Jacques* (scallops) with a parsley-butter sauce is another star-studded beginning, as is the daring lamb sweetbreads tossed with sweet peppers. A new twist on the classic shepherd's pie is the blood sausage covered with a layer of mashed potatoes and topped with a béarnaise sauce. The roasted lamb rubbed with garlic is marvelous, and the veal kidneys with an onion *confiture* is another fragrant, rich, tasty choice. The half dozen or more desserts might include a crisp lemon-coconut pastry, Grand Marnier soufflé, or warm apples lightly cooked on a bed of thin, flaky pastry, topped with Camdeborde's own prune-Armagnac ice cream.

The simple interior is stark and inexpensively accented with a few photos, and the service is somewhat rushed when tables are full. It is not a place to relax and think romantic thoughts. However, the wonderful food makes up for this tenfold. It is a place where you will eat very well, and for the price, it is perhaps one of the best meals you will have in Paris.

LE BISTROT DU DÔME ($, 8)
1, rue Delambre
Métro: Vavin, Edgar Quinet
For a full description, see Le Bistrot du Dôme in the fourth arrondissement, page 90. All other information is the same.

TELEPHONE: 01-43-35-32-00
OPEN: Daily: lunch noon–2:30 P.M., dinner 7:30–11:30 P.M.

PRIX FIXE
Lunch and dinner: 195F (29.73€), 3 courses, BNC
ENGLISH SPOKEN
Limited

RESTAURANT PASCAL CHAMP ($, 16)
5, rue Mouton-Duvernet
Métro: Mouton-Duvernet

TELEPHONE
01-45-39-39-61

OPEN
Tues–Sat: lunch noon–
2:30 P.M., dinner 7–10:30 P.M.

CLOSED
Mon, Sun; major holidays, Aug

RESERVATIONS
Advised

CREDIT CARDS
MC, V

À LA CARTE
200–225F (30.49–34.30€),
BNC

PRIX FIXE
Lunch: 89F (13.57€), 2 courses,
99F (15.09€), 3 courses, both
BNC; dinner: 119F (18.14€),
3 courses, BNC; lunch and
dinner: 159F (24.24€),
3 courses (wider choice), BNC

ENGLISH SPOKEN
Yes

No matter when you go or what you order, this exemplary neighborhood restaurant is well worth the trip. It is just far enough from the usual tourist haunts around Montparnasse to keep it from being "discovered," and that is just the way local patrons prefer it. Like many of his young colleagues, Pascal Champ trained at the temples of haute cuisine in Paris before striking out on his own with his wife, Virginie, and one other helper. By virtue of hard work and talent, they have earned a respected place in the hearts and minds of their customers, and now with many readers of *Great Eats Paris*.

In the kitchen, Pascal employs a light modern touch while adding an inspired spin to his seasonal and weekly menus. He cooks with the freshest possible ingredients and uses only prize-winning cuts of beef, lamb, and veal. The two- and three-course lunch menus offer superb dining value: you might begin with a rabbit terrine, followed by a fresh Scottish salmon or his own *magret de canard,* and end with a selection of cheese or fruit crumble. Note that the 119F (18.14€), three-course dinner menu has exactly the same choices as the 99F (15.09€) three-course lunch, making lunch the clear-cut choice in terms of savings, since you sacrifice neither quality nor quantity. At either lunch or dinner, however, if you order the 159F (24.24€) three-course menu, you have almost carte blanche with everything on the à la carte menu.

Exciting choices here include *escalope de thon aux senteurs de Provence* (fresh tuna with herbs), lightly cooked veal with creamy mashed potatoes, and a lemon pork confit served with honey-ginger sweet potatoes. If chocolate is your passion, the chocolate mousse floating on orange sauce and dotted with strawberry hearts is your dish. Equally tempting is the cinnamon-flavored *tarte Tatin* with a scoop of vanilla ice cream melting onto it, giving it that wonderful creamy taste. When dining here, plan to enjoy a fine bottle of wine from Pascal's cellar, which includes vintages from the best producers in France.

Fifteenth Arrondissement

This vast and generally untraveled region for most Paris visitors is exemplified by La Tour Montparnasse, which looms from the intersection of the sixth, fourteenth, and fifteenth arrondissements. It is the tallest, and by some standards the ugliest, building in Europe, but on a clear day the view from the top is spectacular. In this basically middle-class residential area you will find corners of charm, specifically around the Village Suisse, an expensive complex of antique shops selling everything imaginable at prices reserved for Arab sheikhs. Stretching along the River Seine are high-rise apartments and a new park with walking paths and benches for enjoying the views.

LEFT BANK
La Tour Montparnasse

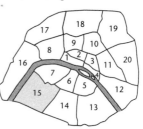

BRASSERIE LE SUFFREN (1)
84, avenue de Suffren
Métro: La Motte-Picquet–Grenelle

TELEPHONE
01-45-66-97-86

OPEN
Daily: 7 A.M.–midnight;
continuous food service noon–
midnight

CLOSED
Sun in Aug, NAC

RESERVATIONS
Not accepted after 12:30 P.M.
for lunch or 8:30 P.M.
for dinner; never accepted
for terrace

CREDIT CARDS
AE, MC, V

À LA CARTE
135–180F (20.58–27.44€),
BNC

PRIX FIXE
Lunch and dinner: 86F
(13.11€), 2 courses, 110F
(16.77€), 3 courses,
175F (26.68€), 3 courses,
all BC

ENGLISH SPOKEN
Usually, and English menu

Everyone in the neighborhood goes to Brasserie Le Suffren. You can, too, if you find yourself near Invalides, are wandering on a Tuesday or Sunday morning on boulevard de Grenelle—one of the best street *marchés* in Paris—or are hungry before or after seeing a film down the street at Kinopanorama, the biggest movie house in the city. Sitting at one of the outside terrace tables provides terrific people-watching in this comfortable middle-class area.

Basic brasserie standbys of salads, *choucroutes,* beef tartare, roast chicken, oysters, and desserts are served nonstop by a rushed crew of black-clad waiters, whose tolerance for tourists is sometimes stretched quite thin. But I had only sympathy for this overworked waitstaff, which is constantly on the run, each waiter handling more tables than unions in America would allow five or more waiters to serve. So long as you don't expect to develop a personal relationship, you won't find the service rude. The three good-value menus are always available, but only if you eat inside. That shouldn't be a problem, but try to avoid the stuffy upstairs area.

HARDEL RESTAURANT (5)
8, avenue du Maine
Métro: Falguière

TELEPHONE
01-45-44-39-41

OPEN
Tues–Fri, Sun: lunch noon–
2:30 P.M., dinner 6–11 P.M.;
Sat: dinner 6–11 P.M.

CLOSED
Sat lunch, Mon; NAC

RESERVATIONS
Preferred

CREDIT CARDS
MC, V

À LA CARTE
Not available

PRIX FIXE
All menus available for lunch
and dinner: *menu salade,* 80F
(12.20€), salad and dessert;
menu rapide, 85F (12.96€), *entrée*
and *plat;* children's menu, 76F
(11.59€), 3 courses; *menu
gourmand,* 140F (21.34€),
3 courses; bouillabaisse, 165F
(25.15€); all menus BNC

Sitting in a dining room packed with French diners, eating reliable food with lots of nice little extras . . . that is what dining at Pascal Hardel's restaurant is all about. Another appealing feature for many is that you can eat dinner at the unheard-of hour of 6 P.M. (considered late afternoon by the French) and tailor your prix fixe meal to fit not only your budget but the size of your appetite by mixing and matching *entrées, plats,* and desserts into whatever combination suits you.

The pretty pastel dining room is light mauve. Open seating along the street has comfortable high-backed chairs around well-spaced tables. There are some banquettes, a potted palm for show, and a small bar as you enter. The lunch bunch is strictly French *bourgeoise;* the dinner guests are a mixed bag, but all are looking for more than the usual glitzy, quick Montparnasse fast-food fix, which seems to be the rule, not the exception, in the *quartier.* In addition to the bargain prix fixe meals, Hardel pays attention to pleasing details: a bowl of peanuts on the table to accompany your apéritif, cookies and chocolates served with after-dinner coffee, and always courteous, prompt service.

The food consists of a varied repertoire of top-quality products served in generous portions. For a dependable appetizer, the salad topped with slices of smoked duck is interesting. The *feuilleté d'escargots, jambon, et champignons à la crème d'ail*—snails, ham, and mushrooms encased in pastry with a garlic-cream dressing—or the fish terrine with chive sauce are other good openers. The best main courses are grilled lamb chops, salmon, and the house specialty, *la bouillabaisse de Marseilles,* a Mediterranean fish stew combining seven types of fish and seafood. All the dishes are garnished with a choice of *gratin dauphinois, frites,* spinach, carrot custard, or rice. If you are like me and think a day is incomplete without something chocolate, try the *surprise pour chocophile* (a new twist on an old theme)—orange mousse with chocolate sauce. Any of the ice creams are good, especially the blockbuster *Coupe Hardel*—rum-raisin ice cream smothered in caramel and hot chocolate sauces with whipped cream covering the whole thing.

ENGLISH SPOKEN
Yes

LA CHAUMIÈRE (15)
54, avenue Félix-Faure
Métro: Boucicaut

Today, restaurant patrons are searching for pleasant, casual surroundings and more choices for less money. The talented young chef Oliver Amestoy and his delightful Australian wife, Marie, have risen to the challenge, consistently giving their patrons more than their money's worth, both with the food served and the warm welcome extended by Marie. As a result, La Chaumière is filled to overflowing for both lunch and dinner, making reservations absolutely essential.

Amestoy's top-quality fare, served in nourishing, solid portions and pleasingly presented, begins with generous *entrées* of rounds of warm chèvre cheese resting on crispy potato pancakes. His fresh crab ravioli in a delicate roe sauce and his smoked Scottish salmon with blini on the side underscore his skill with fish preparations. Main courses also lean heavily on fish—imaginatively paired with interesting sauces and garnishes—such as salmon and langoustines flavored with a sweet pepper sauce and accented with onion fondue. Besides the fish, one of my favorite dishes here is the tender lamb, roasted to pink

TELEPHONE
01-45-54-13-91

OPEN
Daily: lunch noon–3 P.M., dinner 7–11 P.M.

CLOSED
Aug

RESERVATIONS
Essential

CREDIT CARDS
AE, MC, V

À LA CARTE
Entrées 58F (8.85€), *plats* 99F (15.09€), desserts 50F (7.62€), BNC

PRIX FIXE
Lunch and dinner: 130F (19.82€), 2 courses, BNC (desserts 50F, 7.62€)

ENGLISH SPOKEN
Yes

perfection and served with baby green beans and creamy potatoes. On a recent visit, when I asked for a light vegetarian *plat,* I expected the usual array of whatever vegetables the kitchen had on hand. This simple approach would never do for Oliver; instead he whipped up an imaginative flaky *croustade,* filled it with fresh garden vegetables, and sprinkled cheese on top. It was absolutely wonderful, and my four other dining companions eyed it longingly. I suppose you might call it a Parisian pizza . . . but that wouldn't begin to do justice to his delicious improvised creation.

Desserts are positively heaven-sent, and most must be ordered when you first place your meal order. With a selection that includes Grand Marnier soufflé, flaming *crêpes Suzettes,* apple tart flambéed in Calvados, and *bombe Alaska,* it is almost impossible to choose. From a purely theatrical standpoint, the *bombe Alaska* (baked Alaska) receives top billing from me. In fact, the night I ordered it a group of proper Parisians were sitting at a table next to me. They had finished their meal, paid for it, and were getting up to leave when they saw my flaming *bombe* served. After one look, they promptly sat down and ordered three to split among themselves. There was not a bite left on any of our plates.

When dining at La Chaumière, remember, this is Paris, where dining is not meant to be hurried, especially when spending the evening in a nice restaurant. Be patient—good things always come to those who order another bottle of excellent wine. Any wait will be worth it at La Chaumière, which, once tried, will go straight to the top of your list of Paris dining favorites.

LA GITANE (3)
53 bis, avenue de La Motte-Picquet
Métro: La Motte-Picquet–Grenelle

TELEPHONE
01-47-34-62-92

OPEN
Mon–Sat: lunch noon–
2:30 P.M., dinner 7–11 P.M.

CLOSED
Sun; major holidays, one week
at Christmas

RESERVATIONS
Advised

CREDIT CARDS
AE, MC, V

À LA CARTE
160–200F (24.39–30.49€),
BNC

Capacity crowds arrive for both lunch and dinner in La Gitane's seventy-plus-seat dining room and secluded, plant-bordered summer terrace. Situated across from the antique dealers in the Village Suisse and only a métro stop from the Eiffel Tower, it has become an address dear to the hearts of bistro lovers.

When you step inside, you immediately understand what the French mean by a good *quartier* bistro. The menu, handwritten on hanging blackboards around the room, changes often, reflecting the freshest market ingredients and the chef's inspirations. Those with healthy appetites will appreciate the well-constructed repertoire of *pot-au-feu, cassoulet, boudin noir,* and simply poached fish with light sauces. In the cooler months look for stuffed cabbage, *petit salé aux lentilles,* and steaming *choucroutes.* Good wines are modestly priced, and the desserts, especially the apples spiked with Armagnac and the *baba au rhum,* are as rewarding as the rest of the meal.

L'AMANGUIER (10)
51, rue du Théâtre, at rue Georges-Citerne
Métro: Avenue Émile-Zola

L'Amanguier began at this address, then added three other central Paris addresses to form a small chain. It was a hit because it developed a successful formula and stayed with it: efficient and pleasant service, reasonable prices, and good food served seven days a week. However, to prove that cash is king, and everything is for sale at the right price, they have sold the other three of their restaurants, which now have Le Petit Bofinger signs hanging in front of them.

The original L'Amanguier, with its pretty garden setting, continues to provide consistent quality in both service and food, with many appealing selections and an ever-changing list of seasonal specialties. There are three options at L'Amanguier: two *formules* that include two or three courses from anything on the menu, or you can order any *entrée, plat,* or dessert sold separately. In addition to the seasonal dishes, there are a handful of favorites you can always rely on: crab cocktail, foie gras on a bed of greens, steak served with potatoes and a green salad, *magret de canard,* and chocolate *tarte,* crème brûlée, or apple crumble with custard sauce for dessert.

TELEPHONE
01-45-77-04-01

OPEN
Daily: lunch noon–2 P.M., dinner 7 P.M.–midnight

CLOSED
Never

RESERVATIONS
Advised

CREDIT CARDS
AE, MC, V

À LA CARTE
Entrée 40F (6.10€), *plat* 80F (12.20€), dessert 38F (5.79€), BNC

PRIX FIXE
Lunch and dinner: *Le Séduisant,* 90F (13.72€), 2 courses, *Le Menu Gourmand,* 130F (19.82€), 3 courses, both BNC

ENGLISH SPOKEN
Yes

LE BISTROT D'ANDRÉ (21)
232, rue St-Charles, at rue Leblanc
Métro: Balard

Hubert Gloaguen purchased this old, tired restaurant and restored it to its original status, as a canteen for workers from the Citroën factory that once dominated this arid corner of the fifteenth arrondissement. The simple, bright interior now honors automobile pioneer André Citroën with large photographs of Citroën and his factory as it was in the old days. True, the bistro is far from the thick of things, but sometimes it is interesting to get away from all the tourist hoopla and see Paris from a Parisian's viewpoint.

TELEPHONE
01-45-57-89-14

OPEN
Mon–Sat: lunch noon–2:30 P.M., dinner 7:30–10:30 P.M.

CLOSED
Sun; holidays, NAC

RESERVATIONS
Advised for lunch or for 3 or more

CREDIT CARDS
V

À LA CARTE
145F (22.11€), BNC

PRIX FIXE
Lunch Mon–Fri: 65F (9.91€), 3 courses, BNC; children's menu, 43F (6.56€), 2 courses and a surprise, BC

ENGLISH SPOKEN
Yes

The best time to come is at lunch, when the place is wall to wall with a good-looking *quartier* crowd, their jackets off and their sleeves rolled up. The rushed service is efficient, considering the number of tables each waiter must serve. Other reasons to make this a lunch stop are the Monday to Friday bargain-priced, 65F (9.91€), three-course prix fixe menu, served in addition to an à la carte menu, as well as the large salads and daily *plats*. A recent prix fixe lunch included *la salade du Bistrot* (ham, potatoes, and tomatoes) or endives mixed with nuts to start; either salmon with sorrel and rice, a *faux-filet* with pepper sauce, or *andouillette à la moutard* for a main course; and finally a choice of *fromage blanc* or the *dessert du jour*. In the evening the scene is much calmer, and there is no prix fixe menu, but the à la carte prices are reasonable and the food is always worth the trip. If you are a wine enthusiast, Gloaguen's changing wine list made up of little-known French wines at very attractive prices merits special attention.

NOTE: There is a nonsmoking section. Also, to avoid a long, dull métro ride, take the No. 42 bus, which will drop you off across the street from the restaurant.

LE PETIT BOFINGER (4)
46, boulevard du Montparnasse
Métro: Falguière, Duroc

For a complete description, see Le Petit Bofinger, page 93. All other information is the same.
TELEPHONE: 01-45-48-49-16

OH! DUO (11)
54, avenue Émile-Zola
Métro: Charles-Michels, Avenue Émile-Zola

TELEPHONE
01-45-77-28-82

OPEN
Mon–Fri: lunch noon–2 P.M., dinner 7–10:30 P.M.; Sat: dinner 7–10:30 P.M.

CLOSED
Sat lunch, Sun; holidays, first week in May (call to check), first 3 weeks in Aug

RESERVATIONS
Recommended

CREDIT CARDS
MC, V

À LA CARTE
140–195F (21.34–29.73€), BNC

A reader writes: "Dear Sandra: We wanted to write to you about Oh! Duo, . . . by far the best meal of the trip. The service was impeccable, the staff constantly smiling. The food was, as I told *la patronne*, *ne pas de la cuisine, c'est un rêve*. We seriously considered just returning to this one restaurant every night. Please rave about this in your next edition." Consider it done. I am happy to rave about Oh! Duo because there is so much to rave about.

I first found out about this hidden restaurant from a friend who lives nearby. Because I follow through on all tips, I went for dinner. Judging from reader letters such as the one above, many *Great Eats Paris* readers have also found this gem and applaud everything about it. The decor reflects the restaurant's name—it includes a whimsical collection of photos and posters of Parisian people and animals together in twos. The seating at the correctly set tables allows for pleasant conversation and maybe just a touch of romance, especially upstairs by the window. The service and welcome from chef/owner Joel Valéro's wife, Françoise, is friendly and always helpful, and Joel does his own shopping at Rungis.

The four-course prix fixe menu is definitely the best value. To whet your appetite while contemplating the delicious decisions ahead, you will have a *mise en bouche*— a tiny bite or two of cool cucumbers in cream or pieces of seafood. The offerings are seasonal, but the popular *foie gras maison* is always listed as an *entrée*. In the late spring, look for a warm leek *tarte,* a fresh spinach salad liberally sprinkled with gizzards, chicken liver terrine with an onion *confiture,* or thin slices of raw salmon marinated in lemon and coriander. Rabbit in some form is always a main course possibility, and so is the duck filet served with a light honey-and-vinegar sauce. Watch for fresh fish, lamb chops, and the *choucroute maison;* the *plat du jour* is always a good bet. All the main courses are liberally garnished with potato gratin or purée and fresh spinach or another vegetable, if you wish. Profiteroles with honey and chocolate, ginger-scented crème brûlée, and sugar-dusted, warm apple slices fanned into a circle are only a few of the pleasant finishing touches awaiting you. Finally, the wines are fairly priced.

You see, there is *always* plenty to rave about at Oh! Duo.

PLANET-CYBER CAFÉ (12)
173, rue de Vaugirard
Métro: Pasteur

Six computers are up and running from 10:30 A.M. to 8 P.M. every day but Sunday at this landing pad for Web surfers and email junkies, which is run by the Ajzner brothers. At this location, you can order a cheeseburger or pizza, along with soft drinks and beer, to keep you going another hour on the Internet. There is also a second location in the sixth arrondissement at 12, rue de l'Eperon, Métro: Odéon. That site has twenty computers (one Mac, nineteen PCs), but no food, only beverages.

PRIX FIXE
Lunch and dinner: 118F (17.99€), 2 courses, 148F (22.56€), 4 courses, both BNC

ENGLISH SPOKEN
Yes, and English menu

TELEPHONE
01-45-67-71-14

EMAIL
planet@cybercable.fr

OPEN
Mon–Sat: 10:30 A.M.–8 P.M.

CLOSED
Sun; NAC

RESERVATIONS
Not accepted

CREDIT CARDS
None

À LA CARTE
15–30F (2.29–4.57€)

INTERNET PRICES
1F (0.15€) per minute, 50F (7.62€) per hour, 200F (30.49€) for 5 hours

ENGLISH SPOKEN
Yes

S. ET D. FILOCHE (2)
39, rue du Laos
Métro: Cambronne

TELEPHONE
01-45-66-44-60

OPEN
Mon–Fri: lunch noon–2 P.M.,
dinner 7:45–9:45 P.M.

CLOSED
Sat–Sun; week between
Christmas and New Year's,
July 20–Sept 1

RESERVATIONS
Advised

CREDIT CARDS
MC, V

À LA CARTE
None

PRIX FIXE
Lunch and dinner: 146F
(22.26€), 2 courses, 169F
(25.76€), 3 courses, both BNC

ENGLISH SPOKEN
Yes

"S. et D." stands for Serge and Danièle Filoche, the husband and wife team at this little bistro, which is unknown to most Parisian visitors but very well known and respected by a devoted coterie of substantial regulars. Here you will experience a real taste of the food and service of an old-fashioned, family-run restaurant, which is too rapidly disappearing in Paris. The small, comfortable room is understated and sedate, and the service by Danièle and her one helper is gracious. The honest, traditional food aims to please—and it succeeds—with a warm broccoli vinaigrette served with sliced tomatoes and hard-boiled egg slices, a smoked duck salad, and a rich *cassolette* of snails and *pleurottes* (oyster mushrooms). Tender lamb with tomatoes (*provençale*), several fresh fish choices, beef, and French delicacies that Americans often disdain—veal kidneys in a lemon sauce and liver braised with truffles—round out the main dishes. For a light ending, it would be hard to top the melt-in-your-mouth *oeufs à la neige* floating in a caramel-flavored custard.

TY BREIZ (13)
52, boulevard de Vaugirard
Métro: Montparnasse-Bienvenüe

TELEPHONE
01-43-20-83-72

OPEN
Mon–Sat: lunch 11:45 A.M.–
2:45 P.M., dinner 7–10:45 P.M.

CLOSED
Sun; major holidays, 3 weeks in
Aug, sometimes 1 week in
December

RESERVATIONS
Advised

CREDIT CARDS
MC, V

À LA CARTE
100–135F (15.24–20.58€), BC

PRIX FIXE
Lunch and dinner: 65F (9.91€),
3 crêpes, BC

ENGLISH SPOKEN
Yes, with English menu

The message on the restaurant's business card says, *Les délices de la Bretagne peuvent également s'apprécier à Paris.* Or, "The delicacies of Brittany can also be enjoyed in Paris." And, of course, they mean right at Ty Breiz, which is as cute and cozy as a Breton *crêperie* can be. The blue-and-white, beamed dining room is decorated with Quimper pottery and old farm implements. There is also a carved wooden bar and an open kitchen, where you can watch the chefs adeptly turning out at least thirty variations of this popular comfort food. Savory buckwheat crêpes (*galettes*) are filled with mouthwatering combinations of eggs, meat, fish, cheese, and creamy sauces. The servings look huge but they are surprisingly light, and believe it or not, you will find yourself ordering a dessert crêpe . . . maybe a flambéed *crêpe Suzette* or a fancy Berthillon ice cream creation with rum-raisin ice cream and rum sauce hiding under a mountain of whipped cream. To keep the experience authentic, order a pitcher of cider to go with your meal, but be careful. If you are not used to this sort of strong apple drink, a little can go a long way. If crêpes are not on everyone in your party's wish list, there are three salads. The *californienne* is over-flowing with avocados, artichoke hearts, tomatoes, ham, and hearts of palm. Order *l'assiette lyonnaise* and dig in to pistachio-flavored sausage, potatoes, cheese, tomatoes, and toasted *pain Poilâne,* or if you prefer fish, then the *l'assiette nordique* lands you a filling meal—it has smoked salmon, *tarama,* potatoes vinaigrette, and green beans, as well as toasted Poilâne bread.

NOTE: A kir will be offered to *Great Eats Paris* readers who show the guide.

Sixteenth Arrondissement

RIGHT BANK
Avenue Foche, Bois de Boulogne, Jardin d'Acclimitation, Musée Marmottan, Musée d'Art Moderne de la Ville de Paris, Musée de l'Homme, Palais de Chaillot, Passy, Trocadéro

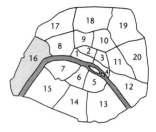

The sixteenth arrondissement, along with the seventh, is one of Paris's best addresses, especially around avenue Foche, where real estate prices are geared to oil moguls and multimillionaires. Elegant shopping can be found along avenue Victor Hugo and rue de Passy. The Trocadéro area, with its gardens, views of the Seine and Eiffel Tower, and complex of museums in the two wings of the Palais de Chaillot (built for the 1889 World Exhibition), forms the nucleus of tourist interest. At night the lighted fountains bring back the glamour of Art Deco Paris. Not to be overlooked is the Musée Marmottan, one of the hidden treasures of Paris museums. Bequests and gifts have enriched the collection so much that it rivals that of the Musée d'Orsay in Impressionist art, especially the collection of works by Monet.

AU CLOCHER DU VILLAGE (6)
8 bis, rue Verderet
Métro: Église d'Auteuil (exit Chardon Lagache)

Wine presses and old baskets hang from beams, posters plaster the ceiling and walls, a copper samovar graces the bar, a huge wooden four-door icebox hovers in the corner of the small room off the kitchen, and enough trinkets and treasure to open a shop fill the restaurant. True, it is cluttered, but it all works to create a homey setting for provincial country dining at Au Clocher du Village. Reserve a table for a 1 P.M. lunch or a 9 P.M. dinner and you may be the only foreigner there, either in the main room or on the beautiful summer terrace. Admittedly, it is not close and the métro ride is long, but trust me, it is worth the extra effort and time it takes to get there, especially on a warm day when you can sit outside.

The food is prepared in the traditional fashion and served by a staff who banter back and forth with long-time customers. When ordering, stick with the daily specials or the grilled meats and avoid the *haricots verts* (green beans). For starters, the mammoth plate of *crudités* or the artichoke hearts are good dishes. If you like apple tart, theirs is served warm with a tub of crème fraîche on the side to ladle over it. Or, if chocolate mousse is your downfall, here it is served in a big bowl *à volanté,* which means you can have seconds.

TELEPHONE
01-42-88-35-87

OPEN
Summer: daily, lunch noon–2:30 P.M., dinner 7:30–11 P.M.; winter: Mon–Fri lunch and dinner, Sat dinner only (same hours)

CLOSED
Sat lunch and Sun in winter; NAC

RESERVATIONS
Essential for a table outside

CREDIT CARDS
MC, V

À LA CARTE
175–190F (26.68–28.97€), BNC

PRIX FIXE
Lunch (winter only): 110F (16.77€), 3 courses, BC

ENGLISH SPOKEN
Yes

DRIVER'S (1)
6, rue Georges-Bizet
Métro: Alma-Marceau

Framed uniforms, crash helmets, and autographed photos of famous race car drivers decorate the walls at Driver's, a classy little bistro owned by Jean-Charles Karmann and Stéphane Muller, the nephew of Michel Dubose, a well-known driver on the Formula I racing circuit.

But you don't have to know or care a thing about racing to appreciate the good food and excellent value offered by the two-course prix fixe lunch for under $15, which includes not only the wine and mineral water but coffee. Then again, the à la carte menu won't send your budget into overdrive either, and neither will a bottle of decent wine. The stick-to-your-ribs food kicks off with snails, lentil salad, or baked eggs with salmon. It picks up speed with rabbit, pork, grilled *tournedos,* or *boudin noir* served with smooth mashed potatoes. Then you coast to the finish with rice pudding, *pain perdu,* or a winning *tarte Tatin* with crème fraîche.

TELEPHONE
01-47-23-61-15

OPEN
Mon–Fri: lunch noon–2:30 P.M., dinner 7 P.M.–midnight; Sat: dinner 7 P.M.–midnight

CLOSED
Sat lunch, Sun; holidays, Aug

RESERVATIONS
Advised

CREDIT CARDS
AE, MC, V

À LA CARTE
165–175F (25.15–26.68€), BC

PRIX FIXE
Lunch: 80F (12.20€), 2 courses, BC (wine, mineral water, and coffee)

ENGLISH SPOKEN
Yes

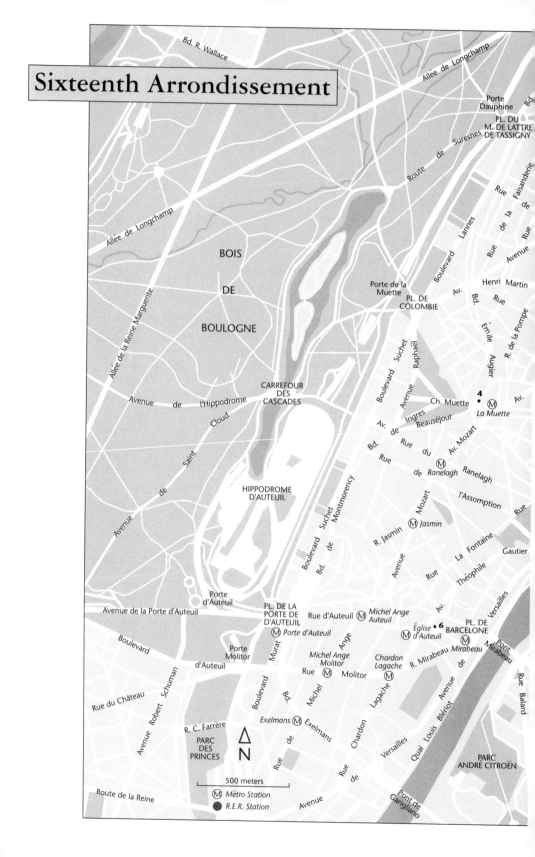

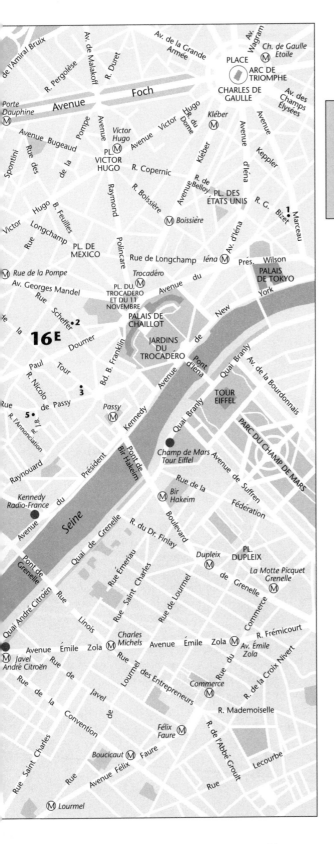

LA PETITE TOUR ($, 3)
11, rue de la Tour
Métro: Passy

TELEPHONE
01-45-20-09-31,
01-45-20-09-97

OPEN
Mon–Sat: lunch noon–
2:30 P.M., dinner 7:30–
10:30 P.M.

CLOSED
Sun; Aug

RESERVATIONS
Essential

CREDIT CARDS
AE, DC, MC, V

À LA CARTE
350–390F (53.36–59.46€),
BNC

PRIX FIXE
Lunch Mon–Fri: 150F (22.87€),
2 courses, BNC

ENGLISH SPOKEN
Yes

If only once during your stay in Paris you decide to have an exceptionally fine meal, you will not be disappointed by choosing Christiane and Freddy Israel's La Petite Tour in Passy. Offering marvelous food and service in a quiet, formal atmosphere, La Petite Tour is a dining pleasure you will remember long after leaving Paris. The food, a blend of classic French with modern overtones, relies on first-class products, precise preparation, and elegant presentation. Even the house dog, a golden Lab named Foster, has a sense of grace and style as he lies contentedly by the doorway.

If you are here in the fall, order Israel's specialty: masterfully cooked wild game. One of the most outstanding dishes is the robust venison stew with whole baby vegetables. It is almost impossible to list all the other specialties, as the menu is long and changes with market availability and the seasons. Always on the menu, however, are the delicate lobster bisque and the *filets de sole aux mandarines* (sole in a light mandarin sauce). The *caneton aux pêches* (duckling with peaches) is delicious, and so is the simple *fricassée de poulet au vinaigre* (stewed chicken in a vinegar sauce). The veal liver with raisins or bacon or the *filet de veau à la crème aux champignons* offer wonderful new interpretations of these French staples. No matter what your *entrée* and *plat* may be, you must save room for one of the picture-perfect desserts, especially the time-honored *pêches Pantagruel* or the blissfully light *île flottante*. In the spring and early summer, the *mille-feuille aux fraises* (flaky pastry layered with cream and fresh strawberries) is spectacular.

La Petite Tour has also recently added a new 150F (22.87€), two-course lunch menu (*entrée* and *plat* or *plat* and dessert), putting their fine dining within reach of many. The selections change daily and include *entrées* such as *terrine de canard* or *St-Jacques* (duck or scallop terrines). Freddy's famous tarragon chicken fricassee and duck with green pepper sauce alternate with fresh seasonal fish. If you have dessert as one of your courses, you may select one from the à la carte menu. Of course, a full à la carte meal does not fall into the budget category, but while sipping a cognac, I am sure you will agree with the many other readers who have been here that this delightful meal is well worth the extra money it may cost in return for the memories you will treasure of a truly fine dining experience in Paris.

LE BISTROT DES VIGNES (5)
1, rue Jean Bologne
Métro: Passy

At Le Bistrot des Vignes, stylish Passy inhabitants appreciate the contemporary bistro cooking as well as the excellent-value two-course lunch menu (pairing an *entrée* and *plat* or a *plat* and dessert). The upmarket mood is set as you are seated in the bright hot mustard yellow dining room punctuated by multicolor chairs. The menu promises good things ahead, with colorful salads of fresh vegetables, a dainty crêpe filled with fresh herbs and crayfish, grilled sausage served with *aligot,* lusty *plats du jour,* and always fresh fish. Reassuring desserts that ignore all calorie considerations include a bourbon crème brûlée and profiteroles for those wanting more of a sugar fix to end their meal. Special monthly wines are listed on the blackboard, and they offer a good opportunity to taste something new and different.

TELEPHONE
01-45-27-76-64

OPEN
Daily: lunch noon–2:30 P.M., dinner 7–10:30 P.M.

CLOSED
Sometimes in Aug (call to check)

RESERVATIONS
Advised

CREDIT CARDS
AE, MC, V

À LA CARTE
Entrées 40F (6.10€), *plats* 89F (13.57€), desserts 40F (6.10€), BNC

PRIX FIXE
Lunch: 95F (14.48€), 2 courses, BNC

ENGLISH SPOKEN
Yes

LE SCHEFFER (2)
22, rue Scheffer
Métro: Trocadéro

This is the part of Paris where the scarf is Hermés, the watch Cartier, the little outfit Chanel, and everyone has had a busy day at the boutique. That is why it is a bit of a surprise to discover Le Scheffer, a typical Left Bank bistro—right down to the big dog napping behind the bar, turn-of-the-twentieth-century posters, and original tile floors—where the kitchen dishes out generous and authentic food. A meal with a glass of the house vintage will ring in for around 175F (26.68€), which is reasonable considering the price of real estate in this blue-blooded corner of Paris.

The well-heeled crowd—foreign as well as French—plan repeat visits for the familiar dishes supplemented with daily specials. The encyclopedia of bistro eats includes lentil salad topped with slices of rare duck, cold green beans quickly tossed with a vinaigrette dressing, slabs of pâté and terrine, grilled lamb and beef, the usual organ meats, a spicy *andouillette,* fresh fish, and conventional desserts featuring seasonal fruits, chocolate, whipped cream, and anything else to try to bend a diner's willpower.

TELEPHONE
01-47-27-81-11

OPEN
Mon–Sat: lunch noon–2:30 P.M., dinner 7:30–10:30 P.M.

CLOSED
Sun; major holidays, week between Christmas and New Year's, NAC

RESERVATIONS
Advised

CREDIT CARDS
AE, MC, V

À LA CARTE
170–180F (25.92–27.44€), BC

PRIX FIXE
None

ENGLISH SPOKEN
Yes, with English menu

RESTAURANT DES CHAUFFEURS (4)
8, Chaussée de la Muette
Métro: La Muette

TELEPHONE
01-42-88-50-05

OPEN
Daily: 5:30 A.M.–10 P.M.,
continuous service

CLOSED
Dec 25, Jan 1, May 1,
Aug 13–27

RESERVATIONS
Suggested for lunch

CREDIT CARDS
MC, V

À LA CARTE
130–145F (19.82–22.11€),
BNC

PRIX FIXE
Lunch and dinner: 70F
(10.67€), 3 courses, BNC

ENGLISH SPOKEN
Yes

Famed chef Joël Robuchon considers this quarter-century-old, family-run café one of the capital's last outposts of home cooking. Quite a tribute. If you want to experience the type of family-run operation that seems to be on its way out in today's Paris, Restaurant des Chauffeurs is indeed a good example, where the second generation of the Bertrand family is now in charge.

The restaurant has been collecting anecdotes and acquiring patina for years, and it is easy to imagine that the hard-core regulars leaning against the bar know all the stories. Another group of habitués sit at the sidewalk tables, assessing and evaluating what upscale Parisians in Passy are wearing this year. The almost-readable, purple-ink menu features trucker-size portions of French comfort food. A typical selection might include a bowl of vegetable soup or marinated leeks, followed by sole *meunière* with steamed potatoes, roast chicken, fresh fish, or the house mainstay, liver with bacon and tomatoes. The desserts are simple versions of *clafoutis,* rice pudding, and fruit *tartes.* With a pitcher of house wine, $20 or so will see you out the door.

Seventeenth Arrondissement

The seventeenth is a sprawling area that includes leafy boulevards and upscale residences if you stay southwest of rue de Rome. The Palais des Congrès is here, a convention center with restaurants, several movie theaters, and the first stop in Paris for the Charles de Gaulle airport bus. The northeastern part of the arrondissement is scruffy as it merges with the eighteenth.

RIGHT BANK
Palais des Congrès, Parc Monceau

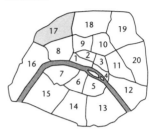

SEVENTEENTH ARRONDISSEMENT RESTAURANTS

($) indicates a Big Splurge

Seventeenth Arrondissement

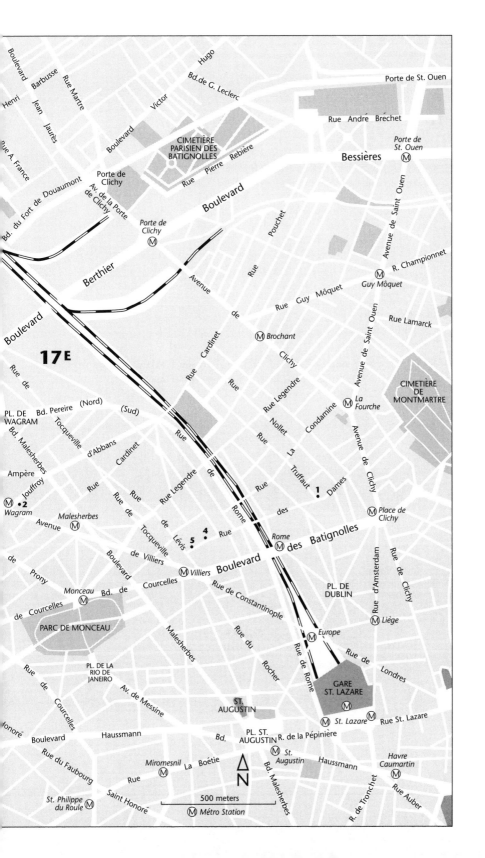

Boulevard Henri Barbusse

Rue Martre

Rue Jean Jaurès

Rue A. France

Hugo

Victor

Bd. de G. Leclerc

Boulevard

Porte de St. Ouen

Rue André Bréchet

CIMETIÈRE
PARISIEN DES
BATIGNOLLES

Rue Pierre Rebière

Porte de Clichy

Av. de la Porte de Clichy

Bd. du Fort de Douaumont

Porte de Clichy Ⓜ

Porte de
St. Ouen

Bessières Ⓜ

Avenue de Saint Ouen

R. Championnet

Berthier

Avenue

de

Pouchet

Rue

Rue Guy Môquet

Guy Môquet

Rue Lamarck

Boulevard

Rue Cardinet

Rue

Ⓜ Brochant

Clichy

Avenue de Saint Ouen

Avenue de Clichy

CIMETIÈRE
DE
MONTMARTRE

17ᴱ

Rue de

PL. DE
WAGRAM

Bd. Pereire (Nord)

(Sud)

Bd. Malesherbes

Tocqueville

d'Abbans

Ampère

Jouffroy

Ⓜ •2
Wagram

Cardinet

Rue

Rue

Rue de

Rue Legendre

Malesherbes Ⓜ

Avenue

de

Tocqueville

de Villiers

Rue Legendre

Nollet

Rue

La

Condamine

Ⓜ La
Fourche

Avenue de Clichy

Rue

Truffaut

Rome

de

Rue

des

•1 Dames

Ⓜ Place de
Clichy

Rome

Ⓜ des Batignolles

5 • • 4

Lévis

Rue

Ⓜ Villiers

Boulevard

Boulevard de Courcelles

Rue de Constantinople

PL. DE
DUBLIN

Rue d'Amsterdam

Rue de Clichy

Ⓜ Liège

Prony

Monceau

Bd. de

de Courcelles

PARC DE MONCEAU

Malesherbes

Rue du

Rocher

Rue de Rome

Ⓜ Europe

Rue de

Londres

PL. DE LA
RIO DE
JANEIRO

Av. de Messine

GARE
ST. LAZARE
Ⓜ

Rue de

Courcelles

ST.
AUGUSTIN

Ⓜ St. Lazare Ⓜ

Rue St. Lazare

onoré

Boulevard

Haussmann

Bd.

PL. ST.
AUGUSTIN R. de la Pépinière

Havre
Caumartin Ⓜ

Rue du Faubourg

Miromesnil

La Boétie

Ⓜ St.
Augustin

Haussmann

Bd. Malesherbes

Rue

Rue

St. Philippe
du Roule Ⓜ

Saint Honoré

△
N

500 meters

Ⓜ Métro Station

R. de Tronchet

Rue Auber

CHEZ FRED ($, 8)
190 bis, boulevard Péreire
Métro: Péreire (exit boulevard Péreire Nord), Porte Maillot

TELEPHONE
01-45-74-20-48
OPEN
Mon–Sat: lunch noon–2:30
P.M., dinner 7–11 P.M.
CLOSED
Sun; holidays, NAC
RESERVATIONS
Advised
CREDIT CARDS
AE, DC, MC, V
À LA CARTE
235F (35.83€), BNC
PRIX FIXE
Lunch and dinner (served till
2 P.M. and 10 P.M.): 150F
(22.87€), 3 courses, BC
ENGLISH SPOKEN
Yes

Owner Alain Piazza has all the familiar bistro elements going full-tilt at Chez Fred, including a crew of career waiters who never fail to remind you just who is boss. Their sometimes gruff service shouldn't deter you from coming, however, because when the food awards are handed out, Chez Fred continually finds itself in the winner's circle. It is a colorful spot, known for its bistro-style cooking, which is meant to be eaten, not admired. The inside is 1930s *grand-mère,* with beveled mirrors, old pieces of china displayed here and there, tightly packed tables, and a collection of umbrellas, hats, and Parisian street signs.

At the entrance, a big table overflows with first-course temptations: marinated mushrooms, herring, *céleri rémoulade, museau de boeuf,* pâtés, terrines, and assorted salads. The *plat du jour* promises a reliable week's worth of dishes: lamb on Monday, *petit salé* on Tuesday, *tête de veau* on Wednesday, *pot-au-feu* on Thursday, *boeuf à la mode* on Friday, and on Saturday, lamb again. In addition there is a full range of Lyonnaise offerings, truly wonderful if you love *saucisson* or *andouillette.* This is the place to ignore your diet and indulge in dessert because the chocolate cake with rich dark chocolate frosting and the crème brûlée are by themselves worth dieting for a week once you get back home.

CHOCOLAT VIENNOIS (5)
118, rue des Dames
Métro: Villiers, Rome

TELEPHONE
01-42-93-34-40
OPEN
Mon: lunch noon–3 P.M.,
dinner 7–10:30 P.M.; Tues–Fri:
lunch, tea, and dinner noon–
10:30 P.M.; Sat: lunch and tea
noon–7 P.M.
CLOSED
Mon tea, Sat dinner, Sun; major
holidays, NAC
RESERVATIONS
Advised for lunch
CREDIT CARDS
MC, V (100F, 15.24€,
minimum)
À LA CARTE
50–160F (7.62–24.39€), BC

If you are strolling along the colorful rue des Levis shopping street (don't miss the excellent Monoprix at the corner of rue des Levis and rue des Dames), Chocolat Viennois is a good place to stop for lunch, dinner, a quick cup of chocolate topped with whipped cream, or a pastry and a nice afternoon cup of tea from Mariage Frères. The wood-paneled interior of this cozy restaurant looks like a mountain chalet, with tables tucked into corners—and special ones reserved for nonsmokers, a real plus in Paris. If you see something you like, chances are it is for sale, from the painted wooden fruit and flower arrangements to seasonal trinkets and the chocolate and sugar tins on display. The lineup of taste temptations ranges from huge salads, *raclette,* and fondue (both available for dinner and Saturday lunch) to quiches, savory tarts, and meat-based dishes. Desserts such as apple strudel, fruit crumble with cream, and an unpardonably rich chocolate cake served with vanilla ice cream and chocolate sauce will make most dieters wear a hair shirt for a week.

NOTE: Tables are reserved for nonsmokers. Also under the same ownership is Le Patio Provençal, next door (see page 250).

EMPIRE STATE RESTAURANT BUFFET AND MONTE CARLO
Empire State: 41, avenue Wagram (15)
Monte Carlo: 9, avenue Wagram (16)
Métro: Charles-de-Gaulle-Étoile, Ternes

What! Fifty francs for a three-course multichoice lunch? In Paris? Two blocks from the Arc de Triomphe and the Champs-Élysées? Impossible—there must be a catch.

No, there's no catch. Just beat your feet to either the Empire State Restaurant Buffet or its cousin just up the block, the Monte Carlo. From the street you will see only a signboard on the sidewalk touting the prix fixe meal at the Empire State. The restaurant is in the basement, and frankly, I expected to see down-at-the-heel *clochards* (bums) with plastic sacks and old ladies in fuzzy slippers occupying the tables. Well, *quelle surprise!* I found secretaries, middle-management types, and other savvy diners enjoying a wide array of self-service food, all brightly displayed along a cafeteria line like something you would expect to see in an airport. Seating is on plastic-covered chairs at Formica tables in a room surrounded with posters of U.S. and French films. There is even a non-smoking section. It is all quite nice and pleasant.

The Monte Carlo is on the same side of the street, just a block or two up avenue de Wagram. It opens onto the street and has a glassed-in terrace, so you can't miss it. It has the benefit of being open 365 days a year from 8 A.M. until 11 P.M. with continuous food service. Here the prix fixe is available only until 3:30 P.M., but after that, a tray piled high would come to only 85F (12.96€). If you don't want a large lunch, both restaurants have one-dish salads, main courses, and good-looking desserts. Though the Monte Carlo has different hours, its prices, food, and other information is the same as for the Empire State.

PRIX FIXE
Lunch: 98F (14.94€), 2 courses, BNC; dinner: 140F (21.34€), 3 courses, apértif, BNC

ENGLISH SPOKEN
Yes

Empire State

TELEPHONE
01-43-80-14-39,
01-40-80-17-73

OPEN
Mon–Fri: 11 A.M.–3:30 P.M.

CLOSED
Sat–Sun; holidays, NAC

RESERVATIONS
Not accepted

CREDIT CARDS
None

À LA CARTE
85F (12.96€), BC

PRIX FIXE
Lunch: 48F (7.32€), 3 courses, BNC

ENGLISH SPOKEN
Very limited

Monte Carlo

TELEPHONE
01-43-80-02-20

OPEN
Daily: 8 A.M.–11 P.M., continuous service

CLOSED
Never

RESERVATIONS
Only for large groups, which are seated upstairs and served a set menu

Even though you are in Paris, where even the cheapest meal is usually prepared well, and this one is, you still cannot expect delicate soufflés or subtle seasonings on wild game. What you see is what you get, and for the best choice and freshest food, get there early. The prix fixe lunch changes daily and could include a yogurt with fruit and ground roundsteak garnished with fries, vegetables, and a roll. Aside from this incredible deal, everything is priced individually, from the rolls and butter to the apple tart (whipped cream extra).

NOTE: Both restaurants have a nonsmoking section.

FÉLIX (6)
99, rue Jouffroy d'Abbans
Metro: Wagram

For a full description, see Pépita in the eighth arrondissement, page 178. All other information is the same.

TELEPHONE: 01-42-27-26-16
OPEN: Mon–Fri: lunch noon–2:30 P.M., dinner 7:30–11:30 P.M.; Sat: dinner 7:30–11:30 P.M.
CLOSED: Sat lunch, Sun; major holidays, NAC

JOY IN FOOD (1)
2, rue Truffaut, at rue des Dames
Métro: Rome, Place de Clichy

TELEPHONE
01-43-87-96-79

OPEN
Mon–Sat: lunch noon–3 P.M.

CLOSED
Sun; major holidays, Aug

RESERVATIONS
Advised; required for group dinner

CREDIT CARDS
None

À LA CARTE
50–100F (7.62–15.24€), BNC

PRIX FIXE
Lunch: 60F (9.15€), 2 courses, 75F (11.43€), 3 courses, both BNC

ENGLISH SPOKEN
Yes

If you think *vegetarian* means only lentils and brown rice, you have not had a meal at Joy in Food. I found this place a few years ago when I was walking by on my way somewhere else, and the clean white-and-blue interior caught my eye. The tempting aromas beckoned me; I had to try it and am glad I did. The imaginative vegetarian cuisine and the final bill, which matched the size of this tiny restaurant, made it a natural choice.

The young, dynamic owner, Naema Aouad, puts on a virtual one-woman show as she cooks and serves from her compact, open kitchen. Since the last time I was here, she has added more seating and a baby boy named Ryan. She was able to take over the shop next door, knock out the wall, and increase the seating capacity to forty-five. By 12:30 or 1 P.M., all the seats are taken by diners who appreciate her health-conscious meals and no-smoking policy. Aouad works with organic products as much as possible, and she goes into the country to select her vegetables directly from growers. Every day, patrons can depend on having a savory *tarte,* a *plat du jour,* and a choice of omelettes. Assorted crudités, crisp salads, vegetable pâté, and onion soup are the tempting starters. Even hard-core dieters succumb to the chocolate cake with pears, the rhubarb and orange crumble, or the apple cake filled with raisins, dried apricots, and cinnamon—order it warmed for best effect. Organic wine, beer, and cider are served in juice glasses along with banana milkshakes, fresh fruit and vegetable juices, and herb tea.

NOTE: Parties of ten or more can reserve Joy in Food for dinner, when the restaurant is normally closed.

LA PETITE AUBERGE (7)
38, rue Laugier, at Villa Laugier
Métro: Ternes, Péreire

Joël Decloux and his gracious wife, Jackie, continue to build on their success, and each time I return to La Petite Auberge I find it better than the last. Decloux is a dedicated chef, always experimenting and improving his repertoire. He does it all, from making bread twice a day to creating the beautiful desserts. The polite, dignified service headed by Jackie fulfills the expectations of the most discriminating patrons, as she pays attention to the little details that make the difference between a mere meal and fine dining.

No matter what you order from the seasonal menu, you will be pleased. Star springtime *entrées* are the *ravioles d'escargots de bourgogne au beurre de roquefort* (ravioli filled with tender snails in a roquefort butter sauce) and the *mosaïc de légumes, coulis de tomates fraîches*—lovely spring vegetables dressed in a tomato sauce. The main courses are all special, but if you like lamb and it is on the menu, please order the roast lamb, served with an eggplant garnish and a potato pancake The salmon dusted with herbs, the veal liver in a light honey cream sauce, and the filet of beef with shallots and potatoes *dauphine* are other equally marvelous choices.

When you are seated, you will be asked if you want dessert. Yes, you do! And just hope you are not alone, so you can share several. All arrive at your table looking like works of art that belong in a museum. The light and flaky *mille-feuille* (puff pastry filled with rum cream) are the best in Paris, and the Grand Mariner soufflé is a soft, cloudlike dream. In the spring and summer, treat yourself to the *feuilleté des pommes tièdes aux noix* (leaves of flaky pastry layered with apples, nuts, and spices) or the *terrine de chocolat amér aux zestes d'oranges* (a rich, orange-flavored

TELEPHONE
01-47-63-85-51

OPEN
Sept–April: Mon, dinner 7:30–10 P.M.; Tues–Fri, lunch noon–2 P.M., dinner 7:30–10 P.M.; Sat dinner 7:30–10 P.M.; May–July: Mon dinner, Tues–Fri lunch and dinner (same hours)

CLOSED
Sept–April: Mon and Sat lunch, Sun; May–July: Mon lunch, Sat–Sun; major holidays, Aug

RESERVATIONS
Advised

CREDIT CARDS
MC, V

À LA CARTE
None

PRIX FIXE
Lunch and dinner: 140F (21.34€), 2 courses, 170F (25.92€), 3 courses, both BNC

ENGLISH SPOKEN
Yes

dark chocolate terrine). After dinner, coffee is served with chocolates and madeleines.

La Petite Auberge continues to be my top choice for a special celebration meal. When you go, order a bottle of the featured wine of the month, sit back, savor the fine food, and toast to the fact that you are dining so well in Paris.

L'ÉCLUSE CARNOT (14)
1, rue d'Armaillé
Métro: Argentina, Charles-de-Gaulle-Etoile

For a complete description, see L'Écluse in the sixth arrondissement, page 137. All other information is the same.

TELEPHONE: 01-47-63-88-29

LE PATIO PROVENÇAL (4)
116, rue des Dames
Métro: Villiers, Rome

TELEPHONE
01-42-93-73-73

OPEN
Mon–Fri: lunch noon–2:30 P.M., dinner 7–11 P.M.

CLOSED
Sat–Sun; major holidays, NAC

RESERVATIONS
Advised for lunch

CREDIT CARDS
MC, V (100F, 15.24€, minimum)

À LA CARTE
125–189F (19.06–28.81€), BNC

PRIX FIXE
None

ENGLISH SPOKEN
Yes

The Patio Provençal, owned by Frederic and Stephan Poiri, the two brothers who run Chocolat Viennois next door (see page 246), is a charming slice of Provence deep in Paris. Bright yellow and greens mix with earth tones, lavenders, and oranges to create the feeling you are dining in the sunny south of France. The first room is appealing, with arbors over the tables and tiled and mirrored booths, but it gets noisy and congested, so you are better off asking for a table in the skylighted garden next to the real Provençal fountain. Almost everything you see around you is for sale, except the lovely framed prints of Provence and the dried floral arrangements. The food is, of course, all about the south, featuring eggplant, squashes, fish, lots of garlic and onions, hearty soups, and seasonal fruit-based desserts. It is a delightful respite for a light lunch or dinner in a part of Paris few visitors ever go.

LE PETIT BOFINGER (12)
43, avenue des Ternes
Métro: Ternes

For a complete description, see Le Petit Bofinger, page 93. All other information is the same.

TELEPHONE: 01-43-80-19-28

LE PETIT BOFINGER (3)
10, place du Maréchal Juin
Métro: Péreire

For a complete description, see Le Petit Bofinger, page 93. All other information is the same.

TELEPHONE: 01-56-79-56-20

LE PETIT SALÉ (11)
99, avenue des Ternes
Métro: Porte Maillot

Warning: Le Petit Salé is not for the timid eater!

At this little hole-in-the-wall, where heaping plates, good fellowship, and crowded tables are the rule, the substantial specialty is *petit salé:* salt pork cooked with vegetables and lentils and served with a big basket of crusty bread to mop up all the wonderful juices. If salt pork isn't your passion, there are other choices: house terrines, *cassoulet,* and *andouillettes*. In the summer, cold meats, big salads, and light desserts are on the menu. Le Petit Salé has a good cheese selection, and the *tarte Tatin* is worth every filling bite. Order a bottle of Chinon or Gamay de Touraine to go with your *petit salé* or any other meat-inspired main course. Do note that lunchtime can be a madhouse, so schedule your arrival accordingly.

TELEPHONE
01-45-74-10-57

OPEN
Daily: lunch 11:30 A.M.–3 P.M., dinner 7:30–11:30 P.M.

CLOSED
Never

RESERVATIONS
Advised

CREDIT CARDS
AE, DC, MC, V

À LA CARTE
160–185F (24.39–28.20€), BNC

PRIX FIXE
None

ENGLISH SPOKEN
Limited, with English menu

LE RELAIS DE VENISE—LE RESTAURANT DE L'ENTRECÔTE (13)
271, boulevard Péreire
Métro: Porte Maillot

Le Relais de Venise, better known as L'Entrecôte, is on every Parisian's cheap eats map, and it should be on yours. You cannot call for reservations, because they do not take them. As a result, you must go early or very late, because there is almost always a line waiting outside. The waitresses are something else: direct from hell, but they don't seem to deter the meat-loving flock from coming back time and time again. The long-standing formula for success has been widely imitated but never bettered. They offer just a single meal: for 121F (18.45€), you are served a salad and an *entrecôte* steak with *pommes frites*. Desserts designed to make the finals at a Betty Crocker bake-off are extra and so is the wine. All this is served to an appreciative audience in a cheerful room with a mural of the Grand Canal in Venice along one side. In warm weather, tables are set on the sidewalk and are hotly contested.

TELEPHONE
01-45-74-27-97

OPEN
Daily: lunch noon–2:30 P.M., dinner 7–11:45 P.M.

CLOSED
Some holidays, July

RESERVATIONS
Not accepted

CREDIT CARDS
MC, V

À LA CARTE
None

PRIX FIXE
Lunch and dinner: 121F (18.45€), 2 courses, BNC (desserts are extra: 35–40F, 5.34–6.10€)

ENGLISH SPOKEN
Sometimes, depending on the mood of your waitress

LES MESSUGUES (9)
8, rue Léon Jost
Métro: Courcelles

TELEPHONE
01-47-63-26-65

OPEN
Mon–Fri: lunch noon–
2:30 P.M., dinner 8–10:30 P.M.

CLOSED
Sat–Sun; holidays, Aug

RESERVATIONS
Advised

CREDIT CARDS
AE, DC, MC, V

À LA CARTE
None

PRIX FIXE
Lunch and dinner: 140F
(21.34€), 4 courses, BNC;
dinner: 184F (28.05€),
3 courses, BC (wine, kir,
and coffee)

ENGLISH SPOKEN
Yes

Les Messugues is a prized gem well worth searching out, because once you've discovered it, you will have found one of the best-value meals of your trip to Paris.

The setting is beautiful and so nicely arranged and appointed that I feel as though I am dining in someone's lovely home. The two rooms are small and intensely romantic, with hurricane candles, soft music, and masses of fresh flowers. It is the perfect place to dress for dinner and spend a marvelous evening enjoying a fine French meal with someone special. My friend's comment during our meal really sums up the feeling everyone has about Les Messugues: "Anyone cooking and running a restaurant with this much feeling and attention to detail deserves to be a great success."

The service by owner Alain Laforêt is flawless, and the cooking by Gérard Fontaine is nothing short of remarkable for its quality, variety, and presentation. Only two prix fixe menus are served, and in the evening, you start with the house apéritif, which is served with a bite-size appetizer. While fresh fish is the mainstay of the menu, it by no means overshadows the rest of the offerings. For dinner you will have a choice of five or six *entrées* and *plats,* assorted cheeses, and dessert. As with the rest of the menu, the dishes change to reflect the seasons and inspiration of the chef. You might start with a salad of lightly poached vegetables, topped with a block of house foie gras. For your *plat,* if it's the early spring, you might have a choice between filets of red mullet resting on a *fondue* of vegetables, *filet de plie* (similar to sole) steamed and served with fresh asparagus, or grilled trout. Tender *pot-au-feu de boeuf* is surrounded by colorful vegetables, and perfectly prepared beef *tournedos* comes in a mustard sauce. The duck with *morilles* (morel mushrooms) is a rich choice, and so is the liver served with reduced balsamic vinegar. The desserts are works of art, especially the *fondant au chocolat sauce café* (dense chocolate cake with a coffee sauce), the pear dressed in warm chocolate sauce, and the *gratin de fruits chaud,* which makes a light, refined ending. Coffee arrives with a plate of Fontaine's truffles and candied citrus, ending a wonderful meal you will want to repeat as often as you are fortunate enough to visit Paris.

LE STÜBLI (10)
11, rue Poncelet
Métro: Ternes

Everyone who knows me well knows how much I like going to street markets, even in my own hometown. When I am traveling, a stroll through any local *marché* is the best way I know to see how people live day to day, not to mention the best way to discover firsthand what I can expect to be served wherever I am dining that evening. One of my favorite permanent street markets in Paris is along rue Poncelet. I like to go early when it opens, then go to Le Stübli, the best German/Austrian bakery this side of the Rhine, and order a steaming coffee or hot chocolate and a slice of apple strudel. If I go later, I never miss a piece of their *schwarzwälderkirschtorte,* known as *la véritable forêt-noire,* a black forest cake that is positively illegal it is so rich.

A nice thing about Le Stübli is that you are not limited to pastries. Upstairs, above the pastry shop and counter, they serve a full breakfast, a delightful lunch, and afternoon tea. Across the street is their deli, Le Stübli Delikatessen, where you can purchase ready-made salads and dishes to warm up later on . . . especially nice if you are staying in an apartment. Here they have a handful of wiggly green metal tables and chairs, sitting directly on the street, boldly positioned between white lines of a parking space and the gutter. If I am here for lunch on the run, I stop by the painted cart in front and have the French equivalent of *le hot dog,* white sausage on a warm sesame or poppy seed roll, slathered in cooked onions. Be careful, the juice could drip to your elbows.

TELEPHONE
Pâtisserie and tearoom: 01-42-27-81-86; deli: 01-48-88-98-07

OPEN
Mon: deli only 10:30 A.M.–3 P.M.; Tues–Sat: breakfast, lunch, and tea 9 A.M.–7:30 P.M.; Sun and holidays: breakfast 9 A.M.–1 P.M.

CLOSED
Pâtisserie and tearoom on Mon; 3 weeks in Aug

RESERVATIONS
Not necessary

CREDIT CARDS
MC, V

À LA CARTE
35–100F (5.34–15.24€), BNC

PRIX FIXE
Breakfast: 55F (8.38€), 145F (22.11€), both BC; lunch: 90F (13.72€), 2 courses, 114F (17.38€), 3 courses, both BNC; *le snack:* 52F (7.93€), 2 courses, BNC

ENGLISH SPOKEN
Yes

RESTAURANT BAPTISTE (2)
51, rue Jouffroy d'Abbans
Métro: Wagram

When evaluating a restaurant, two of the questions I always ask myself are, "Would I come back, and would I recommend it to my friends?" On both counts, the answer for Restaurant Baptiste is a resounding yes! It has been open only a short time, but it does not give off that "we're just getting started" aura. The cooking is as deft and modern as the high-backed rose-colored chairs and miniature flowers that grace each beige-tablecloth-draped table. The past is also treated with respect, as evidenced by the original multicolored 1930s tile floor . . . and by the sensible selection of honest bistro fare. Start with a salad of mixed greens, liberally tossed

TELEPHONE
01-42-27-20-18

OPEN
Mon–Fri: lunch noon–2 P.M., dinner 7:30–10:30 P.M.; Sat: dinner 7:30–10:30 P.M.

CLOSED
Sat lunch, Sun; major holidays, Aug

RESERVATIONS
Recommended

CREDIT CARDS
AE, MC, V

À LA CARTE
None

PRIX FIXE
Lunch: 125F (19.06€),
2 courses, BNC; dinner: 148F
(22.56€) 2 courses, 180F
(27.44€), 3 courses, both BNC

ENGLISH SPOKEN
Yes

with fresh herbs and a walnut vinaigrette. This leaves plenty of room for the tender veal chop on a confit of carrots, potatoes, and artichoke hearts or for any of the fresh fish offerings, all of which are garnished with a pastiche of vegetables. Desserts are excellent, including the apple and raisin crêpes and the chocolate fudge *tarte,* both of which must be ordered at the beginning of the meal. The short, well-conceived wine list can be expensive, but not if you order by the glass or half bottle.

Eighteenth Arrondissement

I'm not from Paris. I'm from Montmartre.
—Longtime Montmartre resident

Montmartre captivates visitors with its picturesque winding streets, magnificent view of Paris from the steps of the Sacré Coeur, and its history as the heart and soul of artistic Paris at the turn of the twentieth century, when the Moulin Rouge and Toulouse-Lautrec were at their peak. It was also here at the site of the Bateau Lavoir that Picasso and Braque developed Cubism and modern art was born. Today, Montmartre is more like a village: a jumble of secret squares and narrow alleyways make up the "Butte," or hill, where the white-domed Sacré Coeur Basilica sits majestically. Montmartre is also a study in contrasts, as nostalgia mixes with the crass commercialism of Pigalle and the place du Tertre, a mecca for tourists and third-rate artists hawking their dubious wares.

RIGHT BANK
Montmartre, Sacré Coeur, Marché aux Puces St-Ouen (Paris's largest flea market)

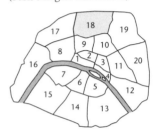

EIGHTEENTH ARRONDISSEMENT RESTAURANTS

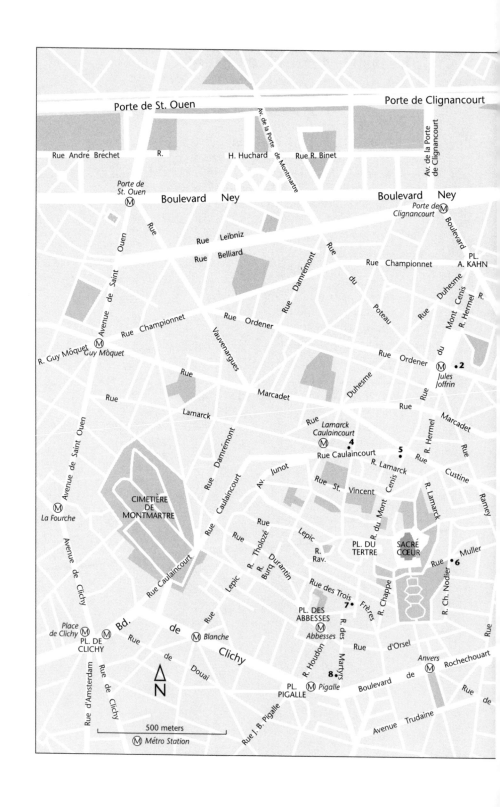

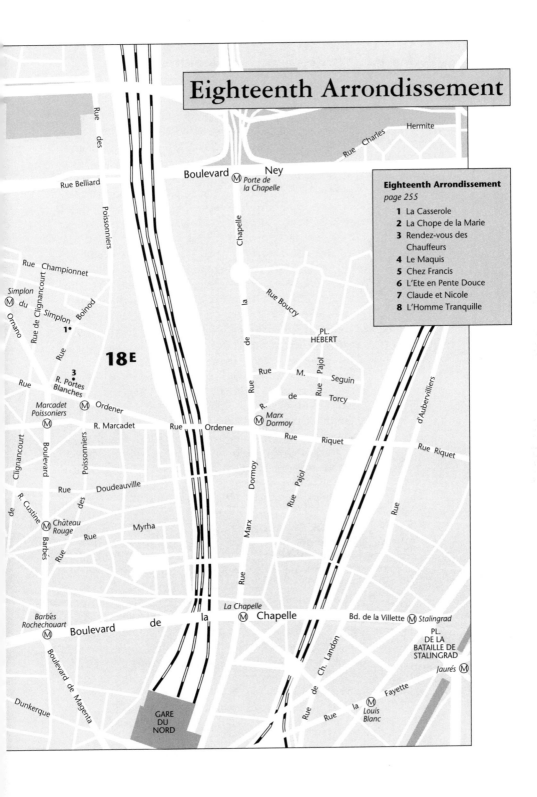

Eighteenth Arrondissement

Hermite

Rue Charles

Boulevard Ⓜ Ney
Porte de
la Chapelle

Rue Belliard

Poissonniers

Chapelle

Rue des

Rue Championnet

Rue Boucry

Simplon
Ⓜ du
Ornano

Rue de Clignancourt

Simplon

Boinod

1•

la

de

PL.
HÉBERT

Rue

Pajol

Rue

18E

3
R. Portes
Blanches

Rue

M.

Seguin

Rue

de

Torcy

Rue

R.

Marcadet
Poissonniers
Ⓜ

Ⓜ Ordener

R. Marcadet

Rue   Ordener

R.
Ⓜ Marx
Dormoy

d'Aubervilliers

Rue   Riquet

Rue Riquet

Clignancourt

Boulevard

Poissonniers

Rue   Doudeauville

Dormoy

Rue Pajol

Rue

de

des

R. Custine

Ⓜ Château
Rouge

Rue

Myrha

Marx

Barbés

Rue

Rue

Barbés
Rochechouart
Ⓜ

Boulevard   de   la

La Chapelle
Ⓜ Chapelle

Bd. de la Villette Ⓜ Stalingrad

PL.
DE LA
BATAILLE DE
STALINGRAD

Jaurés Ⓜ

Boulevard   de   Magenta

Ch. Landon

Dunkerque

GARE
DU
NORD

de

Rue

Rue

la

Ⓜ
Louis
Blanc

Fayette

CHEZ FRANCIS (5)

122, rue Caulaincourt, by the steps at rue du Mont Cenis

Métro: Lamarck-Caulaincourt (No. 80 bus stops at the door)

TELEPHONE
01-42-64-60-62

OPEN
Mon, Thur–Sun: lunch noon–2:30 P.M., dinner 7–10:30 P.M.; Wed: dinner 7–10:30 P.M.

CLOSED
Wed lunch, Tues; Oct 1–8

RESERVATIONS
For Sun lunch

CREDIT CARDS
AE, MC, V

À LA CARTE
150F (22.87€), BNC

PRIX FIXE
Lunch and dinner: 120F (18.29€), 3 courses, BNC

ENGLISH SPOKEN
Limited

Chez Francis is the type of restaurant I could come to every day and feel at home. Overseen by hardworking owner Felicité Erguy, its mood is perfect old-fashioned Paris: a bustling and cramped dining room with varnished paint, yellowing walls, smoky mirrors, and interesting Montmartre habitués sitting at their regular tables. On Sunday, the restaurant is alive with high-spirited family groups lingering on the covered terrace over a leisurely three-hour lunch.

The rich southwestern-inspired cuisine is from the old school and pays no attention to calorie watching. Serious followers of this type of cooking will adore the wide selection on the prix fixe menu. First-rate *entrées* include *terrine de Périgord, jambon de Bayonne,* and *salade landaise* filled with chunks of foie gras. The specialty is paella, and it's simply not to be missed if this is one of your favorites. Other top choices are the *confit de porc,* the *escalope de veau aux pleurottes et crème* (veal with mushrooms and cream), and the *fricassée de poulet basquaise* (tender chicken in a tomato-based sauce). After such a sumptuous meal it is hard to contemplate dessert, but if you can, try the *oeufs à la neige* or the *gâteau Basque.*

Later on, wander back up the hill to the top of Montmartre, stand on the steps of Sacré Coeur, and gaze over all of Paris lying at your feet. It is an experience you will not soon forget . . . I guarantee it.

CLAUDE ET NICOLE (7)

13, rue des Trois-Frères
Métro: Abbesses

TELEPHONE
01-46-06-12-48

OPEN
Tues–Sat: lunch noon–2:15 P.M., dinner 7:30–10:30 P.M.; Sun: lunch noon–2:15 P.M.

CLOSED
Sun dinner, Mon; 2 weeks in June (dates vary), last 2 weeks in Dec

RESERVATIONS
Not necessary

CREDIT CARDS
MC, V

À LA CARTE
None

The surroundings might lack elegance, but Claude et Nicole's Montmartre spot is bursting at the seams with eager, cost-conscious diners seeking *les temps perdu . . .* and finding it. The food offers no gourmet ruffles or flourishes, but the plentiful, good, filling fare is priced to please. A meal here starts with familiar dishes, such as *oeufs dur mayonnaise,* homemade terrines, eggy-rich quiche, and *jambon persillé maison.* Homemade *frites* grace the three main-course choices, consisting of two or three lunch and dinner *plats du jour* and steak (ask for it if it isn't on the menu; it costs an additional 10F, 1.52€). Cheese, crème caramel, fruit *tarte,* or their own yogurt will wrap it all up. It's simple and successful because it never tries to be more than it is . . . a decent cheap eat in Paris.

PRIX FIXE
Lunch: 72F (10.98€), 3 courses, BNC; dinner: 90F (13.72€), 3 courses, BNC

ENGLISH SPOKEN
Limited

LA CASSEROLE (1)
17, rue Boinod
Métro: Simplon, Marcadet-Poissonniers

For a dining experience in an atmosphere found nowhere else on this planet, head for La Casserole. It was opened forty-five years ago by Bernard Dubois, who served as General Eisenhower's personal chef when the general was in Versailles. Dubois is still at the restaurant, but he has turned the day-to-day operation over to Daniel Darthial.

La Casserole is the type of restaurant where you can take spirited in-laws, your kids, your mom, and your spouse and everyone will love it. Located on the back side of Montmartre, it consists of several rooms festooned with an endless assortment of knickknacks, stuffed animals, plants, doodads, fishnets, seashells, cooing birds, pots, pans, fans, feathers, flags, banners, and badges, all hung on the beams, ceilings, and walls, in the windows and over the door. No space has been left unadorned, including the unisex toilet, which you absolutely must see to believe. When I asked how often the paraphernalia was dusted I was told, "Once a year, when we are closed in the summer. It takes us two days just to take it down, and another two to put it all back." Once you see it all, you will wonder how they do it in such a short time.

But what about the food and the service? They are both great. The portions are generous, the service friendly, and the diners fun to watch and be with. In the fall and winter, all sorts of wild game tops the list of favorite dishes to order. During the rest of the year, traditional preparations of robust French standards keep everyone well fed and happy. Look for goose, the most tender *blanquette de veau* in these parts, chicken, duck, and grilled steak, all liberally garnished with large servings of potatoes. The desserts are all made here, including the ice cream. Especially recommended is the *péché casserole*. *Péché* means "sin," and sinful this is, but oh, so good. It consists of chocolate cake with vanilla ice cream, chocolate sauce, and whipped cream and is served in its own casserole. Less sinful, but still dangerous, is the

TELEPHONE
01-42-54-50-97

OPEN
Tues–Sat: lunch noon–2 P.M., dinner 7:30–10 P.M.

CLOSED
Mon, Sun; holidays, 3–4 days at Easter, mid-July–mid-Aug

RESERVATIONS
Essential

CREDIT CARDS
MC, V

À LA CARTE
185–200F, BNC

PRIX FIXE
Lunch Tues–Fri: 75F (11.43€), 3 courses, BC; lunch and dinner: 130F (19.82€), 3 courses, BNC

ENGLISH SPOKEN
Absolutely

homemade nougat ice cream with a honey, orange, and caramel topping.

NOTE: If you plan to come here around a holiday, call to make sure they will be open. Sometimes the restaurant closes an extra day before or after a holiday.

LA CHOPE DE LA MARIE (2)
88, rue Ordener
Métro: Jules Joffrin

TELEPHONE
01-46-06-46-14

OPEN
Mon–Sat: lunch noon–
2:30 P.M., dinner 7–11 P.M.;
Sun: lunch noon–2:30 P.M.;
music Fri–Sat: 8 P.M.–midnight

CLOSED
Sun dinner; NAC

RESERVATIONS
Required for Fri and Sat night,
advised otherwise

CREDIT CARDS
MC, V

À LA CARTE
None

PRIX FIXE
Lunch: 50F (7.62€), *plat du jour; petit menu,* 75F (11.43€),
2 courses; *grand menu,* 90F (13.72€), 3 courses, all BNC;
dinner: *petit menu,* 95F (14.48€),
grand menu, 100F (15.24€),
both BNC

ENGLISH SPOKEN
Yes

At first glance there doesn't seem to be anything special about La Chope de la Marie. It looks like hundreds of others . . . with long lines of paper-covered tables in a brightly lit room and a bar on one side. However, the food and the weekend entertainment put it in a class by itself. On Friday and Saturday nights from 8 P.M. to midnight, you can come for dinner and listen to live Montmartre music, performed by two accordionists and one guitarist—for no additional cover charge, and no increase in regular menu prices. Reservations are required. At other times, it is a convenient choice on the back side of the Butte de Montmartre for an abundant lunch or dinner.

The prix fixe menus, which offer good eating and appealing choices, start off with plates of smoked salmon, *chèvre chaud, crudités,* escargots, and salads laden with calamari, crayfish, or scallops. Then you can try roast veal with braised endives, *dorade* (sea bream) with steamed potatoes, or one of the house specialties: *filet de canard sauce miel* (tender duck in a honey sauce) or *confit de canard pommes à l'ail* (preserved duck with garlic potatoes). Finish with a *charlotte au chocolat,* profiteroles, or *feuilleté aux fraises,* which are all made here.

LE MAQUIS (4)
69, rue Caulaincourt
Métro: Lamarck-Caulaincourt

TELEPHONE
01-42-59-76-07

OPEN
Mon–Sat: lunch noon–2 P.M.,
dinner 7:30–10 P.M.

CLOSED
Sun; major holidays, NAC

RESERVATIONS
Advised

CREDIT CARDS
MC, V

Montmartre is full of greasy spoons dedicated to scooping in the tourists and, in the process, turning off the locals. Well protected from this dining circus is Le Maquis, one of the increasingly hard-to-find restaurants *de quartier* that inspires a loyal following who value sound food at consistently fair prices. The fifty-five-seat dining room is rather formal, with linen tablecloths and waiters clad in black. In the summer, the tiny terrace along the front is a good vantage point for the Parisian hobby of people-watching.

Owner Claude Lesage, who has been here for more than twenty years, does all the baking, including the breads. His seasonal menus are dedicated to traditional dishes, which are beautifully prepared from the best ingredients. The *carte* changes twice yearly, and the prix fixe lunch and dinner menus are different each day, so it is virtually impossible to describe all the possibilities. If I am here in the late spring, I look for fresh asparagus vinaigrette, the house foie gras on a bed of chilled greens, roast veal with just-cooked zucchini, *lotte* (monkfish) with pesto, fresh sautéed scallops, or the leg of lamb with a trio of fresh vegetables. I never miss one of Claude's tempting desserts, which I always hope will include raspberries on a cinnamon crust, chocolate *fondant* with Cointreau, or *tarte Tatin* with crème fraîche.

À LA CARTE
Entrées 48F (7.32€), *plats* 95F (14.48€), desserts 38F (5.79€), BNC

PRIX FIXE
Lunch and dinner: 106F (16.16€), 165F (25.15€), both 3 courses and BC

ENGLISH SPOKEN
Yes

L'ETE EN PENTE DOUCE (6)
23, rue Muller
Métro: Château Rouge

If you want to get away from all the tourist hype and downright disgusting food served in the lee of Sacré Coeur, make L'Ete en Pente Douce your destination. The restaurant occupies an enviable position on the park side of Sacré Coeur and boasts a terrace that is shaded in the summer and a smaller glass-enclosed one across the front. Inside, seating is at marble-topped bistro tables under a frescoed ceiling. There are no *entrées* served, but the main courses are so liberally garnished that you don't need a starter. If you are here in the late autumn, you probably won't be sitting outside, but you can enjoy one of the chef's specialties: mushrooms, both wild and domestic, cooked in a variety of unusual ways, including an *appel-strudel aux cepes, crème Anglaise* (apple strudel with mushrooms and custard sauce) and *nougat glacé aux cepes, coulis de fruits rouges* (a mushroom-nougat ice cream with red fruit sauce). At other times of the year, you can order one-plate meals, large salads, cheese and fruit plates, and vegetarian dishes all accompanied by an assortment of the chef's homemade breads and pastries.

NOTE: When you are in the Latin Quarter, be sure to stop by their other location in the fifth, La Fourmi Ailée (see page 109).

TELEPHONE
01-42-64-02-67

OPEN
Daily: lunch noon–3 P.M. (Sat–Sun till 4 P.M.), tea 3–7 P.M., dinner 7 P.M.–midnight

CLOSED
Never

RESERVATIONS
Accepted for inside seating only, not for the terraces

CREDIT CARDS
MC, V

À LA CARTE
100–130F (15.24–19.82€), BNC

PRIX FIXE
None

ENGLISH SPOKEN
Yes, ask for Martine

L'HOMME TRANQUILLE (8)
81, rue des Martyrs
Métro: Abbesses, Pigalle

TELEPHONE
01-42-54-56-28

OPEN
Tues–Sat: dinner 7:30–
11:30 P.M.

CLOSED
Mon, Sun; several days
between Christmas and
New Year's, Aug

RESERVATIONS
Necessary, unless you arrive
early

CREDIT CARDS
MC, V

À LA CARTE
Entrées 38F (5.79€), plats 64–
80F (9.76–12.20€), desserts
38F (5.79€), BNC

PRIX FIXE
Dinner: 118F (17.99€),
3 courses, BNC

ENGLISH SPOKEN
Yes

For almost fifteen years, Catherine Le Squer has been cooking here—with the help of her mother, who makes all the terrines, and Caryl, who waits on all the tables. Casual observers might think this is just another Montmartre-Pigalle eatery dedicated to luring in tourists, plying them with cheap food and drink, and then gouging their wallets. Not so. This family-owned restaurant, open for dinner only, is out of the mainstream of Pigalle grunge and just far enough from the tourist traps in Montmartre to maintain its character. The funky interior has a design-by-garage-sale esthetic. Collections of coffee grinders, pitchers, and bottles sit in clusters around the room. Candles are lit at night, aging posters are taped to equally aging yellow walls, and there is the usual bouquet of fresh flowers and assorted green plants. Tables are set with paper maps and chunky wine glasses.

Start with a pitcher of the drinkable house wine and order one of the terrines to spread on chunks of fresh bread. Vegetarians are catered to with the *assiette végétarienne,* which pairs a vegetable terrine (spinach, celery, and carrots) with an assortment of the evening's veggies. You should skip the fish—most of it is frozen—but don't hesitate to order the healthy portions of curried pork chops, grilled lamb chops, or the honey-coriander chicken. Dessert specialties include fruit crumble and a slice of chocolate *fondant* that is so popular with the regulars they have threatened not to come if it is ever taken off the menu. From start to finish L'Homme Tranquille provides a basic, fairly priced meal in a section of Paris where this is not easy to find.

RENDEZ-VOUS DES CHAUFFEURS (3)
11, rue des Portes Blanches
Métro: Marcadet-Poissonniers

TELEPHONE
01-42-64-04-17

OPEN
Mon–Tues, Thur–Sun: lunch
noon–2:30 P.M., dinner
7:30–11 P.M.

CLOSED
Wed; NAC

RESERVATIONS
Not necessary

CREDIT CARDS
MC, V

If you are willing to go where most other mortal tourists fear to tread, if what you want is a square meal for a song, go to Rendez-vous des Chauffeurs. This nostalgic throwback is an honest-to-goodness neighborhood hangout where the decor has been given a minimum of attention and importance, but certainly not the food.

Nouvelle cuisine never caught on here, and neither will any other passing food fad, but the restaurant is always packed with a comfortable clientele eager to lap up the adored cornerstones of French home cooking. The bargain *du jour* is definitely the 70F (10.67€) three-course meal, which includes wine. It is served for lunch and dinner, but never on Sunday or holidays or after 8:30 P.M. Starting with a plate of *crudités, saucisson sec,* or radishes with butter, continuing on to a garnished *plat* of roast chicken, tripe, steak tartare, or steak, and down to the last bite of *pâtisserie,* a meal here is a very filling and satisfying experience that all economy-minded diners in Paris will appreciate.

Additionally, English is readily understood here, as the owner, Janot Rocchi, spent twenty-seven years in the United States in New York, Arizona, and Hawaii.

À LA CARTE
110–125F (16.77–19.06€), BNC

PRIX FIXE
Lunch and dinner (until 8:30 P.M. every day except Sun): 70F (10.67€), 3 courses, BC

ENGLISH SPOKEN
Yes

Twentieth Arrondissement

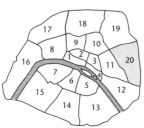

The twentieth arrondissement is proletarian, intensely ethnic, and at times, radical. The northern section, Belleville, is a cultural melting pot. Ménilmontant, in the southern part, is where you will find the Cimetière Père Lachaise. Within its winding maze of paths you can visit the graves of Balzac, Colette, Molière, Jim Morrison, Gertude Stein, Edith Piaf, and Oscar Wilde, to name only a few of the famous—and infamous—people who rest here.

TWENTIETH ARRONDISSEMENT RESTAURANTS

Les Allobroges ($)   **265**

($) indicates a Big Splurge

LES ALLOBROGES ($)
71, rue des Grands-Champs
Métro: Maraîchers (see directions)

If you didn't know about Les Allobroges, you wouldn't come here, let alone be able to find it. However, Paris' smart set has definitely found it, and they have been happily traveling to this outpost neighborhood ever since chef Olivier Pateyron and his wife, Annette, opened the doors. The two small dining rooms display pictures and posters of farm animals on the walls, and there are big pots of daisies in the windows. Seating is at comfortably spaced, properly set, linen-covered tables.

With a cooking style that respects the classics, Pateyron creates dishes that represent all that is modern and refreshing about Paris dining. Everything he prepares tastes clean, unmasked, and satisfying. The two sensational value-priced menus are definitely the way to go. The cheaper one allows a choice of *entrées,* only the *plat du jour* for the main course, plus cheese and dessert. The more expensive option offers six or eight choices for every course and includes most of the best from the à la carte side. For many visitors, the addition of the *toute légumes* (all vegetable) menu rates highly and adds another reason to include this among the top dining selections in Paris.

The house foie gras plays a starring role in many of the starters. One classic is the *gallete de pommes de terre au lard et fois gras,* a crisp potato pancake holding a generous amount of foie gras. Two other remarkable dishes are the *ragoût d'asperges et foie gras chaud* and the foie gras terrine in a thyme *gelée.* The salad with herbs and a showering of parmesan is a lighter, springtime palate-pleaser that allows you to give plenty of serious consideration to the second courses. If you love lamb, definitely order the *souris d'agneau braisée et ail confit,* a melt-in-your-mouth tender lamb served with roasted garlic cloves. Otherwise, have the succulent, golden roast chicken—a divine preparation you must order when booking your table. Inspired desserts will beguile you with a bread pudding accented with a *fromage blanc* sorbet, a pear meringue with pistachio sauce, and a lovely strawberry soup.

Not only are vegetarians not ignored at Les Allobroges, they are attended in gourmet style with the small all-vegetable and fruit menu. It changes often, but on my last visit it included a mixed salad with tomato confit and an eggplant caviar to start, then a vegetable

TELEPHONE
01-43-73-40-00

OPEN
Tues–Sat: lunch noon–2 P.M., dinner 8–10 P.M.

CLOSED
Mon, Sun; major holidays, Aug 3–27

RESERVATIONS
Essential as far in advance as possible; required if you need parking (only at lunch)

CREDIT CARDS
AE, MC, V

À LA CARTE
230–260F (35.06–39.64€), BNC

PRIX FIXE
Lunch and dinner: 100F (15.24€), 185F (28.20€), both 4 courses and BNC; menu "tout légumes" (lunch and dinner): 150F (22.87€), 3 courses, BNC

ENGLISH SPOKEN
Yes

ragout with a potato pancake and light chervil cream sauce. Finally, for dessert was one of Pateyron's famous *feuilleté de rhubarbe*—sweet rhubarb encased in a buttery, flaky pastry.

NOTE: Admittedly, Les Allobroges is off—way off—the beaten track. You might be tempted to take a taxi, but the ride could cost more than dinner. The best way to go is the métro. Get off at the Maraîchers stop, walk down rue des Pyrénées to rue des Grands-Champs and turn right, then walk until you come to the restaurant at No. 71. If, by chance, you are driving, free parking is available, but only at lunchtime, and you *must* notify the restaurant when you book your lunch table that you will need parking.

University Restaurants

Institutional food, even in Paris, is nothing to write home about, but it *is* cheap. CROUS (Centre Régional des Oeuvres Universitaires et Scolaires) runs university restaurants known as Restos-U that offer so-so food at unbeatable prices. These restaurants serve four-course meals that include both cheese and dessert, but not drinks. Anyone with an international student ID can buy meal tickets (cash only) either at the main office or during mealtimes at any of the sites listed below. The following list of CROUS Restos-U includes those that are most convenient, but it is by no means exhaustive. For a complete list, consult the main office.

It is important to know that a visit to the CROUS main office will get you more than a cut-rate meal in Paris. The office is also a place to book a bed in a student residence, arrange a cheap trip, or buy a discounted ticket for sports or cultural events. Of course, you must be a student and present your international ID card to qualify for any of the bargains.

CROUS RESTAURANTS IN PARIS

MAIN OFFICE: 39, avenue Georges Bernanos (5th)
MÉTRO: Port Royal
TELEPHONE: 01-40-51-36-00, 37-10, or 37-14
INTERNET: www.crous-paris.fr
OPEN: Mon–Fri 9 A.M.–5 P.M.
CLOSED: Sat–Sun, holidays, Aug

The following information is good for all the CROUS Restos-U listed:
LUNCH: 11:30 A.M.–1:30 P.M.
DINNER: 6–8 P.M.
CREDIT CARDS: None, cash only
SINGLE MEAL TICKETS: 30F (4.57€)
ENGLISH SPOKEN: Usually

Assas, 92, rue d'Assas (6th), 01-46-33-61-25;
    Métro: Notre-Dame-des-Champs
Bullier, 29, avenue Georges Bernanos (5th), 01-44-41-
    33-44; Métro: Porte Royal. This is the only site
    open on weekends and school vacations.
Censier, 31, rue Geoffroy-St-Hilaire (5th), 01-45-35-
    41-24; Métro: Censier-Daubenton

Châtelet, 10, rue Jean Calvin (5th), 01-43-31-51-66;
Métro: Censier-Daubenton

Citeaux, 45, boulevard Diderot (12th), 01-49-28-59-40
or 41; Métro: Gare de Lyon

Cuvier-Jussieu, 8, rue Cuvier (5th), 01-43-25-46-65;
Métro: Jussieu

Dareau, 13–17, rue Dareau (14th), 01-45-65-25-25;
Métro: St-Jacques, Glacière

Dauphine, avenue de Pologne (16th), 01-44-05-43-88;
Métro: Porte Dauphine

I.U.T., 143, avenue de Versailles (16th), 01-42-88-85-
59; Métro: Exelmans

Mabillon, 3, rue Mabillon (6th), 01-43-25-66-23;
Métro: Mabillon

Necker, 153, rue de Vaugirard (15th), 01-40-61-54-40;
Métro: Pasteur, Falguière

Glossary of French Words and Phrases

Eating out should be pleasurable, but negotiating an incomprehensible menu can ruin a meal. This glossary of French menu terms and phrases—all those used in *Great Eats Paris* as well as many others you may need or encounter—is designed to help make sure there will not be a difference between what you want to eat and what you actually order.

General Phrases

good day, hello	*bonjour*
good evening	*bonsoir*
good-bye	*au revoir*
Excuse me.	*Excusez-moi.*
Do you speak English?	*Parlez-vous anglais?*
I do not speak French.	*Je ne parle pas français.*
I do not understand.	*Je ne comprend pas.*
please	*s'il vous plaît*
thank you	*merci*
You are welcome.	*De rien.*
no	*non*
yes	*oui*
Where is the bathroom?	*Ou est la toilette?*
Do you have . . . ?	*Avez-vous . . . ?*
open	*ouvert*
closed	*fermé*
annual closure (for vacation)	*fermeture annuelle*
on vacation	*en vacances*
holiday	*jour ferrié*

Days of the Week

Monday	*lundi*
Tuesday	*mardi*
Wednesday	*mercredi*
Thursday	*jeudi*
Friday	*vendredi*
Saturday	*samedi*
Sunday	*dimanche*

Numbers

one	*un (une)*
two	*deux*

three	*trois*
four	*quatre*
five	*cinq*
six	*six*
seven	*sept*
eight	*huit*
nine	*neuf*
ten	*dix*
eleven	*onze*
twelve	*douze*
thirteen	*treize*
fourteen	*quatorze*
fifteen	*quinze*
sixteen	*seize*
seventeen	*dix-sept*
eighteen	*dix-huit*
nineteen	*dix-neuf*
twenty	*vingt*
twenty-one	*vingt-et-un*
twenty-two	*vingt-deux*
thirty	*trente*
forty	*quarante*
fifty	*cinquante*
sixty	*soixante*
seventy	*soixante-dix*
eighty	*quatre-vingt*
ninety	*quatre-vingt-dix*
one hundred	*cent*
one thousand	*mille*

Time

What time is it?	*Quelle heure est-il?*
At what time?	*A quelle heure?*
today	*aujourd'hui*
yesterday	*hier*
tomorrow	*demain*
this morning	*ce matinS*
this afternoon	*cette après midi*
tonight	*ce soir*

Eating Out

I am hungry.	*J'ai faim.*
I am not hungry.	*Je n'ai pas faim.*
I would like . . .	*Je voudrais . . .*
I cannot eat . . .	*Je ne peux pas manger de . . .*
I am a vegetarian.	*Je suis végétarien(ne).*

I would like to reserve a table . . .	*Je voudrais réserver une table . . .*
for___people.	*pour___personnes.*
for this evening.	*pour ce soir.*
tomorrow at___o'clock.	*demain à ___heures.*
We have a reservation.	*Nous avons réservé.*
a nonsmoking area	*une zone non-fumer*
May I have . . .	*Puis-j'avoir . . .*
a glass of	*un verre de*
a bottle/a carafe	*une bouteille/une carafe*
a plate	*une assiette*
silverware	*couvert*
a fork	*une fourchette*
a knife	*un couteau*
a spoon	*une cruillère*
a napkin	*une serviette*
rare	*saignant (almost raw)*
medium	*à point*
well-done	*bien cuit*
to take out	*à emporter*
There must be some mistake.	*Il doit y avoir une erreur.*
That is not what I ordered.	*Ce n'est pas ce que j'ai commandé.*
This isn't fresh.	*Ça n'est pas frais.*
I would like to speak to the headwaiter/ manager	*Je voudrais parler au maître d'hôtel/patron.*
The bill, please.	*L'addition s'il vous plaît.*
I think there is a mistake in the bill.	*Je crois qu'il y a une erreur sur l'addition.*
Thank you, that was a good meal.	*Merci, c'etait un très bon repas.*
headwaiter	*maître d'hôtel, maître d'*
manager/owner	*patron*

French Menu Terms

addition	restaurant bill
à la carte	from the menu (not part of prix fixe menu)
amér	bitter
amuse bouche (or *amuse gueule*)	small nibbles eaten before food is ordered
apéritif	before-meal drink
assiette (de)	plate (of)

biologique	organic foods and wines
boissons (compris ou non-compris)	drinks (included or not included)
bouteille de	bottle of
campagne/campagnard	country style
carafe d'eau	pitcher of tap water
carte	menu
carte des vins	wine list
chaud	hot
choix	choice
commande(er)	order (to order)
compris	included
dégustation	taste or sample
déjeuner	lunch
digestif	after-dinner drink (liqueur)
dîner	dinner
entrée	first course
espace non-fumer	nonsmoking area
ferme	farm fresh
fermé	closed
formule	set-price menu, also known as *prix fixe* or *menu*
goût(er)	taste (to taste or snack)
gratuit	free
gros(se)	large
hors-d'oeuvre	appetizer
jardinière	garnish of fresh or cooked vegetables
jeune	young
léger	light
maigre	thin, no fat
maison (de la)	house (in the style of, or made in house)
marché	market
mélange	mixture
menu	set-price menu, also called *prix fixe* or *formule*
menu du marché	a menu using fresh produce from that day's market
mets selon de la saison	according to the season
offert	free
ouvert	open
petit déjeuner	breakfast
pièce	a piece of something
plat	main course
plat du jour	dish of the day
prix fixe	set-price menu
repas	meal
saison (suivant la)	season (according to)

salle	inside eating area
sans alcool	without alcohol
selon le marché	according to market availability
service compris	service charge included
supplement, en sus	extra charge
sur commande	made to order
volonté (à)	at the customer's discretion

French Food Terms

A

à point	medium rare
abats	offal
abricot	apricot
agneau	lamb
aiguillettes	thin slices, usually of duck breast
ail	garlic
aile	wing
aïoli	garlicky blend of eggs and oil
alcools	spirits
aligot	puréed potatoes with melted *cantal* cheese and garlic
allummettes	fried matchstick potatoes
aloyau	beef loin
amandes	almonds
ananas	pineapple
anchoïade	puree of anchovies, olive oil, and vinegar
anchois	anchovy
andouille, andouillette	chitterlings (chitlins or tripe) sausage
aneth	dill
anguille	eel
anis	aniseed
artichaut	artichoke
asperge	asparagus
au four	baked
aubergine	eggplant
avocat	avocado

B

baba (au rhum)	yeast cake (with rum sauce)
baguette	long thin loaf of bread
baies roses	pink peppercorns
ballotine	"small bundle," usually meat or fish, boned, stuffed, and rolled
banane	banana
bar	sea bass

barbue	brill
basilic	basil
basquaise	Basque style, with ham, sausage, tomatoes, and red pepper
bâtard	similar to a baguette, but with a softer crust
bavarois	custard made with cream and gelatin
bavette	skirt or flank steak
béarnaise	hollandaise sauce with tarragon and shallots
béchamel	white sauce with milk, onion, nutmeg
beignet	fritter, usually batter-fried fruit
Belon	flat-shelled oyster
betterave	beet
beurre (blanc) (rouge)	butter (sauce with white wine and shallots) (with red wine)
bien cuit	well done
bière/demi/ordinaire	beer/draught beer/cheapest beer
bifteck	steak (can be tough)
biscuits	cookies
bisque	shellfish soup
blanc (de volaille, de poulet)	breast (of chicken)
blanquette	stewed meat in rich white sauce
blanquette de veau	veal stew with onions, mushrooms, and cream
blette	Swiss chard
bleu	blood-rare or almost raw (for meat)
boeuf à la mode	beef marinated and braised in red wine
boeuf au gros sel	boiled beef with vegetables and coarse salt
boeuf bourguignon	beef cooked with red wine, onions, and mushrooms
boeuf en daube	beef cooked with red wine and vegetables
boeuf mode	beef stew with carrots, onions, and red wine
boire	to drink
boisson	a drink
bombe	molded, layered ice cream dessert
bordelaise	sauce with red wine, shallots, and beef marrow
bouchée à la reine	sweetbreads in pastry
boudin blanc	white sausage made with chicken or veal
boudin noir	pork sausage made with blood
bouillabaisse	Mediterranean fish and shellfish soup
bouilli	boiled
bourride	a fish stew like bouillabaisse, but without shellfish
braisé	braised
brandade de morue	creamed salt cod
brioche	bun, usually made with eggs and sugar
brochette	meat on a skewer

brouillé	scrambled
brûlé	dark caramelization
bulot	whelk, a type of marine snail

C

cabillaud	fresh cod
cacahouètes	peanuts
café	espresso
café allongé	weaker espresso, more water
café crème/au lait	with steamed milk
café décaféiné/déca	decaffeinated coffee
café double	double espresso
caille	quail
calamar	squid
Calvados	apple brandy
canard	duck
caneton	young male duck
canette	young female duck
cannelle	cinnamon
carbonnade (flambade)	charcoal-grilled meat/beef stew with onions and beer
carotte	carrot
carré d'agneau	rack of lamb
cassis	black currants
cassolette	casserole
cassoulet	casserole of white beans with combinations of pork, duck, lamb, goose, and sausage
céleri	celery
céleri rave	celeriac
céleri rémoulade	shredded celery root salad with herbs and mayonnaise
cèpe	dark brown mushroom
cerfeuil	chervil
cerise	cherry
cervelas	pork sausage with garlic; can also be fish or seafood sausage
cervelles	brains
champignons	mushrooms
chanterelle	wild mushroom
chantilly	sweetened whipped cream
charcuterie	cold cuts; terrines, pâtés, sausages; also a shop selling these and other deli items
charlotte	molded dessert, usually lined with ladyfingers
chasseur	sauce cooked with mushrooms, shallots, white wine, and tomatoes
châtaigne	chestnut

chausson	filled pastry turnover
châvignin	sharp goat cheese
cheval (à cheval)	horse (with a fried egg on top of food, not the horse)
chèvre	goat cheese
chevreuil	young deer
chicorée	curly endive
chiffonnade	thin strips, usually vegetables
chiperon	Basque word for squid
chocolat (chaud)	chocolate (hot)
chou (rouge)	cabbage (red)
chou farci	stuffed cabbage
chou frisée	kale
chou-fleur	cauliflower
choucroute	sauerkraut served with smoked meats
choux	cream puff
choux de Bruxelles	Brussels sprouts
ciboulette	chive
cidre	apple cider
citron	lemon
citron vert	lime
citron/orange pressé	freshly squeezed lemon/orange juice
civet	game stew, with wine, onion, and blood
civet de lièvre	stewed hare, thickened with blood
clafoutis	thick batter filled with fruit and baked; served warm
claires	oysters
clementine	small Spanish tangerine
cochon (de lait)	pig (suckling pig)
cochonnailles	assortment of pork sausages and pâtés served as a first course
coeur	heart
coeur de filet	best part of beef filet; chateaubriand
colin	hake
compote	stewed fruit
concombre	cucumber
confit	meat cooked and preserved in its own fat
confit d'oie	preserved goose
confiture	jam
contre-filet	cut of sirloin steak
coq-au-vin	mature chicken stewed in red wine
coquelet	young male chicken
coquillages	shellfish
coquilles St-Jacques	sea scallops
cornichon	tart pickle
côte	rib, chop

côte d'agneau	lamb chop
côte de boeuf	beef rib
côte de veau	veal chop
coulis	purée of raw or cooked vegetables or fruit
courge	squash
courgette	zucchini
couscous	granules of semolina; a spicy North African dish with semolina, various meats, and vegetables
crème anglaise	custard sauce
crème brûlée	custard with a brown-sugar glaze
crème caramel	custard with caramel flavoring
crème fraîche	fresh thick cream with the consistency of yogurt
crêpe	thin pancake
crêpe Suzette	thin pancake flambéed with Grand Marnier liqueur
crêpinette	small, flat, grilled sausage
cresson	watercress
crevette rose	prawn
crevettes	shrimp
croque-madame	toasted ham and cheese sandwich with an egg on top
croque-monsieur	toasted ham and cheese sandwich, no egg
crottin de Chavignol	small, round piece of goat cheese
croustade	bread or pastry case, deep fried
(en) croûte	in a pastry case
cru	raw
crudités	raw vegetables
crustacés	shellfish
cuisses de grenouilles	frogs legs
cuisse de poulet	chicken leg
cuit (au four)	cooked (in the oven)

D

dauphinois	scalloped potatoes
darne de saumon	salmon steak
datte	date
daube	meat stew with red wine
daurade	sea bream (or whitefish)
demi-boutille	half bottle
demi-litre	half litre
diable	reduced sauce with cayenne pepper, shallots, and white wine
dinde	turkey
dorade	red sea bream (not as good as *daurade*)

duxelles	chopped mushrooms and shallots sautéed in butter and mixed with cream

E

eau (minérale)	water (mineral)
eau/gazeuse/minérale/ ordinaire	water/carbonated/mineral/tap
eaux-de-vie	fruit brandies
échalote	shallot
écréme	skim milk
ecrevisse	crayfish
émincé	thin slice of meat
encornet	squid
endive	chicory
entrecôte	beef rib steak
épaule	shoulder of lamb, pork, etc.
éperlans	smelts
épices	spices
épinard	spinach
escabèche	fried fish, marinated and served cold
escalope	thinly sliced meat or fish
escargot	snail
escarole	slightly bitter salad leaves
espadon	swordfish
estouffade	slowly stewed dish
estragon	tarragon
étouffée, à l'	stewed

F

façon	way of preparing a dish
faisan	pheasant
farci	stuffed
faux-filet	sirloin steak
fenouil	fennel
(en) feuilleté	(in) puff pastry
fèves	broad beans
ficelle	a very thin, crusty baguette
figue	fig
fines de claire	crinkle-shelled oysters
fines herbes	mixture of parsley, chives, and tarragon
flageolet	small, pale-green kidney bean
flambé	flamed
flamiche	cheese pie with leeks or onions
flan	custard tart
flet	flounder
flétan	halibut

florentine	with spinach
foie	liver
foie de veau	calf's liver
foie de volaille	chicken liver
foie gras	duck or goose liver
foie gras cru	raw foie gras
foie gras d'oie (canard)	fattened goose liver (duck)
foie gras mi-cuit (frais)	foie gras barely cooked
fond d'artichaut	heart and base of artichoke
fondant	chocolate dessert
fondue (du fromage)	
(savoyarde)	melted (cheese) (bread dipped into melted cheese)
fondue bourguignonne	pieces of beef dipped and cooked in hot oil
forestière	garnish of wild mushrooms, bacon, and potatoes
forêt-noire	a rich fudge cake with a cherry topping
(au) four	baked
fourré	stuffed
fraîche, frais	fresh or chilled
fraise	strawberry
fraise de bois	wild strawberry
framboise	raspberry
fricassée	stewed or sautéed fish or meat
frisée	curly endive
frit	fried
frites (pommes)	french fries
friture de mer	small fried fish
froide	cold
fromage	cheese
fromage blanc	creamy cheese served for dessert with sugar
fromage de chèvre	goat cheese
fruits confits/frais/secs	candied/fresh/dried fruit
fruits de mer	shellfish
fumé	smoked

G

galantine	boned meat, stuffed and glazed
galette	pancake, cake, buckwheat crêpe, flat pastry
gambas	large prawns
garni	garnished
gâteau	cake
gâteau de riz	rice pudding
gaufre	waffle
gazeuse	fizzy, carbonated
gelée	aspic
genièvre	juniper berry

génoise	sponge cake
gésiers	gizzards
gibier	game
gigembre	ginger
gigot (d'agneau)	leg (of lamb)
girofle	clove
girolles	wild mushrooms
glace	ice cream, also ice
glaçons/avec des glaçons	ice/on the rocks
goujons	small catfish, breaded and fried
graine de moutard	mustard seed
grand cru	best-quality wine
grasse double	ox tripe
gratin dauphinois	scalloped potatoes
gratin savoyard	potatoes baked with cheese
gratiné	browned with bread crumbs or cheese
grecque, à la	cold vegetables cooked in a seasoned mixture of olive oil and lemon juice
grillade/grillé	grilled
griotte	morello cherry
gros sel	rock salt
groseille	red currant
gruyère	hard swiss cheese

H

haché	ground or chopped
hachis (parmentier)	minced or chopped meat or fish (shepherd's pie: minced beef covered with mashed potatoes)
hareng	herring
haricot vert	green bean
haricot de mouton	mutton stew with white beans
haricots blancs	white beans
homard	lobster
huîtres	oysters

I

île flottante	floating island, poached meringue in custard sauce topped with caramel; used interchangeably with *oeufs à la neige*
infusion	herbal tea

J

jambon	ham
jambon cru	salt-cured or smoked ham, aged but not cooked

jambon de Paris	cooked ham
jambon persillé	chunks of ham in a molded parsley aspic
jambonneau	pork knuckle
jambonneau de canard	stuffed duck leg
jarret	shin
joue (de boeuf)	cheek or jowl (beef)
julienne	slivered vegetables
jus de fruits	fruit juice

K

kir	apéritif made with crème de cassis and white wine
kir royale	kir made from champagne instead of wine

L

lait	milk
laitier	made with milk
laitue	lettuce
landaise	cooked in goose fat with garlic, onion, ham
langouste	small freshwater lobster (sometimes called crayfish)
langoustine	smaller than *langouste*
langue (de boeuf)	tongue (beef)
lapereau	young rabbit
lapin	rabbit
lard	bacon
lardon	cured, thick bacon
laurier	bay leaf
légumes	vegetables
lentilles	lentils
liégois	with juniper berries or gin
liégoise	sundae made with coffee or chocolate ice cream
lièvre	wild hare
lotte	monkfish
loup de mer	sea bass
lyonnaise, à la	Lyon-style, usually with onions and/or sautéed potatoes

M

mâche	lamb's lettuce
madeleine	small tea cake
magret de canard (oie)	breast of fattened duck (goose)
maïs	corn
mandarine	tangerine
mange-tout	snow pea

mangue	mango
maquereau	mackerel
marchand de vin	sauce with red wine, stock, and shallots
mariné	marinated
marjolaine	marjoram
marmite	stew served in a small pot
marquise au chocolat	rich chocolate mousse cake
marron	chestnut
médaillon	round piece or slice
méli-mélo	assortment of fish served in a salad
menthe	mint
merguez	very spicy sausage
merlan	whiting fish
mesclun	mixture of of baby salad greens
meunière	rolled in flour and cooked in butter, parsley, and lemon
meurette	red wine sauce made with mushrooms, onions, bacon, and carrots
mi-cuit	semi-cooked
miel	honey
mignonette	small cubes of beef; coarsely ground white or black peppercorns
mille-feuille	pastry with many layers, usually filled with pastry cream
mimosa	garnish of chopped hard-boiled egg
mirabelle	yellow plum
moelle	beef bone marrow
mont blanc	chestnut dessert with whipped cream
morceau	piece
morille	wild mushroom
mornay	béchamel sauce with cheese
morue	salted or dried codfish
moule	mussel
moules marinère	mussels cooked in white wine with shallots
mousse	light whipped mixture containing eggs and cream
mousseline	hollandaise with whipped cream
moutard	mustard
mouton	mutton
mûres	blackberries
muscade	nutmeg
museau de boeuf (de porc)	vinegared beef (or pork) muzzle
myrtille	European blueberry
mystère	ice cream dessert; also meringue filled with ice cream and covered in chocolate sauce

N

nappé	covered with a sauce
nature	simple, plain, no sauce
navarin	lamb or mutton stew with root vegetables
navet	turnip
niçoise, à la	in the style of Nice; made with tomatoes, onions, anchovies, and olives
noisette	center out of lamb chop; small rounds of potato; hazelnut
noix (de coco)	nuts (coconut)
normande, à la	Normandy style, with cream and mushrooms or cooked in cider or Calvados
nouilles	noodles

O

oeuf a la coque	boiled egg
oeuf brouillé	scrambled egg
oeuf cocotte	soft boiled
oeuf dur	hard-boiled egg
oeuf en meurette	egg poached in red wine sauce
oeuf poché	poached egg
oeufs	eggs
oeufs à la neige	whipped egg whites poached in milk; served in a custard sauce (used interchangeably with *île flottante*)
oeufs au jambon/lard	ham/bacon and eggs
oeufs au plat	fried eggs
oie	goose
oignon	onion
omelette nature	plain omelet
onglet	beef cut similar to flank steak; can be strong tasting and tough
opéra	chocolate and nut layer cake
oreille	ear
os	bone
oseille	sorrel
oursin	sea urchin

P

pain	bread
pain au noix	rye or wheat bread with nuts
pain complet	whole-grain bread
pain de seigle	rye bread
pain grillé	toasted bread
pain perdu	French toast

pain Poilâne	round loaves of dark bread baked in wood-fired ovens
palourde	type of clam
pamplemousse	grapefruit
panaché	denotes any mixture
pané	breaded
papillote	cooked in parchment paper
parisian, à la	with mushrooms in white wine sauce
parmentier	dish with potatoes, usually mashed
pastis	anise liqueur
pâté	finely minced and seasoned meat, baked and served cold as a rich spread
pâté en croute	pâté in a pastry case
pâte à choux	cream puff
pâtes (fraîche)	pasta (fresh)
pâtisserie	pastry
paupiette	slice of meat or fish rolled up and tied, usually stuffed
pavé	thick slice of meat
paysan, à la	country style, with vegetables and bacon
pêche	peach
pêche Melba	peach with vanilla ice cream and raspberries
pêcheur	refers to fish preparations
perche	perch
perdrix	partridge
persil	parsley
petit gris	small snails
petit pain (au cumin/pavots)	roll (with caraway or poppy seeds)
petit salé (aux lentilles)	salted pork/pork sausage (with lentils)
petits-pois	peas
pétoncle	scallop
pichet	carafe, usually of house wine
pied (du porc)	foot (of pork)
pigeonneau	young pigeon, squab
pignon	pine nut
piment(é)	red pepper (spicy)
pintade/pinteadeau	guinea fowl
pipérade	Basque dish of scrambled eggs, pepper, ham, tomatoes, and onions
pissaladière	anchovy, tomato, and onion tart
pissenlits	dandelion greens
pistache	pistachio
pistou	sauce of basil, garlic, cheese, olive oil; sometimes stirred into fish soups

plat	still, uncarbonated
pleurotte	oyster mushroom
poché	poached
poêlé	pan-fried
poire	pear
poire belle Hélène	poached pears with vanilla ice cream and hot chocolate sauce
poireau	leek
poisson	fish
poitrine	breast of meat or poultry
poivre	pepper
poivron (rouge, vert)	sweet pepper (red, green)
pomme	apple
pomme au four/en robe des champs	baked potato in its skin
pomme de terre	potato
pommes à l'huile	cold boiled potato salad with oil dressing
pommes dauphines	mashed potatoes, shaped into balls and fried
pommes frites	french fries
pommes lyonnaises	fried slices of potatoes with onions
pommes mousselines	mashed potatoes
pommes nature	boiled or steamed potatoes
pommes parisienne	fried potatoes tossed in meat glaze
porc (carré de, côte de)	pork (loin, chop)
pot-au-feu	boiled beef with vegetables
pot-de-crème	individual custard dessert
potage	soups
potée	rich soup or stew with cabbage and pork
potiron	winter squash, often called pumpkin
poularde	fatted hen
poule au pot	chicken hen stewed with vegetables
poulet (rôti)	chicken (roasted)
poulpe	octopus
poussin	small chicken
prairie	small clam
pressé	squeezed
pression	draught beer
printanière	springtime array of vegetables
profiterole	pastry puff filled with ice cream and covered with chocolate sauce
provençal(e)	cooked and served with tomatoes, garlic, and onion and often with the addition of eggplant, anchovies, or olives
pruneaux	prunes
purée	mashed

Q

quenelle	dumpling, usually fish, veal, or poultry
quetsche	purple plum
queue (de boeuf)	tail (of beef)
quiche Lorraine	*tarte* made with eggs, cream, and ham or bacon

R

raclette	melted cheese on boiled potatoes, served with cornichon pickles and pickled onions, and raw or dried ham or beef
radis	radish
ragoût	stews
raie	skate fish (stingray)
raifort	horseradish
raisins (secs)	grapes (raisins)
râpé	grated or shredded
rascasse	scorpion fish
ratatouille	eggplant, zucchini, onions, tomatoes, and peppers, cooked with garlic and olive oil
ravigote	thick vinaigrette
reine, à la	with chicken
rémoulade	sauce of mayonnaise, capers, mustard, herbs, and pickles
rillettes (porc)	coarsely minced spread of duck or pork, served in earthenware pot
rillons	pieces of crisp pork belly
ris (d'agneau, de veau)	sweetbreads (of lamb, veal)
riz (sauvage)	rice (wild)
rognon	kidney
romarin	rosemary
roquette	rocket or arugula
rosbif	roast beef
rosé	pink; meat cooked rare, but no longer bleeding
rosette	dry pork sausage from Lyon
rôti	roast
rouget	red mullet
rouille	cayenne and garlic-seasoned mayonnaise served with fish soups
roulade	rolled and stuffed meat or fish

S

sabayon	a thick, sweet, wine-based dessert sauce
sablé (au beurre)	shortbread-type cookie
safron	saffron

saignant	rare, still bleeding
salade	salad
salade chiffonnade	shredded lettuce and sorrel in melted butter
salade mixte/des foies de volaille	mixed salad/with chicken livers
salade verte	green salad
salé	salted
sandre	pike or perch, a freshwater fish
sanglier	wild boar
sarrasin	buckwheat
saucisse	small fresh sausage
saucisson (sec)	small sausage (hard, dry sausage eaten cold)
sauge	sage
saumon (fumé)	salmon (smoked)
saumonette	sea eel, dogfish
sauté	browned in fat
savoyarde	flavored with gruyère cheese
sec, sèche	dry
seîche	squid
sel	salt
selle	saddle of meat
soja	soy
sorbet	sherbet
soubise	onion sauce
soufflé/Grand Marnier	light, fluffy egg dish/with Grand Marnier
souris d'agneau	slow-cooked lamb knuckle
St. Pierre	John Dory (fish)
steak au poivre	filet steak with green or black peppercorns
sucre	sugar
suprême de volaille	chicken breast filet

T

tapenade	purée of black olives, anchovies, capers, olive oil, and lemon juice
tarama	mullet roe made into a spread
tartare	chopped raw beef served with raw egg
tarte	open-faced pie
tarte Tatin	caramelized upside-down apple pie; served warm
tartine	buttered baguette, open sandwich
terrine	baked minced meat or fish; molded into a crock and served cold
tête, tête de veau	head, calf's head
thé	tea
thon	tuna
tian	provençal gratin, cooked in an earthenware pot

tiède	warm
tilleuil	linden flower tea
timbale	cooked in a pastry case or mold
tisane	herbal tea
topinambour	Jerusalem artichoke
tortue	turtle
toulouse	savory *tarte* or pie
tournedos	slices of beef filet
tranche	slice
travers de porc	spare ribs
tripes à la mode de Caen	beef tripe, carrots, and onions cooked in cider and Calvados (apple brandy)
tripoux	Auvergne dish of sheep's tripe and feet
truffaude	fried mashed-potato cake with cheese, bacon, and garlic
truffe (blanche, noire)	underground fungus (white or black), very expensive delicacy
truite	trout

U–V

vacherin	dessert of baked meringue with ice cream and fresh cream
vapeur, à la	steamed
veau	veal
velouté	cream of
veloutée	veal or chicken cream sauce
verdure	salad greens, green vegetables or herbs
viande	meat
vichyssoise	cold leek and potato soup
vieille prune	plum brandy
viennoiserie	catchall term for croissants and various other pastries
vin blanc/rouge/rosé	white/red/rose wine
vol au vent	flaky pastry shell
volaille	poultry

W–Z

xérès	sherry

Index of Restaurants

WINE BARS